BY DOROTHY CANFIELD FISHER

Fiction

Gunhild
The Squirrel-cage
Fellow Captains (*with* Sarah N. Cleghorn)
Hillsboro People
The Bent Twig
The Real Motive
Understood Betsy
Home Fires in France
The Day of Glory
The Brimming Cup
Rough-hewn
Raw Material
The Home-maker
Made-to-Order Stories
Her Son's Wife
The Deepening Stream
Basque People
Bonfire
Tourists Accommodated (A Play)
Fables for Parents
Tell Me a Story
Seasoned Timber
Four Square
Something Old — Something New

Nonfiction

Corneille and Racine in England
A Montessori Mother
Mothers and Children
Why Stop Learning?
Our Young Folks
Paul Revere and the Minute Men
Our Independence and the Constitution
A Fair World for All
Vermont Tradition: The Biography of an Outlook on Life

Translations

Papini's Life of Christ   Tilgher's Work

VERMONT TRADITION
The Biography of an Outlook on Life

Vermont Tradition

THE BIOGRAPHY OF AN
OUTLOOK ON LIFE

By DOROTHY CANFIELD FISHER

*The present contains nothing more
than the past. And what is found in
the effect was already in the cause.*
HENRI BERGSON

Boston
LITTLE, BROWN AND COMPANY

W

The author wishes to thank the following for permission to use material from their books:

Walter Hard for lines from "An Empty House" from A MOUNTAIN TOWNSHIP. Copyright 1933 by Harcourt, Brace and Company, Inc.

Henry Holt and Company, Inc., for "Good-by and Keep Cold" and "Stopping by Woods on a Snowy Evening" from NEW HAMPSHIRE. (Copyright, 1923, by Henry Holt and Company, Inc. Copyright, 1951, by Robert Frost.) "Spring Pools" from WEST-RUNNING BROOK by Robert Frost. (Copyright, 1928, by Henry Holt and Company, Inc.) "The Pasture" from COMPLETE POEMS OF ROBERT FROST. (Copyright, 1930, 1949, by Henry Holt and Company, Inc.)

Published simultaneously
in Canada by McClelland and Stewart Limited

PRINTED IN THE UNITED STATES OF AMERICA

CONTENTS

Contents

VERMONT TRADITION
The Biography of an Outlook on Life

PRELIMINARY REMARKS
With Something about the Author

WHY do I think I know anything worth writing down about Vermont tradition?

Here are my credentials. I have lived in Vermont ever since 1763, as my father always laughingly put it. That statement is no wisecrack. Here as in other settled (some people call them stagnant) communities, family history often and vividly recounted becomes as real to every generation as personal experience. I know my great-grandmother, who died before I was born, as intimately as I remember her children (great-aunt and great-uncles to me), who talked so incessantly about her. That great-grandmother was not born till 1787, hence she spent her first four years in the doubtful period when her parents were called "outlaws" by the New York gentry, and "profligate banditti" by the Governor-General of Canada. Hence also she must have known almost at first hand everything about the community migration north into the wilderness from New Milford. All her life to her deathbed, so I gather from what was told me about her, she never for a minute stopped telling and retelling stories about old life in Vermont.

Her son, my Great-uncle Zed, passed them on to me. Of course all the older generation joined him, but I enjoyed those stories best when he told them. He seemed prodigiously old to me — and he must have been pretty old, for he remembered the War of 1812. At least he always claimed to, though the records show that he was not far from his second birthday when the Treaty of Ghent was signed. That date would place his adolescence and early manhood at a period when exuberant sentimentality was all the rage. None of it rubbed off on Great-uncle Zed. On the contrary his temperament was a throwback to the Age of Enlightenment. Pope's "Essay on Man" he regarded as the last word in English poetry. He had a Voltairian feeling for narration — clarity and order always building up to a climax which illuminated some trait, mostly a foible, of human nature. He had also a Voltairian delight in deflating balloons of pretentiousness with a sly innocent-sounding question. We were inseparable. See one, the other was near. An odd couple we must have looked — the stooped, wizened old man, stumping along with his two canes, and the tousle-headed school child, tagging after him, drinking in every word!

It takes, you see, very few lifetime-memories to span and preserve a couple of centuries, provided the interest is there to retain and record. In our family the interest never flagged. At any age I would gladly have run a mile to hear yet another version of how it was that Grandfather, as a little boy, met a big black bear on the road, as he was taking some wool to the carding mill at Manchester. . . . "See there, those stones by the brook, they are what's left of the foundations of the carding mill. The overshot water wheel was over there, where the banks are higher. You *do* remember don't you, Dolly, what a carding mill was?"

Of course I knew all about the small local carding mills in the late eighteenth century — ignorant though I was about the current tariff-wall against foreign woolens.

I would have been willing, I say, to run a mile, but I never needed to stir out of my tracks to hear all those old-time chronicles. The ancients who surrounded my little girlhood in the "Brick House" — great-uncles, great-aunt, reinforced by all their attendant cousins and in-laws and venerable cronies — everyone of them was touched with the mania for minutely detailed history, and was eager to pour that lore of the past into the eager little pitcher I was.

Yet such personal qualifications are not unusual. Plenty of other people in Vermont have family roots going as far and as deep into the past as mine.

So I cite a special privilege of mine in our doctor's wonderful collection of Vermontiana. Every old community has, of course, saved some of the records of its past, or the past of its region. But the library built up by Dr. Russell is incomparable. For in addition to taking care of Arlington's health, he has made it his business to bring together all the printed books, pamphlets, magazine articles, Old Home Week speeches, et cetera, et cetera, about Vermont, that he could buy or beg during the forty years of his life here. He has far more than merely what has been printed. His general-practitioner's intimacy with his patients, and their respect and affection for him, have given him the chance to save from destruction an enormous number of old-time records of everyday, everyman life not to be found anywhere else — some of them not even in the Vermont Historical Society's collection at Montpelier.

It happens this way: the doctor finds an elderly patient forlornly pawing over the confusion of papers left in her grandfather's battered pine desk. She says, with a sigh, "Oh dear! I know I ought to do something about these old records and deeds and diaries. But what? My nephews and nieces live in modern skin-tight apartments. They haven't an inch of extra room. And anyhow, they wouldn't know what to make of all this." Even as she speaks, she knows what to do, "Here, Doctor, you take them. They'll be safe with you."

Or there is the case of the gnarled old land-surveyor in a nearby town, who keeps on living and keeps on surveying long after anybody else would have given up. His father before him was the town surveyor. Their two lives covered nearly a century and a half. The house is crammed with their records. Finally, having outlived his own generation, and all of his children, the old fellow lets go. What can his busy twentieth-century grandchildren do? Like most people they are absorbed in earning their livings and bringing up their children. They have no interest in the hundreds of untidy yellowed papers, left in closets, in bureau drawers, in dusty shoe-boxes in the upper part of the barn. It wouldn't be showing decent respect for the dead just to burn the whole lot — but the old house must be emptied and sold. And then Dr. Russell, who brought them and their children into the world, and closed their grandparents' and parents' eyes, asks if perhaps they would like to have him take over that scrambled-together disorder of papers? Of course they would.

And so on and so on. The result is always the same — by the bushel-basket, everything — crumpled tickets for the stagecoach that used to run to Troy, century-old geographies, maps of the town, letters from a boy who died in the Mexican War, recipes for soap-making, almost undecipherable diaries, deeds for land sold in the eigthteenth century, account-books, inventories. Much of it is junk; but some of it throws new light on the way our ancestors managed their lives. The valueless and the invaluable, all jumbled together, are carried up the steep narrow stairs and stored under the slant ceilings of the upper story of Dr. Russell's big house. A gold mine of information for anyone with patience to dig and sift.

But a writer needs so much more than copious information! Patient digging is only the beginning of composing a history, and it is no history I have in mind as I begin this book. What I pray I may have skill to do is to see how Vermont history shaped, molded and created Vermont character. A biographer, about to write a man's life, looks intently at the record of external events of that life, asking himself, "How did those facts influence what the man became and did?" That's the way I hope to look at Vermont history. I am setting myself to write the biography of a community. Not its history, but the influence of that history, through the ups and downs of nearly two centuries, on the development of a community's personality. What I hope to chronicle is the growth of the tradition by which the people of Vermont, by and large, live, measure the relative importance — to them — of the diverse elements of human existence, decide what makes life worth the great effort of living.

And what is it — the Vermont tradition?

To those of us who live here it is as familiar and life-giving as air or water, and as difficult to define in terms of human satisfaction. Can any words bring home to a reader in New Orleans or Singapore the tang of an upland October morning, the taste of a drink from a cold mountain spring?

Certainly it is nothing fixed. Vermonters are fiercely unregimented (I hope the reason for this trait will be made plain in later pages). They will argue with each other and with the Road Commissioner hour after Town-Meeting hour, about where to put a culvert. They disagree with one another more often than they seem to agree. Yet, although you can't predict exactly what they will do in any situation, you can always make a close guess as to the *sort* of thing they will do, and — more or less — what they will say while doing it. And what they will refrain from saying.

Casting about as I set to work on this book, to find some general principle underlying this elusive agreement in diversity, my mind went back to the winter of my girlhood, long ago, when with my artist mother I spent many weeks in Madrid, mostly in the Prado Museum. My mother was a Vermonter of undiluted blood-stream, but all her long life she set herself against the implications of the tradition into which she had been born. She measured the values of life on quite a different yardstick. We looked together at the great paintings in Madrid but we saw different things. My mother was lifted out of herself into rapture by the impact of color and line, by the radiance of light-suffused air. Her emotions centered in — and ended in — objects seen in space. On my side, I saw what would be seen by any young person conditioned, as I had been, by much studio talk: the harmonious colors, the solidity and weight of the admirably drawn figures, the exquisite relations of light and shade. Art at its glorious best made me joyfully aware of beauty.

But for me, even in youth, art meant an enrichment of human life. Through my mind, as we looked together at Velasquez and Goya and El Greco, ran a train of thoughts alien to anything in my mother's mind — thoughts about men and women in their ceaseless Pilgrim's Progress, about our responsibility for each other's misery and happiness, about injustice (those pitiable Velasquez dwarfs set me off on this), about nobility — the artist standing proudly, palette in hand, about the enjoyableness of healthy animality — The Drinkers.

In other words, although in Spain, I was living by Vermont tradition, before I even knew what it was. My mother was not.

This tradition is basically concerned with the conduct of human life. It is not, like some other traditions and fine ones, *primarily* concerned with mathematical formulae, with the orbits of the stars, with the vibrations of sound waves creating musical notes, with mystical religious speculation, with the structure of rocks. The basic, primary concern of Vermont tradition is with the conduct of human life.

A word of warning: the phrase "concern with the conduct of human life" might have in your ear an overtone of the virtuous intention to give happiness to others. If you do hear that overtone, you are imagining it.

In a wry standoffish way, Vermonters have a normal amount of interest in other people's well-being. Kindness is practiced among us to an average degree. So is pity, although practically never expressed in words, always and very clearly in action. Pity and kindness are normal human instincts and Vermonters are normal.

But the "virtuous intention to give happiness to others," no. That would imply rearranging other people's lives for them! Vermont tradition is based on the idea that group life should leave each person as free as possible to arrange his own life. This freedom is the only climate in which (we feel) a human being may create his own happiness. Nobody else can do it for him. Happiness may not be the purpose of human life. For all we know that purpose may be something better. But at least we are convinced that the pursuit of happiness is a natural human right and no temptation of the devil.

We are also sure that happiness comes only from within the human heart, not from outside circumstance. All of us have been puzzled by people who seem to have everything to live for, who are fathers or mothers of promising children, who are themselves prosperous, healthy citizens — yet who wish they were dead. And all of us have known others, half-crippled with arthritis, who don't know where the next meal is coming from, yet who are cheerfully eager for whatever the next day may bring. Such improbable contrasts bear out our conviction that each individual character (a word we often use to sum up the net balance of urges and inhibitions) like the curves and loops of each individual thumb-print, is always different from all others. To be sure, character influences everyday activities and hence can be guessed at, vaguely, by observing actions. But character itself lies deep and secret below the surface, unknown and unknowable by others.

It is the mysterious core of life, which every man or woman has to cope with alone, to live with, to conquer and put in order, or to be defeated by. It follows then that efforts from the outside to meddle with this inner personal sanctuary are as apt to do harm as good.

Vermonters take this attitude for granted, understand one another when they act on it. Unfortunately visitors from other regions, accustomed to a freer flow of emotion — anyhow of words about emotions — mistake it for indifference or dislike. The result is friction — a good deal of friction, I'm afraid — rebuffed good intentions and bruised feeling on one side, and on the other side surprise at being considered unfriendly, but no attempt to become more approachable.

For the Vermonter's impulse is to distrust and dislike hasty short-cuts to intimacy. Not for him the casual social gestures of the summer tourists — calling strangers by their nicknames the day you meet them, saying "darling" to a woman of whom you don't know much nor much like what you do know, laying your hand with an affectionate gesture on the shoulder of a man who has just been introduced to you.

Yet I insist that you are wrong if you suppose cussedness alone makes the Vermonter hold back from somebody who pretends to pick the beautiful blossom of friendliness when the seed of it has only just been planted. He is acting on a deep conviction that true love and strong lasting friendship are rare events, of slow growth, that they are mysteries to be treated with respect, even with awe and reverence; and that since none of us understands himself or others very well, only after long summering and wintering has given the chance to observe what people do, and so to guess what they are . . . only then, occasionally, can a few of us hope to share life intimately with one another.

In every generation many human beings have sensed this remoteness from their fellow men. Frequently it has moved them to laments of desperate self-pity — as for example Matthew Arnold with his "unplumb'd, salt, estranging sea" in which we mortal millions are islands kept apart by echoing straits. Without rhyming words, without any words at all, Vermonters soberly but not sadly accept this separation as an example of the way life often is. If they were moved to speak of it, they might put it, "If so it be; so be it! Let's make the best of it."

"The best of it" in this case, as always when theory has to be adjusted to the facts of life, works out as something of a compromise. Everyone has the right to — the need for — privacy. Yet everyone must have some group life. That stands to reason. Insanity is always just around the corner from absolute solitude. So, to arrange a framework that fits human nature at least as well as a harness fits a work horse, the wisest solution, all things considered, so it seems to us, is to keep society — the community, the group, the family — off the individual's neck as much as possible, to give everyone enough freedom to be himself, so that he can develop *on his own steam* whatever is best and most vital in his nature. Unshakably we hold these truths to be self-evident: that life is not worth living unless every individual can get air enough to breathe deeply and freely. But nobody can help him do his breathing. It is an intrusion to try.

I do not claim that there is anything original in this doctrine. Plenty of teachers, writers, thinkers — Emerson, John Stuart Mill, Pestalozzi, Montaigne — have believed in it. What I find notable about the way it is followed in Vermont is that here it is far from being confined to a few intellectual theorists, such as Mr. Emerson, secure in his clean quiet Concord study, or John Stuart Mill with money enough to hire a woman in a white cap and apron to bring in his afternoon tea. In Vermont this abstract principle forms the actual literal basis of life for the majority of plain, ordinary people in ginghams and blue jeans, standing toe-to-toe with the need to earn every cent of their livings, and slugging it out with poverty all the days of their lives, generation after generation. This, I maintain, is a phenomenon worth looking into.

Again, I do not claim that Vermonters are fenced off from the rest of mankind by their special social outlook. Folk customs, habits of thought are no respecters of state lines — or of national lines. Not to speak of wide sections of New Hampshire, Maine and elsewhere, there are — I have met them wherever I have wandered — people who wouldn't know how to find Vermont in a geography book and yet who have a natural affinity for what we think of as our way of life. Be they Basques from St.-Jean-Pied-de-Port, Pennsylvania Quakers, Iowa farmers, or Norwegians on the Sognfjord, I recognize them, I keep them always in mind as my brothers and sisters in spirit. If I do not cite their example in detail on the following pages, it is partly because for them I lack what I have abundantly for Vermont — a solid foundation of recorded fact — even more because the focus is always clearer when the field is narrowed. Naturally my best chance of understanding the how and why of theory and practice is here, at home in my own country.

Least of all do I claim that anything like this personal Bill of Rights is or ever has been *universally* accepted anywhere. The desire to assert one's own importance by bossing or pushing someone else around sprouts in the human heart as vigorously as thistles in a cow pasture. Some temperaments are incapable of the self-discipline of the "hands off" code, with its corollary: "Keep your mouth closed even when you know your neighbor is a fool and is making the mistake of his life."

Some temperaments, not many! Travel through Vermont — north, south, east, west, from Pownal to Canaan, Guilford to Highgate — nowhere will you find a township where overwhelming majority opinion does not support this unwritten law: that, except where the safety of others is in danger, everyone must be allowed to do, think, believe whatever seems best to him; that equality before the law is only the first step. Equality must extend to the protection of everybody's personal dignity, within the community, for the backroad farmer and his wife bringing butter and eggs to the kitchen door, no less and no more than for the owner of the plywood factory. And this not by anyone's enlightened sufferance. By unquestioned right. By a right so taken for granted that nobody talks or thinks about it. Is this obligation honored in practice? Yes and no. What ideal is ever completely realized? But it is the bull's-eye which Vermont tradition all over the state holds up for us to shoot at. We miss sometimes. But when we do we are ashamed.

Are you saying to yourself that this idea does not sound like much as the deepest aspiration of a human group? A root does not look like much. It is a stringy bundle of brown fibers, uninteresting in shape, held together by a tough skin. But plant this dull-looking fiber in mother earth, let it be watered by rains, fertilized by the rich blessings of decay, and acted upon by the mighty principle of growth, what diverse forms of life spring from it — wood, leaves, flowers, fruits! Thorns too. Perhaps if your contacts with Vermonters have not been too fortunate, you may think there are more thorns than anything else. But if you live here, year after year, casting in your lot with us, I think you will come to see that many other qualities, good, bad, magnificent and mean, grow on the tradition-tree which has sprung up from that strong old root.

What qualities am I talking about? Here is one example: from the start most Vermonters have been farmers, and pretty good farmers at that. But they never have been superlative farmers like those in the more fertile parts of Germany and France, or in the richly productive region of the Pennsylvania-Dutch countryside. No Vermonter ever padlocks his wrist to the plow and throws away the key. He regards his land as a tool to be used; not as an idol, demanding worship every waking moment by father, mother and children as soon as they can toddle away from the cradle. He is not the kind of farmer who holds nothing in the world so important as getting good seed into a thoroughly fitted field, in the right season, on the right day for sowing. A life-and-death battle for a political principle could be raging just over the hill from such a farmer and he would plant his seed and let the battle go as it would.

Nothing like that in Vermont! If a special Town Meeting should be called in haying time — perish the thought! — about a matter involving what the Vermonter thinks of as human liberty, with a close decision in prospect, no Vermont farmer ever lived who would not stick his pitchfork into a cock of hay, drive to town and cast his vote against any measure which seemed to him to increase society's pressure over the individual man or woman. And as for a literal battle with a Hitler gang of totalitarians or Russian Secret Police over the hill from his hayfield, the Vermont farmer and his hired man and his fourteen-year-old son would be there with their rifles, and his wife and little girl would be carrying them their dinner in a basket.

That is, he would be there if he really saw what was at stake. He might miss that meaning, being about as quick and about as slow in imaginative uptake as most human beings. But let the issue stand clear before him, and he is under a compulsion to take sides. And there is never any doubt about which side. The dedicated to-have-and-to-hold-till-death-do-us-part type of farmer, ardent lover and faithful husband of the soil, can go on religiously getting in the hay when it is time to get in the hay, without bothering his head about a Hitler's or a Stalin's winning an election or a battle. The Vermonter loves something better than the soil. Everybody does best that which he gives his whole heart to. Farming is not the Vermont farmer's *first* concern, hence is not done with as much skill here as in some other places. We all know this, regret it a little, but accept it, since it is in the nature of things. You can't have it both ways.

That is all very well, but there are few opportunities to battle with muskets and pitchforks or ballots for the right as God has given us to see the right. How does the Vermont tradition stand up to the undramatic tests of day-by-day living? To me it seems to enrich that living with the note of serenity which Emerson defined as "joy fixed and habitual." A pinched, austere, northland sort of joy, do you think? Maybe so, but it suits us.

This won't do. Generalized description such as I have been writing always lacks the breath of life. The only way to understand people is to know them. And to know them you need to live with them. So let's start back at the beginning, and share the lives of the men and women who have made Vermont what it is.

In telling this story, I mean to do my best to be impartial, not to let prejudice distort the meaning of evidence, not to hide cracks with putty, rose-colored plaster and fancy paint. I shall try to strike as fair a balance as I can between what Vermont and its tradition has, and what it lacks — since it stands to reason that regions, people, periods of civilization, are like individual human beings in that, if they have one kind of good qualities, they can't in the nature of things have the opposite good qualities. Nobody can be both restfully quiet and thoughtful, and at the same time exhilarating, magnetic and stimulating. In short, I have simple-heartedly, perhaps simple-mindedly, promised myself not to let my interpretation of fact go beyond what the facts warrant.

Of course, every writer promises himself to live up to that excellent code. But only the driest dry bones of a chronological skeleton can achieve it. "James Knox Polk was elected President in 1844." That is a safely objective statement. No one can dispute it. But to venture a suggestion as to how Polk happened to be nominated and why he defeated Henry Clay — that is to embark on the fog-shrouded sea of interpretation. On that sea, I hereby launch my craft.

For the chronologically arranged list of established, recorded events in Vermont history has already been worked out by competent scholars. Another one is not needed. The task I have set myself is to pick out from the heaped-up jumble of material at hand those facts and those only which bear on my subject, and having picked them out, to add them up into before-and-after, cause-and-effect sequence till they tell the truth.

It can't be done. The choice, the leaving out, the adding up — the whole process calls for judgment. The only kind of judgment human beings have is personal judgment. Where there is personal judgment, there can easily be personal bias.

So I warn you that, in honesty, the title of this book should read, "What Vermont Tradition Means to Me."

PART I

PART 1

CHAPTER 1

No Scalps, No Tomahawks,
No Master Race

IN 1760 Montreal surrendered. French rule in Canada was ended. The colonial militia attached to the British Army was no longer needed.

As they stood up for the last roll call, many men of that militia answered to names now to be found on the voting lists of one or another Vermont town. What had brought those great-great-grandfathers and uncles of ours into the war?

We do not know. Family tradition, garrulous about plenty of nonessentials, gives no hint in answer to that question. It seems reasonable to guess that they knew and cared little or nothing about the distant bloody heaps of dying cannon-fodder at the battles of Hochkirch, Kunersdorf or Minden, the smoke from thousands of German and Austrian burning homes. They may well have felt that it was of no use worrying about such faraway miseries, because as a matter of plain fact, a war was almost always going on in Europe. The only clue they have left us as to their motives is that they never used the world-historian name of "The Seven Years' War," but called it, accurately enough from their point of view, "The French and Indian War." Evidently the gist of the matter for them was whether the English colonies should remain fenced in along the seacoast, their outpost settlements exposed always to surprise Indian raids, sometimes under French leadership, always with French backing — raids often unspeakably bloody, more often, quick, rush-and-grab jobs where a few frontier families were carried off to Quebec or Montreal, there to be sold to the highest bourgeois bidder. Not a bad investment of venture capital that! A big return if ransom could be squeezed out of relatives still safe in New England. Or, if not that, at least cheap labor from competent unpaid house servants. Possibly, like recruits in some other wars, they had no clear idea what it was all about. They were British subjects. It is fair to assume that none of them dreamed that in a little more than a decade after the Peace of Paris they would be cheering their own Declaration of Independence. So they enlisted, and although they heartily disliked the gold-laced, tradition-bound, Braddock-like, martinet British officers who commanded them (a dislike returned by those officers with compound interest) they stuck it out in their unmilitary, prickly, provincial way by the side of the British regulars until suddenly it was all over. They were mustered out and could start hoofing it back home.

"Hoofing" it was, for most of them. Seacoast men could be returned from Montreal by ship; others went part of the way on lake-sloops or canoes to Fort William Henry. From there to Hartford, Litchfield or New Milford, Connecticut, there was nothing for it but a long hike through the virgin forest.

A hardship? Not at all! Many of those returning soldiers found the weeks spent in this journey among the best of their lives.

Consider their situation: they were vigorous young men, in the flower of their age — very like the G.I.'s we have known lately returned from Europe or the Far East. They were hard as nails or they would not have survived what lay behind them, perils, forced marches, exposures. Hunters and fishermen from boyhood on, they were perfectly at home in the American wilderness. For months and years they had seen comrades die to their right and left. But they were alive! In the fight just ended their side had won. And now, so far as they could foresee, they were free from military life forever. No more standing at attention! No more officers to salute! Now they were going home.

Their way home followed rivers and lakes alive with salmon, trout, pike and bass, along well-blazed trails through forests thick with deer, bear, beaver, but with almost no animals dangerous to a group of men camping out together. Peter Kalm, the Swedish scientist, who traveled through much the same country about this time in the eighteenth century, recorded in his notebook many an exclamation at nature's bounty. "The people of this region," he says, "can eat like lords." And like lords our ex-G.I. fore-fathers did eat — the best cuts of venison, the freshest fish, bear steak, beaver-tail, wild pigeon, turkey — what a change from

army rations of tough salt horse. Full of broiled trout and venison steaks, they expanded into unbuttoned American freedom
after their taut years of British army regulations. They had only
to reach out a hand for fuel for campfires — roaring, luxurious
campfires, since now there was no need to guard against a surprise
attack.

More and more this empty country attracted the young men
who later were to come back and call it Vermont and home.
They moved slowly, allowing themselves many an exploring side
trip. They had no fixed time schedule to meet, for no one back
home in Connecticut or Massachusetts could tell how long the
journey should take. No one even knew, indeed, whether they
were still alive to make it. They were wakened by no bugler's
reveille. Early or late as it pleased their fancy, they roused themselves, refreshed as young Antaeuses by their rest hours on the
earth. With the ever renewed godlike appetite of youth, they fed
voraciously on exquisitely flavored, vitamin-crammed eating. For
them, day followed golden day of glorious vacation between the
vexations of military discipline and the responsibilities of family
life. No finicky British subaltern to rage over their unmilitary
bearing; and, as yet, no neat, trim, young wife, or clean, tidy
mother to be shocked by their clothes, smelling to heaven of
sweat, rancid bear's grease and last week's fish, or by their faces
dark with dirt, smoke and unshaven beards. They wiped their
greasy fingers on their buckskin pants or on their hair, consulted
with their camping comrades over the compass, and set off on the
next lap of the journey with their long Rangers' lope, carefree as
they never again would be in all their lives.

How can I feel so sure about all these details? Well, of course
I do not have the minutely accurate information historians give
us about every move in the Battle of Bunker Hill. But the story
came to me with a rich wealth of color and of feeling that no
document can transmit. Again, let me remind you how few links
are needed in the chain of oral tradition to span a scant two
hundred years. A certain Israel Canfield of New Milford, Connecticut, lately officer of colonial troops, was one of a group of
fellow soldiers, Western Connecticut men too, all mustered out
of the British Army in Canada. As they came home they hap-

pened to make one of their nightly bivouacs on the site of what is now the village of Arlington. They liked the look of the valley, then swarming with beaver, and marked it as their future home. That Israel Canfield was the grandfather of the same Great-uncle Zed who filled my eagerly listening ears with the old legends, as they had been told to him. He carried the account forward: how a few years after that first visit, Israel Canfield and his friends and cousins came back, this time with their young wives and children, bringing iron kettles, feather beds, a cow and a horse for most families, an ax over everybody's shoulder who wasn't carrying a rifle, to found early in the 1760's the town where my folks have paid taxes ever since.

Here, let me break off the narrative for a few pages to consider the astounding good fortune which guided our forefathers' steps. Most of their descendants — including the present generation — have never given thanks enough for being born in such a fatherland. We love it — yes — but hardly any of us have ever thought of Vermont as a particularly lucky state. Why would we? It is usual to call a region "favored by its climate" when sitting outdoors in shirtsleeves is comfortable all the year around. Generally also the phrase "rich in natural resources" suggests a place where the inhabitants make easy money by gathering products of one kind or another very cheaply compared to the price other people are willing to pay for them.

Now, obviously Vermont cannot qualify under either of those popular definitions. Except for brief periods in the summer, sitting down in shirtsleeves outdoors is anything but a temptation. And as for products which can be sold to other people for cash, Vermont's "natural resources" — potash, marble, granite, maple sugar, lumber, milk and "accommodations for tourists" — they have, all through our history, cost a formidable deal of labor before they could be exchanged for dollars. No oil wells, no deep-sea port for world commerce. No nuggets of gold. No Garden of Eden here — a living to be earned by much sweat of the brow!

Yet, looking back over the whole chronicle we can see in our history one stroke of good luck after another. Sometimes Vermonters have recognized these windfalls and have been grateful for them. Sometimes our folks, being human, have winced and

cried out very loudly under the bludgeonings of their own blessings. Most often of all, knowing little of what was happening
elsewhere to other people, we have taken for granted without a
thought the something better being handed to us.

Among the many happy accidents which have blessed the
course of Vermont's history, none is perhaps more important,
psychologically speaking, than the cheerful peacefulness of relations between Indians and the white people who settled our state.
Neither party deserves credit for establishing this tolerant, live-
and-let-live attitude. It did not result from enlightened social
policy like that of the Quakers in early Pennsylvania. It just happened. Without conscious choice, the newcomers followed a pattern which had been built up long before the first axes rang in
our Vermont woods.

For centuries Vermont had been empty, had not been for
Indians a place of permanent habitation to be defended against
trespassers. It had been a thoroughfare, a sort of corridor through
which they came and went on their travels. The deeply forested,
well-watered region was also a marvelous hunting and fishing
ground, but that was no reason for intertribal warfare. Indians
hunt for food, not to amuse themselves, and all through the North
Woods country – in the Adirondack foothills, in Canada, as well
as in Green Mountain valleys – game was in such prodigious
proportions that anywhere any Indian hunter could shoot as
much as he cared to eat or carry away.

Indian relics found by Vermont plowmen, by gardeners, or by
delighted little boys, are arrowheads lost by red men hunting
deer or bear, not by red men trying to kill each other. With
very few exceptions, Vermont had not been a battleground for
Indians. Its beaver meadows, its swarming-with-game forests,
its swarming-with-fish streams might have been called the "come-
and-help-yourselves-folks" country. Its air was darkened period-
ically by incredible multitudes of migrating wood-pigeons, not
by hate. Its ground was not soaked with human blood.

That sod never has been soaked with human blood, either of
white or red men. Again, I repeat, this radiant good fortune was
the result of luck, not of planning. During the three-quarter-
century of intermittent war between France and England, it lay

...and between the outpost British colonies and Canada.
..s plenty of fighting close to the westward — at Fort
.. Henry, Ticonderoga, Crown Point — but not on the
..ore of Lake Champlain.

..id, after that war was ended, when Israel Canfield's family,
and others like them, came in, year by year, built houses, began
to clear land for farms, they displaced nobody, burned nobody's
tepee. Nor did they look to Indians as though they were ruining
the wilderness, all of it, as a hunting-ground. Before an acre
could be planted, a huge number of enormous trees had to be
chopped down, burned, stumps rooted out. For a long time, the
tiny plots of cultivation were separated by miles and miles of
unbroken forest. The few Indians who wandered hunting through
those woods had no premonition — unlike more numerous, more
settled tribes elsewhere along the American frontier — that before
long it would have to be war to the knife between the white
man's way of life and theirs.

It is difficult for us now to realize how empty the country was.
One authority estimates that in 1764, just as the first wave of
settlers began to trickle in, there were not more than three hundred inhabitants, white or red, in the territory. That would work
out as less than two persons to a modern township. While such
a figure can be nothing more than a guess, it bears out — for what
it is worth — the tradition that there were no Indians to be afraid
of. Nor did any of the scattered few met with, here and there,
claim possession or feel strong attachment to any particular section as home.

From this setting, it followed that by superlative good fortune
neither Indians nor the early Vermont homemakers saw any
reason to fear, and so to hate, and so to kill one another. Thus
when Vermonters tell old-time stories to our children and grandchildren, we have nothing to hide, even from the youngest, in
the record of our "relations with the Indians." There was no
blood — even shed in self-defense — on the hands of those lively,
downcountry young folk who came north to Vermont after 1763.

Neither do we have to hang our heads at the memory of
ignoble, shyster, land-grab tricks, to do the Indians out of their
title to land. Such tricks were common in many other colonies,

particularly so in the Province of New York. There Lords of the Manor, their greed limitless almost beyond belief, by skillful manipulation of Indian place-names and uncertain boundaries, stretched the grant of a few hundred acres into several thousand acres for which the Indians received nothing. Nothing! Not even a patient hearing when they appealed to the white man's courts, standing stunned, bewildered before colonial commissions and councils and assemblies, pleading for just a little of that fair play which — so we like to tell ourselves — is the foundation stone of the sturdy Anglo-Saxon way of life.

It might have turned out differently! The early history of the New England colonies as of other North American colonies is full of self-righteous oppression of the Indians, of bland assumption that Indians had no rights whatever. We cannot reasonably think that if the white settlers in Vermont had found Indians in their way, they would have hesitated to drive them out as callously as other white people of that period. They would have killed them without remorse if they thought the alternative was to be killed by them.

They were very much the same kind of people as those who — also soon after the French and Indian War — left their homes in Virginia and Pennsylvania to found new ones in Kentucky and Tennessee. Why wouldn't they be? Same stock, same British colonial standards, same date. Those southern mountaineers battled through years of anguish and hatred, of savage abominations on both sides, of slaughtered children, both white and red. For generations after the last red enemy had been exterminated or driven west of the Mississippi, the white mountaineer conquerors remained suspicious, trigger-happy feudists with a startlingly high rate of homicide. Vermonters never had to endure any such trauma of fear and blood, and throughout its history the Vermont homicide rate has been extremely low. Is it entirely fantastic to question whether this difference can be due merely to coincidence — to wonder whether an important, perhaps the deciding, factor may not be the contrasting emotional atmospheres during the character-forming early years of the two communities.

As a matter of fact, our early Vermont ancestors' feeling went a great deal beyond toleration. They rather admired and often imitated the few stray Indian hunters who, with their strong-smelling wives and dirty, bright-eyed children, occasionally came padding on their moccasined feet down the Green Mountain trails into the settlements. It no more occurred to our forefathers to shoot Indians than we would shoot wandering gypsies. They themselves were as ardently hunters and fishermen as any Abnaki. Their descendants still are. Outsiders laugh derisively at the amount of expensive session-hours our legislatures devote to debate on the "open season" for deer, or the money to be voted for stocking trout streams. The family-size groups of Indians passing through the forests in the early years, and sharing with Vermont settlers what seemed in those days the inexhaustible abundance of fish and game, were understandable and congenial to the rough-and-ready, outdoors, family-sized groups of white settlers. Racial minorities, if they are small enough and do not threaten economic competition, are always fairly safe from mass prejudice.

I wonder if for some time you have been asking yourself how my picture of friendly good-fellowship can be reconciled with the war whoops which ring out from so many pages of the fragmentary Vermont local and town histories in our attics and on our public library shelves? That would be a natural question. You would never guess the explanation if you did not happen to know about Vermont from the inside. The point seems to be that not much Vermont history was written down until the literary-historical folk legend of the American settler had been firmly established. This showed the heroic white pioneer planting corn with one hand and with the other shooting down treacherous redskins who hated all whites on sight. For many sections of our frontier, that picture (although its gory details tended to be touched up and highlighted by frequent retelling) was true enough. By the late eighteenth and early nineteenth centuries when white settlers began to appear in numbers west of the Appalachians, the Indians they met were far more warlike than the Vermont Abnakis, were more numerous, were better organized, and fully understood the meaning — to Indians — of the white man's coming. No amiable Squanto greeting now! From Pontiac's War on, it was a life-and-death struggle for survival.

As the battle lines moved westward, the Indians grew more desperate, and almost as well armed as the whites. Infuriated attack means infuriated defense, and to forestall attack, more and more terrible assaults. The hellishly vicious circle, around which the Indians and white settlers of the United States trod murderously on each others' heels, is folk-stuff for all Americans — alas!

The Indian raid, bleeding scalps, naked, yelling savages, grim pioneers shooting to kill, brave wives close behind, reloading the long rifles . . . all this, time and time again, has been flashed before the eyes of movie-goers. There were no movies in the mid-nineteenth century but plenty of sensational stories had fixed that horrible picture in the imaginations of readers rather inclined, as human beings are, to be fascinated by horrible details. Some of the early writers of Vermont local history were clergymen — the only ones with free time for writing books — and almost all were amateurs, writing at a date when traditions of scholarly accuracy in research were not common in provincial America. One of these historians was Miss Abby Maria Hemenway, author of many volumes and preserver of much valuable information because she wrote when many people in Vermont towns and villages were still alive who could remember early days. She was an amiable and highly esteemed spinster lady, still read in Vermont. One of her town histories recounts a settlement's narrow escape from total slaughter at the hands of bloody-handed savages. One day a band of warriors came stealthily to a lookout place from which they could look down on the village. Their intention was to burst upon the town the next night with fire and tomahawks and destroy it all. But some of the white settlers had been chopping in the woods near the lookout place *and had left their axes there.* (Italics mine.) The Indians, seeing these so much larger than their own tomahawks, thought that the men who used them must be giants, and stole away back to the wilderness. The authoress did not mention how anybody ever heard of the terrible intentions of the Indians and the reasons for giving them up.

By definition, early-nineteenth-century spinsters and small-town clergymen were inclined to respect convention. Marauding Indians were a literary convention of the period. As they took up the task of setting down the local chronicle of the towns where they lived, they felt justified in filling in the many gaps and blanks in their information with their best estimate of what probably took place in Vermont because all the best writers agreed that it took place elsewhere. And they felt no responsibility for indicating which of their statements rested on document or reasonably reliable word-of-mouth testimony, and which had no backing at all beyond their "it-could-have-been-so-it-*must*-have-been" guesses.

When they wrote down a chapter title like "Demons of the Forest," not one of them noticed, judging from what they wrote, that there was an almost total lack of Vermont record or tradition to justify the heading. Such a title was too juicy to give up, was too confidently expected by readers. What sort of mollycoddle history would Vermont have if it recorded nothing about scalping-knives heroically warded off from our great-grandmothers by lion-hearted husbands and lovers?

So it is that hardly an early "history of Vermont" refrains from dragging in every detail of the Indian raid on Deerfield. That was a dreadful event, but people writing the story of Vermont seldom or never so present it that their readers fully take in the fact that Deerfield is in Massachusetts and the raid took place sixty years before the arrival of a single white settler in Vermont. The Schenectady massacre was even more distant both in time and location. But the reflection from its flames are often red on pages written about Vermont. The site of Fort Dummer, to be sure, is within the present limits of our state. But when it was attacked in 1724 as part of a military operation commanded by white French officers, it was accurately regarded as a Massachusetts outpost. At that date there was no Vermont. And Rogers's horrible "punitive expedition," when armed white men slaughtered the helpless women and children of the St. Francis Indians not far from Montreal, has no more place in Vermont history than Pontiac's War, except for the irrelevant fact that going and coming the Rangers cut across what were, much later, to be the northwest and northeast counties of our state.

After the fall of Canada, even these diligent searchers for thrills could find no shooting. No burning log cabins, no atrocities on either side, as the white settlers cleared their homesteads. Nothing until the Revolution, and surprisingly little even then. Once more, Indians were hired as mercenary troops by a white army — this time by the British. The scattered settlements north of Rutland were thought to be in danger, and from them all but the hardy pioneers, abandoning their half-built cabins, their partly cleared cornfields, moved down, for the duration of the war, to the safe (because more thickly settled) towns further south.

That exodus was nuts to the old-style writers. Yet when we skim off their rhetoric, all that remains is a commonplace to post-World-War ears. It was merely an evacuation of the civilian population ordered by military authority as a wartime precaution. Those very few who paid no attention to the order to leave the war zone were in danger. The other white settlers who came to the safe region south never saw or heard an Indian either on their way south at the beginning of the Revolutionary War, or, when after a few years' absence, they returned to their homes in the north. Throughout the hostilities between the British Army and the American colonies there is nothing in the records to show that in Vermont the Indians, always acting under military orders from the conventionally organized British military machine, shot more than a few scouts, carried off more than a few prisoners.

The raid on Royalton furnishes a significant yardstick. Here (my authority is Hiland Hall's painstaking *Early History of Vermont*) under the command of a white officer, the attackers burned twenty houses, killed two men, carried away some thirty prisoners, "destroyed many head of cattle and committed other serious depredations." The small number involved did not, of course, lessen the suffering of the Royalton victims; but when we compare this raid with the massacre at Wyoming, Pennsylvania, and at Cherry Valley, with Butler's fire-and-sword sweep through the Mohawk and Catskill country and remember that neither before nor after Royalton was there any other even moderate-size Tory or Indian attack on Vermont settlements, it becomes easier to understand why no lasting hatred of Indians was burned into Vermont hearts, why after the Revolution life went on with as profound an interrace peace as during the decade before it.

Does the tone of the last few paragraphs suggest disrespect towards those earlier town historians? No, for those early amateur writers of our local histories, we rightly feel much gratitude. When they restricted their work to the local level, they performed a valuable service by reporting both what they saw around them, and what had been told them by their elders. Writing, as they did, at a date when two lifetime-memories stretched back easily to the first settlements, they gathered and preserved an enormous amount of history's raw material. There are many of these local historians. By checking one account with another, it is possible for a modern to sift out the significant from the mass of haphazard and undigested anecdote. When this is done, those poorly printed old books give us a convincing picture of early days in Vermont *as they seemed to those who lived through those days.*

As for me, I am under a personal obligation to them. For to one of those florid mid-century writers I owe the first faint stirring of my own mind, used as an intellectual tool. It happened this way:

Sitting cross-legged one rainy day on the floor of the attic of my great-grandmother's house, where I spent a good deal of my time in my childhood, I pulled a shabby old book out at random from a dusty pile. The first yellowed pages were exciting reading. They ran something like this: "Snatching up a few of their poor belongings, the terrified settlers fled into the wilderness, leaving their homes behind them to the attack of the ruthless painted savages. Women clutching their helpless babes to their bosoms, weeping little children clinging to their father's hands, they stumbled along the trail to the south. Every instant they expected to hear the wild scream of Indian war whoops; at every turn of the path they dreaded to see a tomahawk hurtle through the air close to their heads, and strike quivering in one of the great maple trees. The twang of the deadly Indian arrow seemed to sound in their ears as they desperately hastened through the darkening gloom of night falling around them," and so forth, and so forth, and so forth. "Hot stuff," as you can see.

Sixty-five years ago the little girl in the attic read it, with thrills and chills of excitement very familiar to all children of that period, for whom the tomahawking, scalping Indian was as familiar as, for medieval children, the horned and cloven-footed devil of the miracle plays; as for British children, the hunchback of the wicked Mr. Punch. But it was a little Vermont girl who was devouring those sensational pages. Like all Vermont children, she had listened to many and many stories about early days as her grandfather, great-aunt, great-uncles ran on endlessly about their youth and the lives of their parents before them. There were occasional Indians in those stories, but never any tomahawks, scalping knives, nor the faintest fear of Indians.

Inside the head of the child sitting cross-legged on the attic floor there began — I can feel it now — one of the most prodigious intellectual efforts a modern brain can make, a doubt of what is set down on the printed page. I stopped reading and stared, trance-like, at the underside of the brown slanting roof-board above my head.

When this extraordinary inner upheaval had settled down a little, I drew a long breath and looked again at that description of terrified flight from murderous savages. This time, as if some words had been underlined in invisible ink which now showed clear on the page, I read "*expecting* at any moment to hear" . . . "*dreading* to see a tomahawk" . . . "the twang of the arrow *seemed to be* in their ears."

Yes, I am grateful for that awakening experience, for although it takes no effort at all to swallow the printed page in great gulps, and though chewing is hard dry work, there is no question as to which method results in nourishing the brain.

My gratitude goes further. Read with attentive eye for "invisible ink underlinings" those amateur historians turn out to be not only diligent but, considering their lack of critical and scholarly standards, surprisingly honest. They never claim, in so many words, that a single Indian attack — unprovoked or otherwise — was actually made in peacetime on a Vermont town or isolated farm. And they do set down with abundant supporting detail as to time, place, name of family visited, many an instance of the friendliest good feeling . . . the smiling, indulgent memory of some Indian, often his wife too, who came and went peacefully among white newcomers. Nearly every Vermont town had in its early days its "Indian Pete" or "Indian Molly," who caught fish or shot deer for a living, made do-funnies out of birch-bark (there are some of those in my attic this minute) and moccasins out of deerskin to sell to the white people, brought their sick children to be doctored by the white woman most noted in the settlement for her nursing and curing skill, borrowed the iron "kittle" from their white neighbors for the boiled venison they inexplicably liked so much better than broiled, and always returned it scoured clean with sand.

One such living, historic relic of the past lasted on into my own childhood here in our own Battenkill Valley. Her name was not "Indian Molly" but "Icy." No, nothing aboriginal about the name. It had been Louisa, pronounced "Lo-eye-sy." She was already very old by the time I was big enough to notice her, a small, wiry, straight-backed ancient, her dark-brown face calm, quiet, good-natured, deeply lined. She had no home, I think. At least she was always on the move. Everybody's home was hers if she wanted to come into it. Looking out of the farmhouse window, a great-aunt would say, unastonished, "I see Icy coming up the road. Maybe she plans to settle with us for a while."

There was always room in the big, old-time farmhouses, and Icy was not particular where she slept. Although she intensely disliked the regularly recurring chores of housework she made herself welcome and useful in many ways. She prepared horseradish root for table use. Everybody depended on Icy's horseradish. And she was always glad to lend a hand to any special, and hence interesting, household operation going on — boiling down cider, doing a washing, making a quilt, drying corn, feeding the cosset lamb or the feeble little runt baby pig, brought into the house to keep him from being smothered under the vast flanks of his heedless mother. When she had had enough of that household she departed as imperturbably, as good-naturedly, as she had come. She never gave reasons for what she did. She was never called on to account for her actions. Nobody knew where she had gone, till, perhaps, a neighbor reported, "Icy's staying up to Silas Kent's now."

All through my childhood Icy thus came and went as the older "Indian Mollies" had, in town histories. Presently, of course, old age came, even to her. She could no longer tramp the roads in all weathers, as had been her delight.

What happened then? The Ladies' Benevolent Society of the Congregational Church raised money to build her a little house of her own. It still stands. Our children and grandchildren know it by sight. Tiny, convenient, compact, it was just right for a very old person to manage.

As long as she lived, the Town provided her with what she needed. After her quiet death, the Town buried her, a good funeral too, at public expense. Some years before her death, she herself had bought out of her horse-radish money, saved year by year, a marble tombstone as good as anybody's. The inscription on it reads:

MISS ICY PALMER,
BORN SEPTEMBER 1824
DIED JULY 1911
Rest in Peace . . . asleep in Jesus

I never look at the epitaph without a remorseful qualm. How unimaginatively callous we were all those years. Why did she need to die before acquiring that title of respect? *We* should have called her "Miss"!

CHAPTER 2

The Settlers

GOING back to pick up the story of those lively mustered-out young soldiers, our first Vermont forefathers, one easy-to-make misunderstanding must be put straight. Much as they relished the camping-out freedom of their trip home they were not in the least wild-hearted "mountain men" revolting against domestic cleanliness and civic duty. A holiday time between the military discipline back of them and the tidy domesticity ahead was all very well, but only as a vacation. None of them felt the slightest temptation to drift permanently into the easygoing, dirty, irregular ways and elastic morals (as they seemed to white men) of semibarbaric life. For they were young New Englanders. Most of them were serious, most were literate, all were brought up to be provident and responsible. And almost without exception every one of them had a home waiting for him down in the settled Western Connecticut or Western Massachusetts country, either in his parents' house, or in one of his own already started with a young wife before he went off to military service against the French and Indians.

So they pushed on gladly to those homes in the low, snug farm and village houses, and were welcomed with a furor of joyous affection, excitement and relief exactly like that given by their families to returned soldiers of today, or of any day.

At this point, there is a pause in the forward flow of the story as later Vermonters knew it. Nothing happened at once. In most cases a good many months passed, sometimes several years, before the decision was made to trek north and settle in the Green Mountains. Cautious older-generationers had to be talked around; the fiancée or the young wife with young children reassured; plans discussed with neighbors; family and personal savings put together to finance the purchase of the new homestead; an immense deal of contriving, and deciding which things to take along.

And then they were off. Their parents stood at the door of the old home to wave them good-by, to call out, "Wait! Wait! Did the Dutch oven get packed?" Or "Neighbor Bentley's son is coming back soon to fetch his wife and baby. Send us a letter by him to tell us how you're getting along." (For all these home-spun people could and did write letters.)

North-bound through Western Connecticut and Massachusetts, carefully keeping to the east of the line of the Province of New York, went wave after wave of these young homemakers — long-legged, sinewy lads, pouring with their young wives and little children into the forests and glades of the new, safe, wel-coming land where they displaced no other homemakers. So swift was the rising up of these sons and daughters of Connecticut and Massachusetts (fewer from Rhode Island) farmers, that General Burgoyne in a private letter to Lord George Germain, dated in August 1777, wrote, "The Hampshire Grants, a country un-peopled and almost unknown in the last war [only fifteen years before] now abounds in the most active race on the continent."

Set to write of that peaceful, cheerful swarming out from the old hives to found new communities, a Vermont pen begins to dance and gambol, to toss its head and gallop down the page like a colt let out from the barn to spring sunshine. For it was spring-time — no matter what the season of the year — to those forward-looking young people stepping confidently along the roads and trails leading them to the future.

They passed first along the earthen roads of settled old rural regions, small plain homes tight against all weather, with square stone chimneys, piles of firewood at the back, lilacs beside the front door, lilies of the valley on the north side, big rosebushes and peonies on the southern side, and clean, many-colored clothes hung out to dry, like household banners proclaiming the scrubbed cleanliness within. Just such homes — only, oh vast, immeasurable difference to young hearts, homes of their very own! — were they planning to set up when they reached the Promised Land. In the bulging packs carried by the family horse (often cared for and trained from its colthood by the young husband in the years when he too was a colt) were blankets and pillows and clothing and yards of homespun linen. They were gifts from the parents they were leaving. In almost every pack which went into Vermont was a book or two from the small, prized collection on the shelf under the family clock; a root from the peony in the front yard; a slip taken from the old lilac bush. Such a great-great-grand-mother peony blooms now in my own home garden, a great-great-great-grandchild of one in the front yard in New Milford from which most of our Arlington people came in the 1760's. Such an old volume of Shakespeare was, a generation or so ago, finally read to pieces by farmer cousins of mine. There had been two in the old home in Connecticut and two children went out to the Grants. The son was given the tragedies, the daughter the comedies. That group of the Canfields grew up, they used to say, laughingly, knowing not a word of *Coriolanus* or *King Lear*, but with quotations from *As You Like It* and *Twelfth Night* a part of every day's life. Not too bad a fate, they thought.

All that first part of the trip the young settlers were in home-land country, even though they might never have been there before. The farmer who stopped hoeing corn to come to the side of the road for a talk might by his looks have been their father. The boys who were helping him might have been their younger brothers, silent, attentive, their eyes lighting up at the sight of young folks setting out to new land, to a new life they could shape to their own tastes. All along that first stage of the journey the way was embroidered with leisurely sociable talk. There was no hurry. They had no train connections to make. They could pitch their overnight camp as well in one place as another.

Sometimes a farmer's wife, recognizing them by their looks as belonging to her own kind of folks, came to the door and called, "Come on in. I've just finished churning. Have a cup of butter-milk, won't ye?" They stopped. The horse dropped his head to crop the grass in front of the house. The children squatted down to play with the puppy. The baby, from where he was securely tied on top of the pack, was taken down to kick his heels on the floor or murmur greedily in his mother's arms as he nuzzled her for his dinner. They took the foaming buttermilk with thanks, and began to answer questions about where they were going. Kneading her great lump of bread-dough, the farmer's wife might say, "My man and I are too old to go. We've got a good place here, anyhow. But our second boy's just back from the war, and he and the girl he is going to marry are kind of thinking about the new land up in the Grants. He was wondering the other day about how you'd take hold to buy land there? Ever since he was a baby, we've been saving up to help him get started when he married. We could buy him a pitch — if the land's as good as folks say?"

"It's uneven. In places it's as rich and black as a good kitchen garden. When the Connecticut militia were mustered out in Canada I came through there on the way home with three-four of the other boys from our town. Of course we took notice of the land. All of it ain't good. Most of it grown up to monstrous great trees. But under the trees, there were places where you could run your ramrod clean down, good loose loam, all the way. And when the trees are cut, you can burn 'em and make potash, all you have time to look after. Potash is worth gold-money, you know, any day of the year, in Albany and Montreal. Any amount you want to take in."

"But won't you have trouble with York landlords? Seems though I'd heard some talk . . ."

"No, no, nothing to that. The Governor of New York is always trying to pick a quarrel with any New England governor. The folks who run New York hate Yankees like us. But you know how that ended — the King sent word that the New York line is to run twenty miles east of the Hudson. New York lawyers are smart, but even they can't kick up any dust against that. The King said it so plain. We've paid for our land, hard money. We'll keep to our side of that line."

"How about Injuns? We hear that the settlers out west in the Mohawk country been having trouble."

"No Indians in the Grants at all. Only just a few that come and go with their families to hunt and fish. They're Abnakis, anyhow, not Iroquois. They're decent folks. We'll get along with them."

"How does a person get his land up there?"

"Why, you buy it from a sort of land company. People put their money together to buy up a whole town at once. The Governor of New Hampshire (he's the one that's selling it), won't deal for anything less than a whole township at a time. But then these proprietors that buy it, they'll sell small lots to farmers, or sawmillers, or anybody who wants to settle there. They make some money on the trade, sure, but so do the merchants who buy a shipload of sugar from Jamaica, tons of it, and then sell it by the hundredweight to storekeepers — and they sell it by the pound to us. Nothing wrong with that. We bought our land that way. We paid for it, some from savings our folks gave us, some from my back pay to the militia, though that never came to much. Some we saved ourselves. I've been working for my father since we married."

"But now," from the young wife, "we're going to have a home of our own, of our very own."

She said that almost two centuries ago, but if you listen with your inner ear, you can hear the ringing lift of her voice. For the words she spoke then are spoken now, have been spoken from time immemorial. They bring up sweet memories to older people who have long been drawing strength and stability from a home of their own. They shine like a bright arrow pointing into the future for young adults beginning to be restive under their parents' roofs. From the Connecticut and Western Massachusetts homes where the young settlers passed, many and many a big son and tall daughter rose up to follow that bright arrow.

When they stayed overnight, they slept under the stars in fair weather, or snug in a quickly constructed lean-to of hemlock boughs. The young folk from the farmhouses, after the chores were done, sometimes went out to sit for a while to talk or sing around the campfires of the travelers. The next morning they stood beside their parents, at the barn door or in the kitchen garden, waving with friendly envy. "Save a pitch for us. One with good fishing. We'll be after you soon."

"First come, first served. Don't wait too long. There's good fishing everywhere!"

This was a time of ferment. From century-old communities, north, south, all through the colonies, such young family groups were streaming out towards new homes. The movement had been going on, sometimes fast, sometimes slow, ever since Plymouth Rock and Jamestown. But now that the French and Indian Wars were over, it swelled into a sort of human tidal wave. And this migration was not only more numerous and farther-roaming, its quality was changed. Imperceptibly, over the years, these frontier folk had grown to be totally different from their first ancestors on the American continent — those brave, enduring, homesick Europeans, lost without the framework around them of the familiar Old World society, not yet realizing, not daring to realize, what new freedom lay outside that rigid framework.

These young men and women bound for Vermont were typical of the new outlook. They were Americans. Thanks to more than a century of family experience, they felt at home anywhere under the American sky, on American soil. They took casually and unsurprised the ferocious American winters, the tiger-pounce of American mid-summer heat. Young husband, young wife alike, they strode out into the huge continent as if stepping into their own front yards. Well, the continent *was* their own front yard — theirs for the taking — as the English countryside had never been for their forefathers; as the old country still was not, in their day, for people of their "station in life" who had not crossed the Atlantic.

In eighteenth-century England, harsh old laws and granite-rigid social caste lines were slow to change (in fact many of them did not begin to crumble in England until well on in the second half of the nineteenth century). Working people, tenant farmers' families might help to keep the ground of the Manor forest cleared by picking up dead twigs or dry branches blown down by a storm. (Hence it is that "windfall" has come to mean a stroke of great good fortune.) But woe to the cottager if the authorities found a green stick with freshly cut stem in the little shed back of his kitchen! Only the gentry at the Hall ever enjoyed the luxury of a wide fireplace constantly replenished with blazing logs. The farmers going in to pay their rent might, from afar, catch glimpses of its brightness, but it was one of the gratifications and cheering comforts of life from which poor folks were excluded.

In these teeming American forests, to stroll along, ax in hand, free to cut what one pleased — since these were "our own trees" — was for the men of colonial times a wish-dream realized, as if a

city wage-earner's wife of today should dream that she was
stepping in and out of Fifth Avenue shops with the merchandise
free to every hand.

The century passed far from the watchful eye of the servants
of the Manor had developed in the New England men of the late
eighteenth century a masterly accuracy with the ax. Unlike their
European forefathers, those first Vermonters never broke their
hearts trying to burn the wrong kind of wood. They were deeply
erudite in forest-lore. All the fuel anybody could burn was theirs
for the cutting — dry split pine for kindling, for quick summer
cooking; massive sticks of green oak for the lasting backlog,
armfuls of dry hickory and yellow birch and rock-maple for
the all-day-long, steady, smokeless, heart-warming flames of mid-
winter. We need waste no sympathy on them because for days at
a time they bent their backs to lay by the year's store of fuel.
They were stout backs, and young, and it was his own hearthfire each man was feeding.

They were at home with the trees as their English-bred forefathers had never been. In the same way they were at home with
wildlife, which in England had been forbidden to plain people
like their ancestors. Hunting was reserved for landowning gentry
by complicated British game laws enforced by terrible penalties.
The proprietors of the land, who already had all the food they
needed, not only owned every acre of soil but also every wild
thing that might add vitamins and protein to a farm family's
diet. Even the humble, prolific rabbit was forbidden to plain folk.
The very smell of a savory rabbit stew, if it reached the bailiff's
nostrils, was a proof of wrongdoing that might lead to a prison
sentence; or if the Lord of the Manor and his employees were
notably humane, a beating or a savage tongue-lashing which a
poaching gray-haired father must receive in unresisting submission to his betters, his children looking on, and learning the
tradition by which they were to live.

More than a hundred years of freedom lay between such
memories and the young western New Englanders who went up
into the forests and open glades of Vermont. They never felt the
slightest inhibition in pulling the triggers of their long squirrel
rifles. They knew the exact meaning of every track in the snow,

of every rustle in the summer woods. They feared none of the animals swarming about them. The appearance of a bear crossing a clearing caused no panic. Quite the contrary! It roused the tingling excited enthusiasm of the hunting spirit, so much exalted (as part of upper-class life) by the old-country tradition.

Thus, through the whole range of daily activity, they took hold of life, as they would have said, "by the handle, not by the hot end," neither with cringing apprehension, nor with the raw swagger of the newly emancipated. For it never occurred to them to doubt that they were first-class citizens — "as good as anybody."

Such they were, the vital young people who settled Vermont, eagerly surging up from Western Connecticut and Massachusetts, on foot, on horseback, or with ox-cart. Some of them came in big companies, a number of the young folks of the same township traveling together and choosing home-sites near each other. The children in such a group went on playing with each other uninterruptedly, both along the way and after they had stopped to sink roots into the new soil. Stability of human relations came with them, along with brass kettles, books, and homespun blankets. Sometimes a single family by itself moved slowly along with young children, the iron skillet dangling on top of the pack. Sometimes it was a single man, without any pack-animal, only a knapsack on his back, a rifle on one shoulder, an ax on the other. He was going to "start things" for his folks who would join him the next summer. By neighborhoods, by families, singly, they all knew what they would find, they all pressed forward zestfully to measure their strength against the wilderness.

They were coming not as exiles or refugees from persecution, or because of failure at home. It was their free wish to come. Almost without exception, they were in those joyful first years of young maturity, when the authority of the older generation is being thrown off. They were going to make these new homes as *they* wanted, not to fit the ideas of Great-aunt Eliza, or the fussy housekeeping ways of Mother, or the old-fashioned notions of Father.

Prepared as they were by training and temperament, and with this prospect beckoning them on, it is no wonder that their young hearts were not darkened as the farm clearings grew smaller, more widely spaced, and the dirt road dwindled to a rough blazed trail winding among the trees. Did they feel no homesickness as mile after mile was added to their distance from the routine of settled civilization? Not a trace, from anything we have ever heard. They were young. Their spirits rose to boisterous heights of fun and good-fellowship.

We can understand that. Even today, softened as we are by dependence on push-button conveniences, most of us are delighted to spend high sums to enjoy an outdoor vacation from responsibility. We have all known campers, trail-riders, or hikers, back from a month in Canada or the Rockies. They are brown as to face, relaxed, reposed as to spirits. What they tell us does not sound enlivening. They have been cold and wet. Their meals have been seasoned with wood ashes; wild storms have blown down their tents; porcupines have in the night eaten what was planned for breakfast; they have been all but blinded by smoke from campfires built of rain-soaked wood . . . and as they remember and talk about these misadventures, their eyes sparkle, their faces glow. They have been drinking from some source of vitality far too deep to put into words.

Like the fragrance from old pillows stuffed with balsam needles, there lingers in Vermont memories just such an aroma of outdoor freshness, breathing through the stories of those first days. The particular stories remembered in different towns vary greatly in detail one from another. They are alike in one quality. In none of them is there any melancholy — never the note of "An Exile from Erin" or "Lochaber No More." Here is one example:

Have you by chance ever driven over Route U.S. 7, north from Williamstown? If you have, and if the day was fine, you have, no doubt, like other motorists, stopped your car to admire the view at the Pownal Turn. Nobody who has seen it can forget the complex, harmonious composition of its two green and smiling valleys, diverging in a V from below where you stand at the look-out place. For those with old Vermont memories in their bloodstream, the spot has an added touch of poetry. For, so tradition has it, the pioneer trail also passed this way and this very spot was an accepted overnight halting place. Eight to ten rough miles ahead was Bennington, already something of a settle-

ment even before the full flood of northbound homesteaders.
In his private journal, James Duane, the New York City lawyer,
on his scouting trip to look over the country he confidently expected to rule as Lord of the Manor, noted with satisfaction his
admiration of the pleasant village homes of Bennington, and that
it had "a genteel church" — the adjective being natural to a genteel Yorker.

There was little that he, or any other New York proprietor,
would have called genteel about the lively bands of vigorous
young country folk from hard-working, successful farm families
in Connecticut and Massachusetts who were journeying up to
make their homes on land for which they did not intend to pay
rent to James Duane, because they had already bought it from
Governor Wentworth.

As one such group, bound for Bennington, sat around their
last-night-out campfire, joking, singing, drinking cider (if there
was any of it left in the gallon jugs), playing games, the talk
chanced to turn on a rivalry between the big girls of the crowd
as to which was the best horsewoman. Their older (a little older)
married brothers and sisters egged on the brags. "I'll bet on
Peggy!" "I'll back Mehitabel!" Wagers were laid, a modest purse
was put together to be given to the girl who would be the first
to ride her horse into Bennington village.

Next morning the laughing racers swung into their saddles
and set out, hell-for-leather, along the trail, with their backers
yelling the eighteenth-century equivalents of "Go it, Molly!"
"Do your stuff, Nell!" There were no gray heads among them,
hence nobody shuddered forebodingly at the thought of one of
the horses catching a hoof in a root across a trail, of young brains
beaten out against a tree trunk, of what might happen if one of
the riders should take the wrong branch where the trail forked.
No, they cheered and threw up their hats and waved their kerchiefs. If they had not had little children and household gear to
see to, some of them would have been off themselves in that
glorious reckless plunge forward — so like their own exhilarating
plunge into the unknown hills and valleys before them.

Does this anecdote strike you as improbable? Are you thinking,
"Oh come now, it is only during the last few decades that young

women have learned to ski, to swim, actually to *enjoy* bodily exertion!" Yes, of course, during the Victorian nineteenth century, the heroines of romance were physically frail, clinging-vine, white-cheeked, sofa-women, who depended on their husbands for all decisions except about what dresses and hats to wear. That picture was probably close enough to life . . . to the only life most of those novelists thought worth recording, although George Eliot's farm women were neither frail nor clinging! A good many theories have been advanced to explain the odd (and to us rather disagreeable) behavior code of the Victorian lady. Some lay it to tight lacing. Others label it an example of "competition by conspicuous display." They point out that, like the super-duper mink coat of today, the wife who never lifted her hand to earn gave notice to the world that her husband was an exceptionally good provider. More probably, I think, nobody planned it that way. In the age of expanding profits from trade and industry, when factory production, division of labor, specialization of skills were taking all the old home crafts (spinning, weaving, salting down winter meat) out of the housewife's hands, when cooks and cleaning-women could be hired for a tiny fraction of her husband's income, and when it reflected credit on a husband to have his wife idle, it must have required extraordinary internal drive to keep a middle-class woman from drifting into languidly ornamental uselessness.

It is odd that few Victorian-American writers — from say James Fenimore Cooper on — checked their conception of the innate character of women by what was well known about their own grandmothers. In the rural regions of eighteenth-century America, by the harsh rule of survival of the fittest, there were very few frail women. The frail ones died early. There was no sofa in any house on which anybody could recline — just look at any collection of colonial antiques — no chair in which anybody could lean back. Furniture was fashioned by and for the people who sat up straight unless they were so sick that they were bedridden. Such women did not depend on their husbands for decisions, or for courage. They did not scream at the sight of a mouse — nor at the sight of a catamount.

*   *   *

The cynical wisecrack that history is only a fable which happens to be believed makes sound sense when it is turned inside-out. For traditional folk stories tell us about the inner history, the admirations, the aspirations for a good life, of the generations who have thought them worth preserving and repeating. It is significant, then, that the race to Bennington became famous, in a moderate Vermont way, over a small corner of this region. Everybody up and down the settlements in that part of the new country heard about it, knew which girl had breezed in first, cantering her horse for witnesses to her victory, up to the Bennington tavern where every man-jack turned out to applaud her.

The sequel is even more significant for the light it throws on Vermonters' scale of values.

In time that girl-rider married, had children, had grandchildren. Years later, a traveler stopped overnight at the tavern (by then modernized as a "hotel"). "Is she still alive?" he asked the clerk. "That woman . . . I mean the one who, running her horse all the way up from Pownal, got to Bennington first of her group of settlers?"

"Oh, yes, she's still alive. Pretty old, of course, must be quite a bit over seventy. She lives in the third farm after the right-hand turn beyond the bridge."

Out of curiosity, with a tourist's urge to take in all the sights of the town he finds himself in, the traveler went out to the farm. A rosy little girl was picking up chips back of the kitchen door. He doubted if so young a child could have heard a story so old, but he put his question to her.

"That was my grandmother," she said proudly. "Yes, she lives here!"

"Could I speak to her a moment?"

"Well, no, she's not at the house this morning. She's out in the upper field, plowing."

Something is told about the spirit of a people by the stories they chance to hand down, by the kind of women they admire.

Another story, another setting. This is concerned with one of the young husbands and fathers, who came a season ahead of his family, axed out a clearing, built the first log house, planted corn in the rich land between the stumps, harvested it, and, putting up a great store of firewood, stayed on in the new cabin through the winter, trapping and hunting in order to have some fur to exchange for cash, come springtime.

It was over Wilmington way, I think, that such a solitary settler prepared to live alone through the winter in his newly built cabin. To his door there arrived one wildly stormy day in late November an Indian family, father, mother, sturdy little boy and baby. They, too, were out for a winter of trapping. They had no shelter. The white man took them in, at first till that great snowstorm had passed and then — why not? — as housemates for the winter.

Neither spoke a word of the other's language. But they managed by gestures to make each other understand the plan for peaceful living. A line was drawn down the middle of the cabin floor. Wavings of arms and fingers and noddings of heads said plainly, "This side for Indians. This side for white man." Both were to have access to the life-giving fire on the hearth.

For many months, in peace and tranquillity, the two races lived side by side — the baby the only one to cross the line uninvited. They shared each other's meat; the white man had a little bag of precious salt, enough for a grain or two on broiled bear steak and roast saddle of venison. With perfect confidence each left the cabin when he pleased, sure that the other side of the line would leave untouched his own small store of treasures . . . the ax, the blankets, the growing pile of furs.

When spring came on and the ice in the brook melted, the white man saw that the Indian boy was eying his fishing-pole with a longing which he recognized from his own boyhood. In the mute language of gesture he asked if the lad would like to go fishing. A light sprang up in the black eyes, like a reflection from his own blue eyes at twelve.

The Indian boy took from the fireplace one of the charred sticks they used for pencils. On a piece of birch-bark he sketched the pole, a thinner stroke for the stout linen line, ending with a jiggle for the wonderful metal hook . . . beyond the scope of Indian craftsmanship. He patted the picture, then he patted his own chest. Next he drew a fish, and through it a line dividing it in two. One half was for us Indians, the other — so said the energetic forefinger — would belong to the man who had loaned pole, line and hook.

The white man laughed, took down the pole from the pegs where it had lain all winter, and passed it over to the Indian boy. From that time on, joy to the dark-skinned lad and plenty of broiled fish for his elders, for the streams in those days were swarming with trout. One early settler happened to mention in writing that he and his brother, both young lads, caught a bushel-basket full of trout in an hour.

As the sun grew warmer, the Indian family saw no point in living any longer under a roof, and with many wordless friendly farewells packed up their few belongings, lifted the papoose, bigger and plumper than he had been the autumn before, and were off to a wilder, freer, less trammeled life than even the Vermont settler they left behind them.

He had a tale to tell his own children on the great day in early June when into the clearing came the little cavalcade from the old Connecticut home. His boys ran shouting to meet him, their voices ringing like bells in the silence of the forest. Then came his wife on horseback, holding the baby girl, twice the size she had been when her father last saw her.

There is, of course, no record of what he said to her. But since my great-greats were close to him in age and tradition, in circumstances, in taste and standards, and since I know them pretty well through their letters, through the records of their actions, through what their grandchildren have told me about them, I think I know that what he felt was, "Oh my wife, my love, when you come the meaning of life springs up like a fountain. With you and the children here, I am a whole man again, deep-rooted in hope, faith and joy." But I am sure that he put none of that feeling into words. Probably what he said was something like this: "I've got a line of pump-logs rigged up right to the door. You won't need to go to the brook for water. Little Delia's fat as a pig, ain't she?"

It was a language his wife understood as well as he.

One could go on setting down early Vermont memories, town by town, from Bennington in the south to Newport on the

Canada line. But there is a limit to the interest anybody can feel
in other people's family legends. Still, I can't hold my hand from
putting in one more, partly because I know all the details, since
it concerns my own forebears, partly because it reaffirms my conviction that the traditional, submissive, husband-obeying wife,
who loved to be commanded by a male, if she ever existed anywhere outside mid-Victorian fiction, certainly was not a Vermont
product; most of all because, at least by implication, it throws
light on a much debated, often misunderstood, chapter of Vermont history. It runs as follows.

When the Israel Canfield whom we met in the chapter before
this reached home after his wanderings, he waited only until he
got together money enough to pay for a plot of northern wild
land. Then he put the question to his young wife: would she
consent to leave the comfortable home in New Milford and strike
out with him to found a new home in the tall timber of the
Hampshire Grants.

Her eyes kindled at the prospect of building life together "on
their own." Of course she would. But she made one condition.
She had been a skillful spinster (in those days the word meant
what it said — a woman who could spin, not an unmarried girl)
and she had a good store of household linen, sheets, pillow-cases,
towels, coverlets, all spun and woven by her own hands. Nothing
could induce her to expose the contents of her hope chest to the
rigors of hard water. Her husband must promise her a site fit for
decent laundry work.

"All water's wet," said the puzzled Israel, "however can you
tell whether it's hard or soft?"

As soon as his wife and mother could stop laughing at his
masculine ignorance, they burst out together, "You take along a
piece of soap and wash something in it. If you get a lather, it's
all right. If not, move on."

He agreed to that test. The journey was made. The two horses
of their little cavalcade crossed the southern line of Arlington
town, where many of the New Milford people had arranged to
settle. From then on, the young matron of 1764, my great-great
grandmother, washed her way, mile by mile, northward. She
had a piece of homemade soap in the pocket of her riding skirt.

Wherever the trail crossed a brook, she slid from her saddle, stooped over the clear water, wet, soaped and rubbed her handkerchief.

But the water was hard. Most Vermont water still is. It runs over the abundant marble and other limestone rocks, later so valuable to Vermont. To this day the teakettles of most Arlington houses are coated thickly with a deposit of lime. Not a hint of foam did she get from her soaping. She wrung the handkerchief out, hung it on the back of her saddle to dry, mounted again, and with her half-vexed, half-laughing, altogether good-natured husband, rode on to try the water of other brooks.

"He must a-thought," so my great-uncle used to mimic the old rustic vernacular, "she were a-goin' to land 'em clear up in Canady."

They did not need to go as far as that. Close to the northern boundary line of Arlington, almost seven miles from where she began her quest, the brook beds change by a quirk of geology from limestone to slate. In this water the New Milford soap foamed up blithely into a lather fit to delight the heart of any woman who loved good linen — are there any who do not?

Holding out the good news for her husband to see, "Here's where we'd better settle," she said. So they did.

There, in an open-front log camp — like those used nowadays by summer vacationers in the Adirondacks — they spent the first few months of our family's hundred-and-ninety years of Vermont residence. The men-folks with the help of neighbors put up a well-constructed, winter-tight house lower down the stream. Into this they moved, before winter. That house is as good as ever, and is still one of the Canfield homes.

But only two generations later, by the time my grandfather was born, the rich top layer of leaf-mold had washed away from the arable land. It became apparent that the quality of the soil, to put it conservatively, was not quite up to that of the water. To be entirely frank, the land chosen by my great-greats was about the least rewarding of any in the district. These fields of sand and cobblestones explain the intermittent nature of our family residence. We have never sold that old farm, nor did we ever move away, permanently. But, since early in the nineteenth century, no Canfield has fought the losing battle of trying to wring all of his living from those lean, beautiful and much-loved acres. Instead, most of us have been forced to sharpen our wits in training for one or another profession, success in which meant years in city exile. I alone — for a writer needs nothing more than a typewriter and an R.F.D. mailbox within reach — have had the good fortune of spending not only a great deal of my childhood, but forty-six mature years very close indeed to the spot where the first Arlington Canfields started housekeeping.

When the horses were unsaddled at the end of the trip, so family tradition runs, my great-grandmother's mother stuck into the deep sand beside the soft-water brook the riding switch she had cut from the old willow beside her Connecticut home. It took root and grew. When I was a little girl, my elders called my attention to it and told me the story. In fact, as elders often do, they told me the story many times. But, my eyes on the willow tree, I never minded how often they repeated. By that time it was huge and very old and leaned low across the brook as if bowed down by the weight of its great age. It leaned lower and lower. Time went by. I grew up, married, settled in the low frame house where I am now writing — barely more than a good outfielder's throw from the riding-switch willow. When my children were growing up, the old tree died. It stood with its browned and ancient bones, like an unburied skeleton. Finally in what we call "a big windblow," the storm broke it off close to the ground. It fell across the brook beside which it had lived for so long. We said good-by to it.

But when my first grandchild began to walk, I noticed that a fresh green and yellow shoot of willow was springing up from . . . could it be from a root of the old tree? . . . a seed . . . who knew? . . . something which had never died at all, but still lived. It has gone on living, and now it is tall enough to shade my oldest, growing-up granddaughter, as she halts there on her way to college.

As you get along in years, you come to see that there are poems and symbols which need no words to sing their meaning.

When I was young, I naturally considered that story as belonging exclusively to our family. It was only when I began to read widely in Vermont lore that, to my naïve surprise, I found, scattered liberally through town histories, plenty of big willows — far too many for credibility — all certified to have sprouted from a Connecticut or a Massachusetts riding switch thrust into the moist edge of some local brook.

There are those whose idea of local history is that it has value only when it can trace with accuracy the line of some long-vanished road, and can settle the question as to whether it swerved a little to the right or a little to the left in climbing a steep grade. For such literal fact-searchers, an unlikely number of riding switches proves beyond a doubt that oral folk tradition is untrustworthy. So it is, if the scope of history, local or general, is limited to establishing, through evidence written down on paper, whether such-and-such an event took place on Tuesday the eleventh or on Wednesday the twelfth. Certainly human memory, especially elderly memory, is notoriously undependable about dates and single facts of the past.

But only occasionally does the error of a day, or a week, or even a year, make any noticeable difference in our understanding of the long, continuous tradition of human communities — step by step from the distant past up to today, guiding, enriching, laying the foundation for all our thoughts about government, about our life with others. History is worth reading when it tells us truly what the attitude towards life was in the past. That is what history means to everyone except the most fact-bound pedants. And folk-testimony seldom misrepresents the general attitude towards life of several generations ago. The story of the young wife's riding switch, carried from the old home and taking root beside a Vermont brook, may be in some cases an imaginative fancy, not a literal statement of what happened. But it is a fancy which never would have occurred to the mind of the Oregon Trail pioneers as something which *might* have happened at the end of those grueling months of plodding across the immense expanses of the Great Plains and of the terrible climb over the Rocky Mountains.

The often-repeated tale of the willow switch from Connecticut or Massachusetts bursting into new life in Vermont means that the journey here was never regarded as long or hard, as shutting the door on the past, as withering inherited character-buds, habits of thought, loyalty to old traditions.

That symbolism rings true to everything we know about these first settlers. Whether they had set out singly or in groups, former neighbors hurried to flock together again once the journey was finished. Shared community memory is a strong bond. Fundamentally they were — and their descendants still are — western New Englanders. The slight changes from established patterns, which in time have produced a special Vermontish flavor, developed slowly without conscious plan, as these young people worked out their dream of a life organized as they thought "fit and proper," throwing themselves headlong into the task before them. "Headlong" their activity was in every way. Almost overnight the clearings grew wider, longer, more thickly filled with cabins of friendly homemakers, lending a hand to raise a new rooftree, joining with equally uninhibited energy in boisterous amusements. They danced a good deal, our Vermont forefathers, the old quadrilles, which they never gave up for waltzes. As a little girl I have heard old people talk relishingly of the evenings when you only had to blow a conch horn from your door to bring in sixteen couples ready to stamp it out till midnight. They ate like gourmets: venison, partridges, bear steak, trout by the bushel, squirrel stew, corn bread, corn-meal mush, baked beans, wild berries of every variety, dried or preserved with maple sugar. Each family of them made a hogshead of maple sugar for the year's sweetenin'. They smoked the haunches of the deer shot in their prime, eaten months later. They rendered into birch-bark pails the great slabs of fat from the bear just going into hibernation. It was wonderful for everything, bear fat was, so we used to be told, for tasty shortening in cooking, for greasing thick winter boots, for slicking down hair, for the wooden axles of the first wooden ox-carts.

Very occasionally, between seasons, food nearly gave out and they lived on small rations, these periods of near-fasting probably not at all injurious to their health. Incomparably skillful axmen and reasonably competent, rough carpenters, they soon added to their cabins a shelter for their family cow, for the horse. No more than shelters, but their animals were as hardy as their owners, grew a thick winter coat of fur under the longer hair of their pelts, and throve on what they had.

Many of these grandfathers of industrialism were born with an instinct for machinery. They soon contrived sawmills and gristmills, using power from the streams pouring downhill all around them. The great hardwood trees, which had to be cut to make clearings, they burned in enormous bonfires. Out of the heaps of ashes, they refined potash and carried this valuable cash crop once a year or so, by packhorses or by knapsack, over the constantly widening trails to Albany, to Hartford, to Boston, to Lake Champlain for water transport to Montreal, according to the part of Vermont where they lived. From these deep-water ports (yes, all the above were so considered in those days of shallow-draught vessels!) they came back with metal tools needed in their operations, with shoe buckles, a yard of fine lawn for a sweetheart's best handkerchief, twists of tobacco, news of the great world, and a book or two (not of sermons) to add to the many-times-read volumes on the cabin shelf.

Not that their lives, so satisfying to them, looked comely to conventional people. A Reverend Mr. Perkins, passing through on a missionary trip, some years later, reported cabins filled with smoke, poor beds, fleas, a lack of comfort so complete as to be dismaying.

The settlers themselves were not dismayed. They were young.

Also it is to be remembered that the Reverend Mr. Perkins was not an objective observer. Like the Reverend Dr. Timothy Dwight and several other white-collar observers of early Vermont good cheer, he had an ax to grind, a theological ax. He was outraged that people so frivolously indifferent to the fine points of theology should be so absurdly light-hearted, vital, and happy as Vermonters obviously were. Timothy Dwight specifically predicted that nothing but corrupt government could be expected from Vermonters who had so secular a view of human life. The Reverend Mr. Perkins detected in these rough-and-ready young folks, living without lawyers or law courts, and yet without disorder or crime, and with so few churches compared to the number of schools as to horrify him, a familiarity with the

heinous heresy of John Locke in his *Letters on Toleration;*
that "religion should be organized to promote goodness; not to
preserve the metaphysical subtleties of sectarian theology." The
Reverend Perkins was quite accurate in perceiving this tendency
among Vermonters. It exists to this day.

Also, accustomed as this black-broadcloth-clad clergyman was
to the special table delicacies, soft, padded comforts and prefer-
ential treatment lavished on the clergy by respectfully admiring
churchwomen in his New Haven social tradition, he suffered ac-
cutely from the rude, crude conditions he was forced to share
with these buckskin-clad, boisterously life-enjoying Vermonters.
His journal overflows with the most heartfelt self-pity. Like a
dismal refrain through his recital of the miseries of his Vermont
tour runs the entry, day by day, *"Nothing to drink but brook
water."*

The settlers, like all young people, were thirsting for life
itself and drank it from deep sources beyond his comprehension.

They were young. The communities around them were made
up of other young people. They did not even see the lacks in
household gear, in comfort, in neatness, distressing to visitors
from the more settled colonies. For their sons and daughters, as
the children grew, they set up schools, and were proud to make
provision that every child of Vermont should learn how to read
both print and script, write his own letters, figure enough to
keep his own accounts.

They had Town Meetings like those to which they were
brought up. In them the young citizens stood, dressed in their
best suits of brown homespun, broad-shouldered, lean-faced,
proud that they ran their own communities, looking forward into
the future with clear, untroubled eyes.

They were young. They were surrounded by friendly neighbors, near enough to dance with, to exchange work with, to call
on for help, not near enough to break the blessed freedom of
every family to live as it thought best.

It seemed too good to be true.

It was too good to be true.

PART II

CHAPTER 3
A Chat Between Neighbors

THE subject of the next section of this book is the dispute between the early settlers in the Green Mountains and those few men in the neighboring Province of New York who held either official government positions or grants to enormous tracts of land. This dispute was a long one, running from the early 1760's to 1791.

The narration of what happened during this era of bad feeling has been set down in many books, with meticulous accuracy as to dates, names (complete with middle initials), factual doings. Some of these accounts of the swaying struggle are long, intricate, exhaustive, scholarly. Some are shortened to a length more easily absorbed by a hasty modern reader. None of them is impartial and objective. How would they be, written by human beings as they were?

Some show the Vermont settlers as heroic American patriots. The trouble with this point of view is that the word patriot implies fatherland, to which the devoted patriot is willing to sacrifice himself, and the oddity of the Vermonters' political situation during those first years makes the object of their devotion hard to pin down to anything solid and tangible. The early Vermonters were willing to risk their lives — yes, did risk their lives — but for an idea rather than a geographical fatherland.

Other Vermont histories, written in the more modern style, feel the now-in-fashion urge to discover a sawdust stuffing in such words as "patriotic" and "heroic." The avowed purpose of these later debunking histories is to strip off from the actors in the early Vermont story their theatrical Robin Hood costumes, and to show them as shabby land-speculators.

These two opposing schools have, curiously enough, one sizable element in common. They both start their books with the literal factual beginning of the fight. Concerning the centuries of "build-up" in old-country England and her colonies, which set the stage for this blazing up of resistance by Vermont settlers to New York landlords, not a word is said. But every fight starts long before the first blow is struck. Here, as always, we cannot grasp the meaning of action until we see it as the result of long, special conditioning.

Where, I asked myself, was I to find information about that conditioning? Vermonters were then as we are now, plain people of the kind who earn their living by their own work. It seemed unlikely that public records would have much of anything to say about the opinions, feeling, daily lives, personalities of the equally plain people who, centuries ago, were their British ancestors, or of the farming folk of New England, who were their more immediate forebears. History, as a rule, is not much interested in the anonymous common man who expresses his convictions and emotions in deeds not words. Powerful and articulate individuals are much more picturesque, as well as easier for a historian to study and portray. I expected to find abundant material about the New York "gentry" — so called — and little or nothing about the tenant farmers who rented from such proprietors the land they worked on. Was authentic documentary evidence to be found anywhere, I wondered, bearing witness as to how those Hudson Valley tenant farmers felt toward the framework of their daily lives, which of course would have become the framework of the daily lives of the early Vermonters if they had accepted the government of the Province of New York.

Such doubts were short-lived. I was fairly snowed under by evidence on my problem in the reports of colonial officials, in the publications of law schools, of local and state historical societies, in scholarly theses and erudite volumes written by and for professional historians — the sort of book where three lines of text at the top of a page are followed by twenty lines of fine-print footnotes listing sources, references and supporting quotations.

Obviously this all-too-plentiful information had to be boiled down into an account simple and straightforward enough to hold the attention of readers, weakened as our power of attention is today by doubly compressed digests, tabloids, five-minute surveys of the situation of the world. That task seemed impossible. It continued to seem impossible until I realized that I could not make clear to others what, often enough, because of the technical language, was vague and baffling to me.

So I set myself to see what those learned words meant in human lives, to translate, as best I could, into straightforward, man-to-man meanings, each of the cautiously qualified statements of scholars, the "provided thats" of accurate lawyer language. The effort was worth while. From those legal words (which I have been obliged to look up in the dictionary, one by one), from those literal citations quoted by historians, from official reports made by governors and lieutenant governors to eighteenth-century London, there rose before my eyes a vivid picture of human beings. You may see it as I do.

Here it is:

First of all, where did our settlers live before they traveled northward? Consider the roster of a few townships in southwest Vermont: the founders of Arlington came mostly from New Milford, Connecticut — fifteen miles from the New York lines; Manchester, just north of us, from Amenia — now in New York State, then troubled border country; Poultney folks, most of them from Berkshire County, Massachusetts, with a few from the Connecticut county just to the south — both separated by only a surveyor's line from New York; Cornwall, Vermont, was settled from Litchfield, Connecticut — twenty miles from New York; Salisbury and Rutland, Vermont, from the district around Salisbury, Connecticut — only five miles from the New York boundary.

From any of those districts, in the days before the migration, say in the 1750's to the 1760's, a squirrel-hunting lad, roaming in the woods, might casually step over an unmarked line into the Province of New York. From anything he could see, there among the trees, he'd never know that he had crossed a boundary. But he would have stepped from one world into another, out of a world with social ideals looking towards the future of our American nation, into one where the social ideals were based on acceptance of the British past.

He would have seen no difference in the woods, in the air, in the ground under his feet, except that in general the land looked

much more fertile, less stony, lay more level to welcome the plow
— and yet had fewer people in it, by far, than in his own neighborhood.

Finding the faint trace of a trail, and following it on the chance
of its leading to a settlement, he would have been surprised to
find no house in such a fine farming country. Hardly a stone in
the rich black earth. Splendid great trees, open glades where wild
grass grew thick enough to fill a barn with hay. But there were no
barns. Great patches of blackberry bushes hung thick with fruit,
ungarnered.

Very different all this, from the thin, stony soil of his own
hilly birthplace. Yet everywhere in his home district there was a
network of roads. They were poor and narrow, but vastly better
than this deer trail. And there were always houses and people
around.

His mother would probably be out at this minute in a berry-
patch with a crowd of neighbor women from nearby farms.
They would all be in neat, clean, poor, linsey-woolsey dresses,
which they themselves had spun, dyed, woven and sewed. Each
one would be carrying a great basket, made at home the winter
before, in front of the leaping hearthfire while the head of the
house read aloud from *Gulliver's Travels* or *Robinson Crusoe*.
After the summer day's fruit-picking, the heaped-up baskets
would be carried back to the neatly kept, low, frame houses
where the old folks had been left to take care of the babies, the
hens, the cosset lambs, and the calves and colts in the barn.

The tall lad with the rifle had eaten since morning only a dry
piece of bread. But he came from a plain farm family and was not
used to comforts. And there was this splendid feast of fruit.
Cramming the luscious berries into his mouth, he wondered why
nobody had picked them to put up in sugar for next winter's pies.

Not so many brooks, he noticed, as in Connecticut. After all
day in the woods, he was now so dry he would gladly have drunk
brook water, although it was not considered wholesome. Cider or
ale sat better on the stomach, people thought. Tea for women,
rum for older men. He swung his long legs in a wider stride.
Surely there must be farmhouses in such rich country. Yes, he
caught sight of a roof. Someone was moving in front of a small,

low, stone house. Sure enough, the trail, now a path, turned to lead him there. He followed it briskly, his spirits rising at the thought of a drink, perhaps a neighborly invitation to eat a bite after many hours without food, a chair to sit down in after a long time on his feet, and a chance to pass the time of day. He had not spoken since long before noon.

He saw now that the figure moving to and fro in front of the roughly built house was a lad of about his age, carrying pails of water from a large, fair brook that ran at some distance from the house. The boy was poorly and shabbily dressed. So was the squirrel-hunter. But the squirrel-hunter was clean, and smelled clean. Not the water-carrier. He was barefooted, his feet calloused and dirty. The Connecticut boy wore well-oiled, deer-hide moccasins which he had sewed for himself the winter before.

"Well, the water's clean, anyhow," thought the newcomer and asked in a civil tone for a drink.

The boy with the pails stared. "You can take all you want out of the brook," he said glumly. He went on into the house, and shut the door. It was made of slabs, sagging, askew, so that it could be shut only with a slam.

The boy from Connecticut knelt by the brook, took a long drink, stood up wiping his mouth, and looking at the building. Its unhewed stones were so roughly put together ("Father wouldn't let us build a stone wall in a back pasture so kim-kam as that," he thought) and it had so few windows and such small ones that to his eye it looked more like a little barn or a fort than anybody's home.

The other boy now came out with the pails empty, and stopped to dip them full.

"Here, let me have one. I'll help you. Pay for my drink," said the Connecticut boy, smiling dryly. He was used to people who lightened their talk by ironic turns of phrase.

The other boy did not smile. He clutched the two pails. "Where you from?" he demanded suspiciously.

"Near Salisbury. My folks live on a farm there." Something about the boy's blank, doubtful face made him add, "That's in Connecticut, you know. Maybe I've come over the line without knowing it."

"I *thought* you talked queer," said the New York boy. He handed over a pail, "If you're not from around here, I guess it's all right for you to come into the house."

The squirrel-hunter had no idea what the other boy meant. But he had been rigorously trained to keep his mouth shut about what he did not understand. He asked no questions, filled his pail, trudged behind his companion to the shut door.

It was opened a crack by a woman of his mother's age. Like his mother, she was dressed for work in linsey-woolsey. Her dress was poor, as all dresses in that material were, but unlike his mother's, it was not clean, nor whole. Some wisps of hair straggled down from under her cap.

"It's all right," the boy told her. "His father is a farmer. He's from over the line. He talks the way they do, too, kind of drawly. He lost his way in the woods."

The woman opened the door to a single, dark, cluttered room. From a chair beside the hearth a toothless older woman hauled herself up, hobbled over to the tousled bed, took off two pillows, and pushed them down between the bed and the wall.

The Connecticut boy looked surprised.

Remembering his manners, "How are you, ma'am?" he said to the younger woman, setting the full pail down. Then to make sociable talk, as he would have spoken to his mother about a handy household contrivance, he went on, "Do you know, ma'am, there's an easier way of getting water into your house than pails. Around us, all the houses and barns have it. In wintertime we take long augers and bore out the center from straight tree trunks, to make what we call a 'pump-log.' Some places, they do it at the sawmill. Then, come warm weather when the ground's thawed, you dig you a ditch, lay your pump-logs in it, end to end, put one end in the brook, and you have good water running into a trough, right in your back kitchen. Doesn't cost a cent either. Water runs down hill, you know. You could borrow the auger, if you haven't got one, from most anyone in our neighborhood."

The woman and boy looked at him strangely with an expression he did not understand. In the tone with which she would have said, "Don't talk like a fool," she said, shortly. "We're tenants."

The Connecticut boy gaped, not seeing the connection. She thought he had not heard her, and repeated more loudly, "I said, we're *tenants*."

"But — but — but ma'am, what — ? We have neighbors who rent their land, and they have pump-logs and water running in their kitchens and barns."

"Don't their landlords take half-rights or quarter-rights when they sell their leaseholds? Ours do. Water in this house would make the place worth a lot more. *He'd* get half. Everything you do to improve the place is money in *his* pocket. There's plenty there a'ready, I always say, that he never earned. There's no sense in our working the skin off'n our fingers to hand over more to him. If we got water running, so it'd be handy, he'd push us off the place to get his half-rights. I'd rather carry pails all my life."

The squirrel-hunter understood none of this. Not a word. "I never heard of selling a leasehold. And I don't know what quarter-rights or half-rights are." He tried to explain, "It's not that I don't know about renting land. My married brother rents his farm. He pays so much every month. Part of what he pays is rent, part goes to pay for the land. He calc'lates that in eight years the farm'll be his, all paid for. It'll be a nice place too." He carefully avoided looking around him. "He's set him up a little sawmill on his brook. You know, with a big wheel, doesn't take much water. My father helped him dam the brook. He saws by pondsfull. Mostly on rainy days, when he can't work outdoors. He's sawed enough boards out of trees on his own land to build on an ell to his house. They've got two boys and a baby girl, they need more place to put the children. Their house has four rooms now."

The woman and boy pounced on him with a jeer for his improbable tale. "D'ye expect us to believe *that?* He can't hide a sawmill from the rent collector."

"What's the *rent collector* got to do — ? Why should he hide — ? What's *any*body got to do with his mill?" Even to their ears, his astonished wonder rang true.

"Why, he don't know. He really don't know," said the boy to his mother.

"He *would* know if he lived this side of the line," said the
woman. To the stranger, "Our landlords don't 'low anybody to
have a sawmill but them. What's more, you have to buy every
sawed stick you use from them. Any price they want to ask you.
You dassent buy from any other sawmill, even if it's miles nearer,
and sells boards for less."

"How do you mean — you don't dare?"

"It's in the lease. You have to sign a lease. All kinds of things
in it, you agree not to do. If you *do* any of 'em, he gets his lawyer
to make out a writ of ejectment and puts you off. But even if you
could saw out boards, yourself, 'twouldn't do you no good. You
can't cut any of the good trees on your land. They're for the
landlord. That's in the lease too. If you make a mistake and cut
down trees you're not supposed to, he gets his lawyer to make
out a writ of trespass against you."

"*Trespass* for cutting trees on your own land?"

"Ain't our own land. They won't sell it. None of 'em. Except
to each other. They won't let a real farmer buy it. They want to
keep farmers under their thumb. They stole it for nothing from
the Indians, or bribed somebody in a law office to make out the
grant. And they're bound they're goin' to have everything that
anybody can make off it, for themselves and their families, for
ever and ever." She spat, "Perpetual rent to their heirs and assigns
forever — that's in all their leases."

"Who do you mean — 'they'?" asked the visitor.

The boy of the house said angrily, "A dozen or so tradin' storekeepers, folks from New York City, or Albany, that got to the
land before any farmers did."

The old woman by the fire stirred, shook her head, made an
uneasy warning gesture, "Look out, now! You don't know for
sure he's from Connecticut." She got up, went again to the bed,
moved the pillows to a darker corner and laid an old blanket
over them.

"Don't pay no attention to her. She's got them pillows on
the brain," said the younger woman. "She thinks everybody is
a-spying out what we've got that would be worth taking on
distraint. I tell her I keep the house looking so poor nobody would
ever think we had a shillin's worth of anything."

"Restraint?" asked the visitor, "Did you say restraint?"

"Distraint."

He blinked.

"Didn't you never hear of the law of distraint? You surely *are* from Connecticut! Everybody over this side the line knows what distraint is. If you don't do what they say you signed to do in your lease, or if they *say* you haven't done it, they can come in and take possession, and turn you out. And they can prove anything on you in the courts. Every one of 'em has a lawyer in his pocket. Granny's always afraid they'll take her pillows when they do. They're good goose-feather, and she thinks the rent collector looked hard at them when he came. *I* aim not to let him into the house, but they do what *they* like. Granny's sure he wants them pillows for his own bed."

The barefooted boy said impatiently, "Granny's got things mixed. Distraint don't let 'em take your furniture and things — only the place and the improvements you've made. They couldn't take her pillows."

"Not by law, they couldn't," cried the old woman. "I don't say it's one of the things in the lease. But they do take things. There's allus a great hullabaloo when they come in on distraint, and I tell ye, they take anything they can carry off. And then they can prove in a law court you never had it. My mother had a good pewter . . ."

They hushed her, exasperated. "That pewter teapot! You've told about that a hundred times!"

The Connecticut boy was too much astonished to keep the shut mouth which was manners. "But I never knew that there was anything to do to keep a rented house, except pay the rent on time. What else do you have to do over here?"

The woman shook her head and passed her hand over her eyes, "Different things in different places," she said listlessly. "Down Westchester way, I hear farmers have it good. But wait till that landlord dies. The tenants'll have to take whatever his son wants. It depends on the landlord. You can't do anything against what he says. This patent here is a bad one. We're 'at will' tenants." She laughed sourly, "That means the landlord's will, not our'n. Any year he wants to, he can tell us we can't stay on. But he won't, most likely. He's got such a bad name, he can't get tenants. Not more than ten houses in ten square miles.

"One thing we signed to do is to give so many days a year working with a team at the sawmill. That's where my man is today. He had 'lotted on cutting the corn. It's all ready. Ought to be cut before first frost. But he has to go for sawmill work the day *they* say. And so will he — " she jerked her head towards her son — "when we're gone. And *his* son after him for ever and ever."

The visitor said reasonably, "Well, around us, folks work out their taxes on the town road. Isn't that the same thing?"

"No, it ain't. If you don't like the man you have to take orders from, you can pay the tax in cash, can't you? No such chance for us. Or you can vote a mean-acting road commissioner out of office, can't you? Our men have to do their work-stint, no matter how mean the sawyer at the mill is. The one at this mill is a rascal. My man hates him. When he comes home at night after his day working at the mill, he can't hardly get his breath, he hates the sawyer so. He can't get any good of what he eats, for days, the sawyer's so mean. But he's signed to work for him in the lease. So he has to. But you'd better believe as long as we have to buy our boards at *that* mill, we'll never build on to the house. I'd enjoy to live decent, but we'll go on living in one room like pigs in a sty, before we'd build. *He'd* get it — the landlord — anyhow, half-rights of the sale price. We'd be working for him."

The visitor looked around him to find a way to change the subject. Being a boy, he took little heed of dirt and disorder, but he noticed now, in wonder, that he saw not a single book in the room. In his plain and rustic home a shelf beside the mantelpiece held the Bible, a copy of *Surveyors' Rules*, *Gulliver's Travels*, an old arithmetic, a book of children's stories, a battered *History of the World*, and — often — a volume of Locke or of Newton, borrowed from the local doctor. No books here at all, he noticed, and not a scrap of paper or any way to write on paper. At home his father's long-legged, stand-up desk always had on it an ink bottle and some quill pens.

He wished he had not come, made a step towards the door, but remembered his mother's lessons in mannerliness and tried to make a neutral, polite remark to his hostess.

"I passed a fine berry patch, up along the trail. Best blackberries I ever saw. I suppose, ma'am, you'll soon be putting up yours. Before frost."

"Not me! I'd have to buy the sugar at the landlord's store."

The boy from Connecticut wrinkled his forehead, perplexed. She went on. "That'd mean more money in his pocket. I'll tell ye how he gets that sugar. He sends his Negro slaves out here to cut down the good trees on our land that *we*'re not to touch or he'll get us fined for trespass. His blacks do the work for nothing — only what they eat, and most of what they eat they grow themselves, and no pay for hoeing it, either. They raft the wood down the creek to Hudson's River, and then to his landing, and load it on a ship. He sends it to Jamaica and sells it for sugar and rum. Don't cost him much of anything, in cash, you see. Well, nobody need think I'm a-goin' to buy that sugar. He makes it hot for you if you buy it off anybody else. You always used to sign in your lease never to let a stranger stay overnight in your house. That's not in leases any more, but 'they' don't like it if you do."

The visiting boy had been edging towards the door, but at this he stopped short, staggered. "Not let anybody stay overnight! What does that have to do with . . ."

"You might buy something from him. Sugar maybe. That'd do 'them' out of their profits on the goods they sell in their stores. Or maybe," she added, "it was just one more thing they could bring up against you, to get a 'jectment writ on you. The Governor's a Lord out of the old country. Some say he wants to treat us tenants fair. But even he can't get anything done in the courts, if 'they' don't want it. Their lawyers make their living mostly out of writing 'jectment actions and writs for trespass."

"But lawyers don't decide lawsuits. It's the jury that does."

"Tenant farmers aren't good enough to serve on juries. Not unless they've got a lot more money than most of us. Law in New York's against it. No poor farmers on juries."

"Why don't you *change* the laws?" The Connecticut boy was astonished at their lack of spunk. "You can vote, can't you?"

They laughed.

"You don't really mean you can't *vote!*"

They laughed again.

The old crone by the hearth drew a whistly breath and broke in, "Did you ever hear the tale about how this province was settled? I'll tell ye the way it was told to me.

"The English fit the Dutch about a hundred years ago and took this province. Well sir, before they let a single farmer in on the land, they sent over a shipload of lawyers from England — everyone of 'em with black broadcloth on his back and fine linen at his neck, and a pen behind his ear. The sails of the ship were black and they had black men for sailors that were deef and dumb.

"Then them British lawyers put their heads together to figger out what kind of laws would let *their* kind of folks make the most money, and that's the way it is in New York Province. The storekeepers that turned landlords, them and the lawyers, mostly live in New York City and Albany. They never work a stroke, they never earn a ha'penny by anything they *do* — live off rents and quarter-sales when leaseholds are sold, and water-rights and mill-rights, and selling the good lumber they keep for themselves.

"Their women don't work a stroke either. They have black slaves to wash their clothes and cook their food and take care of their babies and wait on 'em. Did you ever go to Albany? No? Well, if you did, you'd see that every fourth person on the street there is a black. They've got them slaves where they want them — right down where they'd like to have us, if they could."

The barefoot boy protested, "Their blacks have it good. They get more to eat and more to wear than we do."

The old woman cut him short, "They treat 'em all right the way they treat anybody all right, as long as they've got him where they want other folks to be, down, so they can't help themselves. But let a black lift one finger different from what they tell him to — or maybe they just get so they don't like his ways any longer — they sell him across the water to Jamaica. Down there, the Negroes are worked to death on the plantations, in short order. And I tell ye, they wish they *was* dead, long before they drop over. All the blacks here know that. When they find out they're being sold, they try their best to kill themselves.

But the white folks won't let 'em. They have to forfeit the price of the sale if they don't deliver the slave. They send a guard all the way down to New York City to the ship that's goin' to take'em to Jamaica to make sure they don't jump overboard. And maybe the slave they're selling is the one who took care of their old grand-daddy after he got childish."

She was almost out of breath, but she heaved, gasped and went on, "The landlords and the lawyers don't do any of their own work and they don't do any of their own fightin' either. Our boys that are in the militia will shoot all right against Indians or French. But they won't back up a sheriff serving a 'jectment writ on a tenant farmer. Their own folks are tenants, mostly. So the landlords get the British regulars. Them redcoats will march anywhere they're told, and when they get there, they'll do anything. They get paid to. They'll kill anybody their officers tell them to shoot at. That's the way the regulars make their living. It's all the same to them, whose house they burn down, so long as they get their pay." Her wheezing stopped her.

"All that's not really so, is it?" the boy from Connecticut asked amazed, turning to the younger woman. "It's a story she's made up."

"Well, that foolishness about the ship of lawyers with black sails and deef-and-dumb sailors comin' over before settlers were allowed, that's just old woman's talk. She heard that told in some other old tale, I guess. She does get things mixed up. But the rest of it's so. My mother, when she was a girl, saw sailors fishin' a black woman out of the river, where she'd jumped overboard tryin' to drown herself before she'd die under the whip in Jamaica. My mother used to tell how she couldn't sleep nights after she heard that black woman screechin'."

The Connecticut lad's boyish face took on a sick, shocked expression. He looked young, innocent, harmless.

The tenant wife gazed searchingly at him. She looked from him to her son and back. "Do you — ?" She stopped, fumbled with her crumpled cap-string, finally asked, "Do you know how to read?"

The Connecticut boy forgot his manners again. "Why, *yes!* Don't you?" This was the explanation of the house without a printed page in it, nor so much as one sheet of paper or a quill pen.

"Where would I learn?" she asked dryly. "I've heard tell that when the Dutch had the running of things, they used to keep up the schools — but since 'they' have taken over, they've seen to it that there ain't no schools for poor folks on farms. They say 'twould make farmers independent-minded if they could read and write. And that, they *won't* have."

"Some of our folks over home in Connecticut grumble because schools cost so much tax money, and my folks say the teachers don't get paid much. But in all my life I never heard of people who don't want any schools at all."

"You never lived in the Province of New York," answered the woman, "or you'd have heard of plenty who don't want schools — except for *their* young ones."

The barefooted boy said now, "Were you thinkin', Ma, of gettin' him to read next year's lease?"

The woman looked at the beardless, ingenuous face, "I might," she said. She put her hand to the mantelshelf. Under a piece of old iron, there was a folded paper. She took it down, looked at it, her face working anxiously. "Would ye really tell us *honest* what it says?" she asked, and held it out to the lad. But before he could take it, she snatched it back, wailing, "How'd I *know* if you really told us or not. How'd I ever know if *anybody* told us honest or not. A person that can read — they could tell us anything. And then it might turn out all different. The lawyers can just take our hides off and hang 'em on a fence to dry — so long's we don't know our letters, we can't do a thing. We don't know what *any*body's up to."

The Connecticut boy had never in his sixteen years tried to think what life in a world run by printed and written documents would be to a person who couldn't read. The only illiterates in his experience had been an occasional half-witted schoolmate, who could not learn his letters. It was evident that this family, for all their dirt and rough ways, were not in the least half-wits. Now that he was a little used to them, he saw that both the woman and her son had fine, well-set eyes, good foreheads and shapely hands. He was touched and abashed by the shamed dis-

tress in the woman's face. He took the paper soberly and gently
from her hand, and said with deep earnestness, "I promise I'll read
it to you, *honest*, just what it says. Why wouldn't I?" He added,
meaning to be helpful, "And if there's something I don't understand — I don't know much of anything about laws of course —
I'll ask my uncle about it and come back and tell you. He's a
lawyer!"

The word exploded in the room like a bomb.

The woman fell upon him with a shriek, snatching the paper
from his hand. The boy put up his fists and rushed at him in a
rage. "You told me your father was a farmer!" he shouted
furiously.

"I warned ye, ye'd better be careful what ye said in front of
a stranger," sobbed the old woman. She snatched up the pillows
and limped out of the back door with them.

The visitor defended himself with energy, "My father *is* a
farmer," he cried. But he hastily stepped outside. "I told you
he was. And he is."

They hooted at the idea, "A lawyer — brother to a farmer!"

"Why, my grandfather is a farmer. My uncle's father is a
farmer. John Adams is son of a farmer."

"A lawyer — *son* of a farmer." They stared at him darkly.

"You better go," said the woman.

"I'm going!" he said with emphasis.

But as he plunged into the trail leading back to where he had
come from, he heard a shout. He turned. The boy was running
after him. The woman stood in the black hole of the door.

"If you were thinkin' of tellin' on us," said the boy, panting,
"'twon't do ye no good. We wunt be here next winter. We're
going to cross Hudson's River, and move on into the Jerseys —
where you can own your own land — if we have to swim for
it."

The boy from Connecticut was hungry and tired. But it was
nothing to be hungry and tired after a day in the woods. Inside
that stone-heap of a house he had felt sick. He drew in deep
breaths of the fresh air. That was better. He would be all right,
he thought, as soon as he got home. At the bright thought of

home, he quickened his pace. In a moment, he was out of sight of the tenant's house.

His name could have been Ethan or Ira Allen, or Remember Baker, or Thomas Chittenden, or Israel Canfield, or Seth Warner. Many of the young people who a few years later began to settle Vermont, the Allens, the Bakers, the Chittendens, the Warners, were born and brought up where opportunity was equal for all, yet only a few miles from that invisible boundary line. They brought with them — living as the buds on any symbolical willow riding switch — two sets of downcountry memories: one of self-governing, self-respecting independence, the other clear fore-knowledge of the bitterly contrasting governmental system of the Province of New York. Thus they were doubly prepared when the time for decision came. But the time was not yet.

You don't believe a word of what you have just been reading, do you? It does sound incredible, as though a fiction-writer, temporarily acting as historian, had slid off from the dry, papery crackle of documents, into the never-never land of imagination. Nevertheless, every single detail of that conversation is backed by some statement of that period, written or printed, some memoir, letter, deed, diary, official report, will or lease. This first-hand supporting material was recast in the form of con-versation for a simple reason: talk is carried on in words which mean something definite, concrete, and understandable to men and women who are talking, words, therefore which can be counted on to carry a direct meaning to the minds of readers un-trained — as most of us are — in the subtleties of lawyer language.

I do not undervalue the use of Latin-derived abstract terms. They are, as a rule, much better fitted than rough-and-ready Saxon for expressing the minute distinctions, shades of thought required by scholars in their effort to define precisely exact truth beyond any chance of misunderstanding. But such dictionary words seldom carry voltage enough to kindle our imaginations with a spark. Although the meaning is identical, there is a world of difference at the receiving end between a news item beginning, "A sanguinary encounter took place," and an eyewitness saying,

"I saw bloody men killing each other in a fight." Again: "Lee now ordered Jackson to initiate a turning movement against Hooker's right flank . . ." adequate though that wording is for military archives, it arrests the reader's attention hardly more than last week's weather forecast. Any page of *The Red Badge of Courage* tells us more of what the Civil War meant to the men who fought it.

Or, to come closer to our subject, I ask you to look closely at this document presented by Dr. Irving Mark in his splendid book *Agrarian Conflicts in Colonial New York* as a typical example of Hudson Valley land tenure:

> It was a conveyance, dated 1766, by Philip Philipse of a "fee farm" of eight acres, which reserved an eight-pound perpetual rent to Philipse, his heirs and assigns forever. Milling and mining rights were reserved to the grantor in conveyances of this century, as were quarter or half-sale rights which entitled the grantor to a quarter or a half of the sales price when the estate was sold. For non-fulfillment of obligation, the deed included a right of distraint which permitted the landlord to re-enter and retake possession.

That is excellent exposition. Objective history could not be more lucidly written. But I ask you, suppose I had quoted that passage just as it stands, instead of making it part basis for the talk between a New England lad and New York rentors, would its terms have made your blood run cold? If so, you are more sensitively awake than I. For at my first reading everything about it was so alien to my experience, seemed so remotely formalistic, that my attention slipped from it like a shoe on a banana peel, without even noticing the Doomsday color of the provision, "rent to be paid forever."

Perhaps you were capable of seeing and feeling the flesh-and-blood misery bound up in those cold legalistic provisions. I needed close study of them and much reflection upon a society where the law courts were in the power of the very clan which profited by proving that there had been "non-fulfillment of obligation," to understand the full terrifying meaning of an accusation from a landlord that a tenant of his had not lived up to all the clauses in a lease? It meant — as they used to say in tough forty-niner gold diggings — that the defendant "wouldn't have a Chinaman's chance" for legal protection. It meant a threat looming over the tenant's home, such as Milton put into magnificent poetical words, all the more arresting because they are shadowy and mysterious:

> But that two-handed engine at the door
> Stands ready to smite once, and smite no more.

Do you think this is going too far, getting fantastic, to wrap around the fears of a poor, illiterate tenant farmer the cloth-of-gold of Milton's verse? I don't admit it. I would be no Vermonter if I felt that a menace to any human life's security is more tragic than to another. The tenant farmer was illiterate through no fault of his own, his poverty has nothing to do with his human dignity, and he, like any son of man, felt ominous threats as keenly as you or I.

The words "mill-rights" lie so thin and colorless on the page we can fairly see through them the parchment on which the lease was written. You must look hard at them before you see that they are strangling hands, stifling efforts for better housing for men and women and their children. When you read on a printed page "half-sale rights" you can hardly be blamed for skimming rapidly on, hoping soon to come to the end of the chapter. Only when you hear some human being using those words in a report of his own life do they come home to you as a form of spiritual murder, as smothering to death the natural wish to improve one's home, one's own barn, one's own fields. To make head or tail out of the Yankee-Yorker dispute, we must start long before it began, remembering that every generation is rooted in the past and looking toward the future. We must go back as a psychiatrist does, very far back, and trace the constant interaction between human beings and the outside circumstances of their lives which made both parties to the dispute what they were in the late eighteenth century. Always we must be on our guard against measuring other periods by the yardstick of our present ideals and prejudices. We must try, difficult though it is, to see events through the eyes of those, then living, who hoped, feared, sometimes despaired, in the cause of the long struggle to carry on and hand down what we today are proud to call our American Heritage.

But this program calls for a monstrous deal of work both for author and reader! Moreover, it halts the flow of the story of what happened in a New World province in one century to go back to other centuries in English history where the two sides stood up against each other before ever the Dutch were put out of New York.

Is the following proposition a fair one, I wonder? I don't see why not. If you don't feel you can accept the "Chat Between Neighbors" as true on my say-so, you will find in the back of this book the complete statement with dates, facts, place-names, proper names, quotations from documents, from which I deduced the picture shown in this chapter. You can get an idea of what kind of reading this collection of facts provides by the following samples, a few out of many.

John Watts, British Eastern Boundary Commissioner of the Province of New York from 1753 till the Revolution obliged him to return to England, reported to the Ministry in October 1777 [this was the very month and year of Burgoyne's defeat at Saratoga, which meant the collapse of the British effort to separate New England from the Middle States]: "As the counties of Albany, Dutchess, and Westchester, in the Province of New York are in an absolute state of vassalage, being all tenants at will to Rensselaer, Livingston, Beckman, and Philipse, I do therefore advise administration to have a bill brought into Parliament to declare the above enormous grants and patents extravagant, and therefore vacated.

"I would then advise that the Crown by proclamation declare that all the present tenants be free from their vassalage, and that everyone may be a freeholder of such farm and premises which he now holds for ever, on condition that they not only return to their allegiance to the King, but that in person they take up arms and assist His Majesty in reducing the rebels to subjugation. This, My Lords, being done, *would instantly bring you at least six thousand* able farmers into the field, without one shilling expense to the nation."

Frederick Jackson Turner ("The Old West") tells us that one of the most important factors in restraining density of population in New York, in retarding the settlement of its frontier, was the land system of that colony, which imposed feudal tenures and undemocratic restraints, and which exploited settlers.

Sir Henry Moore, 1765–1769, British Governor of the Province of New York [speaking of the New York law courts] " — in effect the issues of a cause depended not so much on the right of a Client as on the breath of a Judge."

Governor Colden of New York in 1763 warned the Lords of Trade in London of the danger if New York's claim to Vermont were given up, "that the *republican principles of New England would be extended.*" *

No amount of editorial arrangement could reduce the material to a simple, easily followed chronological narrative. The complexity of the main theme calls for much skipping about from colony to province to colony; for flashbacks to old-country antecedents, to forecasts of the future; for repetitions where a point already noted briefly in the text needs detailed re-examination. There are many people who are bored by historical detail. If you are one of them, and if you will take "Chat Between Neighbors" as true, read straight on from the end of this chapter.

But if you find yourself skeptical either of my good faith or of my ability to interpret historical documents, I hope it isn't asking too much of you to slip a bookmark in here, and turn over to the proofs that the two ways of life shown in this chapter represent two contrasting social ideals. There are people who are not bored at all, but interested, by documentary detail. Such readers will certainly find their attention held by the facts underlying one of the strangest of our history's many strange phases — the existence, close together, side by side, of two antagonistic outlooks on life,

---

* I put in the italics here and in the other quotations scattered through this book. My idea was to call attention by italics to a single phrase which had no especial interest to the eighteenth century (or earlier or later) writer, but which, it seems to me, throws light on the general attitudes I am trying to portray.

each an end product of extremes reached by the slowly swaying English social pendulum.

Those who were to be the first settlers of southwest Vermont grew up, the majority of them, in the hotbed of radical democratic ideas along the western fringe of New England. They needed only to look across an imaginary line to observe in the Province of New York the most coherent, purposeful, powerful, and consistent attempt ever made on the soil of the North American continent to create an exact copy of the legalized caste system of rural England in a very reactionary period of English history. That they did look, that they did see, is proved by their actions, by their spoken and written words. They made it manifest that they not only understood, but detested everything about the government of New York Province as it affected people like themselves, ordinary, hard-working dirt farmers.

Boundary disputes of one sort or another were common in those days. Plymouth felt aggrieved by the encroachment of Massachusetts Bay. Both of them accepted the findings of an arbitration commission. At different times, Massachusetts and Vermont claimed part of New Hampshire. In neither case was there widespread discord. When agreement was reached, the decision was accepted without lasting hard feeling.

The land grant quarrel between Vermonters and New York landlords was something different — and why wouldn't it be? Almost as if they were part of a planned laboratory field test in sociology, the Green Mountain Boys had been conditioned for generations, by inheritance, tradition, environment to reject and rebel against the particular form of caste-gradation — poor, landless tenant laborers, separated socially, economically, politically from their "betters" (the owners of land) by an unbridgeable gulf — on which an attempt was being made to found the social system of the Province of New York.

Thus the pride with which we look back rests on a base vastly more worth while than the mere fact that our side won. Reticent by habit, ashamed as we are of any suspicion that we may be boasting even to ourselves, we seldom speak of our thought — but still the thought persists, a beacon to guide when we grope for our way through the dark. "In the good fight our forefathers stood up to be counted. Their struggle was not provincial, isolated, ephemeral. It was part of the world-wide battle for human rights — the plain people against enslavement by the crafty, the powerful, the ruthless. That war is never-ending. It started before recorded history. It is still going on. In it our old Vermont story, threadbare with familiarity to us, often totally unknown to other Americans, was only a small skirmish on the edge of the greater field. But no one can doubt under which flag it was fought."

CHAPTER 4

In Subordination Forever

THE REVEREND JOHN TAYLOR in his journal (1802) of a missionary tour through the Mohawk and Black River region of New York:

> The same evil operates here as in many parts of this Country — the lands are leased. This must necessarily operate to debase the minds and destroy the enterprise of the settlers. If men do not possess the right of sale, they never will or can feel independent. The Americans can never flourish when on leased lands; they have too much enterprise to work for others or to remain tenants. I find that they are greatly depressed in mind and are losing their animation.

A New York petition from tenant farmers in 1795 demanding an investigation of the Livingston terms for leasehold:

> They are oppressive and burthensome to the last degree, unfriendly to all great exertions of Industry, and tending to degrade your Petitioners from the Rank the God of Nature destined all Mankind to move in, to be Slaves and Vassals.

Modern business men feel that it is wise policy to forego an immediate profit, if enforcing the letter of a contract will drive into bankruptcy the man with whom the contract was made. Earlier generations thought otherwise. It was their idea that fear of punishment is the surest enforcer of commercial integrity. Total loss of a few accounts, they thought, would be more than balanced by the prompt payment of others. The New York landlords acted on this principle in disputes with their tenants.

All through the eighteenth century such disputes recurred. On one of the Livingston patents, settlers (between two and three thousand) from the Rhenish Palatinate felt that they had been given a dirty deal. When they complained, no satisfaction was forthcoming. They were hard-headed, vital people, and rebelled. British regular troops were called in to suppress them. They were hard to frighten and revolted again. Were suppressed again. After a decade of this intermittent violence, most of them moved on to Pennsylvania.

> As a result [writes James Truslow Adams], from that time on, no Germans who could possibly help it, settled in New York, and the great stream of immigration went almost wholly to swell the numbers of the Quaker colony. Whereas if its earlier members had been better treated, it would have helped build up the great valleys of the Hudson and the Mohawk.

In 1731 New York and Connecticut made a peaceful and reasonable rectification of the uncertain boundary line between them. By this arrangement, a jog along the Sound (Greenwich, Stamford, et cetera) was brought into New England. There is no record that the least objection was voiced by any inhabitant of the territory which came under Connecticut jurisdiction. In return, New York took over a narrow strip to the north. Here (as official correspondence between Governors shows) the transfer was less popular. Men from Ridgefield, Connecticut, crossed over into land recently surrendered by Connecticut . . . "and in a riotous and tumultuous manner pulled down and burnt a dwelling house, and cut down and destroyed timber and fences, and still persevering in their evil dispositions, threaten to commit the like again."

Ethan Allen was born not five years after this "riotous and tumultuous" expression of dislike for the jurisdiction of the Province of New York, his birthplace being less than a day's horseback ride from Ridgefield. If your guess is that, as he grew up, he did not often hear people talking about that violent protest, I think your guess would be wrong. From what we know of country life anywhere, and of the Connecticut feeling against the province, we can be pretty sure that the episode was told and retold with admiring folk elaborations around the hearthfires known and frequented by the Allens. But the point is not worth insisting on, for this was only a curtain-raiser for the big show which began soon after.

Not only Connecticut but Western Massachusetts was involved.

The Berkshire mountains and adjoining country offered an ideal site for disputed titles. A wide stretch of territory might belong to Massachusetts or to New York, depending on which vaguely phrased royal charter should finally prevail. An extra snarl came from the common belief — it amounted practically to common knowledge — that both Livingston and Van Rensselaer claimed vastly more land than they had ever legally bought from the Indians. Why then should any tenant be fool enough to go on paying onerous rent to a landlord with no right to collect it, when a much better bargain could be struck by dealing direct with the Indians or with a Massachusetts agent who was satisfied with a reasonable fee for acting as middleman?

"Why indeed?" thought many tenant farmers, and began to act on what they thought. The altercation started with orderly suits at law, no rowdy barn-burning. But the pleas and demurrers of legal pettifogging seemed endless. Tempers rose on both sides. It ended in something very like civil war.

Here is a passage from one of those detailed studies which historians write for other scholars to read, every statement supported by citations from official documents:

> In July 1753, Livingston through an armed band of retainers, made effective his refusal to renew leases to tenants who had accepted Massachusetts titles. These men burned George Robinson's house and carried off the wheat from Loomis' field. The Massachusetts reprisals which followed intensified the border violence. A Livingston tenant, Van Deusen and his son were arrested and his land granted to a claimant who was willing to take a Massachusetts title. On July 28, 1753 Governor Clinton [New York] issued a proclamation for the arrest of those involved, a copy of which was forwarded to Lieutenant Governor Phips. Under this proclamation Hallenbeck was arrested. In addition, another troublesome Livingston tenant, Joseph Paine, was imprisoned for cutting down some of Livingston's trees. Aroused by these events, the Boston government protested that while it had released the Van Deusens on bail, Hallenbeck was held in a Dutchess County prison without bail. Clinton answered with an announcement that Hallenbeck had made good his escape. [Quite a few tenants arrested for insubordination

managed to walk out of prison — apparently the jail attendants were not very enthusiastic about co-operating with
landlords.] By the end of 1753 New York authorities were
still insisting on their rights. The Massachusetts General
Court professed its willingness to compromise, but restated
its . . . etc. etc.

This sample is plenty, I should think, to explain why I do not
propose to tell the complete story — we would lose the forest in
the thick-standing trees.

But if we are to understand Vermonters, we must know the
main events of those years because the conflict was foreground
stuff for most of the men and women whose mature lives make
up that history's first chapters. All through their formative childhood and adolescence, the young people of Western Connecticut
and Western Massachusetts were stirred, thrilled and horrified as
they learned about the ups and downs of this bitter wrangling.
You may be sure that what they heard was never told im-
partially — no suggestion that there might be two sides to the
quarrel. All their folks were fiery partisans for the independent
farmer, whoever he might be, against the whole tribe of landlords.

If you lived, as a number of our Vermont forebears did, in
Woodbury, the Cornwalls, Salisbury, or closer still, as Ethan
Allen did, to the troubled country and its border warfare, you
called out to any passer-by coming from the north: "Any word
from the Livingston tenant fight? What's doing over on the
Bateman patent?" Whatever news he brought was carried by
somebody in your family over the back trail to Uncle Elihu's
house, where they too were all breathlessly following the events
of the front-line battle. In their turn, Uncle Elihu's folks would
send out to tell their neighbors. In no time, everybody for miles
around you would have heard the latest installment in the constant bickering.

Perhaps it was that the alarmed Livingston had written, as he
did in May 1753, "Infection will soon be general, and then no
man that has an estate in this Province or perhaps in North America, will be safe to call it his own." Or perhaps the day's bulletin,
by exception, made people burst into hilarious laughter, as on
August 11, 1753, when Henry Van Rensselaer sent this note to

Robert Livingston: "The New England People Intirely Intendth to Take you, Dad or alife." It was a relief to despise him for a pig-headed Dutchman who did not know how to write English even though his family had lived under British rule for close to a century.

Or perhaps it was terrible news — that Van Rensselaer had armed some of his paid employees, and taken a savage house-burning, crop-destroying revenge on one and another homestead. This set everyone's pulse to pounding. Do not forget that the New York tenant farmers, thus punished by their landlord's private army, were family men with wives and children, left homeless by such reprisals. They were close to the boundary line. Many of them fled as refugees and were taken in by Connecticut and Massachusetts farm families. Is there the faintest possibility that the children in those farm homes who listened to such tales remained emotionally untouched?

Today we are jaded with drama. Some of it we recognize as faked. Only occasionally does the flat flicker on the movie screen fool us into gripping the arms of our seat, our breath coming fast. For a moment — not longer. We know by experience that in the last scene, the oppressor-villain will be foiled. And calamities and convulsions we know to be real — newspaper reports of earthquakes in Peru, famines in Pakistan — are not much felt because they are so far from us as we sit tranquil, the arm chair pulled close to a warm radiator. Yet violence in a form we can understand rouses us, even today. Let an automobile crash through the guard rail, plunge down an embankment killing a car full of people — they may have been total strangers to us, but how many of us join in the procession, kept moving by exasperated state police, driving slowly past, to catch just a glimpse of the spot where death was waiting, as somewhere along the road it may be waiting for us!

Think then what it must have meant to a back-roads New England family with no newspaper, no radio, no telephone, no mail service, to have a neighbor stop for a dipper-full of water and tell what with his own eyes he had seen take place only a couple of hours ago at a well-known farmstead — where you had often gone for a friendly visit, or to buy a young pig for fattening — a bloody hand-to-hand fight on the doorstep, armfuls of blazing hay flung through the door of the house into the kitchen-living room, the barn set on fire, the home burned down, the growing crops destroyed.

"They tore it up and trampled it down! As good a wheat crop as you ever saw! In two weeks more it would have been ripe for cutting. They went through it like wild animals. In no time it was all gone. And they burned the house down. The whole neighborhood of us put it up in a work-bee, not five years ago. Henry and Maria had just got a new room built on for their little boys. The landlord's men wouldn't even let Maria take out her blankets or her kitchen dishes. Everything they had in the world was burned to the ground in twenty minutes."

Could any Connecticut or Massachusetts family listen with indifference to such a tale? Or forget it as soon as the narrator, white in helpless rage, had gone on? Or look out across their wheatfield, next year's bread, ripening to gold in the August sunshine, without an inner shout of thanksgiving that, owning their own land, they were safe!

Do we Vermonters, perhaps, read too much into all this because it so closely foreshadows the danger from the same landlords which only a few years later was to menace our own hard-pressed federation of towns? We think not. Others share our view. In one of the studies published by the Berkshire Historical Society, the author, F. L. Pope, in an often-quoted passage, describes this New York-Massachusetts border-tenant-and-landlord war as "nothing less than a death-struggle between free-land-tenure and independent town organization of the Massachusetts Colony, and the antiquated feudal system under which the adjacent territories of the Province of New York were held and governed." Later in his well-documented paper he adds that the inhabitants in the eastern portions of the Livingston and Van Rensselaer manors had long "chafed under the exactions of their landlords, and the continual taunts of their neighbors still further to the east in Massachusetts who, holding their lands in fee under the Boston government, regarded them as little better than slaves and vassals of the lords of the manor."

* * *

As round after round of this match was fought out close at hand, the boys and girls in Western Connecticut farms were growing up. There were too few farmers in the Hudson Valley. There were too many in Western New England by the end of the French and Indian War. There was little even tolerably good land left open there. Where could the young veterans, the G.I.'s of that period, go when they married? Where could they start their new homes? For in New England at that date, every self-respecting new home was founded on land owned by the home-makers.

Just over the line there was plenty of land, with a welcome to any farmer who wanted to settle on it. It was much better land too (as fifty years ago the Earl of Bellomont, then governor of the province, had said) than what was left in New England. It was not only fine for farming, but had the incomparably valuable, wide and safe highway of Hudson's River, leading to markets. Both upstream to Albany, and downstream to New York City, that smooth waterway was ready to carry to willing buyers anything the land could produce. In a time when roads were few in number, and for most of the year, intolerably bad in quality, it was a fabulous advantage to have that great arm of the sea, with no rapids, no falls to interrupt the floating rafts of lumber, the seagoing vessels, the sloops, the fleets of smaller boats, which carried goods up and down to buying centers. The rich but underdeveloped province had in it, outside its cities, less than a third of the population of Connecticut or Massachusetts. On one side more people than there was land for — on the other a vacuum.

Any historian addicted to the "economic-man theory" would back with his last dollar his certainty that a tidal wave of settlers would during the eighteenth century constantly pour over the line from New England to take up the fertile New York holdings. More than economics is needed to understand why the dividing line, although it lay thin as a piece of cotton twine on the floor of the forest, materially so nothing-at-all that a baby could toddle across it, yet stood up like any dyke of Holland, keeping back the tides of vigorous active youth, swelling higher and higher in the New England states.

* * *

As months, as years went on, the hot dispute grew hotter. Livingston wrote direct to the governor of Massachusetts protesting that the "Boston people" were winning over his tenants. The revolt kept spreading. Van Rensselaer tenants took it up, with Robert Noble as their leader. Noble's farm at Claverack lies about thirteen miles west of the present Massachusetts border, only twenty from the northwest corner of Connecticut. News of the goings on there traveled quickly over the "grapevine" communication system to wherever our great-greats of that period may have been living.

Noble was no illiterate, log-shanty farmer, scratching a living in the bush. He was one of Van Rensselaer's tenants but he also had been an officer in the colonial army. In a class-conscious, England-copying society, this gave him the standing of a gentleman. That a man who could have sat down to dinner with any of the landlords chose to take sides with the downtrodden renters — that was news which the busiest New Englander would gladly stop work to hear.

In February 1755 (Ethan Allen was then a tall, bold lad of eighteen) New York constables went out to arrest the former officer as ringleader of recalcitrant tenants. But Noble's followers were armed. They also had as leader a man experienced in war. They, mere tenants, fought back, captured the constables and took them off to jail. Where could a jail be found willing to hold New York constables in custody? Where do you suppose? In the Commonwealth of Massachusetts. This was getting dangerously close to intercolonial war.

Noble's supporters stood guard over his house. The landlord's private army carried off some of them to New York prisons. In return Noble's "troops" captured several of their employees, and lodged them in the jail at Springfield, Massachusetts.

By April of 1755 it was evident that the armed bands of Livingston and Van Rensselaer even reinforced by local constables were not strong enough to capture Noble. It would take more men than proprietors had money to hire, to overcome the unpaid farmer forces. The government of the province ordered Noble's arrest. Plenty of evidence exists to show that the phrase "the government of the province" meant the landed proprietors. A large

armed force went out to Nobletown commanded by a sheriff of
the province. The house was surrounded, the garrison called on
to surrender. It refused. Shots were fired by both sides. In the
confused account of the fracas which has come down to us,
through later court testimony, what stands out most strongly is
the passionate intensity of the defenders. "I will not go out until
I am killed!" "If I go out I must die!" — strange burning words
to come from plain English-speaking farmers. In the end some
broke through and escaped, many were taken prisoners. One of
those who preferred being killed to capture was shot to death.
Some doubt there must have been as to whether the killing was
justified, for the deputy who fired the fatal shot was arrested
— but at once he was released on bail and never brought to
trial.

Nobody can reasonably blame a court officer for doing his ut-
most to serve a duly executed writ or warrant. That is his sworn
duty. But when government becomes a tyranny . . . ? Is it per-
versity or a healthy instinct that makes us choose for our popular
heroes Robin Hood, not the Sheriff of Nottingham; Wilhelm Tell
not Gessler; which sets our blood racing faster when we remember Patrick Henry's great climax: "If this be treason, make the
most of it!"

Through all these years of never-ceasing unrest, how many of
the boys and girls who later were to settle Vermont saw from
their homes a distant column of smoke and, running out excitedly
to an upland pasture, saw that it was billowing up from the burning house of a neighbor! How many of them stood in tight-lipped
excitement to watch a company of men with rifles tramping by,
on their way to help out a New York farmer besieged in his own
home! When a shadow fell across the threshold of their open
doorway no farm family could know what tragic, or heroic, or
pitiable figure would appear — perhaps a neighbor or cousin in
homespun, rifle in hand, his face blazing with battle-fury. Or the
white-cheeked wife of an ejected New York tenant, who had seen
her home with all her household goods go up in flames. Her husband had been carried off to prison by the New York sheriff and
his posse. She, baby in arms, had stumbled over a forest trail to the

only safety she knew, shelter under the roof of a freehold Massachusetts or Connecticut farm home. Or perhaps it was an exhausted New York farmer, wounded, bleeding, escaped through
a backroom window, fired on by the men who came to take him
prisoner, as he fled across the cornfield he himself had plowed,
planted and cultivated. Can you imagine a New England family
which would not count it an honor to make him welcome?

Ethan Allen, to take him as a typical example for his age group,
lived always within walking distance of most of these battles, often
as his work took him to and fro, within sight and hearing of
fighting. At the date of the capture of Nobletown he was a six-
foot-tall adolescent. He had read Plutarch, Newton and John
Locke. In every generation of his family, from the first American
ancestor to his father, a radical, outspoken liberal, the Allens had
been fiery opponents of all authority which tried to limit the
freedom of any man. He was at the age when it is abnormal not
to be carried away by wrathful sympathy for underdogs putting
up a fight against those who would be their masters.

For a decade longer, as the violent disorders over the line
swelled, diminished, swelled up again — never died out entirely —
he was to go on watching, as a neighbor and friend, these frantic,
futile efforts of New York tenants to escape from a bondage system they detested. We know that his nature, up to the day he
died, was anything but cool and moderate. We cannot understand
the man he became if we do not bear in mind the ideals he inherited from his ancestors, and what he saw with his own eyes —
the blood-stained, smoke-blackened, tear-soaked background of his
youth.

In the light of this full understanding we will not (as some
modern historians do, from the unruffled safety of their own
lives) laugh off as florid speech-making such proclamations as his
when he said that, if Vermonters should be forced to live under
the kind of government offered by the Province of New York,
there would be two hostile factions, "One party would be for
slavery, while the other would be for liberty, which would end
in civil war." (He knew what he was talking about, having wit-
nessed years of localized civil war from exactly such causes.)
"For their genius, polity, temper, spirit and manners would be as

diametrically opposed to each other as they are now, and as liberty is to slavery."

Only if we have forgotten the vital facts of the past, can we label as spread-eagle ballyhoo his cry of wild determination when he said that rather than fail, he with the "hardy Green Mountain Boys would retire into the desolate caverns of the mountains and wage war with human nature at large."

To smile condescendingly at such phrases is rather like smiling at the "glittering generalities" of the Declaration of Independence; or at Garibaldi's desperate "Here we make Italy, or die"; or at "We shall fight on the beaches, we shall fight on the fields, we shall never surrender."

The outcome in all these cases was by no means factually the same, was not at all on the same scale. Nor is the literary quality of the various phrases comparable. Garibaldi's rhetorical defiance was part of the rising from its grave of an ancient European civilization. Jefferson's Declaration was a flourish of trumpets announcing the birth of a brand-new nation which was to become one of the most powerful on the globe. Churchill's magnificently clanging phrases summoned to a desperate last stand a freedom-loving people threatened with extermination.

When Ethan Allen spoke as the voice of the Green Mountain men, he was trying to find words to express the feeling binding them together in the face of danger. In time this feeling brought into being, not an old civilization reborn, not a mighty new nation — only a plain, small, rural American state, never rich, never powerful.

The human values are the same.

CHAPTER 5

The Great Rebellion

FOR fifteen years, a long time in the lives of growing-up young people — the revolt smoldered away among the embers in a dull smother of resentment, now and again flickering up in flames of violence, attacks and repulses, raids and ejectments. Finally in 1766, with a burst of fury, it blazed out into bold active rebellion.

The grounds for discontent were the same as always, but now the field had widened. Beyond Livingston and Van Rensselaer lands, farmers of the Philipse Highland Patent, on the Cortland Manor and in Dutchess and Upper Westchester Counties were joining in the outcry not so much against paying rent as against uncertain tenure, mill and timber reservations, distraint, quarter-sales, and all the other manorial encumbrances. Many of them also denied their landlord's right to act as the owner of land which, by every rule of law and justice, still belonged to the Indians.

As before, test cases were brought in the courts. During one such case, Nimham, the dignified chief of the Stockbridge tribe (active allies of the British in the recent war with France) contended that the Philipse estate had no valid title to some two hundred thousand acres. Just as his representative was about to point out that the deed offered in evidence was obviously fraudulent since the official stamp on it was of later date than the alleged transfer, one of the Governor's Council snatched the document out of his hands and ordered Nimham and those with him to leave the courtroom and go home.

The bewildered Indian tried to have his case reopened. He found that every lawyer in the province had been engaged by the other side. Every single one. Was he allowed, at least to come before the court without legal support and speak for himself? No, this was forbidden to him under the threat of being sent to prison for opposing a grant of the Crown.

The Philipse title was — are you surprised? — upheld by the court. The New York steam roller moving massively forward,

knocked down, ran over and obliterated a mere Indian's claim to
a fair hearing.

The Indians had offered the individual small farmers leases running a thousand years. The triumphant Philipse proprietors now
offered one-year holdings, to be ended at the landlord's will,
granted only on condition that each farmer bond himself for a
thousand pounds to fulfill every one of the many obligations of
the lease.

What next? Irving Mark in *Agrarian Conflicts in Colonial New
York* writes: "The settlers now boldly advertised publicly that
they would reinstate tenants who had been evicted from their
homes by force." Part of their public announcement of this intention reads that they vowed "They would stand by each other
with lives and fortunes, would not suffer any particulars of them
to compound with their Landlords without the rest." They also
"promised to rescue any who were arrested in furtherance of their
movement." Their leader, a farmer named Prendergast, justified
their intention to resist force with force by their knowledge that
in the province their rights "could not be defended in a Court of
Law because they were poore, therefore they were determined to
do themselves Justice and that poor Men are always oppressed by
the Rich." This was a sentiment shared by several of the British
governors of the province who had conscientiously attempted to
make headway against the New York political and legal machine
of interlocking lawyers and landlords.

Here are the names of the leaders of this revolt of tenants: William Prendergast, Elisha Cole, Isaac Perry, Silas Washburne and
Jacob Gonsales. Prendergast was a tenant on Philipse land near
Pawling. He and his young and pretty wife had been married in
the Meeting House on Quaker Hill, past which many of us have
driven on tours through that lovely farming country. Of him, the
New York City newspapers reported that he was a "sober, honest
and industrious farmer, much beloved by his neighbors." His
reason for joining the revolt was no personal grievance of his
own, but, so the same newspapers stated, "because he pitied poor
people who were turned out of their possession."

He was respected and honorable. His angry neighbors looked
to him for leadership. He found himself at the head of a thousand

Dutchess and Westchester County farmers. This force set about freeing their imprisoned comrades. There was little difficulty about this. When they ordered jailors to unlock cell doors, only token resistance was shown them. The jailors, like the New York militia, were not upper-class men.

The "sober, honest, industrious farmer" adopted for his followers from the anti-Stamp-Act movement the name "Sons of Liberty." His leadership so organized and heartened them that in the spring of 1766 the news ran around — "hundreds of tenants are turned levellers and are in arms to dispossess some and maintain others in their own, without rent or taxation." The phrasing of this dispatch suggests that it came from a source unfriendly to the tenants, since the term "levellers" had now become a "smear-word," used indiscriminately for anyone dissatisfied in any way with the political and economic structure which upheld the status quo.

The influential landlords appealed to the authorities for support. Accordingly on April 2 Governor Moore issued a proclamation against the growing rebellion. Some tenants were arrested. A large number of farmers gathered and threatened to break open the New York City jail where they were imprisoned. Another proclamation on April 30 offered a reward for the seizure of specifically named leaders, "and other rioters who have dispossessed parties in Westchester County." On May 6 a reward of one hundred pounds was offered for the taking of Prendergast, Chief of the County Levellers, and fifty pounds for either Munroe or Finch, also leaders. On June 10 the sheriff of Dutchess County (does it surprise you that a landowning Livingston held that job?) reported that a mob of five hundred men had opened the doors of the Poughkeepsie jail and released an imprisoned tenant farmer.

It is hardly possible for us to realize now how profoundly such combined resistance by people of the working classes to ordained authority must have shocked an eighteenth-century community based on the inherent right to supremacy of the rich and well-born. But even today any of us would find it hair-raising to read in the morning papers that New York police were battling near George Washington Bridge with armed farmers by the hundred, that high rewards were being posted for the capture of the leaders of the revolt, that a force of five hundred rebels had broken down the doors of the Poughkeepsie jail and let out a legally sentenced prisoner.

News of that sort today would set the prudent householder of that region to closing shutters and bolting doors. It would likewise act as a magnet to the rash and venturesome. Even more so in 1766! In fact, Matt Jones in his *Vermont in the Making* (Harvard University Press, 1939) for once goes beyond his usual trained historian's aversion to any statement unsupported by a citation from authentic documents, and surmises that Ethan Allen (then in the full flush of his young maturity) may very well have been in the thick of these violent actions, since "it would have been entirely in keeping with his impetuous character" if he had "actually served in these uprisings." For my part, I dare make no more than a guess as to whether or not he was present in body. But it is no guess at all — it is a foregone conclusion — that Ethan Allen was there in spirit, and with him many others of Western Connecticut's younger generation, who were to become the founders of our State.

Chittenden, who as governor was to lead Vermont through the storm, lived in Salisbury, Connecticut, within a few miles of the New York boundary. By this date he was a serious man of thirty-six. The Allen brothers and their associates were young, but men grown. They were all hardy, vigorous, active in mind and body, as little docile in temperament as men have ever been, all keen argufiers about political rights. They had grown up as spectators of the long prelude to this climax of violence. They were masters of their own time, farmers not employees. They were as used to covering ground on foot or horseback as any later Plains Indian. Matt Jones says: "Many of these disturbances took place on territory that practically adjoined Salisbury, Connecticut, the home of Ethan Allen, and it would appear that in this Anti-Rent War we have the progenitor and the pattern of the revolution on the New Hampshire Grants. Allen could not have failed to note the inefficiency of the New York provincial authorities, civil and military, and he must have observed that mobs had their way, *as long as the British regulars were passive.*"

In this case the regulars were soon active. On June 19, the New York Council (almost entirely made up of owners of large acreages) called upon the professional soldiers of the British Regular Army to take the field against American civilians. Among the Albany records there is a memorandum signed by General Gage, dated June 24, 1766, as follows: "This requisition of troops is approved of by every Branch of the Legislature, for they find their Militia is not to be depended upon, and the Rich and Powerful People of the Province are most affected by the Proceedings of the Confederates."

This confidential endorsement stated only what everybody then knew: that the New York legislature was always ready to take orders from the rich and powerful; that Thomas Gage, Major General of the Army, and son of a British viscount would naturally be sympathetic to the wishes of the wealthy ruling class. As well known was the fact that both militiamen and jail-keepers were inclined to sympathize with plain working people like themselves. These facts were in the mind of every spectator in the crowd lining the Poughkeepsie street which leads up from the river, watching the redcoats swing by. They looked formidable in their elaborate battle-dress, now familiar to all Americans because it was the wear of the British troops only nine years later, when they marched out from Boston to Lexington and Concord, on an April morning.

The marching soldiers detested the civilian Americans who stood there staring at them, and the glum crowd detested the soldiers. This we know from an account written by one of the family of a captain in the British Army, describing a short-lived mutiny among British troops in Albany only the year before: "The mutiny was on account of withholding the provisions they were used to receive in times of actual war, and this discontent was much aggravated by their finding themselves treated with a coldness amounting to aversion by the people of the country. They now forgot past services and showed in all transactions with the Army a spirit of dislike bordering on hostility."

We may imagine that the Twenty-eighth Regiment from Albany felt like shouting for joy to find themselves again in action, marching to fife and drum, their arms glittering. They had no reason to feel soft-hearted towards these plainly dressed colonial civilian farmer folk who had shown "a coldness amounting to aversion" for professional soldiers from across the ocean. Their commanding officer, Major Brown, cannot have regretted this chance to get grumbling, mutinuous troops out of the deadly stagnation of barracks life.

Against trained, experienced, military forces, the embattled farmers stood no chance. The big crowds of countrymen with pitchforks and squirrel rifles had been quite able to defend themselves against other amateur soldiers paid by the landlords. They were routed in short order by Major Brown and the hardened fighting men of the Twenty-eighth, who were professionals in the art of warfare, armed as formidably as they had been, a year or so ago, to fire on French and Indian enemies. Fifty of the antirenters gave up and were taken prisoners.

Prendergast's wife begged him to surrender but he was no "sober" farmer now. A brave man with his back against the wall, he fought hopelessly against overwhelming odds. He crazily armed himself with a cutlass (against the field artillery and muskets of the regulars), vowed he would "make daylight show through anyone opposing him" and was so carried away by frenzy that (so it was said by witnesses for the Crown at his trial) he cried "that if the King were there, he would serve him so. For kings have been bro't to, by mobs, before now!"

Of course this one-man opponent of the British Army was soon captured. He was carried off to prison to wait for trial for treason in those times, as in ours, the most dreadful and terrifying accusation that could be made. Sixty and more revolting farmers were in jail with him.

But the rioting kept on. A fresh detachment of regulars was ordered to Poughkeepsie with two field pieces of artillery. An appeal to the British Army for help against their own tenants came from the Van Rensselaers. The Nineteenth Infantry, with a detachment of the artillery train and their fieldpieces, set out for Claverack in response.

By this time the struggle between Hudson Valley landlords and their tenants was no longer an obscure local matter, little known beyond the reach of neighborhood comment. What is called "The

Prendergast Rebellion" spoke so loudly of alarming cracks in the social structure that it was reported in the city newspapers of Boston, Albany, New York City, and points beyond. Here are a few examples:

From the *Boston Gazette*, July 14, 1766:

> For four months past a mob has frequently assembled at the manor of Renslear . . . Jon Van Renslear and the Sheriff of Albany treated inhabitants very cruelly because they would not submit to him as tenants. He came with guns . . .

From the same paper a week later:

> Notwithstanding all attempts to delude and throw them into a Snare, the inhabitants continue fixed as fate in preserving the liberties of their country, their government having treated them with a good deal of severity. . . .

From the issue of August 18, 1766:

> A few men sent to quell rioters have returned, after removing many inhabitants of their illegal (said to be) possessions.

From the *Massachusetts Gazette*, July 30, 1766:

> Boston has received a petition from a number of inhabitants of Nobletown whence they have been driven by the Sheriff of Albany. . . . The inhabitants of Nobletown were driven away as sheep by wolves to Sheffield, Barrington . . . by the Sheriff of Albany and Robert Van Renslear of Claverack . . . and are most distressed.

Those Massachusetts towns were, in those years, not large communities. Everybody knew everything that was going on. In whichever New England town gave them shelter the refugee families from the distressed areas of the New York Manor region were certainly the center of indignantly sympathetic neighborhood talk.

Now, on July 29, with the British cannon still booming, and with feeling everywhere running high, the Special Commission of the Province of New York began its session. The preliminaries were soon rushed through. Over sixty men indicted for "riotous assault and for rescuing prisoners" admitted guilt. They were quickly given various sentences — to hours in the pillory, to fines, to terms in prison. Then the big show commenced. Everyone knew that the landed proprietors were out to make the punishment of Farmer Prendergast an example that would startle and impress all who heard it.

They did just that. The newspapers of the time report a large public audience following every detail of the Prendergast trial attentively, and with sympathy to the point of weeping. And Ira Allen, years afterward, writing of his first visit to Bennington, recalled his memories of this trial in words which showed how familiar he was with the implacable prosecution of that good family man who had never with his own hands harmed another human being.

To guard this American prison, two companies of British regulars had been held in town. They could be seen, every day, on sentry-go, muskets on their shoulders, in their red uniforms with handsome, white, pipe-clayed trimmings. Everyone who saw them there, impassively pacing to and fro, knew that they would with equal impassivity shoot down American civilians if so ordered.

This was only two years before Boston people were treated to the same spectacle of smartly turned-out British soldiers, marching to and fro to overawe the grim-faced, very little overawed Boston street crowds. We have the testimony of an eyewitness as to the mutiny of British troops in Albany a year before this expedition. So we know there was no friendliness felt by Americans who watched the British soldiers. Every passer-by on the street, every visitor from the countryside, knew that the redcoats and their muskets were there because the New York militia, mighty fighters in war against military enemies, were, to quote again the British General Gage, "not to be depended upon by the Rich and Powerful people of the Province" when it came to shooting fellow civilians, farmers and homemakers of their own race, language, nationality and station in life.

And we may be sure that those present who had ridden over from Connecticut and Massachusetts — keen-eyed, Locke-reading levelers as they were — noted that the impressive, distinguished New York Court was composed, almost exclusively, of the richest landlords and land owners of the province, by definition predisposed against the cause of the accused.

An English governor of the province had once removed a New York chief justice from office, partly for sitting in a case which involved his own land. But that had been thirty years before. In a later continuation of Nimham's plea, the Indians begged the then British governor to make his decision *without* the New York Council because, "most if not all the Gentlemen of the Council were either interested in the Lands in Controversy, or *in other Lands which lay under similar Circumstances.*"

James Duane, one of the ablest and most wily lawyers of the province, was in charge of the prosecution. The adjective is not my own invention. He was frequently called "sly" and "wily" by people of his time who admired the success he achieved by those qualities.

The jury, drawn according to New York statute, were all men of substance — which meant that the acquittal or conviction of this tenant farmer rested on the judgment of twelve owners of landed estate. Prendergast, on trial for his life, was allowed no lawyer. He conducted his own defense as best he could. His only helper was his devoted wife. She was young, attractive, with the poise and self-confidence of a member of the Society of Friends, which, even at that date, treated women as spiritual and intellectual equals of men. A newspaper, the *Weekly Post-Boy*, reports that her calm presence of mind "suffered not one circumstance that could be collected from the evidence, or thought of in his Favor, to escape the Notice of the Court."

Thereupon the prosecuting attorney (so the report continues) moved to have her put out of the courtroom "lest she too much influence the jury by her very looks." But the judge was not without humane feeling, for he is quoted as ruling "that Mrs. Prendergast had not spoken unreasonably," and that, if the request were granted, the prosecutor "might as well move the Prisoner himself should be covered with a Veil, lest the Distress painted in his Countenance should too powerfully excite Compassion." He had reason to have "Distress painted in his Countenance," for the charge of high treason against him meant, if he were convicted, frightful torture and slow, agonizing death. The small mouse who had tried to fight was now helplessly in the power of large and powerful cats.

The jury brought in the verdict: "Guilty as charged."

The court pronounced sentence that "the prisoner be led back to the place whence he came, and from thence shall be drawn on a hurdle to the place for execution, and then shall be hanged by the neck, and then shall be cut down alive, and his entrails and privy members shall be cut from his body, and shall be burned in his sight, and his head shall be cut off, and his body shall be divided into four parts, and shall be disposed of at the King's pleasure."

When Prendergast heard this terrible sentence, wrote a New York paper reporting the trial, "he uttered an ejaculatory prayer to God for mercy with such earnestness and looked so distressed that the whole audience were melted into tears." But he quickly regained courage and begged leave of the court to say, boldly, though without avail, "that if opposition to the Government was deemed rebellion, no member of that court was entitled to sit upon his trial." True enough, less than a year before, many well-to-do New Yorkers had taken part in the violent opposition to the Stamp Act. But of course *they* were gentlemen!

All the time the court was sitting, the regulars, turned loose in Philipse Patent, flung themselves into pillaging, plundering and burning. Their officers did not restrain them. Their officers approved. The expedition was planned as a punitive measure to teach the rebellious farmers and all their friends a lesson they would not soon forget. A writer of the time has left this description of their operations: "It is beyond the power of language to paint the horror of this poor distressed people to see their habitations, some demolished, some robbed and pillaged, and others of them enveloped in flames of fire . . . to see themselves at once, in an instant, deprived of all their substance for which they had labored, sweat and fatigued themselves all the days of their lives."

If some younger Connecticut and Massachusetts men — later to be Vermonters — had traveled as far as Poughkeepsie to be present at the trial of Prendergast, how many more seeing the huge pillars of smoke mounting into the air must have dropped whatever work they were doing and rushed across the invisible border line to the rescue! To country people, then as now, a distant curl of smoke above the trees was a cry of distress which no man worth his salt could ignore. Breathless, eager to help, they were stopped by sentries but not driven away — they were allowed to stay that they might see and remember. They saw and they remembered. A public execution was considered the surest method for bringing home to spectators the power and majesty of authority. There, in fields and pastures, the men from Connecticut stood with their New York country neighbors, silently watching the houses burn.

They were small houses, but each was a triumph of human effort. They had not been run up impersonally by a contracting firm, but constructed by neighborly co-operation, beam by beam, rafter by rafter. Here the watchers from over the line saw, marked, and never forgot . . . soldiers zestfully making bonfires out of human hopes.

The next time Vermonters saw the soldiers of King George was at the Battle of Bennington.

The tragic epic had risen to its climax with the conviction (legal enough, since he had resisted the King's troops) fit for a sadistic murderer pronounced on the honest farmer who had been sorry for poor people put out of their homes. Over the whole countryside swept a wave of public revulsion against landlords and lawyers. How do we know that there was such a wave? It is proved by a dramatic documented fact: the Poughkeepsie sheriff advertised in the newspapers for an assistant to help in carrying out the dreadful penalty. In this printed statement he promised that his helper "will meet with a good reward, shall be disguised so as not to be known, and secured from Insults." But to their honor, not one man in the Province stepped forward to get this good reward.

Sir Henry Moore, then British Governor of New York, had, at the urgent plea of the wife of the condemned man, granted a reprieve. Fifty armed horsemen stormed the Poughkeepsie jail (it is not so stated, but we must suppose the guard of regulars had been removed) and opened the doors for Prendergast's escape. But he was a well-informed man, who knew that as a fugitive his family would be reduced to utter destitution because all his property would be confiscated. He chose to wait there till the King's answer was known.

From September to December, the flames of violence died down. The hard feeling continued. Dr. Mark says in *Agrarian Conflicts:* "Bitterly complaining fugitives from New York farms took refuge in Massachusetts and Connecticut, but eventually found their way to the unsettled region that later became Vermont, since the chief land in their native colonies was almost entirely gone. Vermont towns like Manchester, Danby, Dorset, Panton and Poultney appear to have been settled by emigrants from Dutchess and Westchester Counties. Furthermore the events of 1766 deflected the tide of New England immigration towards the same region."

In December, with a thunderclap of unexpectedness, the King's answer was received. Prendergast was not to be executed. Not to be sentenced to a prison term. The King had pardoned him. He could go free. He was joyfully escorted back to his home by a great crowd of friends and admirers, cheering King George with hearty hurrahs.

There were no hurrahs from the powerful upper classes of the province. The home government did not seem to agree with the New York landlords that resistance to their system of land tenure should be punished by torture and death. They were astonished and affronted by this check from the Crown to their efforts to serve the interests of their own class. To them, Prendergast's pardon was inexplicable.

To us, with the records now at hand, the situation is easy to understand. In view of public opinion in the colonies, already unfriendly to the mother country, the London authorities were not at all enthusiastic about using British troops to intimidate American civilians. They were fully aware that the association of ideas with the British Army uniform, thus created, would not make future relations with the colonists any easier. There is a biting undercurrent of criticism in the Earl of Shelburne's letter to Governor Moore: "His Majesty has graciously [*sic*] pleased to grant him his Pardon, relying that this instance of his Royal clemency will have a better effect in recalling these mistaken People to their

Duty than the most rigorous punishment. . . ." And again: "There is room to apprehend that the Sheriff of Albany may have exceeded, if not his legal Powers, at least the bounds of discretion." And the Lieutenant Governor of New York commented, acidly, "The power of the civil authority of New York alone must have been sufficient, had there not been a general jealousy of the powerful combination in the courts of justice in favor of the extravagant claims of the great landed men."

It was in the last days of 1766 that the "agrarian revolt," the "Anti-Rent War" was crushed. The next year, in 1767, Ethan Allen set out alone on snowshoes to see for himself what kind of country it was where settlers in the New Hampshire Grants were beginning to make their homes.

CHAPTER 6

The Roll of Thunder

WHAT did Ethan Allen find in the Hampshire Grant Country?
He found the land and life already described under the chapter
heading, "The Settlers." Evidently it suited him. He took root.

The only sour note in the situation — the hazy legal position
of the territory — was not particularly daunting. Something more
or less like it existed all up and down the colonial frontier.
Original charters were always vague. Often they contradicted
one another. Virginia, for example, with boundaries getting wider
and wider apart as they ran westward toward their destination,
"The South Sea," challenged the jurisdiction, equally valid on
paper, of Massachusetts and Connecticut. Connecticut's lawful
expansion — according to old parchments — toward the South
Sea, was blocked by the hard fact of New York's existence. In
this case a compromise had been adopted, well known and much
quoted by New Englanders in the Grants. The "invisible line"
crossed by our squirrel-hunter in "A Chat Between Neighbors"
had been surveyed approximately twenty miles east of the Hudson River. Further north, between Massachusetts and New York,
while details remained to be worked out, the same limit had been
practically agreed to. Governor Wentworth of New Hampshire
felt on firm ground when he argued that, if in two cases New
York's territory ended at twenty miles from the Hudson, it
should, must and did end there in the third case also; hence
that New Hampshire with rights running "to the borders of
New York" could give lawsuit-proof deeds to all lands now
included in Vermont.

"Not at all!" replied New York authorities. They cited
Charles II's gift to the Duke of York, lately (in 1764) empha-
sized by Royal proclamation, stating that as against New Hampshire, the New York line extended to the west bank of the
Connecticut River.

Did that settle the question? For the moment only. While

Ethan Allen was making his way through the snow, Moses Robinson of Bennington was making his way across the Atlantic to ask the London authorities for a reversal. In due time something like a reversal was issued. Its not-too-clear phrases made the settlers think that their victory was complete. But New York read them as merely postponing decision on pending disputes, in no sense as forbidding new grants, which the big landowners hurried to get on record. From time to time, London put out "cease and desist" orders. New York lawyers found ways to get around all of them. Meanwhile friction grew hotter with every day's events. That, very sketchily, sums up the legal outlook during Allen's first months as a Vermonter.

At the start of their life in the Green Mountains, the young settlers had not given a thought to impending danger. They were like people cheerfully getting ready to plant a garden, absorbed in spading, raking, fertilizing, marking out the plots for this seed and that, which later would feed them and their children. It had been early in the morning for them when they had begun to work, the air had been clear, the sun bright. When had that film of cloud first dimmed the light from the sky? Was that a murmur of thunder off on the horizon? They could not stop to listen, to gaze, there was so much life-giving work to be done.

The mutter of thunder grew louder. The news was constantly more disquieting. It did not come to them by a shellacked and manicured voice speaking through the mystery box of the radio, nor by great headlines shrieking calamity from the morning paper. That the trap had snapped shut on them came, as all news came to them, over the trails, down the streams, a-foot or horseback. Indeed they could hardly have told, any of them, the exact moment when they knew. A scrap here, a scrap there, a phrase the young father had picked up from the talk of men at the neighboring tavern, or something brought home by the lanky son, his eyes wide, his face pale, from a trip with bags of grain to the gristmill.

Sometimes the warning came from a man none of them had ever seen before, a settler perhaps, on his way to look over country far to the north. "Something's brewin' in Albany. I heard talk about it when I came through there. The big-money boys mean business. The landlords and their lawyers are gettin' ready to handle you the way they handled that Prendergast. I thought maybe a word to you now might come in handy. Pass the word around, why don't ye? Me, I'm goin' a long ways from here. They won't catch up with me for a while." Then he rode on, calling over his shoulder, "Best of luck to ye!"

Or it might be an over-the-mountain man, ominously silent about what business might be taking him to Bennington, except to let drop, "Some of the folks over east are saying they might as well make the best of a bad bargain and turn in their New Hampshire deeds for New York leases. A lot of them come from over Boston way, too far east for them to know what it means to hold a New York tenant lease. But we do. We've seen how it works. Something's got to be done. One rotten apple can spoil a bin full. We've got to stick together, all of us who ever saw a Yorker sheriff serve a 'jectment writ.'"

One hint after another. The bright sunshine faded. Stranger or blood kin, every man who came along the trail brought news. As far away as they could see him coming, those early settlers knew that it was bad news. The man working by himself flung down the hoe, the adz, to listen. The men working in company let fall the log they were rolling up on a neighbor's cabin a-building. The mothers laid the babies half fed down in the old cradles. The young dancers gaily swinging their partners at the corners halted their nimble feet. The fiddler's bow dropped from the strings. The tall boys stuffing firewood in under great potash kettles, the women picking berries in a clearing — almost before a word was spoken, they felt the sky darken, heard the ominous crack of a thunderbolt, saw sinister lightning flashes and knew that a deluge threatened to sweep into devastating flood waters those carefully planted seeds, pregnant with the future.

This was the danger the young settlers had always dreaded, although, till then, they had managed to thrust it down deep into their subconsciousness. They had never feared material perils, familiar to them by tradition. Their fathers and mothers, their grandparents, had fought Indians, floods, famines, forest fires — had beaten them — had gone forward over them into life renewed. But this danger was something new to any New England man, this threat to his personal individual status as a free man, the possibility that the great proprietors of the province might take over by law and arms the homesteads these settlers had paid for and labored for, might by force change Town Meeting people, free owners of their own farms, into tenants, who would vote, if at all, as their landlords decided.

New or not, the crisis had to be met. We know how anxiously the young heads were put together in uncertainty, wherever the scattered settlers chanced to meet, on the trails, in the woods, in the Catamount Tavern, before the hearth in a log cabin home. Nothing was really definite, as yet. "We can't be sure — might be nothing but just talk — anyway, we ought to make our plans, we ought to be ready."

They were ready!

This is the way the story is told by Matt Jones. For readability's sake, I compress the passage a little and leave out some of his cautiously legal technical explanations and qualifications, and so do not put quotation marks around the story. It is on pages 282–283 of *Vermont in the Making*. In 1769, as a preliminary to New York ejectment suits, the grantees of the Walloomsac tract had secured appointment of Commissioners to survey and divide this great area among New York claimants. When the surveyor accompanied by the Commissioners reached the farm which Breckenridge had purchased from Moses Robinson (of Bennington) a number of armed Vermonters were found in the field adjoining the house, nominally engaged in harvesting the corn. A New York justice of the peace read the riot act but without avail, and the survey was abandoned.

Legal action however was *not* abandoned. Ejectment suits against Breckenridge and others in like circumstances were brought to trial in June 1770. New Hampshire deeds on which the Vermont defendants based their case were not allowed in evidence by the Albany court, which declared without further hearing that the lands were in the Province of New York, and forthwith gave judgment for the New York plaintiffs. Commenting on this case, Mr. Jones says, "The immediate appeal to force by the settlers under the New Hampshire grants after the ejectment suits went against them at Albany, together with the entire absence of effort to litigate the matter any further, makes it difficult to resist the conclusion that they were advised that their case was unsound at law and that a favorable conclusion could not be expected there."

That, no doubt, is one way to look at the matter. A view rather closer to reality would be that after one attempt it was clear that whether their case was legally sound or unsound, it was not worth the trouble to plead it in a court which prejudged and allowed no argument on the basic point at issue. But Mr. Jones is entirely correct in stating that from then on the Green Mountain Boys relied on force, or rather on a show of force. He makes that clear by citing this episode: In July, 1771, Sheriff Henry Ten Eyck gathered together in Albany a posse of about two hundred men and once more set out for the Breckenridge farm. "As the Sheriff proceeded toward the house, his followers fell away until only about twenty reached it with him." Standing in the nearby cornfield were about a hundred and fifty armed Vermonters who did not "fall away." The door to the house was locked. The sheriff read aloud the writ of ejectment, dread document for many a Hudson Valley farmer. The door to the house was not opened. The sheriff threatened to break down the door. Silently the Vermonters lounging around in the cornfield raised the barrels of their guns and took aim. "Whereupon," so runs the letter written next day to report to Duane, "considering the little probability of success and the eminent [*sic*] Danger attending it he, by the advice of his friends, Desisted." Matt Jones, who, by the way, is far from a partisan of the Vermonters, concludes in these words: "It is apparent that the entire force, whose members, aside from the Albany Mayor and three or four interested lawyers, never had any heart in this task, beat a precipitate retreat, leaving Sheriff Ten Eyck alone."

For us today that scene, with its silent menacing countrymen, with the courage oozing out of the sheriff deserted by his posse, accurately forecasts the outcome of the dispute. That is what happened throughout the long story.

But it is easy to have hindsight wisdom. Nobody at the time could possibly have known what is now plain. To every observer in and out of Vermont the odds must have seemed at least ten to one in favor of the old reliable Albany steam roller. True, the great majority of Vermont settlers were resolute, hard as nails, young enough so that the prospect of a fight was exhilarating instead of terrifying. Yet, to the eye of good sense — and these were men and women brought up to respect good sense — it was sheer insanity to fight back against a government which, as they well knew, during fifteen years of unbroken success had kicked the teeth down the throat of any tenant who dared to resist his landlord's decrees.

Those who threatened them had law courts, shrewdly and ably organized in their favor. The log cabin frontier folk had not a lawyer in their district, nor any way of getting their case considered in a court — in Connecticut, Massachusetts or New Hampshire — where a judgment might be rendered according to its merits. They had no money. There was plenty of wealth on the other side. They had no organized military force, being scattered civilians, in their working clothes; their arms were their own hunting rifles, their ammunition what powder each happened to have in his cabin. Many of them had seen the New York landlords backed by hundreds of professional soldiers, fully armed, with artillery if they needed it, well-officered, hot for action against civilians whom they despised.

Those were the prospects. With a reflex as instinctive as that which snatches a hand back from a hot stove, the men and women of the southwest Grants unanimously shouted "No!" and decided to fight.

As it turned out, they were not insane. Reckless perhaps but with cool heads. For they showed the best of judgment in planning the one line of strategy which offered them a hope. In the interminable discussions always needed before a sizable group of equals can reach a decision, they went over every item they had observed when, from their old down-country homes, they had watched the revolts of Noble and Prendergast. They thought their way through to three main considerations on which, as is shown by the record, they based their sound plan of resistance.

First of all, it was a matter of common knowledge that the non-gentry majority in the Province of New York had no love for wealthy Manor Lords and Patentees. They might give little active help but there was good reason to think they would do nothing to harm plain farmer folk struggling to be free and independent masters of the land they plowed.

A single well-known incident proves the soundness of this assumption. The Governor of New York offered a cash reward of twenty pounds (much more in purchasing value at that time than the hundred dollars of pre-devaluation exchange) for the arrest of Ethan Allen and seven other "rioters" as he called them. Ethan — always something of a cut-up — replied by offering a reward of fifteen pounds for the apprehension of James Duane and Attorney-General John Kempe. A little later, on a dare, he rode to Albany, took a drink at a well-known tavern there, held up the announcement of the promised reward for the arrest of the prominent New York gentlemen, asked the proprietor to be good enough to post it where all could read it, chatted with the people around him, and, in the highest of spirits, rode triumphantly back to Bennington. Not one man-of-the-street in Albany had slipped out of the tavern's back door to inform on Allen and claim the high reward for his arrest. Here's something Vermonters do not forget about their New York neighbors.

From this friendly unspoken sympathy, it followed that the rank and file of New York militia would keep up their passive resistance, so marked in the past. That militia, not always, not all of them, but often and in large numbers, had silently gone on strike when the landed proprietors had called on them to eject or fire on farmers resisting the terms of New York land tenure. Of course nobody could be sure on this point or on any point. Still, trying to peer into the troubled future before them, those early Green Mountain men believed they had better than even grounds for hoping that the militia could be figured not as a minus but a plus.

That estimate was justified by the event. New York militia never marched against Vermonters. William Smith, Chief Justice of the Province of New York, writing to William Eden in England a discouraged explanation of the dismal (from his point of view) lack of progress in the Land Grant dispute, ends his report: "Is it to be wondered at, when from Fear or Affection no force can be persuaded to move against Allen and Vermont?" Speaking for the Vermont side, one of our Arlington older people used to say that we ought to put up, in Montpelier, next to the statue of Ethan Allen, a monument in gratitude to those who helped us when help was needed — a militiaman in colonial New York uniform, flat-footed at parade rest, his musket firmly grounded.

But how about the dreaded British regulars? In Ira Allen's journal he says that the day after he first arrived in Bennington a hard-riding messenger brought in a warning from friendly Quakers on Long Island that the regulars were to be called out again, just as, he adds, they had been in the great anti-rent uprising in the Hudson Valley, in the course of which "Pentergast" had been sentenced to death. Though this news turned out to be a false alarm, the menace was always there! If the redcoats had used their overwhelming power then, might they not use it once more to enforce the decisions of New York courts?

But would they? That was the vital question. The Vermont farmers, putting their heads together, worked out a line of action designed to keep the British regiments in their barracks. There is no evidence that they knew of the sharp reproofs which, after the Prendergast revolt, had been sent from London to the Commanding Officer, the New York Council, and to the Governor for using, to destroy homes and crops, soldiers who had been left in Albany for the purpose of defending the province from outside attack by its military enemies. What they did know was that the New York authorities had based their appeal for help from His Majesty's troops on the fact that during the anti-rent fight lives had been lost. Murder in the course of rioting, they had protested, was sufficient reason for using any force available to restore order.

Very well then, if loss of life was the accepted reason for the use of British troops, there would be no loss of life in the course of the resistance to New York landlords — no matter how precarious seemed the chance of success without recourse to a shooting war.

The astonishing fact is that they stuck to this resolution. All the more astonishing when we remember how incapable the early Vermont men were of accepting what is often called "discipline," meaning obedience to orders simply because orders are given. Every man of them felt himself to be as good as any other. Yet, during the turbulent months and years which followed, in their breakneck rides along the trails together, under stress of life and death (for any man of them captured and taken into New York would have been sentenced to die), in spite of the large consumption of rum (common everywhere at that period), in spite of all this, not one of the always-armed young Vermonters forgot himself and pulled his trigger. That tells us something about their quality, and also about their compelling unanimity of purpose. They knew how to obey the orders they had given themselves. This is self-discipline.

Once more the Vermonters had guessed right. Although, as we now know, New York authorities expected help from the British Army, their petitions were always brushed off with one or another polite excuse. Finally a definite refusal came in terms not at all polite. In 1773, General Gage was moving on to the hot spot of Boston (this was Tea Party year). Unlike Gage, who was the son of a great English nobleman, his successor in New York, General Haldimand, was not even British. He was a Swiss professional soldier, of an exiled French Huguenot family. He had lived his early years among dour, hard-headed, rough-spoken Swiss farmers, not in the least like the docile, respectful tenants on an English Manor. If he had a military man's distaste for unruly people who would not obey orders, that was nothing to the scorn he felt for civilian authorities who could not handle their own problems.

When the New York landlords and lawyers confidently appealed to him to "put down disorders," he told them if the precedent should be set up that professional soldiers are necessary to "control a few lawless vagabonds," it would make the civil authority contemptible. He also pointed out that it is the business of militia to "control domestic disorders" and that the Province of New York had plenty of militia of its own.

"Vagabonds" is an odd epithet for the Vermonters of that time, who were, almost to a man, married, with families in stable homes, to which they were devoted. But "lawless" — yes, that they were, from the New York point of view, and glad to have the fact widely publicized.

From another point of view they were almost unbelievably

orderly in the conduct of life. As a matter of record, from the first settlements, early in the 1760's, to the organization of the state as an independent republic in 1778, there were, in all the western side of the Vermont territory, neither law courts nor lawyers; and on the eastern side, only a shadow, a token of a legal organization, existing on paper. A lawyer, writing in the nineteenth century for other lawyers, in a Massachusetts legal magazine, says, "No sessions of the New York courts were ever held in Vermont; and their jurisdiction, save in theory, never extended over it." Ethan Allen (addressing himself as usual to the world at large) explained that it was the intention of the Green Mountain people "to run this country in accordance with the laws of Almighty God *and those of Connecticut* — till we get better ones." We entirely miss the point of that reference to the laws of Connecticut if we do not bear in mind that it was purposefully intended — and was so understood — as an open, pointed repudiation of land-tenure laws in New York.

For eighteen years a group of human beings, its numbers soon running up into the thousands, managed its affairs without the framework of any formal legal system. As somebody has said of those years, "There were in Vermont, no lawyers, no courts, and no disorders." Each individual town at its own Town Meetings elected certain citizens — no lawyers they — to act as constables and justices of the peace. In that excited group of young people, no crime against man or woman or property, no breaking of the domestic peace of their precariously established "society" occurred which could not be handled by these Shakespeareanly rustic, untrained officers of a self-imposed law.

Here is part of the "Vermont Tradition" not to be forgotten. During this period which lasted long enough for a boy to grow up into a husband and father of a family, no law code was in force over them. Yet their "civic order" was not disturbed. Their own code of decent behavior was enforced on them by their own self-mastery.

The last two paragraphs sound, of course, like partisan ranting unless we keep in mind the distinction Vermonters made — and still make — between the internal tranquillity of their closely knit communities and the fury of their resistance to outside domination. In the course of that resistance there were plenty of disorders, but hardly crimes, unless we accept the extreme pacifist definition and call any violence a crime. Why did the Green Mountain Boys think violence of any sort was necessary? As time went on, it seemed evident that no organized soldiery — either militia or regulars — were likely to move against them. There were many plain Vermonters ready to arm, ride, risk their necks for the ownership of their homes. On the other side, there were not many, perhaps not any, plain Yorkers ready to risk their lives in order to add those Vermont homes to the wealth of the great landowners. As for the gentry of the province, a great scoffing laugh went up from the lean, tough, young frontiersmen at the idea of weapons in the soft, white hands of those indoor men who found it too hard work even to shave their own faces — James Duane would put up with any other ineptitude from a servant of his if he had a good hand with a razor.

Yet, secure though they seemed for the moment from armed attack, the Vermonters could not count on security from legal attack. Sooner or later, some kind of official, Royal inquiry would certainly start taking evidence about this stalemated border dispute. The Green Mountain men needed to plan their protection from that as well as their resistance to military action. It would help them greatly to show an overwhelming majority of bona fide settlers united in opposing New York's claim to overlordship. In the past, British administrators, at the higher level, had expressed a farsighted sympathy with men and women actually on the land, as against absentee capitalists. But mile after mile of misty ocean waves often blurred London's view of colonial affairs. It would not help the Vermont case, when it was argued in England, if New York delegates could point even to a sprinkling of families in the Grants who accepted — no matter how grudgingly — the status of tenants to New York landlords. Those in charge of the Royal Inquiry might well become weary and baffled by conflicting testimony, might, in order to get home for a long week end, take the quickest way out and set the boundary line once for all at the Connecticut River. This would void every title from New Hampshire. All holders of such titles would automatically become legal trespassers in their own homes. They would have two courses open to them: to give up their hard-won homesteads, or to accept whatever terms were offered by New York proprietors. It must never be forgotten that to live under New York jurisdiction meant giving up public-supported, free schools for their children, town-meeting self-government, the election of their own local authorities. Furthermore, such a ruling, endorsed by Royal decree, would be a very different matter from the judgment of a provincial court. Resistance to it might well call out His Majesty's troops, in force.

With opposite desires, Messrs. Duane, Kempe and associates followed the same line of reasoning. They lost no time in offering not too burdensome leaseholds to wavering, already established settlers, and sending in tenants (when they could secure any) of their own to take up unoccupied land. To resist this infiltration, Vermonters could reach no court they considered unprejudiced. What do law-abiding people do, when they have no reason to respect the only law courts available?

The force employed by the loosely organized band of Green Mountain Boys was, on the whole, less ruthless than the average conduct of such vigilante movements. Much of the time it went no further than piercing war whoops from the galloping horse-men, guns brandished, but not fired, some loud-mouthed, hair-raising, verbal threats. In harder cases, roofs were taken off cabins, crops destroyed, some paid pro-Albany organizers flogged. I do not pretend that this was good clean fun — the inside story of any war, hot or cold, makes ugly reading for posterity. But, only a few years later, the Tories in every colony were handled at least as roughly. Also I think it fair to point out that those floggings never approached the sadistic "discipline" inflicted by British naval officers on their own seamen, or the horrors of the public whippings of deserters from the British Army occupying Boston. Furthermore it must be remembered that in that period flogging was an ordinary, familiar form of punishment, considered more humane than many others because it left no permanent mutila-tion. As for the rest of the terrorization campaign by the Green Mountain Rangers, although it is an incomplete excuse to say, "the other fellow began it," still it is worth noting that up to that time in Connecticut or Massachusetts, nothing of the sort had taken place. The Green Mountain Boys could have learned those methods only by watching from their boyhood homes the New York landlords using British regulars, or their own armed employees, to break down farmer resistance.

At that, the noisy Vermonters held their hands from the worst of that manorial ferocity they remembered so well. The transplanted New Englanders followed the New York practice of destroying farm property, but unlike the agents of the Rensselaers, they never rendered women and children destitute by carrying off husbands or fathers to terms of imprisonment. New settlers whose only offense was that they were being used by New York landlords in an attempt to establish title to Vermont land, were sent back to New York, frightened but unharmed in body.

One such instance for which full information has come down, because it was on a larger than usual scale concerned the "settlers" near the mouth of Otter Creek. They were Highlanders, who spoke and understood no English, hence were not subject to the "taint of levelling ideas" which with every New England contact rubbed off so readily on New York tenant farmers. They had been brought from Scotland by British Colonel John Reid and sent into Vermont as his farm tenants on land also claimed by several Connecticut men through purchase from New Hampshire. The intention was of course to secure that possession which is nine tenths of ownership.

These poor Highland Scotch can have had no idea that they were being used as pawns by a New York landlord to establish title under New York law. But the Green Mountain men understood this very well. They rode in to the little settlement, and ordered the bewildered and intimidated Highlanders out of their cabins. Carefully allowing them time to save their household gear, they sent them back to Albany, burned every cabin to the ground and laid waste the fields.

It was by far the most considerable violence on their side. It was also a logical move in the legal warfare. They were cutting off a tentacle of a law-octopus which in years to come was to be repudiated and destroyed by the people of its own province. All the same, those were human families, who were trying, in ignorant good faith, to establish homes. We wish it had not happened. Not that we claim the right to set ourselves up in judgment. If we were back in the same tangled, desperately confused situation, would we not probably, reluctantly endorse this and many another harsh expedient as necessary for the protection of the rights and freedoms which we (and Hudson Valley farmers) *now* enjoy?

We find it harder to take a generous view of the role played by lawyers on the New York side. Far from being merely conscientious professional men doing their best for their clients' interests, they were, as repeated official statements of British governors testify, inextricably and personally bound to the special privilege, large-landowner party. Of James Duane this was particularly true. In this quarrel it was his own purse which was at stake as well as his political and social beliefs.

For he had grants to very large tracts of land in Vermont. As a matter of course he expected to keep these acres in his possession, with subordinate tenant farmers working them, exactly as he had tenants on his many acres in the province. He saw himself as a sound businessman seeking a legitimate return on invested capital. We see him as a man already wealthy, planning to found a still greater fortune on the broken hopes of working people.

One of the original documents of this period, available now to us, is his journal of his survey of this Vermont land, in 1765, a trip on which he passed over a region claimed by him under New York law. An ancestor of mine owned and occupied part of this land by a grant from New Hampshire. I still live on that land. Also, among other Vermont settlers, one of my Arlington great-great-grandfathers, Captain Jehiel Hawley, is mentioned. Mr. Duane says that he and his traveling companion "made advances to him. But he was shy of treating with us. Old Robinson of Bennington shewed the same behavior." But much more important than its personal interest to me is the evidence given by this travel-diary that the Green Mountain Boys accurately foresaw what would happen to Vermont farmers, now free and independent, if they failed in their resistance to the tightly organized political ring called the New York Junto. For in this diary Mr. Duane sets down not only where he and his companion went, and what they thought of Vermont land, but what they would do with it, when they had title. Of the thousands of acres to come into his hands, Mr. Duane planned to set aside a small percentage as a sort of compromise with the landowning mania of the men of the region. Five lots of a hundred acres each in sundry places of his vast claims, he would sell, actually sell outright, New England fashion, to working farmers. All the remainder he would "lease at low rents. This will encourage able Settlers, promote good building and improvements, and be of advantage to us by *drawing a third of the sales when they* transfer their leases." A third, you notice — more than the quarter-sale which, inside the province, was becoming the common claim for New York landlords.

It seemed incredible to a lawyer like James Duane, who had till then carried all before him in the courts, that the landlords would not, in this case as in all the others, emerge victors over those who followed the plow. He was right. It was incredible. If it had not come out the way it did, nobody could ever have believed it possible.

It has even proved almost impossible to write the whole story of how it did happen to turn out the way it did, with the plow-holding farmers still owning the land they tilled, still governing themselves. The narrative has too many details, and it is so recent that most of the details are on record somewhere. To this day, lawyers and historians when they try to take all those details into account, and to follow all the threads of the elaborate spider-web of legal and extralegal action, find it hard to avoid getting wound up in a buzzing confusion.

Fortunately for my readers, I am not writing an exhaustive reconstruction of the Land-Grant dispute. Complete accounts of it are available in ever so many histories to be found in bookstores, public libraries, and in the collections of Historical Societies. I am trying to set down the main sources of Vermont tradition. Now a tradition is a matter of psychology. It is based on the general outcome of numerous events, not on a precise acquaintance with each stage of their sequence, such as is needed to pass a college history examination.

To steer a history-canoe through the details of the boiling

rock-studded rapids of any violent passage in the life of any people anywhere, and come out right side up, paddle still in hand, takes a stronger head than most authors have, or most readers require. For everyone but the specialist, it is enough to know that there was such a passage, such dangerous rapids to shoot, which way the current ran, and into what waters it brought the canoe.

Even in its barest outline, the Vermont drama of those days convinces us that the men and women and children who were its actors could not but be profoundly influenced in character by twenty and thirty years of danger, excitement, by threats from enemies far more powerful than they, by knowing that they could expect no help from outside, above all by total uncertainty of the outcome. They entered those years like any other Western New Englanders. That long ordeal marked them with a special quality. After it, they were not the men and women they had been.

What had they been, when they came up into the Vermont forests? Historians who don't like our tradition, or who think it desirable to debunk the indiscriminate praise of some native writers, sometimes say that no one left the settled regions of Western Connecticut or Massachusetts except the failures, the shiftless folks who could not earn their livings and so were forced to wander on. Such an idea leaves out of consideration the prime factor that most of the first generation of Vermonters were far too young to have had time to try and fail at anything. They were newly married couples, leaving their parents' homes to make new ones for themselves. What else do any young people do when they marry and have children?

But for a quarter of a century destiny hammered those fathers and mothers of young children on the anvil of danger and long-drawn-out suspense. We who have lived now in taken-for-granted safety for nearly two centuries must never forget that for them actual peril darkened the horizon of every day's life, rumbling like the ominous thunder of an approaching storm. From the time their children were babies till they in turn were grown men and women, those hard-working young parents in the Vermont forests faced a skillful, never-ending attack, a long, ingenious effort to take from them a way of life which — to them — made plain people honorable.

There is a good deal more we must not forget. At any time, on any day, when the tension and anxiety grew intolerable, they could have just given up and gone back to Connecticut. There they and their little children would have been physically safe. Certainly not each individual among them was heroic; some of them must have grown very weary of sitting on a ticking time-bomb. The fact remains that they did not give up and go back.

There was another escape from the uncertainty and constant physical danger which hung over them. They could have accepted the living conditions offered by the land tenure system of New York, with all its implications very well known to them. But they considered such living conditions beneath human dignity. This is no guessing hypothesis. Look at the record. People show what they feel by what they do. What the recorded facts show is that with rage, with courage, with endurance — massive foundation stone of human life as endurance is! — these working farmers and their working wives defended, year after year, the principle of equal social and political opportunity for every citizen and equal educational opportunity for every child.

After the lightning-clap from Lexington and Concord, the general swing towards independence powerfully heartened Green Mountain morale. Of course it raised here, as everywhere, a new complication of divided loyalty. My home town of Arlington long carried the nickname of Tory Hollow and a great-great of mine was, because of his English sympathies, exiled and his property confiscated, as was the general American practice during the Revolution. In Vermont the money from this source paid for the cost of government.

Yet, in spite of some division of opinion, the American Revolution brought — at first — to the great majority of Vermonters the comforting sense of being no longer alone, but part of a greater movement. It brought also bright prospects for their own future. Vermonters jumped at the chance to attack Fort Ticonderoga. Later, in a rear-guard action at Hubbardton they stood off the British until St. Clair's troops had made good their retreat.

Joined with Stark's New Hampshiremen, they smashed Burgoyne's raid on Bennington.

The road ahead seemed clearly marked and wide open: to join not only as comrades in arms but as political associates with all other Sons of Liberty. The first necessary move was a get-together unity of all the scattered townships. In the past, such a completely united front had been prevented by the reluctance of some of the citizens of some communities east of the Green Mountains to take irrevocable action against the claims of New York Province.

Almost without exception, the few towns in the southeast corner of the Grants had been settled not by people who had lived their youth so close to New York territory that they personally knew what the New York regime meant to working farmers. They came mostly from further east in New England, where they had seen nothing of what made New York Province distasteful to West Connecticut farmers. The older ones among them had felt sure that some kind of compromise could be found, making life tolerable even without local self-government. But they now received a sharp reminder that King and Parliament might go but that in the new State of New York as formerly in the province, those who had amassed or inherited money and political power intended to stay in control.

A new Constitution had been drawn up for the American State of New York. As Vermonters, east or west of the Green Mountains, read its provisions, it looked to them as if a mighty thin coat of whitewash had been spread over the frowning walls and battlements of a medieval castle. They noted that by the terms of the New York State Constitution only the fairly well-to-do were to vote. The others would take what they got, with no say-so about it. They saw to their horror that the governor was given the power to send the legislature back home any time he disliked the line it was taking. Sore and angry about what they felt was the raw deal they had had in New York courts, they saw with alarm that the appointment of judges in the new state was not only in "safe" hands, but was for life. Quit-rents were to continue. The new state affirmed its claim to all territory formerly granted by the King.

One look at this Constitution sent the Vermont east-siders to stand beside those west of the Green Mountains. General Bayley, leader of the Connecticut Valley moderates, wrote to the New York Committee of safety: "The people, before they saw the Constitution, was not willing to trouble themselves about a separation from the State of New York, but now, almost to a man they are violent for it."

General Bayley gauged the trend correctly. To every separatist meeting — at Dorset, Westminster, Windsor — more and more townships sent delegates, until in midsummer 1777 a really representative Convention boldly (for just then Burgoyne, apparently invincible, was sweeping southward on the Lakes) threw off allegiance to the Crown and drew up for the new and independent Commonwealth of Vermont a constitution which actually did embody its professed intention "to act without Partiality for, or Prejudice against any Class, Sect or Denomination of Men, whatsoever."

So far, so good — in fact excellent. From then on, Vermont could act as a solid political unit rather than a collection of *de facto* committees of safety. But her external relations were anything but solved. With apologies to any old-style historian who may happen to read these pages, let me avoid the confusion of trying to identify each and every rock in this stretch of the rapids by compressing the situation into this sketchiest of outlines: the Americans could not win the Revolution if the vital Hudson River line were lost. Along that line the margin of support was so slight that any shift in it might be disastrous. The New York delegation to the Continental Congress was very much under the control of James Duane and other experienced political in-fighters like him, all of them masters of committee maneuvering. It would not help the barely born American cause to antagonize those influential New York landowners by admitting the Green Mountain people as one of the new American states.

On the other hand, it was very desirable to have Vermont on the American side. Its flanking position, threatening any future British invasion by way of Lake Champlain, could not be disregarded from the military point of view.

We who in our own days have winced at many a compromise

between principle and military necessity, during the two World Wars and afterwards, are not surprised that the hard-pressed Congress shuffled this hot-potato problem rapidly from hand to hand, from committee to committee. Never, in so many words did Congress uphold New York's territorial claim — or Vermont's. It implicitly denied the new state's existence by refusing admittance to delegates from "the people styling themselves inhabitants of the New Hampshire Grants."

The majority of the Vermonters had been hotly pro-American, as can be seen by Ethan Allen's letter to Congress in the chapter about him. A Vermont regiment had been organized to fight with Washington's Colonial Army. Their enthusiasm for the cause of American independence was doused as by a bucket of cold water. Congress was a political body. The New York delegates were politically necessary. The war dragged slowly on.

As far as the Green Mountain people could see, the new American State of New York had the same intentions towards them as the Royal Province. As Dr. Mark puts it: "The wealthy landlords did not fare badly under the new order. New York was not ready to throw off its ancient traditions and accede to the New England system of Democratic land-owning." Nor as time passed did the Continental Congress give any indication of a change of heart. On the contrary: it was seriously proposed there that the disputed territory be divided, all to the east of the Green Mountain Range taken over by New Hampshire, the western slope forced to accept under a practically unchanged New York government practically the same leasehold system which had caused the continually recurring Hudson Valley discontent and revolts for the last hundred years. With his usual sonorous hyperbole, Ethan Allen prophesied that if the Americans won independence from Great Britain, the claiming states of New York, New Hampshire and Massachusetts "would leap at Vermont and rend her limb from limb."

We have now reached the year 1780 — a long, long time since those first, ardent, forward-looking young settlers had come into the Green Mountain forests. Men and women who had been among the first wave of pioneers were now between thirty and forty years old, parents of children in their teens. They had lived all their adult lives in what psychologists tell us is harder on human nerves than actual and immediate physical danger — in suspense.

Back of the leaders, whose bold words history has preserved for us, were thousands of men and women and growing boys and girls, unknown to historians, but very close to us, their not-so-long-after descendants. Throughout the twenty years (more or less) of their young maturity every decision in the ordinary course of their lives had been made to the accompaniment of that never-ceasing dull roll of thunder, threatening storm. The little boys were growing big; they should have a room of their own, and the growing-up daughters too. Other things being equal (that is to say if they were not constantly unsure as to what the next day might bring) it would be easy to enlarge the house as the children grew. Every family had its own woodlot, every man and boy knew how to chop and hew timber and to do rough carpentry. But would an enlarged house be not an addition to their own comfort and decency, but only to the wealth of a landlord? A new settler had come in from Connecticut, a sawyer, who wanted to put up a sawmill on the local stream ten miles nearer than the one they had used. Yes, but mill-rights were especially reserved to the great Patentees by New York land tenure system.

Well, they went ahead, they built additions to their cabins when needed. They built sawmills. They cultivated more fields, they grew more crops and more varied crops. But they did not so gaily spend evenings in the old-time square dances. They did not so lightheartedly sing the old ballads they all knew. They acquired a tight-lipped discipline in endurance, in steady resolution, in a quiet but desperate determination to resist and to go on, which is not a pretty or perhaps amiable part of our tradition, but on which we can, when we need and must, lean with all our weight and know that it will not give way.

It was in this very year of 1780 that an incident occurred which for nearly a hundred and fifty years was practically unknown. There were, to be sure, rumors about it but nothing more substantial than folk surmises repeated vaguely and doubtfully by older people, until, in the Canadian archives, proof of it was discovered.

At that time Ethan Allen was living in Arlington. One day, on our single village street, a stranger came up and gave him a letter. It was from a Tory American, then colonel in the British Army. The news in it was that Sir Henry Clinton, commander of the English forces in America, was willing to make a separate peace with Vermont.

We of today with two dreadful wars in our personal memories can understand much better than our nineteenth-century grandparents that any such proposition from an enemy contains dynamite to people worn down almost to the limit by continued resistance.

There followed months of exciting negotiations between representatives of Vermont and of the British government. They are, now that they are public property, burningly interesting to Vermonters, but probably not to other Americans. The details naturally were known to only a few of the leaders on each side. But it was observed that British forces which had been massing as if for attack on the northern frontier of the rebellious American colonies stopped short. Rumors flew wildly up and down Vermont settlements that a "Halt" had been shouted by the British high command.

Ethan Allen had no more taste for hush-hush diplomacy than for anything hush-hush. He wrote bluntly to the President of the American Congress. "I do not hesitate to say I am fully grounded in opinion that Vermont had an indubitable right to agree on terms of cessation of hostilities with Great Britain, provided that the United States persist in rejecting her application for union with them; for Vermont of all people, would be the most miserable were she obliged to defend the independence of united claiming states; and they, at the same time, in full liberty to overturn and ruin the independence of Vermont."

Nothing could be more open and aboveboard — less like a cloak-and-dagger conspiracy. Just the same, modern Vermonters, who for a hundred and sixty years have proudly, lovingly, waved the Stars and Stripes, feel a little queer about the fact that their forefathers did not at all indignantly repudiate the offer of a separate peace from the British, but carefully weighed the question before them. "If choose they must, would Vermont prefer to live under British rule, which they remembered very well from their early days in Connecticut and Massachusetts — rather than under the laws of New York?"

It must be remembered that Vermonters of that period were not "American citizens," deciding whether to turn against "their" country. The citizenship which they had inherited from their forefathers was British. The very conception of being "American" was brand new. The government of England offered them a continuation of the old citizenship which, unlike that proposed by Hudson Valley landlords, had allowed their fathers to set up a society with free schools, local self-government, honest courts. That prospect certainly was very tempting if, as then seemed probable, becoming "American" meant knuckling under, giving up every principle they had fought for through the weary years of resistance, being forced into second-class civic rank in the most reactionary of all the thirteen states.

There is, of course, a different interpretation: that Allen and Chittenden, then Governor of Vermont, never wavered in revolutionary patriotism, but merely seemed to consider the British proposal as a sort of bluff designed to scare Congress into accepting Vermont on her own terms. This view is possible, plausible. Only I have found no evidence either to support or disprove it.

There does exist, however, positive, written, objective, non-partisan evidence throwing light on how the average run of Vermonters felt about political issues. The same French-speaking, Swiss professional soldier who some years before had refused to send British regulars against settlers in the Grants, was now Commandant in Canada. On General Haldimand fell the task of negotiating an armistice with Vermont. Wishing to find out the sentiments of the Green Mountain people on this project from some other source than the Vermont leaders, whom he did not much trust, he sent a capable secret agent into the Vermont countryside.

After several weeks of intensive field observation, from house to house, talking with all sorts of people, the agent returned. The evidence collected was carefully sifted and weighed. The resulting official report is still preserved — a unique document in the New York-Vermont dispute in that it was composed by an outsider, paid to ascertain the facts, not to advance one side of the quarrel or the other.

The findings of this eighteenth-century Gallup poll were as follows: among the leading men of Vermont, about a third were disheartened and alarmed, inclined on the whole to trust the London Parliament more than the Philadelphia Congress, controlled (as it appeared to them) by the same old gang of the New York Junto, pulling wires in committee rooms.

Roughly another third of the leaders were belligerently anti-British. The last third was uncertain, baffled, could not decide.

But, the agent's report went on, there could be no doubt of where the great majority of Vermonters stood. We have always felt through our pores a certainty of what must have been our forefathers' ruling passion. This instinctive conviction was confirmed in the clear black and white of an official document. As for the "common people," so the report ran, without any qualification whatever, they were ready to "accept any government EXCEPT that of New York."

Whether, when it came to a final showdown, Vermonters would have agreed to enter the Dominion of Canada is a question which never had an answer. Never needed one. Before any public declaration could bring it out into the open, everything was changed by the news of Cornwallis's surrender at Yorktown in October 1781. The British withdrew rapidly from their side of the negotiations and the Vermonters as swiftly from theirs.

There followed another decade of uncertainty, ten whole years of living in suspense. Think back in your own life to a date ten years ago. Then, coming up to the present, step by step, try to remember all the problems for you and those closest to you, which called on you to make the closest guess possible of the future's probable development. To those ten years after American independence was established, add at least another fifteen of the earlier struggle during colonial times, and you may perhaps have a faint realization of the ordeal lived through by those old-time Vermonters. From one year to another, weary but stead-fast, they did, day by day, the best they could, never knowing what was before them.

Because we are proud of our ancestors — and well we may be! — those of us who write books about early Vermonters are apt to portray them as vivid, romantic, spurred and stimulated by constant excitement, like the characters in a historical novel or a movie script. But our forefathers were not in the least dashing young cavaliers waving to full-bosomed young actresses. Ver-monters were then just about what they are now, sober, self-contained, plain people capable of enduring material hardships without self-pity, but no more capable than anybody else of en-joying constant danger, suspense and complete lack of security. They could take it because they felt they had to. But they made no pretense of being cheerful about living in a fort under siege.

Ethan Allen died in 1789, and was given a picturesque mid-winter funeral, which might be called "military" if anything so informal as a gathering of the Green Mountain Boys could de-serve that adjective. So he did not see his side triumph in the contest which had occupied so large a part of his adult life. But James Duane did not die until after the defeat (utterly amazing to him) of his side. He lived to rage impotently over the small token payment agreed to. The whole sum paid by Vermont to New York claimants was $30,000. Duane's share came to $2,621.29. But even this was not paid until two years after his death.

What happened? No minutes were kept of the Senate cloak-room trading then, any more than now. But the story goes that already the North-South struggle for voting control, so domi-nant through the next half-century in the United States, had begun to take shape. Kentucky, with southern backing, could not be kept an organized territory much longer, and fast-growing Tennessee obviously would soon upset the balance still further. A gentlemen's agreement (the polite term for a deal) was arrived at. With one hand the Senate pushed New York lobbyists off the stage and with the other hand (in 1791) opened the door to Vermont as the first state admitted to the new Union.

The long struggle was over. The Vermonters had stuck it out.

CHAPTER 7

Aftermath

IN any period, present as well as past, it is hard to distinguish between the mid-ocean ground swell and the surface waves, splashing around in every direction. We need not be surprised, then, to find some writers dismissing the land grant dispute as nothing more than the scheming of two opposing groups of speculators, each anxious to reap the maximum of profit from its venture. Others with a little wider vision see in it the contest between two systems of agriculture — neither of which is of any importance under modern conditions. There is a grain of truth in each of these views, but both of them fail to explain large sections of recorded data. The breadth, the complexity, the emotional heat of the resistance defy measurement by such rigid foot-rules. Something bigger must have been involved, and that something was brought out clearly as long ago as 1846 — a fruitful year for such a survey, as we shall see later in this chapter — by Professor James Butler of Norwich University in a speech to the Vermont Historical Society, when he said:

> The controversy of Vermont with New York has never been described as its merits, and the richness of material regarding it, demand. No historian hints — what every historian should have clearly shown — that the struggle was not about the price of land, but a conflict between New England and New York *principles* — those of the Puritan and the Patroon — between our township system with local elections and taxes, and New York centralization.

In using those two capital P's, Professor Butler was perhaps carried away by a speaker's fondness for alliteration. There has been very little of the Puritan in Vermonters at any period, and the word Patroon had dropped out of New York's vocabulary when the British took the province in the seventeenth century. But the analysis is sound.

There is no sense to be made out of the many apparently disconnected details of the land grant dispute, except when brought into focus by Professor Butler's key idea. Speaking in 1846, this professor of history was near enough in time to the Vermont struggle against landlordism so that the emotions and ideas underlying it, which we get, if at all, out of laborious searching of documents and books, came to him from the talk of his Vermont neighbors, many of whom had lived through that long ordeal. Interpreted from living contacts, the land grant dispute, brief and isolated though it was, holds the stage for one split second (in calendar time it was for some twenty to thirty years) in yet another scene of civilization's perpetual drama — the past by its dead weight holding down the future struggling up to light and air.

Now, every human activity, like every human motive, is mixed. On the Vermont side in Ethan Allen's attitude and in that of other Green Mountain settlers, along with undeniably sincere talk about human freedom there was also the typically American instinct to make money out of what lay at hand. On the other side, in the New York Province setup, there was much which was fine, "gracious," and agreeable among those considering themselves "social equals." But not for the tenant farmers. And this book is concerned only with the effect of the New York Province rural system on working farmers, since Vermonters were working farmers.

After every qualification has been raised and admitted, what stands out is the Vermonters' savage, exalted certainty that the Justice of their cause forbade compromise, that, in the words of Ethan Allen, they were ready "to eat mouse-meat" before they would let their homes pass into possession of landlords backed by courts organized to protect their special privileges.

Most of the talk centered about land tenure. In our nation, that is hardly a live issue today. Modern large farms are really wholesale agricultural factories, business enterprises which pay money in proportion to the energy, capital and good management put into them. The industrial revolution has eliminated fortunes built up by rents coming in from farmland, in return for no more effort than clipping coupons from a corporation bond. But the ideal at stake is timeless. The essence of landlordism as something to be resisted is still with us. In the old days of the New York Junto, the landlord class was a close-knit minority who, because they had wealth and power, took for granted that they only were fitted to direct the government. Such arrogant minorities are constantly trying to come to power, although landowning is no longer an entrance requirement to their numbers.

The United States has not developed according to Jefferson's dream of an idyllic fraternity based on nation-wide, self-owned, self-sufficient farmsteads. Does that reduce to foolishness the old Vermont insistence on holding land in "fee simple, absolute"? Not at all. To the roughneck early Vermonters, owning land enough to support a family meant personal freedom and their share of political power. Personal freedom and a fair share of political power for each citizen still need defense here and every-where, always will need vigilant and fighting defenders. Vermont's long refusal to accept autocratic rule was such a fighting defense of principles basic to our American way of life. It was recognized as such far beyond the Green Mountains, must have helped stiffen resistance elsewhere. Certainly it must have helped keep alive the resistance of the New York tenant farmers, who living close at hand could see others enjoying the freedom they craved, while they still, as they publicly expressed it, continued to be "Slaves and Vassals." The story of their resistance answers a question which may perhaps have occurred to you: "Wasn't the Yankee-Yorker rumpus a waste of effort? If the Green Mountain settlers had been patient for only a few years, wouldn't the American Revolution have given them everything they asked for?"

The New York Constitution did go part way. It forbade primogeniture, entail, alienation and other incidents of "Knight's Service" tenure. But the relation between the operating farmer on one of the established Manors or Patents and his landlord continued to be about as it always had been. The relation was determined by a civil agreement, expressed by provisions of a lease. The State of New York had no intention of abridging the vested rights of those landed proprietors who, after hesitation, had picked the winning side in the Revolution. Article 36 of the new Constitution was explicitly stand-pat. It provided that "nothing in this constitution shall be construed to affect any grant of land within this State, made by the authority of the said King, or his predecessors." The landlords interpreted this clause as permission to go on doing just what they always had. No one was surprised at that. Indeed, earlier in the Revolution, a radical New York City artisan (being a city dweller and not holding lease-land, he dared speak out) had accurately called the turn. Deploring the entrance of rich, upper-class men, like Duane and Livingston, into Revolutionary councils, he warned his fellow workers that the "Oligarchs will soon subject you either to a British tyranny or to a tyranny of oppression among themselves not much better."

What bears on the subject of this book is that while the rest of New York State was slowly groping its way towards the American way of life, little change was made on many of the old established Manors and Patents. If New York law had been allowed to come into Vermont, the rules and customs of those very patents would have been transplanted into the Green Mountains and those long-enduring social anachronisms would have come with it. Let us consider how long they would have lasted.

Here is the chronology: Vermont had been long self-governing in practice. In 1778, it set itself up with all the political machinery of an independent republic; in 1791 it became a regular member of the United States of America. In that very year 1791, there broke out another of the constantly recurring resistance-efforts of New York tenant farmers. It was in opposition to the sale by auction of the homes of evicted farmers. Trapped and dominated by an all-enveloping system — as the threatened land grant farmers had never been enveloped or dominated — these New Yorkers were more desperate and hence more excitable and violent than Vermonters had ever needed to be. A New York sheriff was killed in this fracas, as never a New York official had been killed in Vermont. This revolt failed, as all preceding ones had failed. By that date Vermonters had lived for thirteen years on land they owned, in homes where no landlord could enter to evict them.

By 1795 there were young people in Vermont, eighteen, nineteen, twenty years old, for whom the old danger that they and their fathers might have been voteless dependents on the will of landlords was no more than a dark old-wives' tale. In that year inside New York another protest was made by tenant farmers. This time it was a petition to the government of the State for an investigation of the Livingston titles, on the ground that they had been fraudulently acquired and were "oppressive and burthensome to the last degree, unfriendly to all great exertions of Industry and tending to degrade your Petitioners from the Rank that the God of Nature destined all Mankind to move in, to be Slaves and Vassals."

This was thirty years after the arrival of settlers in the Green Mountains. Vermonters running their State as part of the Union were in no more danger than you are now wherever you live in the U.S.A. from the conditions denounced in these words of wrath. But there were plenty of Vermonters still alive, although elderly by this time, for whom the words "Slaves and Vassals," theatrical and unreal to modern American ears, snarled and snapped like savage teeth in menacing strong jaws.

By 1811 a whole generation which had lived in full free responsible citizenship in Vermont were now in their turn young fathers and mothers of families. To their children a system of caste subordination was something to study out of books, like the Stone Age, or the Roman Empire. In that year of 1811, there was news in the papers of another explosion in York State. The men with pitchforks had once more attacked the Bastille of hereditary legal privilege. Tenant farmers of Montgomery, Delaware, Dutchess, Otsego and Saratoga Counties, so it is set down in history books, were so violent and dangerous in resenting their continuing subordination that the extreme measure was taken of *proposing* an investigation in the New York Legislature. Nothing came of it. Nothing was done. Those New York farmers remained as they were, that is to say in a status Vermont farmers had, at their peril, refused to accept. For the then younger generation in Vermont, the progress of this attempted revolt by New York farmers was not quite a mere news item in the papers, because they heard their grandparents comment on it with the harsh, shaken voices of emotion beyond control.

In 1839 the heirs of Stephen Van Rensselaer tried to collect four hundred thousand dollars in back rents. The men with pitchforks once more stormed out to fight against bayonets. Once more the bayonets won. In Vermont at that date, there were still living some few tough fellows, eighty-odd years old, who, as the day's news was read aloud to them by their grandchildren, pounded on the floor with their canes and, panting and wheezing, told the old story again, with the old fierce pride in having refused to be less than Americans should be.

It was from wheel chairs or from their beds, that the few aged Green Mountain Boys still above ground listened excitedly to the newspaper reports of the long final wild storm in New York which began in 1841. The farmers of Columbia and Delaware Counties rose again in armed, angry revolt. Sheriffs and their deputies who tried to serve writs of ejectment were tarred and feathered. From the Vermont wheel chairs came memories of the New York sheriff and his posse at the Breckenridge farm south of Bennington. "We didn't take tar and feathers to 'em. Only just the trigger finger crooked and ready. We knew their militia was on our side, and so did they. The folks who are fighting the sheriffs now are the grandsons of those York State militiamen that helped us."

In 1845 another hated New York sheriff was killed by insurgent tenant farmers. "We didn't kill 'em," came huskily from the bedridden old men. "We just yelled at 'em, the way you'd yell at a chicken thief out o' the window. But *we* were on our own land."

In 1846, Samuel Tilden's official report on the New York land system of that date revealed that, on tracts formerly organized as manors and patents, many — very many — of the traditional privileges and incidents of tenure as they existed before the Revolution were still in force, sixty-four years later. In case after case examined, perpetual rent was still being exacted. If any obligations of the lease were not fulfilled, the landlord could still enter homes and farms and take possession. If a tenant sold his leasehold to another, the landlord could (and did) legally claim a quarter or more of the sale price, thus profiting largely on improvements made by the tenant. Conveyances "in fee simple" had plenty of strings attached. In the final analysis, land belonged to landlords, not to the farmers who cultivated it.

This last, long, furious insurrection and the resulting report to the legislature finally produced action. Drastic use of the power to tax, plus an amendment of the State Constitution, ended the eighteenth-century system of land tenures sixty-eight years after Vermonters had taken up arms to resist it.

Most Americans in 1846 were astonished (but not much interested) to learn from the morning newspapers that there had existed up to then, in the heart of the American Federation of States, a region where the law upheld the ancient practices of distraining, mining rights, water, mill and lumber privilege, quarter- and half-rights on alienation, perpetual rents, disenfranchisement for tenant farmers (Oh yes, the law said they could vote, but the landlords told them which way to vote — or else), and all the rest. Most Americans of those days had never heard of those terms. They had not the slightest idea of their meaning even in law, let alone in human lives. They did not much care either, not enough to look the words up in the dictionary. They were as insulated by the technical terms from the meaning of the words as we would be if told that a community was now free from variola and elephantiasis Graecorum.

They were more completely insulated, for we would know that we do not know what those words mean. If we looked in the dictionary we would recognize them, when defined as "smallpox" and "leprosy." Most mid-nineteenth century people who read about the final Hudson Valley farmer revolt did not even know that they did not know what it meant. How could they dream that the familiar words "rent" and "lease" might have other meanings than the harmless business transactions familiar to them?

"What's the matter with renting your farm?" they might ask, "Why do Hudson Valley farm tenants shoot up sheriffs? They aren't the only farmers who rent their land. Why such a fuss about it?"

Anyhow it was of the past, and did not need to be understood. People of today, of every today, have their hands full trying to understand today's doings. What's gone by, is gone by. The people of 1846 laid the morning papers down and went about their business. All except Professor Butler of Vermont. He took in the meaning of the day's news and passed that meaning on in an address to the Vermont Historical Society.

By that date, practically all the original settlers of Vermont were dead. They had come to the end of their years, free men, owners of their own homes, their own land, first-class citizens, voting on their own convictions, with no landlord to punish them if they did not vote to please him. They had died. Their funerals had been held in churches with no privileged pew curtained off to honor the men who owned land and kept it out of the hands of the men who cultivated it. The old Vermonters lay in their graves, in soil set aside for burying-grounds by their Town Meetings, sovereign in the right to do so. They were dead, but they had bequeathed to their children and grandchildren a feeling about human dignity so vital that it lived, deep in the heart, lived — and lives on as tradition.

CHAPTER 8
Ethan Allen

IN telling the story of the land grant dispute, I meant to leave out enough detail to make the narrative readable. I certainly left out a lot. (Let me remind you that the more complete version is printed at the back of this book, available for those who can take it.) But at that, maybe I didn't leave out enough. It is hard to pick one's way around a maelstrom of historical dates and names and places, and not fall in. The suction is a mighty one.

It may do us good to take time off from the complex inter-actions of groups of people and make the acquaintance of one individual human being. What kind of man was Ethan Allen?

In his lifetime, the lawyers and landlords of the Province of New York took Ethan Allen to be a foul-mouthed, low-lived, ignorant bar-fly, an atheist and a cheat. To them, his big words about political equality for working farmers were phony double-talk, part of an astute come-on racket. Of course his real purpose was to put more money into his pocket.

How could they think anything else? The written records show that the upper classes in the Province were set, come Hell, high water or a new British attempt to limit their land-holdings, on making money and keeping political and social power in their hands. They took for granted that such was the purpose of any sensible man. They only did not believe that the lower classes should have political or any other kind of equality of oppor-tunity; they did not believe that anybody believed it. Whoever professed such an idea must be a fake. Their estimate of Ethan Allen was a perfectly natural one. And theirs is the one which historians, looking into the documents of the time, have seen most of. They were fluent and eminent; their letters, diaries, private papers have been carefully preserved.

His Vermont neighbors eloquently expressed their opinion of

him, but in action, not in letters or reports. Their action is known, and it plainly proves that those in Vermont who knew him best valued his sincerity and his prodigious courage, physical and moral; that they shared his political ideas to the last dot of an i, and took them for granted as completely as the gentry of New York took for granted the opposite; that they were glad and proud to have him loudly proclaim to the world their attitude towards life which none of the rest of them were articulate enough to talk about.

Here are two opposing opinions — opinions only. What are the facts of Ethan Allen's life?

The story of anybody's life begins as long before his birth as there are records of his family. Ethan Allen was born in 1737. The record of the Allens goes back for a century before that. In 1632 the first Allen landed from England in Eastern Massachusetts. This ancestor was one of the "Dorchester Company." Their chosen leader was Thomas Hooker, the clergyman who, sixty years before Locke said it, held that "the foundation of authority is laid in the free consent of the people." To set up, on this principle, their own kind of community, Hooker and his followers went out together in 1636 through the wilderness to the as yet unpeopled Connecticut valley, far away (in those days) from the powerful ministers of Eastern Massachusetts. The first Allen went along. Generation after generation his descendants lived in a region where the consent of the governed was taken as the only valid authority.

When Ethan was born, his father Joseph Allen had moved to the new small town of West Cornwall, in Connecticut, within easy walking distance of the line between New England and New York. Here Joseph Allen was elected by his fellow citizens as a selectman. In a New England town the three selectmen form just about all the "governing authority" there is. He was given an even greater honor, he was elected Moderator of the all-important annual Town Meeting. These are recorded facts. They mean that Ethan Allen's father was trusted by his neighbors to be intelligent, honest and forceful.

Like the other farmers around them, the Allens were literate. That working farmers should read, write, do their own sums and have books, was in itself offensive to the landowning gentry now only a few miles away from the Allen home. Every one of the eight Allen children was taught to read and write and do sums. They all had Bible names, except Lucy, and that is the name of a saint canonized in the third century. The family were Anglicans. You'd never guess this, would you, from the rum-soaked legend of the "atheist outlaw Ethan." He never became a communicant, but like his father and his family, he went to church, often, although not regularly. He was never, early or late in his life, an atheist, as the conservatives and orthodox liked shudderingly to call him. He, like numbers of his neighbors, was a "deist." We might now call such people "religious liberals." That so many Green Mountain people were deists shocked the New Haven theologians and the party-line church gentry of New York, as much as if they had been without any moral principles at all, as Timothy Dwight of Yale, and the Reverend Perkins thought them to be. In his religious, political and social beliefs, Ethan Allen did not stand out in contrast to his Vermont community. If he had, he never would have been wholeheartedly accepted as he was, as he is to this day, by the people of his state.

He was a bookish boy and man. Almost without exception Connecticut people of his time had books, a few, one, or many. As a lad, Ethan is known to have read every book in his house, every book he could borrow in the settlement. He knew the Bible intimately. He was so obviously superior in mental quality that the Allen family council decided he ought to have a chance at higher education. In Connecticut that meant Yale. Local district schools did not meet the entrance requirements of Yale. In the nearby town of Salisbury, a minister prepared bright boys for Yale. Joseph Allen, the farmer, somehow raised money enough to send his promising son to study with the Reverend Jonathan Lee.

But the father died.

The death of a father of a large family suddenly shows the quality of the older sons and daughters. If they are conscientious, it means the ending of their childhood as they bend their backs to the burden of the family cares the father has laid down. Ethan Allen bent his back.

He gave up college. He gave up studies with his tutor. He went back to the farm, helped his mother reorganize the family finances and work program so that the younger children could grow up in their own home. Never after this did he have any chance at studying systematically under qualified teachers, as in his youth he had hoped. But he never gave up getting an education. That was a lifelong occupation. As best he could, he went on studying and thinking till the day of his death.

Self-education is the only kind that is really alive. But if it is started at too early an age, the self-taught student is at an intellectual disadvantage. Ethan Allen was always at a disadvantage in logical reasoning and thought, never succeeded very well in writing abstractly about ideas. The extraordinary fire of his personality partly made up for this handicap. He expressed emotions with volcanic power.

The friends and comrades of most boys are usually of their own age, with the same tastes. Ethan Allen shared the liking of the big lads around him for hunting, life in the woods, and noisy, sociable drinking bouts in the tavern. In this world he always had a large circle of hearty cronies, his brothers, his innumerable cousins, his neighbors. Yet it was to a much older, professionally trained intellectual that he attached himself in an admiring, lifelong friendship. The local doctor, Thomas Young, was a cultivated man with a lively mind and socially radical ideas. Later on, Dr. Young practiced medicine and revolutionary politics in Boston, Newport, Philadelphia, always successful, admired, prosperous. Ethan Allen, living at the end of nowhere, never lost touch with him. He went to see him when possible, often consulted him by letter on vital questions of opinion and policy. It was from a visit with this friend of Ethan Allen that in 1777 Vermonters brought back the enlightened, liberal Constitution which, with a few changes, Vermont adopted.

What books did Dr. Young loan to his backwoods boy friend? We know the list. It includes Tacitus, Plutarch, Newton and John Locke — the last name the most vital. Every historian who describes life in New England in the eighteenth century speaks of the widespread influence of Locke. He was read everywhere, on farms, in city homes, by young and old.

Most of us "took" Locke in college, "under" some professor; but few of us now find in our minds any exact memory of what those eighteenth-century forebears of ours saw when they bent their young heads over Locke's pages.

I opened a volume of Locke, and imagined the young Ethan to be looking over my shoulder. Here are some of the sayings which he must have read and talked over with Dr. Young:

> The liberty of man in society is to be under no other legislative power but that established by consent in the commonwealth — not to be subject to the inconstant, uncertain, unknown, arbitrary will of another man.
>
> Being all equal and independent, no one ought to harm another in his life, health, liberty or possessions.
>
> Remember that absolute monarchs are but men.
>
> Though the water running in the fountain is everyone's, yet who can doubt but that in the pitcher is his only who drew it out. His labor hath appropriated it to himself.
>
> As much land as a man tills, plants, improves, cultivates, can use the product of, so much is his property.
>
> . . . all this to be directed to no other end but the peace, safety and public good of the people.

At the time of the Great Rebellion of 1766, and the trial of the farmer Prendergast at Poughkeepsie, Ethan Allen was twenty-nine years old. We may be almost sure that he was among the spectators in the courtroom, watching the New York lawyer James Duane, very near his own age, with his sly, swivel eyes, standing in his fine black broadcloth before a court which was on his side before he opened his mouth. We have documentary evidence that the Allen brothers knew about the trial of the "sober, industrious and kind" farmer which ended in that sentence to long-drawn-out torture and death.

Four years later, Allen was thirty-three years old when, in Albany, watching another session of the Supreme Court of the Province of New York decide once again in favor of landlords and against farmers, he talked to James Duane, face to face, the only time in his life.

We may be sure that on both occasions, Locke's idea that a man owns what he has worked for, was in the mind of the man from Western Connecticut. We may be as sure that the man from New York was concentrating on those technical details of law which, as Senator Fulbright in our times has remarked, have an analogy with the rat-technique of pulling cheese out of a trap without getting caught.

We do not need to guess at the ideas in Duane's mind. We know accurately. Duane's biographer tells us that to his fourteenth year the New York City boy received a "solid classical training, with emphasis on the Latin and book-keeping." "The Latin," in the amount which could be acquired by a boy of fourteen, was not for literary training, but because tags of Latin were common in eighteenth-century British law. Bookkeeping is a study of which there is no mention in the education of Ethan Allen. It was basic to a man like James Duane who practiced it every day of his life.

From fourteen to twenty-one, Duane was apprenticed to a lawyer. His biographer says that during this impressionable period of his youth, his chief duty and work "was to copy almost endless legal documents." He also "read the old year-books assiduously, on Chief-Justice de Lancy's advice that this was the best way to imbibe the spirit of the law. Duane's briefs and arguments bristled with citations from British precedents." No Duane time was spent on speculations about the relation of man to society. His journals have nothing in them but statements concerning only those verifiable facts which were of concern to his personal prospering.

When Duane was twenty-one, he was admitted to practice before the Supreme Court of the Province of New York. His biographer says that the bulk of his business as a young lawyer "consisted of actions to collect debts and of ejectment and trespass," and mentions that his nickname was "Swivel-eye" because of his ability to see what was going on out of the corner of his eye, without turning his head. Every day he wrote down in his journal a minute record of what money he had spent; and no calculation about an investment was so casual that he omitted to add seven per cent interest to any expenditure he had made on his property. He died well to do. When Ethan Allen died he was so out of funds he owed a neighbor for a load of hay. Each man lived his life according to the ideals on which, in his youth, he had formed his personality.

But how about that alcoholism? Yes, Ethan Allen did drink a good deal. But as a neighbor of mine says, "My grandfather always told us that his old folks told him that Ethan Allen didn't drink any more than most men in those days."

Our Arlington doctor-historian says the same thing. "Take a look at the account books of that time," he comments (he has dozens of eighteenth-century account books in his Vermontiana) "So much for shoebuckles, so much — quite a lot — for gin flip; so much — much more — for rum." That's the way it goes for all our ancestors.

"But it didn't mean what it would mean now. In those times, hardly a man had work which kept him indoors. Chopping, plowing, hunting, fishing, riding, surveying lines . . . their blood was oxygenated every hour of their lives. People in those days could take alcohol and they did. It's absurd to talk as though Ethan Allen guzzled rum while folks around him drank lemonade."

His profanity is another matter. It really was a specialty of his, and it came from a personal experience. The experience was reading some of Jonathan Edwards's sermons.

Since his family were neither Puritans nor Calvinists, he had never, till he was a tall lad, chanced to encounter Jonathan Edwards's hell-fire and brimstone. When he did he was horrified. The idea that it might be God's pleasure to condemn to eternal torture the kindest and gentlest of human beings and even little babies, shocked him and made him furiously angry. He was in a frenzy when he thought of the mental suffering of those who really believed in predestination.

Satan and his minor demons were parts of the belief in hell. At a time when even to mention the devil openly (except in a sermon) scared people, the big boy began deliberately to make this kind of fear ridiculous. Many specimens of Ethan Allen's profanity are extant. If you look at them closely you will see that he did not so much take God's name in vain as the devil's.

The second root from which his profanity sprang was his great native gift for the use of language. He delighted in words. His use of the vernacular was the joy of those who in his lifetime heard him, is still the joy of those who hear his spoken words repeated. Like many an untrained gifted man, he did not write as well as he talked. When he took up a pen he often (not always) fell into the high-falutin' style. He did not copy this from the books he read, for they were mostly of noble quality.

But on occasion he could write as well, as passionately, as he spoke. Here is a sample of his writing at its best, taken from an open letter addressed to the Continental Congress, shortly after the taking of Ticonderoga (1775) when he was on fire with enthusiasm for the Revolution: "I wish to God, America would at this critical juncture exert herself. She might rise on eagles' wings, and mount to glory, freedom and immortal honor if she did now but know and exert her strength. Fame is hovering over her head."

If Ethan Allen's father had lived and the boy had gone to Yale, would his professors have tried to make him write like Addison? Would he have lost his ear for folk speech tunes?

His skill in the use of these tunes was always admired by his neighbors. His repeated sayings have come down to us in our special Vermont intonations.

He lived in Arlington and in Sunderland for years. My home is halfway between those two towns. The boom of his great voice still echoes in our valley.

"One Sunday morning, Ethan Allen went to church," so my great-uncle used to tell the story as we jogged along the valley road past the old Allen house, "in the Sunderland Church, right over there across the river. After the service, when the congregation was coming out, he saw that his neighbor's cows had broken through the fence into his cornfield and had spoiled a lot of the corn. He threw his hat on the ground, jumped on it with both feet, and said," (here my great-uncle drew a deep breath into his old lungs to have voice enough to roar) " 'By Godfrey, if I had teeth as long as the old Harry's, I'd tear those cattle till that hillside stank of carrion, as hell stinks of brimstone.' "

Both the old man and the little girl thought that was fine. It fitted roaring, as a good ax-handle fits the chopper's hand. And (notice the careful euphemism "By Godfrey") in spite of such satisfyingly earthy words as "stinks" and "carrion," nothing in it which a decent old man could not tell a child.

His first wife was the kind of woman now called a pill, a lemon, a sour-puss. In Sunderland they said she got out of bed the wrong side every morning of her life. Somebody passing by the Arlington burying-ground and seeing the gravedigger at work, asked him who the grave was for. "For Mrs. Allen," said the digger with a neutral intonation. He added reflectively, "I never dug a grave I enjoyed more." I also was brought up on the story that when plans were being made for transporting her coffin to the church, a Sunderland man made a cordial offer of help in these words: "You could call on any of the neighbors. There's not a man in town wouldn't be glad to help out."

Ethen Allen never pretended his wife's character was different from what everybody knew it to be, but he never philandered with other women. He was an affectionate father to his children. Only once (as far as I have ever heard) did he speak of his bad-tempered wife. That was at two o'clock at night, on the road between my great-grandmother's home and the old burying-ground of Arlington.

This is the way that story goes: Ethan Allen had ridden down to Bennington to pass a cheerful evening with tavern cronies. Some of the lively Arlington boys in the horseplay years of their teens, made themselves weirdly tall by draping sheets from broomsticks held up over their heads, and hid behind the marble tombstones. When Ethan came along, these eight-foot-tall, white specters ran out to the road, screeching that they were devils come to carry him off to hell.

Ethan Allen waited composedly till his voice could be heard, and said, "Go back to your master Beelzebub, and tell him I said:

"I fear him not
For I married his sister."

Sometimes the rhythm of these repeated sayings is long and flexible, as "In the name of the great Jehovah and the Continental Congress." Once you know the way he puts things, this sounds unmistakably his. Sometimes it is tart and brisk, as when a Bennington clergyman in a long prayer was praising God for the great victory of Ticonderoga. After fidgeting in his pew (note that he was again in church), Ethan Allen called out loudly:

> "Parson Dewey! Parson Dewey!
> Don't forget that I was there."

Another well-remembered saying is in this short, trotting rhythm. It has been, I believe, never printed before. Until the modern breaking down of the decorum-fence, it was not considered proper enough to put into a book. Yet it is as mild as milk, compared to what we all read in modern novels.

Ethan Allen had built a cow-shed, so the story goes. Nobody in Sunderland was surprised when it turned out a foot or more too short. A neighbor asked him, "Did you mean to make it that way?" Allen inquired, "What's the matter with it?" The neighbor explained that a considerable part of the animal's anatomy would be exposed to the weather. Allen, with a wave of his big hand, said, good-naturedly:

> "What's a drop of water
> On a damn cow's rump?"

When I was young it was not nice to say "damn" or "rump," so the story was not quoted in general company. Yet it was often used. When an irritable housewife scolded about mud brought in on the kitchen floor, when a fussy grandfather was disagreeable about an ax left on the damp ground instead of struck into the chopping block, someone asked with the deceptively naïve intonation which in Vermont is often used for irony, "What's a drop of water — " and needed to say no more.

Perhaps the most eloquent — and I unashamedly think it very eloquent — of his sayings was one of the two occasions when a rich bribe was offered him to give up his foolish idea that Vermont farmer-citizens could possibly escape being turned into New York tenants. It was after the Breckinridge trial in Albany.

One of the wordless strokes with which history paints Allen's portrait is the fact that, knowing him, the men who held New Hampshire titles chose him to represent them at this, their one effort to present their case in a New York courtroom. He took along with him a distinguished lawyer from Connecticut, Mr. Jared Ingersoll. The two men rode together to Albany. I think we may be sure that at least once, as they planned how to present their case, the name of old Chief Nimham was spoken, he whose proof of fraud had been so competently disposed of in another session of a New York court.

Here is Allen's write-up of the trial: "Most, if not all, the judges and attornies, particularly Messrs. Duane and Kempe which attended the court were patentees under New York and some of them interested in the very patents then on trial.

"The plaintiffs appearing in great state and magnificence, which together with their junto of land-thieves, made a brilliant appearance." [This sentence is a sample of the way in which, occasionally, he was floored by grammatical sentence structure.] "The defendants appearing in but ordinary fashion, having been greatly fatigued by hard labor wrought on the disputed premises and their cash much exhausted, made a very disproportionable figure at court. In short, connection and grandeur being all on one side, easily turned the scale against the defendants."

At the end of the two minutes which it took to dismiss the case, the defeated Ethan Allen walked out of the courtroom, beside an invisible Indian chief. Then an incident occurred, reported variously as to its setting. One version puts it there, in the doorway of the courtroom. Another says that John Kempe and James Duane went to the Albany Tavern where Allen was lodging.

There is no variation in the report as to Allen's answer to the proposition made him by the two New York lawyers. Its cadence made it remembered.

To the tall, roughly-dressed country-man came the attorney-general of the province and the artful, successful, swivel-eyed lawyer, both of them elegant in dress, both of them convinced that they were in the right. Kempe spoke first. They greatly regretted, he said, all this dissension. How much more reasonable it would be to settle the matter peaceably than to keep homemaking, hard-working families dangling in danger, with certain failure before them. The very words with which Kempe ended his remarks have come down to us by oral tradition. "The people settled on the Grants might just as well make the best terms they can with their rightful landlords. We have might on our side, and you know, as all men know, that might often prevails against right." We may be sure that at this point, the farmer Prendergast came to stand invisibly but very present, beside Nimham, as a symbol of the legal power of the Province of New York.

Duane carried the ball quickly through the opening Kempe had made. He told Ethan Allen that if he would give up leading the unhappy Green Mountain men to inevitable defeat, New York landowners would be glad to settle things out of court, by seeing to it that he secured grants to such large tracts of land that he would be a prosperous landowner, with a secure title to many hundreds, or thousands of acres.

This was a proposal to desert principles which had been Ethan Allen's and his father's and his grandfathers' for a hundred and fifty years. This was an invitation to take pay for going over from the desperate underdog side to the sleek-coated, long-fanged, top-dog side. I think we can see John Locke now stepping forward from the past, to join old Chief Nimham and Farmer Prendergast beside Ethan Allen.

Ethan Allen had no words. He reached for his hat, and turned to go. The two distinguished lawyers were at a loss. Had he not heard what they had said? "But — but — " they called after him.

He turned at the door and answered gravely, in his language not theirs:

"The gods of the valleys
Are not gods in the hills."

Somebody has said mockingly that every Vermont baby knows these words before he can say "Mama." There is some truth in this jibe. We have still not been able to think of words blistering enough to reply directly to an ignoble proposition. In Vermont vernacular, the best answer is by implication, like Allen's.

"What do you mean?" asked Kempe.

Over his shoulder, Allen called back a cadenced elliptic response:

"Come up to the hill in Bennington
And the sense will be made clear."

Only a short time later, the first armed resistance in Vermont to a New York sheriff took place near Bennington.

* * *

This story makes it plain that Ethan Allen knew when he went down to Albany to the foredoomed "trial in court," that the Hampshire Grant settlers were ready to stand to arms for their principles.

Another thing is plain — that he was not chiefly interested in feathering his own nest financially. Modern scholarly historians are understandably sick of the florid, hurrah-boys talk about the Green Mountain Boys. Like sensible men they realize that the motives of eighteenth-century people, as in our times, were mixed. But the debunkers do not present them so — some desire for money mixed with much love for an old tradition of political equality among citizens. They ignore the idealistic motives just as the New York gentry did. They never speak of the way in which Ethen Allen took the really wounding refusal of the Vermonters to give him the command of their newly created regiment. That would have been the moment for him to devote himself to the development of his own landholdings, if money had been his aim. But instead he went off, without any rank at all, on a wildly dangerous military invasion of Canada and when that failed was at once carried into three long years of great misery in English prisons.

There is a later document on record which bears on this matter. William Smith, Chief Justice of the Province of New York writing to William Eden in England during the Revolutionary War spoke thus of him:

"Ethen Allen may in my opinion be easily tempted to throw off any dependence on the tyranny of the Congress, and made useful to Government [the British Government] by giving him and his adherents all the lands appropriated to Rebels and making that country a separate government dependent on the Crown and laws of Great Britain."

There is also a letter from Alexander Wedderburn to William Eden of 1775 when Ethan Allen was suffering acutely in a British military prison. Wedderburn suggests returning Ethan Allen and the other prisoners.

But I think something more might be done than merely return them as prisoners to America. I would send to Allen a person of confidence with this proposal: — that his case had been favorably represented to Government, that the injury he had suffered was some alleviation for his crime, and that it arose from the abuse of an order of Council which was never meant to dispossess the settlers in the land in debate between the two provinces. If he had a mind to return to his duty, he may not only have his pardon from General Howe but a company of Rangers, and in the event he behaves well, his lands restored. On these terms he and his men shall be sent back to Boston at liberty. . . . Some of the people who came over in the ship with him perhaps or perhaps Key himself might easily settle this bargain, if it is set about directly.

This kind of proposition worked with Benedict Arnold. Those who play down Ethan Allen do not speak very audibly about the fact that it did not work with him.

Because the Allens bought large tracts of land, it is sometimes said that they were "land-hucksters." But is a man a huckster who buys a large quantity of quinine, intending to sell it to sick people who need quinine? No, he is one of the cogs in the machine of business. Ethan Allen with his wholesale purchase of land, intending to sell it at retail to working farmers, was an American businessman. His interest in making money from the sale of land, like that of Washington, Madison and others, had nothing to do with the Hudson Valley intention to perpetuate in the New World, by means of landownership, hereditary social and political inequalities.

Perhaps an item in a portrayal of Allen's personality is the fact that he left no fortune — just enough assets to take care of his lovely, much-cherished second wife and his children. His two sons (one was named Hannibal and the other Voltaire — just imagine those names in the Duane family) were educated at public expense at West Point.

His second marriage is such a cheering part of his story I can't bear not to share it with you. In 1783, some time after the death of his disagreeable first wife, he met a handsome, well-educated, guitar-playing, youngish widow, with a quick witty tongue and a warm heart. They were married not by a clergyman but by the Chief Justice of the Supreme Court of the Republic of Vermont. Unlike some liberals Ethan Allen did not at all grow more conservative as he grew older.

The story goes — I don't guarantee the literal truth of this one — that when the judge said, "Do you, Ethan Allen, promise to live with Fanny Buchanan, agreeable to the laws of God?" the bridegroom said quickly, "Which God do you mean? If you mean the laws of God as written in the great book of Nature, go on. My sleigh waits at the door."

In that sleigh they rode off into a married life which was as sunny and happy as the first marriage had been dark and sour.

After all, this late happiness does perhaps help us to understand the unique oddity who fitted the Vermont opinion-climate so well. In every generation, Green Mountain people have felt a deep lasting satisfaction in Ethan Allen. We can see that he might not suit other people. He suits us fine. We are proud of the fact that in his later years, people from outside Vermont (those involved in the Wyoming, Pennsylvania, land dispute and in Shays's Rebellion) turned to him for help in what they felt to be a fight for human values. And possibly one of the many elements in the satisfaction we take in him may be the proof that along with other qualities like reckless personal courage, both physical and political, wholehearted devotion to human freedom, a hard head for liquor, great skill as a woodsman and hunter, originality and generosity, he could give and take happiness in the most intimate of human relationships. Perhaps the thought of his natural joy in so natural a thing as good mating is a part of the Vermont tradition. That tradition is sober and self-contained, but it is not in the least morose or ascetic. It has in it little self-tormenting distrust of human nature, and no hatred of natural joys.

This narration has been of facts. It gives little idea of what in his time, Ethan Allen meant to Vermont. It is sometimes said that he stamped his attitude towards life upon our tradition. No statement could be more beside the mark. He and the majority of Vermont settlers had the same attitude towards life. It was from the same sources that they drew their pails full of the same ideas, from such Locke sayings as "The end of government is for the public good and safety." "The end of government is to preserve and enlarge freedom." Allen was not the apostle of this faith. The Green Mountain people did not learn it from him, as his disciples. He was neither ahead of them, drawing them on, nor behind them following their lead. He was one of them.

We tend to think of Jefferson and Lincoln as the creators of the mass opinion for which they were the voices. Because Ethan Allen's loud voice is the one we moderns still hear, shouting from history books, we are apt to think of him in the same way. Carlyle is no longer in fashion, but he has left in our minds a tinge of his "great man" idea, for instance that Frederick the Great was the creator of the Prussian military machine, forgetting that the human material he shaped was already reduced like well-trained horses or hunting dogs to passive submission to command. The human material of the Hampshire Grants had, almost to a man, exactly the opposite tradition, a violent reflex resistance to anybody trying to give them orders.

People who speak of Ethan Allen as a noisy dictator imposing his will on quieter folk do not know Vermonters. They were quiet all right. They still are. But nobody imposes his will on them. If they had not been heart and soul for the resistance movement they would have silently voted him down at their Town Meetings, just as they do now when they disapprove of somebody.

This is no surmise. We have proof of it. After the beginning of the American Revolution, Vermont raised a regiment of militia to serve in the Continental Army. (Quite a story, that regiment had!) The officers were elected by vote, as was usual then. They did not elect Ethan Allen as their colonel. The vote went forty-one to five against him, although he very much wanted the post. They chose Seth Warner, a quiet, unpicturesque man, skilled and experienced in professional military life as Ethan Allen was not.

What they wanted of Ethan Allen was to say what they wanted said, not to tell them what to think or what to do. And what they wanted said to the claims of the New York landlords, was "No!" They felt as though they themselves had spoken when he wrote to Governor Tryon of New York, "Be it known that we will not be fooled or frightened out of our property, and that persons are cowards indeed if they cannot as manfully fight for their *liberty*, property and life, as villains do to deprive them thereof."

Ticonderoga is perhaps the basis of the idea that Allen was the military leader of the Vermont resistance. But no military skill was required to take that old fort, its defenses tumbled down, its token garrison only forty-three men and two officers. The force led by Ethan Allen and Benedict Arnold (the latter much offended to find himself rated as of equal rank with a mere backwoodsman of no military experience) had fifty men to begin with, raised and paid by the Hartford Committee of Safety, together with as many Green Mountain Rangers as could be summoned from their homes in a night's racing from cabin to cabin from Castleton to Shoreham.

Even so, the action of the attackers was a bold one. We know now that nobody was going to be killed. But they did not, as they stepped forward in the night, towards the famous old fortress. They were politically bold, also, since the attack on Ticonderoga took place less than a month after Lexington and Concord. But it required equal boldness from them all. And, as the affair turned out, it required little more than boldness from any of them that night.

The record of facts show that none of the Green Mountain Rangers were cautious about danger. They needed no inspiring leader, sword in hand, shouting "Forward" to get them into a fight. On occasions like the rescue of Remember Baker, like the action at Hubbardton, like the Battle of Bennington, Vermont, men risked their lives, whether Ethan Allen was there or not. What they could not do was talk about their reason for risking their lives.

To point out that they did not need him as military commander, nor to teach them the political principles they were defending does not lessen his importance. He played a role which, judging from the personality of Green Mountain people, then and now, not a single one of the others could have taken. He was their voice. Ethan Allen was almost the only one who had an ardent love for words, as the tool of ideas. This is essentially a literary trait, and in this sense Ethan Allen was a man of letters. And, as a woman of letters, I halt at this spot to protest loudly against an

idea which may have come into your mind, that thus to charac-
terize him is to belittle him.

The fact is, when you consider his life, he was successful only
as a voice, as a man of letters. In practical matters he had a typical
author's ineptitude. Whether in building a cow-shed the right
size for a cow, or in making money out of land speculation, Ethan
Allen showed an engaging and lovable absence of aggressive skill
in forwarding his own interests.

The long impassioned fight of the Hudson Valley tenant farmers against class subordination was begun before Vermont was
settled, was kept up long after Vermonters were running their
own government. Their persistence proves that, like the men of
the Green Mountains, they needed nobody to inform them that
freedom is desirable. They too believed that, whether they got
it from John Locke or out of the American air. The news they
needed to rouse them to sympathy and help for Vermonters was
what the voice of Ethan Allen told them, that up in the New
Hampshire Grants, farmers were gunning for landlords. When
they heard that, they knew what to do.

Ethan Allen's "proclamations," announcements, appeals, sound
nowadays wordy and diffuse. To the people of his time, not only
to Vermonters, the passionate sincerity of these documents
sounded trumpetlike through all his rhetoric. His cuss-words
caught the ear, too, his rhythmic, sonorous defiances, his heavy-
handed sense of humor — they all helped. People remembered
them, passed them along, all the more zestfully because secretly —
as the illiterate and oppressed have always rejoiced in resistance so
secret that it cannot be punished.

That his statements also got under the skin of the governing
class was proved to the great satisfaction of Green Mountain people by the gentry's frenzy of hatred for the Vermont ideal. In
1774 a measure of reprisal was passed in New York, so savage that
it could have come only from people emotionally enraged. Something was at stake far more important to them than their getting
into their hands more land than they had already.

This Act forbade three or more persons to gather against an
order to disperse issued by the civil authorities. (There were no
recognized "civil authorities" in Vermont so this meant the au-

thorities of the Province of New York.) It declared unlawful assumption of judicial power and malicious destruction of property punishable by death. (This referred to the destruction by the Green Mountain Boys of the cabins of settlers sent in by New York landlords to hold land *as tenants* according to the New York system.) Allen, Warner, Baker and Cochran were named as the chief rioters. The New York governor published a notice in the New York newspapers that he might command any violator of this Act to stand trial within seventy days. If the offender failed to appear, he would thereby become a felon, subject to the death sentence. A writer of appallingly bad verse on the side of the Vermonters, commenting on this death sentence for not appearing in court, remarked that not in the Bible nor in Caesar's code could anyone find an Act:

> Which destines man to awful fate
> And hangs and damns without a trial.

James Duane, the New York lawyer, explained that this extraordinary Act was less drastic than the English Riot Act, on which it was based. His legalistic explanation was water on a duck's back to the Green Mountainers, in whose name Ethan Allen at once sent a gay public invitation to Duane, Kempe and other governing Yorkers, to come up to Vermont to see "as good a regiment of marks'-men and scalpers as America can afford." This not very subtle pleasantry was in exactly the right tone for repeating in New York taverns to the accompaniment of guffaws from the drinkers, who took it home to their families, who passed it on to the neighbors, who retold it the next day to all they met, in the grapevine system of communication which has always given illiterates the local news of the day about as rapidly as the linotype gives world news, often more vividly.

Again and again in the Vermont-Yorker dispute, we hear the voice of Ethan Allen laughingly, furiously, contemptuously, eloquently saying what his comrades felt.

He was their "public-relations" man, he "promoted" Vermont's side of the quarrel, and he proved that this role can be ennobled by total sincerity. He meant what he said, he represented men who meant what they did.

He was, as few men are, wildly passionate. Not passionate about women, not about power over others, not about getting money. He was passionate about an idea — the ancient idea that men and women live best and most fruitfully in as much freedom and equality as is possible. He was the voice of Vermont. He still is.

PART III

PART III

CHAPTER 9
And Then What?

A MADE-UP STORY can always end when the author thinks he has come to a dramatic climax. A favorite last page for historical fiction describes the proud moment when after a battle, the flag of victory is raised over the conquered — or defended — ramparts. But this is a true story I am telling. In real life the clock goes dryly ticking on, past drama, out into serious everyday hours. The victors must stop waving that flag, must keep the fire going in the kitchen stove, see to the mending of their roofs, and get the children to bed on time.

Vermont is still here. More than a century and a half has gone by since the day in 1791 which ended the uncertainty, the long anxious tension about its political status. Since then the tension and anxiety felt by most Vermonters has centered on the question: How are we going to earn our livings?

For a while a self-owned farm worked by the whole family seemed, everywhere in America, the obvious and final solution to that problem. Then came the industrial revolution upsetting former values. Fewer of life's necessities — from shoes to lumber-sleds — were made by handwork at home. Some crops had to be raised not to eat but to sell, to get money to pay for factory products. The Erie Canal and the railroads brought competing wheat and meat from fat western lands into eastern city markets. The economic man, somewhat slighted in the preceding pages, steps from the background into the spotlight.

Whether Vermonters realized it or not, the fact was that their impassioned struggle against landlordism with its caste system had won only the first round in their fight for independent survival. The great estate versus small farm question was only a passing phase of an everlasting conflict. The ownership of land now gives neither social privilege nor power over others. Money is power. And in every era or situation, some of the powerful always try to exploit those who can't resist. In the wrestling bout with wealth, no twists and turns long avail to keep poverty's shoulders from the mat. Safety lies in avoiding poverty.

But how could Vermont avoid poverty? How could a self-respecting standard of living be maintained in a district where, as the old joke puts it, the climate is eight months winter, and four months darned late in the fall; a district with a small and static number of people in it; with hardly any mineral wealth; remote from the main lines of communication; with more than half its land tip-tilted so that after a few years of cultivation the arable soil was gone, washed away into the rivers?

The answer to that question is complex. But right at the start one simplification must be made. Vermonters have not held themselves down to the absolute minimum existence, material and spiritual, of the sow-belly-hominy-grits, backward sections. Their scale of life, while they have kept it down to what they have had money to pay for, has steadily been and still is, somewhere near the nation-wide trend of considering the luxuries of one generation as necessities for the next. At present, average families, in average Vermont communities, expect to enjoy such expensive modern comforts as telephones, free libraries, automobiles, decent-quality elementary and high schools, bathrooms, a margin of money in the bank, churches, overstuffed furniture, radios (some television sets), college and professional training for the more intelligent of their sons and daughters, electric refrigerators, record players, clothes enough like everybody's to pass in the city street. Within what we would call "prudent limits" they live, always have lived, in the economic present, not in its past, and they look forward to stepping on into its future. Like anybody.

Now any such plan of living as this runs into figures far beyond the income returned from even the most fertile of our farmland — Iowa visitors, by the way, always laugh when they hear us describe any Vermont land as "fertile." How has this been managed? The recipe is simple, mostly by using heads as well as hands. By taking on some promising sideline to make a little extra money, and putting into it hard work, pretty general mechanical know-how, and ordinary honesty (which in the economic dictionary is called "business integrity"). What this program amounts to is that manufacturing of one sort or another has always paid a large slice of Vermont's store bills, even although many of those side-lines have been high-quality specialized farming.

My grandfather's — even my father's — generation remembered the time when every fair-sized brook in the state furnished the power for a succession of small saw and turning mills, and when the water power on the east side of the state in the valley of the Connecticut River ran larger manufacturing plants. The smaller ones, which were everywhere, were in their beginnings closely geared to farm life. During the growing season the big overshot water-wheels stood still, while the farmer and his sons were work-ing the land. They started turning again whenever continued rain, snow, frozen ground stopped the sequence of plowing, harrowing, seeding, harvest.

Different in character and on a larger scale (though small enough by down-country standards) were, and are, the regular, year-round factories, of which there are many; many more of them than a tourist is apt to notice on a holiday trip over scenic highways. Some of them began operation early in the state's his-tory. They have grown in size and number as the man-power needed on farms and the farm unit type of industry has dwindled. They have always absorbed our excess labor supply. Their pay-rolls help balance many a community budget all over the state. The latest figures I have seen indicate now that rather more men and women are working in them than there are left on the farms.

Back around 1906, when *The Jungle* and similar novels were best sellers, any writer would here have felt bound to discuss the disastrous cleavage, implied by such figures, between solid inde-pendent landowners and a bitter, thwarted industrial proletariat. Some of those writers, already leaning toward class-psychology generalizations, would have gone further and ascribed to the fac-tory hands an inverted sort of pride in their enforced humility. Diana Trilling, brilliant literary critic, detects such a doctrine in the works of D. H. Lawrence, admires, as one of his flashes of poetic insight, his "observation of the satisfaction which a subdued people take in their subjugation." Neither Mrs. Trilling nor Law-rence invented that idea. Old India hands had long been insisting that "natives" feel affectionate respect only for rulers who kick them. Victorian women, it was said, felt lost without a powerful father or husband to boss them.

Nowadays we interpret those symptoms differently. Nobody denies that there was something abnormal in the early, big-factory labor situation, in the situation of colonies in an empire, in the dictum of common law that husband and wife are one person and that person is the husband. Obviously that abnormal element in the situation caused frustrations, neuroses, unrest. What time and events have disproved is the idea, once seriously offered by people in power, that it was normal for people not in power to accept a dominant master without protest. Contemporary women, we note, have not the slightest wish to live like their great-grandmothers, asking their husbands for pocket money; British coalminers supported Lloyd George and continue to support the Labor Party; nor have any of us ever heard of Asians who circulate petitions asking the sahib to come back and kick them.

Am I beating a dead horse? Not entirely. Even today someone may be wondering whether the Vermont tradition of personal independence and human dignity has survived the iron routine of the time clock, the production line, of taking orders from a foreman? Have they bartered their birthright for a full dinner pail? Have they, since they earn so much of their livings in industry, become wage slaves? The only answer to such a question is "Not so you'd notice it, any."

How have they turned the trick? Well, I suppose you will think that I am a little touched in the head if I drag in again that quarrel with the New York landlords. But as I see it, the connection is plain. Victory over the attempt to make them social subordinates not only set up a high standard of self-respecting independence below which every citizen of Vermont feels it unworthy to fall — it did more. With an unsuspected by-product it furnished the material resource to back up and pay for the luxury of adhering to such a standard.

Early deeds often ran into the high hundreds of acres, but when the impossibly steep rocky slopes of the Green and Taconic mountains were deducted, the result in plowable land became decidedly moderate. The pattern of small one-family-size farms was set up. From the first years the Vermont farm family mixed some industrial production with their agriculture. As time went on, they came to mix some agriculture with their industrialism. Both ways the mixture has been a good one. It has persisted. With the ups and downs of fortune, meadows and pastures were bought and sold. Almost everyone who wanted to (and a great many wanted this) could claim as his very own property at least some piece of land, some sort of dwelling.

Agricultural experts accurately point out the defects of this system. Large sections of the state's soil are submarginal, unsuited to farming, never should have been cleared. This is true from the scientific agricultural point of view. But we Vermonters have seen how it looks from a human point of view. Any little patch with room for a house, a garden and enough field-corn to fatten a pig, perhaps to keep a cow, always furnished — long before the economic securities of the New Deal were dreamed of — a positive, reliable form of unemployment insurance, and hence a mighty stiffener of human backbones. When the mill shut down in depression, or wages were cut below the level of normal living, or the foreman turned unbearably cranky, the Vermont factory-hand did not have to grit his teeth and take it. Resistance and the risk of losing his job did not mean extreme suffering and near-starvation for him and his wife and children. Either he or his father, or his uncle, or his wife's father owned a place where in exchange for work he could earn shelter, food enough to get by on, all the firewood needed. Even in the black nineteenth century, no Vermonter was forced to undergo the spirit-crushing anxiety of a coal-miner or steel-worker with wife and children in danger of being evicted from a company-owned tenement. Thus the Vermonter was never forced into that most unmanning sensation, helplessness, was never beaten down into paying for survival by docility. He works or quits the job as if carrying out the vote of a self-organized labor union with a single enrolled member — himself.

But mostly he works. Before long, he and the boss get to calling one another by their first names.

The following section of this book is not intended to present an exhaustive, consecutive economic history of Vermont. A great deal of our economic history has been like that of any reasonably modern area of the nation anywhere. I have chosen certain chapters in our earning-a-living story because their human color gives them a specially Vermontish quality. Also because, though the material setting changes from one to another, the same quality, the same personality runs through them all. To me that seems to hold out a hope that whenever the old clothes of Vermont tradition wear out, it can put on new ones over a frame so powerful that its identity is plain, and that our children and grandchildren will see it zestfully stepping along the road it marked out for itself, so long ago.

CHAPTER 10

Potash and the Will-to-Die

A GLOOMY PROPHET has recently said that the rapid dwindling of the human capacity for attention will soon reduce the art of narrative to a formula like this: "A man lived in the woods. So did a bear. The man killed the bear." Or the other way around, if the author follows the despair-and-frustration literary fashion of our time.

But I hope that day is not yet quite here, because if it were, we would all lose a cheerful reassurance about human life which is often brought to us by leisurely and respectful meditation about apparently trivial details. We would never make the surprising discovery that many of them are not in the least trivial, but when understood, are proofs of universal human solidarity. Of course the exploration which, alone, can take us to that discovery can't be carried out with the brisk speed one uses in tearing last month's page off the calendar. It takes thought. And thinking always takes time.

Every Vermonter with old-time roots here knows something about potash. It is mentioned in ever so many of the letters and other papers piled in our attics, or preserved in historical collections. Plenty of Potash Hills or Potash Roads are to be found sprinkled liberally over local maps. Old account books suggest that its sale was an important financial item in our forefathers' lives. But not much more than this has come down to us twentieth-century Green Mountain folks. That is odd, when you remember the immense amount of research which lovers of the past have devoted to other handcrafts of the past, now never practiced except by an occasional hobbyist — such as spinning with a wheel, forging iron utensils by hand, making rugs.

My own interest was aroused almost by chance, when I happened to notice in a dry county history the fact that in 1791, a thousand tons of potash were sent out of Vermont. A thousand of anything, let alone tons, exported from Vermont as early as that was surprising. I had no answer to the question, "Who in the world could possibly have wanted to buy as much as that?" so the next time I was in Montpelier I stepped into the fine library of our State Historical Society and asked the librarian for information.

He answered readily, "Potash was used in making soap — same thing as lye."

That much I knew already. In childhood I had often hung around to watch my great-aunt make soap, both soft and hard, from lye drawn from the year's supply of wood ashes, and the year's accumulation of grease saved from cooking.

"But," I objected, "the amount of potash you come across in old account books and commerce reports couldn't have been for making soap to wash with. Enough was sent out of Vermont every year to wash the clothes and faces of humanity all round the globe ten times a day . . . in a manner of speaking. In 1791, three hundred tons of potash were produced in one Vermont county alone. That's six hundred thousand pounds and that year two million pounds were exported from the whole state."

The librarian, expert in Vermont statistics, knew these figures too.

He suggested, "It was mostly taken, you know, to cities outside of Vermont — to Albany from down in your part of the state; from up here to Montreal via Lake Champlain and the Richelieu River. Brattleboro records show that lots of it was sent down to Connecticut to the River Towns — Hartford and so on. The local records say, 'Mostly for export!' "

We looked at each other nonplussed. For all his erudition in Vermont history, he knew no more than I why anybody anywhere wanted tons and tons of potash every year. And so far as he had ever heard, nobody else knew. Why wouldn't it, I wondered, be worth while to look into an economic factor which by its great bulk must have left some mark on the human quality of Vermont's formative early years?

When I set myself to this undertaking, I discovered that the underlying facts are not hard to unearth. Plenty of source material is available, although not in the books usually read by literary people. Eighteenth-century reports of commerce, industrial histories, memoranda by the Board of Trade on colonial conditions give full information about the buying and selling of potash. Neither did the subject turn out to be a dry and dusty pebble of detached fact. To my surprise the bushels of ashes in our old Vermont account books proved to be living capillaries in a very old organism — green twigs on an immense, ancient and always rapidly growing tree.

Apparently potash is one of the first true chemicals to be used by mankind, long before anybody had the faintest idea of the nature of chemical change. In Pliny's time, the accidental discovery was an ancient folk tale. And in fact, potash was manufactured and used a thousand and more years before Rome. Some of the earliest glass beads of Egypt were made with it.

The Roman toga was made of wool, and if there is one thing you learn when you begin to look into potash, it is that good quality wool cannot be made without using soap at every stage of its manufacture. Pliny spoke, as of a familiar procedure, of making soap from water which had dripped through wood ashes, combined with hot grease or oil. This transformation of two ingredients into something else quite different from either of them, was far more of a miracle than was ever wrought by the medieval alchemists trying to turn other metals into gold. But apparently soap has always been too familiar to arouse wonder.

Like others of the Roman skills the use of soap in manufacturing woolen cloth became by the middle ages a closely guarded, profitable trade secret. Sight-seers in Florence often marvel at the amount of money spent by the local woolen guilds. To their woolen-working shops, people from all over Europe sent their goods for the mysterious processes of "finishing." Along the wretched, muddy, stony, perilous trails of medieval Europe, plodded trains of pack-horses loaded with coarsely prepared woolen cloth or raw wool. Preyed upon by titled members of the aristocracy who held strategic passes, men, mules and horses finally struggled through the Alps and thence down into Italy and Florence, where woolen cloth could be transformed from its first stiff, smelly stages into the smooth supple folds of fine-quality woolen cloth, one of the most valuable products known to human society of that time.

The citizens of Florence assumed, of course, as people with a trade monopoly do, that this prosperity would last. They had a vision of a boom-town Florence, expanding continuously. They laid out big "surburban developments," mapped and named new streets, on which thousands of new homes and new shops would be built.

But trade secrets are notoriously hard to keep. After a while, the clever Low Country woolen manufacturers learned how to make that combination of potash and oil which we call soap, which the Prayer Book in its seventeenth-century language calls "fullers' sope." They stopped sending those long pack-trains. They bought potash, made their own "sope," set up fulling mills, refinished their own woolens. This was one of the reasons for the end of the boom in Florence. The sketched-out suburban streets remained wheatfields, vineyards, olive orchards. Technological unemployment hit Florence a sledge-hammer blow. Such crises seems to have followed the production of woolen cloth. As we shall see, one hit Vermont.

In the place of Florence rose the thriving cities of the Low Countries, where the woolen guilds grew powerful. To their workshops the British sent their wool. Bruges was rolling in money, Ghent grew richer every day, while Florence slowly subsided to farming and small handcrafts.

But the British government grudged every penny that crossed the Channel. Money ought to stay in England. "Buy of your home-town merchants."

To produce woolen goods of a quality that could compete with that made on Belgian and Dutch looms and "finished" in Low Country workshops, skilled weavers were needed. Ordinary people in England (like ordinary people everywhere) disliked "furriners," especially those more skilled than they; but the British government forced them to accept wave after wave of refugees from religious and political persecution on the Continent, of course with a marked preference for those refugees who knew the secrets of making fine woolen cloth. Bruges and Ghent lost their monopoly. It was their turn to go down before technological unemployment. Bruges fell into a passive trancelike memory of its bustling days. Ghent became just another city.

The English government used every device to safeguard the production of woolen cloth, and to increase it — inside England. The exportation of English raw wool to the Continent was at one time forbidden under pain of death. In Charles II's reign, an act was passed decreeing that all corpses must be buried in woolen shrouds. By the latter half of the eighteenth century (note that this is the period of the settlement of Vermont) the woolen industries employed a million people — a vast number in those days. Wool had become, in a famous phrase, "the flower, the strength and revenue and blood of England." The Lord Chancellor of England sat on a wool-sack.

Throughout this great industry whenever money changed hands, it stayed in England, except for a single item — potash. Soap could not be made without it. Tons were needed every year. The only known source was from burning vegetable matter — mostly trees. When English trees became too valuable and too rare to be burned, it was imported from Riga; with language difficulties, shipping troubles, business misunderstandings. Russia seems to have been Russia then as now. Even without friction of this sort, when potash was brought in from Europe, British money went out of England, a disastrous situation, according to economic theories of that time.

In 1757, Moscarene, in a book entitled *The Manufacture of Pot-Ash in the British North American Plantations, Recommended,* pointed out, "It is computed that there is annually imported into Great Britain and Ireland, Three Thousand Tons of Potash; which, according to a moderate Price, amounts to upwards of One Hundred Thousand Pounds, and this paid to *Russia, Poland* and *other foreign States* in *ready Money.*"

This shocking state of things could not be allowed. In 1751, Parliament passed "An Act for encouraging the making of Pott Ashes and Pearl Ashes in the British Plantations in America."

England fiercely stamped out every attempt in the North American colonies to develop manufacturing. If anybody was to be paid for skilled labor, it was to be the English workman, within England, under the close control of the English governmental and social system. The Americans were allowed to trap beavers and sell the fur in its crude state to English hatmakers, and then buy finished hats from the mother country. They must not make hats. They could mine iron and export it in bulk. They must not (except furtively and outside the law) make their own nails.

But potash now — here was something on which England's "strength and revenue and blood" depended. Here was a manufacturing process which the English actually urged on the colonists.

From September 29, 1756 on, "no duty was to be paid on Pot and Pearl Ashes from America."

By this date those who were to become Vermonters, boys and girls of Western Connecticut and Western Massachusetts, were in their late teens and early twenties, just about ready to marry and set forth to found homes of their own. It was the best of news for them — this demand for a product they could manufacture, which would always be paid for, promptly, and at a high price, in hard money.

From the middle of the eighteenth century, British wool-manufacturers, glass-makers, linen-weavers, clamored for more and more American potash. They never — as far as I can read the record — had too much, never refused any that came in from the colonies. London offered large premiums to those who should import the greatest quantity of pearl and pot ashes. Manuals with exact instructions about making good potash were published in England, sent to the colonies and circulated widely. The process became more and more familiar to Americans. In 1770, potash to the value of $290,000 was exported. By the year 1790, the sum had risen to $840,000. (Bear in mind the fabulously greater value of money in those days.)

It was precisely when the demand for this "American alkali" was rising most rapidly that settlers were moving into thick-wood country. Of course they expected to work hard at felling trees to make clearings and fields. All settlers did in new regions. The astonishing part was that these settlers would not only own the fields they cleared, but be well paid for burning those trees and manufacturing something out of the ashes.

It was no monopoly of Vermont. Hardly. Potash was being

made in this country wherever there were trees to be cut down. But it took more than trees. It required men and women skilled, patient, self-disciplined.

The great *History of Manufactures in the U.S.A.* says of colonial manufacturers, "One class of industries (potash-making) depended for perfection upon carefully observed processes, rather than upon manual skill or machinery." It was a simple proceeding. But a long one. And our simian inheritance makes it particularly hard for human beings to stick at anything that takes a long time to do. It required not only willingness to work hard, but attentiveness and reliability, such qualities as are often known as "character." Vermonters succeeded very well at it. Many colonies far from New England gave bounties for potash. "Potash manufacture was an important incentive in establishing settlements in Carolina, Georgia and other colonies of the American seaboard." South Carolina in 1712 provided a reward of forty shillings a ton for the first five hundred tons of potash shipped out of the country. But (I quote from an article in the *Journal of Economic and Business History*) "All attempts to establish a potash industry in the southern colonies failed. Why? The answer appears to be twofold: poor raw material and poor labor. At practically every step, the production of potash demanded skilled workmanship of a kind not ordinarily obtainable from laborers in the South. The potash industry in New England, on the other hand, had no such handicaps. The forests consisted of trees high in potash content, and the laborers were alert and skillful."

It was, moreover, a familiar skill to the young settlers in the Green Mountains. The industry was already thriving in Connecticut and Massachusetts. One of Ethan Allen's ventures as a young man, before he started northward, was an iron-works in Connecticut which mostly made potash kettles. There was a quick sale for every one.

No wonder the first Vermonters were cheerful. It looked as though they had in their hands a sure formula for success, that is, for stability and personal independence. Not for wealth. It was their great good fortune that neither then nor afterwards did they measure success in terms of an impressive hoard of money. Like other American colonial pioneers, they could grow or make for themselves most of the basic necessities for daily life — food, shelter, fuel. In addition, by producing this chemical so urgently needed by the British textile industry, they could buy and pay for the all-important extras — powder, salt, shot, books, rum, fine lawn, steel tools, shoebuckles. Like the Florentine woolen guilds, like those of the Low Countries, the American colonials who made potash assumed that their monopoly would always last. It did last, with a normal number of ups and downs, during the lifetime of the first generation of settlers in Vermont.

This profitable manufacturing was simple, accurately adapted to their situation and character. Let me put down here, long s's and all, a passage from one of the several manuals of instructions sent over from London. This one is dated 1767, and was widely studied by all potash-makers in the Colonies:

> DOSSIE, R.
> Observations on the Potash brought from America
> London 1767

> Equipment needed for making potash:
> A ftrong iron rod, longer than the depth of the cauldrons, or pans, and flatted at one end, in the manner of a broad chifel, for loofening the alkaline falt from the bottom of the cauldon during the evaporation.
> An iron ladle for raking out the falt; or cooling the ley, if it tend to boil over the cauldron.
> A ftrong broad iron chifel, with a wooden mallet for cutting the falt out of the cauldron, when the whole operation is completed.
> An iron rake, with clofe teeth, for feparating the bits of unburnt wood or coal from the afhes.
> A pair of fmall fcales, with two phials, for trying the ftrength of the ley, in order to know if it be fit for evaporation.

And so on, and so on for many pages.

Our young Vermont forefathers had been brought up among potash-making people, and knew without books that there was nothing to it but soaking wood-ashes in water to make lye, and then, in big kettles, boiling the water out of the lye. Care in handling the ashes, in packing the black solid matter which was left in the bottom of the kettle seemed simple to them, "alert and skillful" as they are called by the *Journal of Economic and Business History*.

What they thus manufactured was worth a good price in cash money. And of prime importance, it was light in comparison to its value. Wheat grew splendidly in Vermont in the early days, and it also had a good cash value. But a pound of wheat had nothing like the value of a pound of potash. It took a good deal of time and a great deal of hard work to transform a big elm tree into five tons of wood, then to burn the wood into ashes, then to extract lye from the ashes and thence, by evaporation, to produce thirty-nine pounds of potash. (I know that this detail will not interest you; but it cost me so much time and effort to find, I can't be restrained from putting it in.) But Vermont pioneers had time, did not fear hard work, an elm tree thus processed could be carried out to market in a man's knapsack, and it meant a respectable sum in cash. Long before roads were built for wheeled vehicles, a couple of pack-horses could carry over the trails a load of potash worth the enormous sum of fifty dollars, ten times what the same weight of wheat would have brought. Fifty dollars was more than a Vermont pioneer of that period would see (except for potash) in months or years — or would need to see for reasonably comfortable living. One more point is worth mentioning — the Vermonter took his potash always to a seller's market. He got a good price for it without any need for aggressive, energetic or even passable salesmanship, a skill in which the Green Mountain tribe has never been especially gifted.

The situation of such an ancestor of ours, the lump price of many months of labor in his pocket, was the same, factually (although not psychologically), as that of a sailor in from the sea, paid off for a year before the mast; or of a lumberjack with a winter's wages, or of a gold-miner, with a bag of yellow dust, just back from the dreary solitude of his claim. This is a familiar situation which traditionally follows a familiar pattern: in a week's wild carouse, every penny is gone. Sellers of alcohol, women-to-be-bought, card-sharpers, aided by professional thieves, fall upon the helpless drunk, rapidly transferring the contents of his pockets to their own. An old folk phrase describes any man on a wild spree as "spending money like a sailor in port."

Such self-destructive behavior-explosions now have a new name. They are called manifestations of a fundamental will-to-die (or at least a will for self-hurt) which, some of us are surprised to hear, is considered by modern psychiatrists (some of them) as basic an instinct as the will-to-live and to enjoy life. We would better look at the evidence on the subject. The only evidence there is comes from observation of human behavior. Psychiatrists have no monopoly of such data.

It is as evidence of this kind that I invite you to look at a small detail in Vermont history which taken as an isolated fact could interest none but Vermonters, and antiquarians at that. No repeated habitual actions of men are meaningless for those wishing to make a little more sense out of what we do with ourselves. Consider as evidence about basic human nature the early Vermonter, far from home, his potash money in his pocket.

He is available as an authenticated history-fact worth thinking about, because we of today know what he did with that lump sum. We do not of course have data to reconstruct the case history of every single Vermont potash seller. But we do have information about a surprising number of them. Our forefathers kept account books, we have records of the purchases they made. All over Vermont, letters, memoirs, accounts, local histories, family talk, tell the same story.

Our eighteenth-century ancestor stepped out from the counting rooms of the export merchants who brought potash into one or another of the deep-sea ports of that time. Deep-sea ports are always marketplaces for the merchandise of the big world. The same ships which were to take his potash back to England to make "sope" had brought to America manufactured articles such as could not be produced in inland American frontier towns. The Vermonter found himself in a sort of Nizhnii Novgorod world's fair. Wherever he looked, up and down the streets of Albany, Montreal or Boston, he saw useful, interesting, comely, skillfully manufactured things for sale; and he had the money to buy them.

From the records left by our ancestors, we learn that in the very first years of life in the Vermont forests, before tools were made by the local blacksmiths, he bought axes, saws, hammers, wedges, and the like. He also bought some of the good things to eat and drink and smoke which could not be produced in the Hampshire Grants home-farm-factories — tea, for instance, molasses, twists of tobacco, and rum, rum, rum (whiskey was distilled at home very early). He bought a limited number of pretty, seemly, presentable things to wear — steel shoebuckles, a few yards of fine lawn for kerchiefs for his women folk; buttons, pins, needles, fine thread; a yard or so of bright ribbon to tie up a pretty girl's hair; occasionally some good quality English cloth to make a coat he could wear at important meetings.

Perhaps most noteworthy is that from the first, these far-from-home country men bought books. Not sermons. Our local lending library in Arlington, organized about a century and a half ago, has in the by-laws of its constitution a provision that at no time should more than one thirty-fifth part of the money spent on books go to the purchase of "books of divinity." When you remember the small amount of cash they ever had in the treasury, you see that one thirty-fifth part of it meant practically nothing at all. And sure enough, in the first purchases made by our local library, there is not one "book of divinity."

This by-law is no local specialty of Arlington. A similar provision is found in the constitution of many and many an early town library in Vermont. John Locke's and Ethan Allen's distaste for theological discussion of orthodox dogmas was a character trait of early Vermonters. What books did they bring back, purchased by potash-money? Very much the varied literary fare we now read — books of travel, biographies, romances, volumes of Locke, books of science such as people took science to be in those days. The single volume of *Robinson Crusoe* could be bought for twenty-five cents. A two-volume history cost a dollar and a half. Gibbon's monumental and very nontheological *Decline and Fall* was in the first purchase made by our small, rustic, unmoneyed Arlington library. Another in that first batch of books was a shocker of the time, *The Mysteries of Udolpho*. All kinds, you see.

These steadily recurring trips from the far forests to the deep-sea ports provided more than material comforts for the first Vermonters. They also provided news from the big world, important-serious news of politics, important-trivial news of what shape of caps were in style. The potash-selling Vermonter heard and brought back to tell his neighbors what was said about noted men in England and in the colonies, listened to gossip about the English king, had a chance to notice when wigs began to disappear, when long trousers began to come in. This contact with the older settlements and through them with the trans-Atlantic world meant a good deal. From the first years of their history, Vermonters have never been shy and abashed (although very reticent) with strangers. Yet they were backwoods folk, living far from the centers of population. They were without the social timidity of the illiterate and ignorant, because they were neither; they were reasonably sure that their best clothes were presentable enough not to make them ridiculous, that they had a passable acquaintance with the news of the day, with books people were reading, so that they could join in ordinary talk.

The selling of potash thus kept our forefathers in touch with the outer world. What they bought with the money, and why they bought it, was decided by the quality of their family life at home.

The Vermonter, far from home, selling his own and his neighbors' potash, was like the sailor in from the sea, the lumberjack and the gold-miner, in that he had been living for long months practically without money. He and his family were not paid in cash for work, they did not pay cash wages to others who worked for them; they "traded" work hours as they traded extra corn for pumpkins or home-knit stockings for home-woven cloth.

One of my grandfather's recollections (he was born very soon after the close of the eighteenth century) of his little boyhood is of the exciting day when a "circus" came to town — an elephant, a lion in a cage, some monkeys. He was eager to go. Nobody in the lively, cheerful community saw any reason why a boy shouldn't have some fun. If his folks could pay for it. The price of admission was seven pence, seven copper pennies. His family agreed. But to collect this cash, about as exotic as the monkeys, his father had to go from house to house, through the whole neighborhood. Yet they were all substantial people, living on their own well-tilled land, in pleasant snug homes, with adequate clothing, both for work and for going to dances, with food not only adequate but first-rate in quality, with a decent education and a few well-read books of excellent quality in every house.

How could a man whose sense of money was adjusted to a few copper pennies keep his head, when, far from home, he had what was then an imposing cash sum in his pocket? There was nobody to watch him. He was in the unsupervised freedom which makes tourists, tramps and sailors-in-port act as they do. Why did he not burn up the town and come limping home, his pockets empty, his head aching, rotten to his bones by an "ill disease," as Vermonters called venereal infection?

Can a claim be made that the early Vermonter was of more than usual virtue, wisdom, self-control? Not in the least. The whole point of this story as of any Vermont story is that he was, then as now, a quite ordinary man, like any other American of his time, of any time. The Green Mountain community was not like the Society of Friends, carefully made up of picked men and women. They were quite anybody. It was not through stoic asceticism that the Green Mountain frontiersman in Albany, or Montreal, or Boston cautiously, thoughtfully, spent the year's cash income on purchasing useful or agreeable things, for his family and himself. He needed no special power of self-discipline. He was doing what anybody in his senses intends to do with extra money, getting out of it the greatest possible satisfaction. Like any mature and experienced person, he knew well enough that the sophisticated big town or city was really only a marketplace in which to show goods for sale. These smartly dressed merchants valued a rustic country man's money as much as anybody's.

One hand was in his pocket, firmly grasping his wallet, the other hand held the shopping list made out before he left home, after long consultation with his wife. It was, be it said in passing, written in a good fair hand, with fewer misspellings, by a long shot, than in George Washington's private writings. All around him, human nature being what it is, there must have been plenty of sharpers, thieves, con men, and loose women. Their hard, sharp eyes quickly turned away from the young Vermont husband and father. They knew he had money to spend, but they also knew that he was not likely to buy what they had to sell. I invite you to look, as if we were studying psychology in a laboratory, at the difference between the Vermont potash-seller and the paid-off sailor.

Their factual situation was similar; but they had arrived there by very different routes. The sailor in from many months at sea had been living in crowded quarters, often in mortal danger from storms, seeing none but rough, callous men, as starved as he for normal human relations. The woodchopper had worked long hours in an isolated camp, had bunked and been shut up with men some of them half-demented because deprived of so many of the ordinary daily human satisfactions. During those same months, the Vermonter had lived with his wife and children and babies. Many learned psychiatrists now think that establishing one's own home by one's own efforts is perhaps the most fundamentally satisfying occupation known to human beings. The Vermonter, like the sailor, had worked very hard, had had no ease, often no comforts. But unlike the sailor, he had not been forced, by cruel and degrading punishments, into slavish obedience to a tyrant-captain. Unlike the woodchopper, he had not been under the dictatorship of a foreman, with hiring and firing powers. He had been neither slave nor master of slaves. He had been a free citizen of a free community building up for his town the tradition that no man gives orders to other men without their consent. Such civic life is as richly satisfying for a community as establishing a good home in personal life.

The early Vermonter, unlike the paid-off sailor and lumberjack, had, in his daily life been constantly supplied with the personality-calories and character-vitamins necessary for health. So he was a normal man, in a normal frame of mind. What he did may, therefore, be considered normal human behavior. This is the justification for my telling you about this inconsiderable item in the inconspicuous history of the plain people who were the first Vermonters.

Looking from that homespun Vermonter to the carousing sailor or lumberjack, we might reasonably feel that the impulse to burn up a year's earnings in a few days of crazed debauch is not basically human, not caused by a deep, imperative will-to-die, but is a result of psychological starvation. Such a comparison gives us ground to ask ourselves whether any man who gets from his daily life the simple, deep, human satisfactions we all need, will feel the instinct to destroy himself or others in any of the numerous direct and indirect ways in which such destruction can be carried out.

We really don't know yet much that is accurate about the springs of adult behavior, human nature being so complex and many-sided. We are much more sure of our understanding of children's behavior, partly because a more or less accurately analytical study has been made by intelligent people of what children do, partly because their behavior is not yet complicated by violently active life-elements such as sex activity and economic responsibility, and partly because they have not had time to acquire much ability to hide their real impulses. So if we look closely at destructive impulses in young children, we have more chance of seeing what causes them.

A little boy comes storming in from the street, sobbing, terrified and furiously angry. A big boy took his precious ball away from him and when he tried to get it back, slapped his face, and went away laughing. Once he is safe inside his own home, he has what psychiatrists gravely call a "destructive behavior explosion."

Anybody who has ever brought up children needs little description of what he does. He screams, he kicks the chair legs, in a passionate gesture he sweeps from the living room table the breakable knickknacks he knows his mother prizes, he flings himself face down on the floor, shrieking that he hates her, he hates everybody, that he wishes everybody were dead, that he were dead.

An inexperienced young caretaker might be alarmed. She might even think that he did wish he were dead. But his mother, especially if he is a second or third child, glances at the clock, sees that it is past his supper time, remembers that he did not have his usual afternoon nap, knows that the loss of his ball is a tragedy for a four-year-old. She does not think that he wishes he were dead. She does not even think there is much of anything the matter with him. In a conversational tone she says to his convulsively agitated back, "Come along, and have your supper. I made custard today. And there are cookies." She lifts him up, leads him to the table, talks cheerfully to him while he wolfs down his milk, custard and cookies (sobs still intermittently shaking him, as he eats). She says, in a casual parenthesis as it were, "We'll get Daddy to make a gate to our yard. When that's shut, no big boy could come inside. You can play there till you're bigger." She tucks him up in bed, and as she kisses him good night, she remarks, "We'll get you another ball, first thing in the morning." He is not dead, he is only soundly and healingly asleep before she leaves the room.

She has seen that he has no desire to destroy himself, or even a definite desire to break the china; rather that he is hungry, tired, frightened, has lost a prized possession, that he has been shaken by a dreadful humiliation — helplessness in the face of aggression. She has met those simple, understandable, not at all unreasonable needs with food, rest, protection and hope.

The accident-prone truck driver does not look much like a frightened and angry four-year-old. But circumstances may have put him in very much the same situation. If it were made possible for him to arrange his life so that he had his fair share of what we know to be not unreasonable psychological needs, his hand on the steering wheel might be steady. This will not always be possible. But it never will be possible in a single case, so long as we go on thinking that he has accidents because of a basic will-to-die.

We look around us and see — exactly as the crape-hangers say — the human world full of madness and horror, full of people who fling themselves down in tantrums, screaming they hate, hate, hate everybody and everything. We see countless others more quietly, less spectacularly, but as surely — in homes and family life, in and out of novels, in business offices, in factories, because they have too much money, because they have too little money — poisoning themselves and others, destroying their own and others' possible happiness by negative and embittered actions. Many theologians, many fiction writers, many psychiatrists tell us that this behavior is inevitable because it is human.

Maybe they are right. But we can see for ourselves that a large part of humanity is hungry, materially and psychologically starved, has not anything like a fair chance to hope for what we all need and long for. How can we be sure that human behavior, mean, hateful, grovelling, aggressive, detestable as it often is, is the result of innate, inevitable qualities of our human race, not of just such spiritual and psychological deprivations as reduced the traditional sailor-in-port to acting like an insane debauchee, as makes a four-year-old explode into hysteria, or as makes a modern truck driver "accident-prone"? That is a question, just a wondering question, not a statement.

There is so little data about what ordinary human beings would be if they were not the victims of some kind of starvation — bodily, spiritual, psychological — that the rustic, backwoods Vermonter with his potash-money is worth standing up beside the sailor with his year's pay, where we can look from one to the other with an attentive eye.

Probably those early Vermonters expected — hoped anyhow — that they could always continue living by the simple economic formula of their beginnings: home-growing and processing of food, home-manufacture of clothing, and most other needs, and a cash crop to pay for merchandise that they themselves could not produce. But the harsh teaching of the school of experience soon taught them, as it has taught almost every generation of their descendants, that hope must learn to accept change without turning into despair. What happened to their potash-money, as the modern world developed, is typical of Vermont economic history. It has not been an easy kind of history to take.

The demand for potash poured in, we have seen, from huge industrial forces in the international give-and-take of the great world of manufacturing and finance. It was cut off by other great global forces, other developments, political, business, scientific. Skill in chemistry was increasing. Scientific analysis, accuracy and logic were just ending the long task of sweeping alchemy off the lecture platform to be carted away to the dump heap. The laboratory began to appear in something like its modern form.

Within a few years of Ethan Allen's birth date, a man named Leblanc was born in France. Probably he had no better brains, but greater opportunities for abstract learning were opened to him because he lived in eighteenth-century France, rather than on a farm in Western Connecticut. In the full meaning of the word "study," as Ethan Allen never had a chance to study anything, he studied the problem — crucially important for the industrial production of his time — how to get more potash.

British statesmen and industrialists had always deeply studied the same problem. But they were men of affairs, steeped in the pre-laboratory idea that reality is composed of facts sizable enough to be seen by the naked eye. Theirs was the "practical" approach. The first fact they saw was that the growing industry of England needed more and more potash. After this, they noted a second fact, that potash is made from wood ashes. Next in impeccably logical sequence came a third fact that the North American colonies were richly forested. From their London desks went out orders to step up the manufacture of potash in the colonies.

Vermonters, as unaware as most people that they were parts of a coherent global whole, energetically stepped up their production. They never dreamed that abstract chemical theory was waiting with a club around the corner. They alertly improved their methods of manufacture. The first patent ever taken out in the new United States Patent Office was given to a Vermonter for a process he had invented to make more and better potash. As time went on, there were storekeepers in our communities. The manufacture of potash at home on the farm gave way somewhat to a division of labor which increased efficiency, as specialization usually does. The storekeeper set up potash works of his own, and hired men experienced in leaching and boiling, to do that work. It was better done, of course. Many farmers brought in their ashes to the store. As our old store account books show, goods for sale, calico, tobacco, rum, silver shoe-buckles and all the rest, had a fixed value in bushels of ashes. The storekeeper readily gave merchandise for ashes, sure of the market for the potash he got from them.

While practical men thus acted in a practical manner, the Frenchman named Leblanc was fiddling around with theoretic abstractions and formulae. By 1800, scientists knew that sodium can replace potash for industrial purposes, and that it can be produced on a large scale by chemical treatment of salt deposits. In Alsace, in Germany, there were — are — huge salt mines. The industrialists of the time thought — and they were right — that this product was not only cheaper and more available than "American alkali," but more stable, more uniform in quality, much better for manufacturing purposes. The warning bells began to sound at the switch. The big machine of technology, rolling ponderously forward, turned off on a new track.

But in Vermont, no premonition of this imminent knockout blow to the cash crop which gave them a modest, satisfactory margin. And for a while, what was happening in the political scene gave them the illusion that business was still good, would always be good.

Leblanc lived just before, during and just after the French Revolution. The wild upset of politics, industry, finance and society of that period was no background for laboratory research, new chemical formulae, and their application to production. He made a beginning. No more. The industrial and profit-making implications of Leblanc's theory were so tremendous that some leading French citizens combined in the effort to put it into practice. Factory production was outlined, was begun. The chemist himself put all his heart into the project.

But like everybody else in France, they were living on the side of a political volcano in full eruption. The blood-and-thunder Napoleonic drama absorbed all energies. The flags of Austerlitz and Jena were streaming in the air. Money could not be found to finance an experimental venture in industry. By 1806 the enterprise, which had not yet moved an inch forward, collapsed. Leblanc, sick with disappointment, committed suicide.

Vermonters could go on, a little longer, with the process they assumed would always continue, cutting down trees to clear the land for agriculture, and burning them at a profit.

The industry even provided one of the few passages in Vermont history acceptable to that traditional definition of "the picturesque" which requires lawbreaking, secrecy, violence and danger. Vermont, of all places, had its period of large-scale smuggling.

After the Revolution, England had been, understandably, not eager to put money into the pockets of former colonists. Every penny spent for "American alkali" was grudged. A tariff was put on potash imported from the new United States into Great Britain. Russian potash still came in free — but still to the accompaniment of friction of many kinds. There were inexhaustible forests in Canada. The British government made a great effort to develop there the making of potash.

But Vermont is very near to Canada. By night (moonless nights that is) flowed a stream of Vermont potash, which later appeared in England labeled as a Canadian product.

Thomas Jefferson's unpopular Embargo early in the nineteenth century was, in Vermont, not only unpopular but disregarded. Smuggling potash to Canada was increased, well organized, met with the same perverse popular sympathy for lawbreakers always enjoyed by smugglers. On Lake Champlain smuggling was done with the traditional cloak-and-sword accompaniments — secret rendezvous by night, mysterious passwords, a ship painted black (it was called the *Black Snake*) which ran in and out of small harbors picking up potash casks brought to the beaches — all good material for storybooks.

During this period, the price of potash rose, because its exportation from the usual Atlantic ports was so greatly reduced by the Embargo. It had brought, for a while, a hundred dollars a ton. The price now rose to three hundred. Dr. C. A. Browne of the Bureau of Chemistry and Soils of our Federal Department of Agriculture, says that "at this time nearly the whole population of some of the northern counties of Vermont and New York, devoted their energies to the manufacture and transportation of potash to Montreal."

But in Europe, men trained in the long patiences of scientific research were going on with Leblanc's research, weighing minute quantities of this and that on delicate laboratory scales. Looking eagerly over their shoulders, impatient for their conclusions, stood active, moneyed nineteenth-century manufacturers. Behind them, the huge djinn of modern industrial production was daily towering taller. In countless of its processes, far more than had ever been dreamed of, sodium was needed. As an essential factor of the industrial revolution, chemical production of sodium from salt deposits soared high.

By 1807 the value of exported potash and pearlash made from wood ashes was $1,490,000. In 1810 (after the removal of the Embargo) the value was $1,579,000. But in 1813 it slid down to $204,000, and thereafter slid to zero.

Leaning over the records of our fathers' lives, we find no indication that they understood what was happening. People seldom understand the connection of individual personal life with the great world scene. Most Vermonters had no idea — in similar cases we also still do not guess — that a distant lever, thrown by incalculable forces, had shut off power from one line and poured it hot, hot, hot along new wires.

All that was apparent to the human eye (which sees so much less than the human brain) was that the demand for wood-ash potash was less than it had been. Unheard-of phenomenon, men who took potash to the warehouse shipping agencies were turned away. Not always. The change came by gradations. There was for some time a market for Vermont potash for our newly organized American woolen industries which were growing swiftly. But presently they too began importing the chemically produced "salts."

The U.S.A. had been one of the great world sources for potash. Before long, as the huge European salt deposits were developed, as industry in all the Western world expanded, as Liebig discovered the undreamed-of agricultural value of potash, our nation became one of the greatest importers of potash, helplessly and alarmingly dependent on the German deposits.*

---

* The mention of Liebig is a reminder of an absurd accusation occasionally brought by professional debunkers against early Vermonters — that they showed an unscrupulous, almost criminal shortsightedness and greed for immediate profit at no matter what cost, because year after year they sent all that potash out of the state instead of returning it as fertilizer to the robbed and impoverished soil. As reasonably accuse doctors in the Middle Ages for not taking antiseptic precautions against infections. Nobody till

A great deal of anxious thought is now being given once more to potash production, not only in the United States, but in all modern countries. In Italy, efforts are being made to exploit the volcanic deposits of lava and leucite. In Palestine, the saline waters of the Dead Sea can be made to yield potash. The salt deposits in Germany will last that country for a thousand years. France has plenty in the deposits of Alsace. Our American technologists are studying ways and means to utilize our many mineral deposits, and to develop the use of potash for agriculture far beyond even the present enormous amount used.

History, making up its categories out of oddly assorted materials, put up on the industry shelf, beside Florence in Italy, and Ghent in Belgium, the small inconsiderable rustic figure of Vermont in America. Each drifted into an eddy, which slowed down, became stagnant, dried up. The main current roared along, far in the distance. The only people who wanted lye made from wood-ashes were old women sot in ancient ways who still saved mutton tallow and bacon fat to make the year's supply of soap. When they died, the name potash left human houses and everyday talk to take its place as potassium in the table of elements in chemistry books. The great potash kettles in Vermont were abandoned. Some of them were left in the fields where they had so long stood on their stone or brick supports, carefully tended fires blazing under them. Some of them were drawn on ox-sleds to serve as roadside watering places. Perhaps you have filled the radiator of your car from such an "iron kittle."

Many of the original settlers of Vermont were still living when, only fifty years after their arrival in the Green Mountains, Vermont had its first encounter with the fact that the other name of life is change. The state with its folk-simple satisfactory economic formula ran head on into a stone wall familiar to humanity from its beginnings, which we mouth-fillingly call by a new name, "technological unemployment."

What would happen now?

Liebig's chemical and physical experiments with soil analysis dreamed that potash was needed for soil fertility. By 1845, the date when Liebig's discoveries became known, not an ounce of potash was leaving Vermont.

CHAPTER 11

No Important Facts or Dates —
Just Some Meditations

UNFORTUNATELY for those who write of the past, it is impossible to talk about two subjects at the same time. Since in real life a lot of things happen at the same time, the written account always comes limping in, far behind the event, looking foolish.

During the forty-odd "potash years" of our economic story, the thoughts of Vermonters were not as intensively centered on potash as the preceding chapter might indicate. In the economic field everything else was happening which naturally would happen. The soil, rich with eons of leaf mold laid over its basic sand, gravel, rocks, produced lavishly whatever crops could grow in a cool climate — wheat especially. Astonishing, isn't it, to think of wheat growing forty bushels to the acre in *Vermont* soil. It had as ready a sale — when did wheat ever fail to have a ready sale in a non-Oriental population? — as potash, but till decent roads were made it was infinitely harder to carry out to the cash-paying markets of the big world. Taxes were paid in wheat, it was bartered with the neighbors for other eatable products of field and garden, and as fast as was physically possible it was, in one way or another, carried out to the always wheat-hungry world.

Everything grew in Vermont. You should read Ira Allen's long, mouth-watering list of the varied farm and garden crops available to early Vermonters in the flush years after fields were really cleared, before the leaf mold deposits began to be worn out and washed away, before the even more fertile (and *level*) lands of Western New York and beyond began to beckon.

But there is nothing unique in this smiling passage of our history. For all the American frontier, clear out to the prairie, the early years were of exuberant fertility — and difficulty of transportation which made it impossible to get these wonderful crops to market.

Hence they were largely consumed by the people who raised them. Such good eating few plain people in other countries have ever had.

My own childhood dates back only to sixty and seventy years ago — "modern times" my grandfather's generation thought — but such a treasure-packed cellar was very familiar to me. I was often sent down, with an old chisel and a hammer, to chip off a week's supply of sweetenin' from the big barrel of dark crystallized maple sugar (white sugar was for company). Or with a basket to bring up potatoes from the bin, carrots from the box of sand, onions from the hanging shelves on which they were spread out, bushels and bushels of them, or — disagreeable sloppy task for a child — to fish out a slippery chunk of salt pork from the brine in a barrel. It was pleasanter to reach down from its hook a flitch of bacon, or a well-smoked shoulder of pork, to carve out a piece of cooking butter from the supply laid down under salt the summer before, to pick out from the water glass six or a dozen cooking eggs, and from the barrels pie-apples (with specks of decay) and eating apples, the sound, red-cheeked Northern Spies which later, polished to brilliance, would light up the side-table in the dining room. Their presence would go far beyond the dining room, and pervade the house with an aroma which, mingled with the smell (not disagreeable to a child) of creosote from the chimneys, became the characteristic odor of home, bringing back childhood with as actual a presence as Proust's famous little madeleine cake. From the pantry upstairs came dried peas for soup, dried beans to be baked for Saturday-night supper, and thick cream, sweet for baked potatoes and gravy, sour for biscuits, from the top of the milk in the great pans crowding the shelves.

It does no harm to celebrate the Horn of Plenty of those days, because the story of Vermont is often told as if it had always been meager, pinched and anxious. But there is nothing in the picture especially characteristic of the Green Mountains. People of my age, brought up in Wisconsin or Ohio or Western New York rural regions, have exactly similar old-time memories of eating affluently at no cash cost. Industrialism has changed all that in Vermont, as elsewhere.

In our economic life there were passages quite different from those in other regions; they became part of our tradition, alive and hence growing — as, I think, our tradition still lives and grows. There were two animals, sheep and horses, then familiar to all country people, which for a long time had a very special position in Vermont life.

The relation of man to the animals he has lived with — from the cave age to the machine age — has been a vital one, to which many scratched-on-rock pictures bear witness.

We became so used to the presence around us of these word-less, flesh and blood helpers that we took them for granted. We never seriously thought about any effect upon us of our relations with them. We have not realized that our personalities must have been altered by our responsibility for them, and our hearts molded by their dependence on us. It has not occurred to us that our long observation of them and their ways, sinking into our sub-conscious, may have helped give us more understanding of the animal each one of us lives with, all his days — his own body.

This eons-old influence is now dimming. Animals have begun slowly to make their exit from our human stage. What will take the place of the animal comradeship which has come along with us from our very first steps as human beings — until now? If we have learned anything from experience, we know that that place cannot be filled by animals as luxuries, or as price tags proving income, or as idle, petted, neurotic parasites. Animals have per-sonalities, as everyone knows who has ever loved one. No more than men and women can they develop to full psychological maturity and dignity of character without any useful part to play in the scheme of things. And now their only recognized genuine usefulness is as companions for children. Our relations with kept animals has nothing in common with the older, organically sound relation, when animals had their allotted places in the great strug-gle for survival.

In the last analysis this struggle to survive has been, in all ages, what has kept us men and women on our feet. Till now. But as always, tomorrow brings change from today. Perhaps what man's growing mastery of science is doing is to give us a new kind of alternative to face — no longer "struggle or die," but "struggle for new goals or rot." The new goal is to raise the plane of human life for all — the intellectual, moral, aesthetic plane. Animals cannot help us to reach the goal. They cannot see it, any more than they can see the beauty of a spacious view from a mountain top. Perhaps the slow, almost unobserved disappearance, of animals as our fellow-workers is a sign of our turn away from the past, towards a new future. The desperate clutch at them as pets, as useless ornaments living in a psychological vacuum, may be due to our unconscious consternation at the departure of so visible a part of our past. Our hearts, if not our minds, are dismayed to see them silently moving towards the exit sign, leaving us alone with the machine — and with each other.

In Vermont the change has come, or is coming, with a speed which makes it plainer to the eye and heart than in many other regions. The "age of animals" lasted long here, in our nonurban state. And while it lasted it had, because of the small numbers involved, a far more intimate connection with human life than in ranches of vast pastureland where the individual identity of animals has long, like that of big-city people, been merged in a featureless mass of great herds or flocks. The life of Vermont men and women has always been colored by the absence of immense numbers of human beings. Our relations with each other have been individual and personal. So with our animals. Our contact with our flocks and herds was close enough so that the difference between one and another individual member of the group (as great a difference in animals as in man) could be recognized. Our personal acquaintance (it has been nothing less) with these sentient beings has been used in Vermont as authentic raw material in the effort to make some sense out of living.

Lest this statement lie passive and blank on the page, as so many abstractions do, I'll give you one concrete example, out of old Canfield family talk.

Although it is a story about sheep, this especial episode is a satiric one, not colored with the weary, sometimes pitying, often exasperated patience enforced on those who take care of sheep. For I never heard of anybody who admired the character of sheep. Even the gentlest human personalities in contact with them are annoyed by their lack of brains, courage and initiative, by their extraordinary ability to get themselves into uncomfortable or dangerous situations and then wait in inert helplessness for someone to rescue them.

But my especial Canfield sheep story has nothing touching or exasperating in it — just laughter, animating meditations on the nature of life, as only laughter can do.

When my great-grandfather was a lad, late in the eighteenth century, he was once sent before breakfast to let out the sheep inside the barn so that they could reach the watering trough. He opened the big door, went to the sheepfold inside, let down its bars, and stood aside to watch the flock, led by the majestically authoritative ancient ram, file sedately towards the door. Around their pattering feet, the dust of the barn floor rose in a thin cloud.

But they did not go out. When the old ram who was their dictator-leader came to the open door, he halted, shaking his great horned head in uncertainty. Behind him, all the flock stood still — patient, incurious, docile, awaiting the orders of their Duce. The farm boy who was my great-grandfather could not see anything to bar their way. He pushed his way through the submissive sheep, till he could see what the ram saw: the just-risen sun sent through a knothole in the barn wall a long ray across the opening of the door. In the dusty air of the barn it looked like a solid yellow bar, about the height of the shoulders of the sheep.

As my young great-grandfather looked, he saw the ram realize his responsibility for those followers of his, who depended upon him to make up their minds. Gathering his haunches under him, he launched himself into the air, sailed over the impalpable ray of light as over a wooden rail — and trotted across the barnyard to the watering trough. The sheep behind him did not question his decision. If their Duce ordered a leap it was for them to leap. The next one in line sprang high, and triumphantly cleared the airy bar of transparent sunshine. The farm boy stared. The third sheep rose into the air, his forelegs doubled up under him to avoid knocking against the ray of light, landed on the other side, proud of his feat. My great-grandfather began to laugh. One by one every sheep accepted the dictum of their ruler that only by a mighty leap could the watering trough be reached. The boy laughed harder and harder. Some of the flock faced with this unexpected challenge, flinched, drew back, hesitated, but in the end every one of them seemed to mutter to himself whatever is sheep-language for "Heil Hitler," tautened his muscles and heroically made the plunge. The farm boy leaned against the wall of the barn, weak with hilarity.

He went in to have breakfast. Over his corn-meal mush he described the scene. His grandfather was there, his father and mother and assorted brothers and sisters. They all laughed, but the grown-ups, in discussing it, made some naturally caustic comments on the idiocy of the follow-my-leader way of managing life.

Years later, the children who had heard that story told it to their children, repeated the comments of their elders and added others drawn from their own later observation of human ways. Not a generation of our folks since then, but have heard that story as a sharp-edged warning about the tiresome, futile and often deadly quality of docile refusal to question the party line — *any* party line. We have been put on our guard and fortified against servility masked as loyalty by a ram which was old and wrinkled a century and a half ago.

CHAPTER 12

Boom and Bust

> If you want to know what a man is really
> like, take notice how he acts when he loses
> money.
>
> OLD PROVERB

MY young great-grandfather's wild fit of laughter over the sheep-homage to the principle of authority was so early that those sheep were just sheep, nondescript and undistinguished, useful for their contribution to stockings, dresses, coats, blankets. They were not at all prized for food, because the taste of mutton was then disliked — still is, by many older Vermonters, still is by most people forced to associate with the bothersome, silly, smelly animals. Every farm had a flock, every farm boy learned how to take care of them. Nobody gave more thought to them than to the mongrel hens picking up their living around the kitchen door.

Yet even while my great-grandfather laughed, distant Europe was distracted by political upheavals, one unexpected result of which was to provide Vermont with a gate through the stone wall of technological unemployment. Once more, as with potash, remote capillaries of production in the Green Mountains turned out to be living parts of the organism of world commerce.

Napoleon's goings on had a great deal to do with the Vermont sheep epic. But before Napoleon was the French Revolution and the beheading of Louis XVI. Our ancestors here kept up with world events, certainly heard about those two faraway events. But we may be sure that they did not dream that the guillotine of 1793 would by a chain reaction open a new era of prosperity for Vermont.

It went this way: the Spanish royal family were naturally outraged by the beheading of a king, any king. Spain became a fervent member of the first European coalition against France. But after Napoleon came to power, he made short work of dominating the Peninsula. A secret treaty of 1800, and another of 1803, laid

Spain helpless before him, involved that country in a war with England, and also (because its aristocracy at that time had neither decency nor strength) in a series of disastrous domestic intrigues. These turned the Spanish nation, politically, economically, socially and legally, upside down and inside out. The customs, laws, ordinances of old Spain bent, broke, vanished. Valuables formerly reserved to the nobility lay open to anyone with energy to step in quickly and help himself.

The valuable objects easiest to appropriate were flocks of the great Spanish Merino breed. Formerly reserved to grandees, they had been until then like so many sacred cows in Spanish economics.

The breed had originated in Africa, had been brought to the Peninsula by the Moors before the discovery of America, and had become a notable source of great wealth. Readers of Don Quixote will remember that huge flocks of these animals crossed and recrossed Spain as early as the sixteenth century. Because they belonged to the Crown and to grandees, and brought in much money, the health and growth of sheep were safeguarded by special privileges. The attempt to export a single one of them was an offense legally punishable by death.

In the free for all, political fight of the early nineteenth century, some of the Spanish grandees took a beating, their huge flocks of valuable sheep being confiscated. People from other lands had long yearned to introduce Spanish Merinos to their own countries. Now, unnoticed in the confusion, Wellington's invading army sent a flock to the British king. But Merinos never throve in the damp, mild, equable British climate. A number were brought to Connecticut by the American minister at Madrid, and several thousands to this country by William Jarvis, American consul in Lisbon. You probably never heard his name. It is revered in Vermont.

Mr. Jarvis, or "The Consul," as he is generally called in Vermont, was born during the American Revolution, son of a successful Boston physician. When he grew up he went into business, signed too many notes for associates and came to the financial disaster which often follows signing notes. With integrity and courage he personally took on the responsibility for large debts.

To make a new start, the then penniless young merchant sailed as supercargo on a ship going on a business venture to Corunna in Portugal. This chance voyage was like the throwing out of the frail, single thread on which a whole web is expertly spun.

At that time it was hard to get Americans to serve as consuls (especially since the young U.S.A. paid no salary, and fees were uncertain). The upright young Bostonian was soon consul at Lisbon. This official position did not at all cramp his business style. He was an honest man but he knew his way around. Early Boston merchants did. When the political, military and economic situation of Spain and Portugal became chaotic misery, Mr. Boston Jarvis in Lisbon and Mr. Connecticut Humphrey in Madrid were on the spot with what was needed.

There is a certain lack of agreement as to the exact procedure of Mr. Jarvis at Lisbon and Mr. Humphrey in Madrid in getting hold of the thousands of precious Merino sheep which from 1810 to 1811 they shipped to the new United States. Mr. Humphrey's story is that when he prepared to return to the United States, a testimonial farewell gift of bars of silver was offered to him. He reports that he said he could not accept this, but would be very glad to take in its place some of the famous Spanish Merino flocks. To which the Spanish officials replied ("the more it changes, the more it is the same thing") that this would be against the law. They couldn't do it. But if Mr. Humphrey cared to get together a flock and put it on ships to America, officialdom would look the other way.

As for Mr. Jarvis's being allowed to purchase the sacred animals, it is said that the armies, French, Spanish, English, then marching and countermarching across wretched and helpless Spain, were made up of soldiers as hungry as all soldiers, and that wherever they came across a flock, they slaughtered for food the sheep which had an almost inestimable value as breeding stock. Another explanation, historically pretty well documented, is that as the French military invaders drove further south into the heart of Spain, the Spanish government (this meant Spanish grandees) found themselves alarmingly short of funds, and by under-the-counter sales turned some of their flocks into cash assets.

Mr. Jarvis himself was discreetly vague about these details of the early stages of great adventure of his sheep importation. When he talked about it — as he did — he saw it imaginatively as what it really became, an enormous help to the struggling economy of the new, poor American Federation of States to which he was sincerely devoted.

Probably all of these reasons contributed to the dramatic crossing of the Atlantic by those worth-their-weight-in-gold sheep. The facts are carefully listed in the reports of the collectors of American ports. To the horrible Goya pictures of "Disasters of War" portraying shrieking Spain, bleeding and torn, these official American statistics add a detail — a couple of Anglo-Saxons, profiting by Spain's misery, taking advantage of the murk of smoke and flame, quietly driving off to their own countries flocks which had been for centuries one of the great sources of Spanish wealth.

From the Byronic and romantic point of view, it was not heroic work. But it was probably the best thing anybody could have done; for from chaos they were salvaging living seeds of great value, the harvest from which in a few decades had spread to the far corners of the globe.

You'd think to read Vermont books about the great Merino years here, that our state was the only place in the New World to which these sheep were taken. That is partly due to our natural provincial vanity; partly to the fact that other American states, having by this time a much more diversified economic life than Vermont, never made an epic out of sheep, as was done in the Green Mountains. The figures show that at the Port of New York between September 8, 1810, and April 26, 1811, fifty-two vessels arrived from Spain on which were shipped over nine thousand Merino sheep. During the same time, eight more vessels arrived, with Merino sheep, "to an undeterminable number." This means that over ten thousand were shipped to New York alone, during a period of eight months and twenty days. Including other ships which arrived from Spain with Merino sheep at different American ports, the total is estimated at 17,197. Out of this number, between four and five hundred were brought to his Vermont farm by Consul Jarvis.

What happened to the rest? In the main their story is easy to trace, for almost all records were carefully kept, because of the value of the breed.

In the Southern ports, their rare distinction did them no good. A contemporary record says: "Evidently the Merinos were not appreciated south of Pennsylvania, where business was very dull. Few sheep were sold. The consignees were ignorant of the care and best management of them, and sheep were soon badly diseased." These animals fell wretchedly sick and died if they were neglected. Like the making of potash, this new source of wealth would flow only if handled with more steadiness, intelligence and patient endurance than could be counted on in labor available in the South at that time. The relatively few animals which were bought seem for the most part to have melted away unnoticed.

In Mr. Humphrey's Connecticut, in Pennsylvania, New York and other Northern states, the sheep were well received, well cared for, the quality of the fleece improved. As a matter of fact, not often mentioned in our legend-lore, a great many of the Vermont Merinos came from the Connecticut Humphrey flocks. But even as early as this, those larger states had their collective eye fixed on industrial production and commerce. Farming was by no means so important to them as other activities.

In Vermont, with potash income fast drying up, this opportunity was eagerly seized.

In Spain the sheep, for centuries the highly prized source of wealth for the grandees, had been much better housed and fed than their dismally poor shepherds. In some sections of America large numbers of these rare creatures were like superior refugees perishing for lack of appreciation of their value. In Vermont in the first half of the nineteenth century, they found a climate cold enough to develop the magnificence of their fleeces, they found sweet upland pasturage, running brooks everywhere; but far more, they found a royal welcome. Vermonters young and old were familiar with sheep, already knew how to take care of them, were not daunted by the amount of work involved. The Swiss often say that the spectacular success of their dairy products, sold all over Europe even in countries with good dairy farms of their own, is due to no secret agricultural formulae but to the fact that all Swiss hired men are high-school graduates. On the same principle the Merinos throve incredibly in the care, not of ignorant half-starved serf-shepherds, but of literate people who, with the help of their families, took care of their own animals.

How those Merinos throve! It was legendary. In fact Vermont Merinos and what they did for Vermont have become a legend in our folklore, with all the exaggerations and omissions typical of folklore. Sheep, when in good health, well taken care of, and in a favorable climate, reproduce their kind with such speed that in no time (so to speak) the few hundreds brought in had become thousands. The moderate-sized flocks which had grazed in Consul Jarvis's Vermont pastures and which he generously sold for low prices to his Green Mountain neighbors grew as if by magic. After some ups and downs in the graph, Vermont had by 1840 more than five sheep to every inhabitant — Pennsylvania and Maine one to each person. There were one hundred eighty-five sheep to every square mile in Vermont as against sixty-five per square mile in New Hampshire.

People of my age used to know old folks who had lived through part of what is sometimes called the "Merino mania." As they told us about it, the period sounded like the tulip craze in Holland, or the South Sea Bubble. Ordinary, family-sized Vermont farms had flocks of a thousand or more. Where there were such flocks, they brought in sums which surprise us now to read about. Leading sheep-growers sold, in a year, from ten to twenty thousand dollars worth of sheep and put as much back in improving the quality of the flock. As farmers they had formerly been well satisfied when their year's work had fed and clothed the family and added a few hundred dollars to the family savings.

The more the Vermont Merinos became known, the greater the demand for them in the big world. The greater the demand, the more intensive and skillful the care given to them in Vermont, the hotter the pride in them, the more ambitious the plans made for developing not their numbers, for Vermont pasturage was limited, but their quality.

Yet the numbers too seem, now, to have been very great. The mountains from which so many trees had been cut off to make potash were turned into fields. Photographs taken toward the last of the Merino epoch show our Red Mountain, on the lower slope of which my home stands. It is now densely wooded to our front door; but then it lay open almost to the top, in a stone-walled pattern of sheep pastures.

There seemed no end to the demand. The world was the market. I can remember when there were old men living in Addison County who had been many times around Cape Horn with a cargo of sheep for Australia. One big flock of Vermont Merinos for breeding was taken by ship to Panama, and under the guidance of the Vermont farm owners was driven through those steep, tropical mountains, through jungles and wild Indians and cactus, down to sea level on the other side. Thence they were taken by ship to California, where they multiplied with fantastic rapidity into vast flocks.

May I at this point pause for another exclamation of self-pity? To try to set down what happened in any corner of history — the complex doings that is, of any group of complex human beings — is a hopeless undertaking. During the years of the nineteenth century when the Merino business was running its exciting course in Vermont, up and down from one soaring climax to another, from one collapse to the next, all the thousand other vital activities of human life were taking place here, as elsewhere — personal, communal, spiritual, intellectual, political. It seems absurd to speak only of sheep, when the War of 1812 was coming and going; when potash-making was vanishing, when with whirlwind speed industrial production was replacing handcrafts; when the Erie Canal was opened, and young Vermonters began to pour west; when some Vermont girls stayed at home, while others by the dozens, by the scores, by the hundreds, went off to the textile mills of Massachusetts; when the California gold rush blared wildly and died down to silence; when Vermont schools improved enormously, and libraries improved — some; when farmers began to experiment with dairy products; when the tremendous drama of the Civil War played out its four year-long tragic acts; when the lumber business, getting at last a chance at transportation facilities, swelled high, made fortunes (Vermont-size fortunes), was crowded out of markets glutted by the pillaged forests of the West and North West. Yet if I am to tell coherently the story of

sheep in Vermont, which certainly had an effect, although an unexpected one, on our Vermont tradition, I must for the time ask
you to stay with me while I stick to my muttons, till the tale is
told.

The printed, written and oral records of the Merino sheep epic
in Vermont show that it seemed, to the people engaged in it, as
permanent a source of prosperity as making automobiles in the
economic life of today. As the prosperity of the woolen guilds
in fourteenth-century Florence. As potash in the late eighteenth
and early nineteenth centuries.

Human beings are apt to lose their heads over the minutiae of
any occupation they take seriously. It is not surprising that the
blood pressure of sober Vermont farmers rose as high over the
technically fine points of their Merinos as that of antique specialists
over the rungs of chairs of differing dates. You would have to read
for yourself to believe that such intensity of feeling, such jeal-
ousies and recriminations, such passionate discussion could have
been based on the depths of wrinkles in a sheep's pelt, the amount
of oil in the fleece, the length and crimp of the wool fibers.

There are handsomely printed old volumes written by Vermont
Merino *aficionados* crammed with carefully compiled and documented statistics about pedigrees, about gold medals, about
weight, about the quality of fleece as shown by measurements of
fibers, about the use made of these fleeces by the woolen mills
springing up all over Vermont. These volumes have portraits of
some of the noted Vermont flock-masters (as they were called),
chin-whiskered men of substance, with yeoman names — Stick-
ney, Rich, Hammond, Crane, Sandford.

There are also portraits of individual prize winners, each one
with a name. This was before the era of photographic illustrations.
The portraits of the sheep are careful engravings, done with such
respectful admiration for the famous animals that some of their
stupid sheep-countenances have an almost George-Washington
dignity. Their names show affectionate familiarity — Old Greasy,
Matchless, Golden Fleece, King of Spain, Old Wrinkled.

More money was involved in sheep-growing than Vermont had
ever seen. A common price for a good animal was eight hundred

dollars. Flock-masters sold an occasional ram for thirty-five hundred dollars. One flock-master in Vermont, just before the end of one of the booms, refused to sell his flock of two hundred sheep for fifty thousand dollars. That may not sound enormous to you. It did — and does — in Vermont.

Not only money but prestige for the State came from the sheep. At a great International Exposition in Paris, Vermont Merino sheep carried off two out of three gold medals, seven out of eight bronze medals. At an agricultural exhibit in Hamburg — yes, Hamburg in Germany — twelve Vermont Merinos were exhibited, the only American sheep shown against nearly eighteen hundred European Merinos. They took two first prizes. These sheep were sold for five thousand dollars to a Silesian breeder.

Purebred Merino rams were sold in large numbers for breeding to South America and Australia. Trainloads of Vermont sheep also fanned out along the rails from the Green Mountain State to — to everywhere in the west in our country, to those great plains which, like the spacious prairies of Argentina and Australia, were admirably suited for sheep-raising.

Did nobody in all this time stop to think that Spain had kept the monopoly of its Merinos only by making it an offense punishable by death to export even one of them? Was no Vermonter ever alarmed by the thought that when all have got the seed, all may have the flower?

Not one. At least in a lifetime's browsing in books on this subject and listening to old folks' talk about it, I have come across not one word of concern on this point.

There is something here which is worth trying to understand. Only a few decades separated the Vermont flock-master from the Spanish aristocrat who had formerly monopolized the Merinos now being sold with an epic disregard of consequences. Yet in those few decades a complete turnover of public opinion had taken place. The spirit of the times, that vast invisible Gulf Stream which carries us all resistlessly from where we are towards where, without knowing it, we are going to be, had shifted its direction. It poured through this small corner of the agricultural-economic field, and swept those chin-whiskered Vermont farmers into a new approach to human affairs. An idea quite unheard of in the past was becoming more and more a recognized part of the present, and — to forward-looking people — the only possible basis for the future.

This idea, which would have seemed like lunacy to the Spanish aristocrats, is that the more widely something of value to all is distributed to all, the better for all.

No, this is not womanish (old-womanish at that) up-in-the-air idealism. It is the recognized base of modern business, expressed in hard-and-fast principles familiar to us, such as "The chances for profit all round are greater in a fast-moving free market than in a stagnant closed one," and "Wide sales at reasonable prices add up to more profit than a high return on a few luxury items," and "Commerce and industry will be choked to death by their own products unsold, unless the masses can afford mass consumption."

Are you laughing at my naïveté in suggesting that the Vermont flock-masters cared for anything except to make all the money they could out of their sheep? I am setting down the facts as I find them, and I ask you to note that the Spanish grandees cared as exclusively for their own personal profits. But their instinct (dating from the past) was to stand guard over a monopoly. The Vermont instinct, based on a divination of the future, was the opposite. In this particular case, both parties failed to call the turn of the cards. The aristocrats lost their shirts. The Green Mountain flock-masters lost those dazzling paper profits.

Do we conclude that neither was successful? That depends on the definition of success. Vermont flock-masters took, and Vermonters reminiscing still take, a sincere pride in the fact — although it was their personal ruin — that the vast flocks in the Argentine, in Australia, on the spacious plains of our own West, grew in large part from sheep born and brought up in the Green Mountains. Could it be that those Vermonters were somehow deficient in grasping the bookkeeper's standards of life-fulfillment? Some of their habits point that way.

For another item in this story is the fact, rather odd in prudent, thrifty people, that although abundant cash flowed through the fingers of the Vermont flock-masters while the boom lasted, not much was left to them when it busted. When the Golden Fleece no longer hung on the Vermont tree, there were mighty few extra dollars left in the families of the flock-masters. The point seems to be that they had never focused all their attention on cash profits, but had cared more about the reputation of their sheep than about the money they brought in.

There was a lot of nonsense about that "reputation." Parmalee Prentice, during a lifetime of open-minded, objective research and experiment in a related field, has shown that some of the technically fine "points" required for the blue ribbon at a cattle show have no bearing on milk or beef production, but originated in ancient Carthage, and are still with us only because of humanity's inertia in questioning long-established customs. The great flocks of sheep outside of Vermont, which had grown up to thousands on plains all around the globe, probably did not have the deeply wrinkled pelt which was a show point, perhaps were not so "oiled" as the fleece of the famous Old Greasy. But they provided tons of serviceable wool for human use, and tons were needed. The small fields of Vermont could not compete at all with such vast sheep-factories, once the factories were stocked.

One sharp peak broke the downward slanting graph. During the years of the Civil War, miles of woolen cloth were needed for army uniforms, and as a substitute in civilian clothing for the cotton no longer coming in from the South. For a while Merino rams once more sold for fabulous prices, one of them bringing five thousand dollars (as much as many a dirt-farmer of that period could have saved out of his lifetime earnings). Then suddenly, after 1867, prices slid down.

No more sheep were raised for wool, only pure-blood Merino rams for stocking flocks in South America, in Australia, and in the West. But after a while, such is the nature of rapidly breeding animals, those distant flocks were numerous enough to need no more. And that was that. Not slowly like the dwindling of potash manufacturing, but with an audible clang, like a clock striking the end of an hour, the sheep business of Vermont came to its end.

What was left?

Visibly and materially not much. For a time the sheep-barns stood empty, or were used to store hay. But it was not worth the cost to keep the foundations, sills and roofs in repair. Little by little the weather-beaten old buildings sagged, leaned, and sank gently into the bramble-covered low mounds which are their graves.

For a while the woolen mills went on operating. They had been the energetic industrial response to the valuable new farm crop, providing a new raw material at hand. The first of these, which had been built even before the earliest years of Merino sheep, had been the carding mills, needed for the production of woolen cloth by women using the spinning wheel. The spinning wheels had multiplied. It was said that in places in Vermont, early in the nineteenth century, the traveler as he rode into a village could hear the hum of the spinning wheels in every house. The machine production of woolen yarn knocked the spinning wheels out of the living rooms of homes, up attic for a century, and thence down into antique shops. Power looms were set up on every stream big enough to furnish power for simple machinery. Those farmers who were especially marked with the yeoman instinct to add some kind of paying business to agriculture did less plowing and planting and drove from neighbor to neighbor collecting wool from their sheep, which they took back to small woolen mills set up and manned by those of their sons who were especially marked with American mechanical-mindedness.

At that time it really did look as though our Vermont economic structure was settled for keeps. To produce raw wool with farming skill, and then on the spot with mechanical skill to spin and weave it into quality yard goods — here was a balanced economy that would last.

That's all they knew! For a while after the end of sheep-raising, the wheels of the woolen mills went on turning. Not having enough Vermont wool to weave, they began to import wool from Australian sheep, the descendants of their grandfather's flocks. But transportation facilities have never been so easy to come by in Vermont as to waste them in uneconomic doings. One by one, many of the small Vermont woolen mills have given up. And now the clock of technology seems to be ticking off to its end one of the most ancient and stable of all human activities — the woolen industry itself. Not only in Vermont, but everywhere, wool has lost its old priority, with the discovery that yard goods which look and feel like wool can be made, fantastically, out of skim milk or chemically treated rocks extruded into threads. Shades of Old Greasy and the Golden Fleece!

The most visible leftovers of the 1,600,000 sheep of the Vermont sheep era are some fine houses. While that fancy money was pouring in and rushing out, some of the flock-masters built excellent homes, large and handsome. They were early enough in the nineteenth century to escape the 1870 and later gingerbread trickings-out. They still stand square, dignified, good-looking, the ornament and pride of their neighborhood. When in the midst of the usual low, story-and-a-half Vermont houses, you see a sizable one of fine proportions, built on ample lines, with many rooms, you can be fairly sure that the money for it came from sheep-raising. You can also be fairly sure that no sheep are now owned by the family living in it.

There are so few left in Vermont (less than nine thousand) that automobilists stop their cars to take photographs of an occasional flock in a pasture near the road. They are mostly near the road now, because there's no leaving them in the remote pasture, high on the mountains where they formerly fed. For two reasons: marauding dogs would get in, as they often did, even during the sheep epic, and, just for the dog-fun of it, playfully slit the throats of dozens of them in a single night. Secondly, those pastures are no more. Weeds covered them, then brush, then saplings, then young trees, then thick forests. When I was a little girl (sixty odd years ago) there were still Canfield sheep on West Mountain, in a high pasture, called the "Downer lot" (the original eighteenth-century owner having been named Downer). My Great-uncle Zed, so ancient that he could walk only with two canes, showed me how he kept track of them from the valley. Sitting on the front porch of my great-grandmother's house, with a long, ship-captain's telescope, he counted the white specks moving to and fro on the greensward of the old pasture. The sheep have long been gone, almost as long as Uncle Zed has, and so has the Downer lot. The only traces of it in the midst of the beech and oak and maple trees are some tumbled-down mossy stone walls dimly marking the boundaries of the pasture that is no longer there.

*   *   *

This chronicle has been a tale of death, the death of hopes that were bright. Have you heard a knell tolling from the pages? If you have, it has come to your ears from some other tradition than that of Vermont. The sheep epic left practically no material traces in the life of our state. But something of lasting, human value was left. In the collapse of the sheep boom, our tradition encountered a new test. It had not been hard in the early years for all Vermonters zestfully to enjoy life without having much money. Could their tradition carry some of them, without deep psychological wounds, through the ordeal, even harder for all men and women, of living on less money than they had had, of having a large income, and then losing it? I answer my own question cheerfully. Yes, it could and it did.

When the sheep industry folded up, the exasperation and disappointment of those who had prospered by it were keen. Of course. But it was not taken as reason for despair. The farmer who one year sold a ram for thousands of dollars and the next couldn't get a dollar for the same animal never dreamed of putting a pistol to his temple, as we hear stock-market operators sometimes do after a big money loss. No women shut themselves up in decaying, once handsome houses, to brood over the shame of being poor. The sons who had looked forward confidently to plenty of money, did not lounge on rotting back porches in apathetic hopelessness. They were off, earning their way through college, or teaching school in a new Wisconsin community. If the back porch began to rot, the flock-master who once had thought he was so rich and now, just like anybody, was poor, jacked it up and put new sills under it. Or if it was too far gone, he tore it cleanly down, sawed and split the debris into fire-wood length and stacked it up in the woodshed, under cover. (I hope you understand I am not talking about literal, material back porches.)

The way this great money loss was taken in Vermont is the justification, I think, for setting the facts down. If it were no more than an account of the Vermont sheep industry, why should you know about it? That Hecuba would certainly be nothing to you.

But no matter where or how or when we live, we are all in the same human boat. It is no idle curiosity that makes us wish to know how other men and women have taken events which are as likely as not to happen to us.

Sweeping economic changes, due to causes beyond anybody's control, have always been as common in human existence as rainstorms. They are a factor in life as old as the bronze age, which certainly put out of business a great many honest, highly skilled workers in wood and flint. We cannot hope to halt such change. Only one thing is partially in our control — how we stand up to those incessant shifts of material circumstance.

The collapse of the sheep prosperity was a dismal event to Vermonters, not to a few, to many. But when I first began asking elderly Vermonters how the economic catastrophe was "taken" by the older generation, they usually faced me with the blank expression which means either "I didn't hear what you said," or "I don't know what you are talking about." Occasionally one of them fished up some such vague answer as "So far as I can remember, things went along about as usual . . . no special changes . . . except that then everyone began to do more lumbering . . . started to build up the dairy herds."

Such answers were so improbable that I widened my research (if academic tradition will permit me to label as "research" anything except consultation of printed or manuscript documents). As a matter of fact, I also consulted documents, I read those parts of local and town histories which are of devastating dullness, but priceless as detailed records of the past. And I kept on questioning people of my age who remembered what their fathers and grandfathers had felt about things in general.

No knell tolled for "reduced circumstances." There were tollings of other knells, plenty of them. Individual personal sorrows, tragedies, mistakes, had been "taken hard." But never the greatest loss in prosperity Vermont had ever known.

There was so much testimony, all pointing the same way, that no one could entertain the slightest doubt about what happened. But why it happened that way remained a puzzling question. Sometimes past motivation is cleared up by transposing the problem into modern dress. I tried that experiment, like this: let us suppose that, through some changes in stock-voting control, a

Mr. Smith loses his position as general manager of a large corporation. Mr. Smith is a capable man and soon gets a job with another firm, but many rungs lower down on the administrative ladder, and at a salary so reduced that retrenchment is called for. The Smiths move into a small house in a less expensive part of town. While far from destitute, they are miserable. Unable to throw lavish parties, they drop — or are squeezed — out of their old circle. Mr. Smith gives up golf. None of Mrs. Smith's former friends come to the new house for a cocktail or a cup of tea. The son, no longer at a fashionable prep school, knows that even if he manages a college education, he will not have the right background to be chosen by a "really good" fraternity. The daughter, with no invitations to country club dances, despairs of meeting a fiancé whom she and her mother would consider suitable. They do not — because at heart they feel it would be beneath them — make any social contacts with their new neighbors. Dust and ashes!

There you have a sound plot-outline for a realistic novel laid almost anywhere at almost any period. Only a little analysis is needed to make it clear that the loss of actual money, representing the price of meat, potatoes, and warm overcoats is not the root of the Smith family tragedy. What really hurts them is the loss of surplus money required as dues for belonging to a social circle, the charm of which largely depends on the fact that a great many other people, who would like to be in it, are excluded. The Smiths can hardly be blamed for being snobs. They are only accepting the scale of values current in their environment. They were brought up to those values. They have brought up their children to measure human happiness by that scale. What is the explanation for the totally different reaction of those Green Mountain sheep-raisers?

It was my friend, the old Vermonter, Dr. Russell, who gave me the clue. His father and grandfather had been prosperous farmers in Addison County where, during the boom, sheep outnumbered human beings by eleven to one. They had been up to their necks in sheep-raising. Their two lives had covered the whole Merino period.

"How did your older generation stand the big comedown when the bottom dropped out of the market?" I asked.

The doctor answered equably, "Well, I never heard they took it as a comedown. They hadn't ever set up to be better than their neighbors just because they made money out of sheep."

Those words, so casually pronounced in that take-it-for-granted tone, brought up before my mind the many families we have all known whose money had come not from Merinos but from oil, or silver mines, or plantation-raised cotton, or Wall Street, or railroads, and who very definitely were convinced that a rise in their income did give them the right to "set themselves up as better than their neighbors." Loss of money for them brought with it the loss — far harder to bear — of social position.

Modern biologists tell us that, as far as innate characteristics go, the average of any human group is about like that of any other. The differences between them are due chiefly to the training (much of it wordless) they receive from those around them as they grow up. "Tradition" is of course another name for such training.

Those men and women of Vermont were not by nature more unworldly than anybody else. If they did not suffer anguish over the loss of fortune, if the personalities of their sons and daughters were not warped by that loss, was it because according to their tradition — the Vermont tradition — an impressive inventory of capital (pleasant and reassuring though it doubtless was) did not raise its possessors in any marked, publicly acknowledged degree above those less wealthy. It could not establish them in a conspicuously superior class in a society so democratic — or, for people who see it that way, so boorishly crude and primitive — that no fixed social hierarchy exists. Consequently to them the loss of money meant no more than the loss of the material objects it might have bought, not the loss of pride or position or gratified vanity. After the crash, the flock-master remained as likely as ever to be chosen justice of the peace or selectman. His wife was not cold-shouldered at meetings of the Ladies Aid Society. Perhaps a simplified statement of the matter might be that the wealthy flock-masters and their families did not think that money lifted them into a superior social class, for a very simple reason — it didn't.

*   *   *

All this took place long ago. But we who by our free choice live in Vermont take much satisfaction that today the old tradition is still going strong here. We do not worry when we see that little cliques form among us, and hold together for a while. We know by experience that they will die before long, from malnutrition. We do not expect the clocks elsewhere in our bustling modern world to regulate themselves by the out-of-date sundial of one small, rural section of America. We can quite understand that many people (novelists especially perhaps) would be repelled by the rude lack of hereditary social gradations in our kind of life, would think it dull and monotonous. We don't find it so. In our personal and human relations we live through all the drama, all the emotional ups and downs we can stand. We can see for ourselves that for many temperaments life would be dreary without social institutions which provide the joy of excluding others from what they would like to have. That joy does not taste very sweet on our tongues. But for those who feel that without it life would be tiresome and boring — well, there are any number of other places in our nation, on the globe, where (of course if they are well-to-do) they will find it easily available. We would not object. Like the Sunderland man making his neighborly offer to help carry Ethan Allen's first wife to her grave, there's not a man among us who would not be glad to help such people get started on their search for that joy — somewhere else.

There are those, I know, who will feel that the flock-masters must have had pinched, arid souls to show no more feeling in the face of calamity. A few pages ago, I asked, "What is success?" I now ask, "What do you mean by calamity?" Personal grief breaks hearts here as everywhere. And here as elsewhere, those who grieve come after long suffering to a vision of sorrow as beauty because it grows out of love. But yes, Vermont is prosaic and dry in refusing to see any putrescent beauty or poetry in decay. It is not part of our tradition to drape emotional crape around a lost bank account.

If there is one idea which nearly two centuries of no leisured ease and of incessantly shifting economic life have beaten into our

collective Vermont minds, it is that human affairs are never un-
changing. And a very good thing, too, even from the practical
point of view. The loss of the past is often anything but a calamity.

If, as Vermonters hoped, potash manufacturing had continued
indefinitely, our steepily tilted land would have been deforested.
The crashing end of sheep-prosperity stopped the flow of money
into some individual pockets, but it was the salvation of our State.

Look back at the Vermont scene during the height of the
Merino epic — it was pictorially lovely, but the erosion-devil must
have smiled broadly to see it: those hilly pastures, laced with sweet
silver brooks (which when the snows melt or hard rains come
always go on a rampage, and gouge out channels down to bed-
rock) the thin, fine, green grass blades, nibbled closer and closer
to the earth by the teeth of the ever-increasing flock; the thousands of sharp-pointed little hoofs cutting the covering sod to
pieces — the stage was all set for a catastrophe like that which,
through goats, has overtaken the Mediterranean countryside, and,
through open cultivation, the hill farms of our American Southern mountains.

Occasionally one of our big pictorial magazines publishes an
article on soil conservation illustrated with horrifying photographs of deeply gullied hillsides, with poor, hopeless farm homes
clinging to the edges of water-ravaged chasms. When we Vermonters turn over such pages, we lift our eyes to our hills and
mountains covered to the top with soil-anchoring trees, and feel
that nobody need try to tell us that the disappearance of a past
way of life is always a loss. Those mossy and forgotten stone walls
buried in the midst of forest trees — we let summer visitors muse
in mistaken poetic melancholy over the bygone homes which,
they assume, used to stand near. It is with cheerful hearts that we
climb over them. They served their time well. But their time is
not ours. And if, as their builders intended, they had been carefully kept up to hold sheep into mountain pastures, our beautiful home state would have been a desert.

CHAPTER 13

Morgans, Knee-breeches and Moving Out of the Past

RESOLUTION passed by the Vermont Legislature in 1939:

J.R.S. 15. Joint resolution relating to 150th anniversary of the birth of the famous horse, "Justin Morgan."

Whereas, this is the year recognized as the 150th anniversary of the birth of the famous horse, "Justin Morgan," which horse not only established a recognized breed of horses named for a single individual, but brought fame, through his descendants to Vermont and thousands of dollars to Vermonters. The name "Morgan" has come to mean beauty, spirit and action to all lovers of the horse; and the Morgan horses for many years held the world's record for trotting horses, and

Whereas, the Morgan blood is recognized as foundation stock for the American Saddle Horse, for the American Trotting Horse, and for the Tennessee Walking Horse. In each of these three breeds, the Morgan horse is recognized as a foundation and, therefore, with the recognition of its value to the horse breeders of the nation, and recognition that it was in Vermont that Morgan horses were first established, therefore be it

Resolved by the Senate and House of Representatives, that a committee consisting of one senator and two representatives be appointed by the presiding officers of each body, respectively, to make some recommendation for the proper recognition of the 150th anniversary of the birth of the horse, "Justin Morgan" and to report to this present session of the General Assembly.

Is it absurd to have in a book about a human tradition a chapter about a certain kind of horse? I can't help it. Morgans really are part of our tradition. Human families in the Green Mountains lived for a century with members of the Morgan horse family. To Vermonters of my age the name has delightful associations.

The remarkable Morgan family history has a place in these pages, as you can guess from the resolution of our Legislature at the head of this chapter.

If it hadn't happened, you'd think we'd invented it to fit our Vermont notions. Yet the story is authentic and well documented enough to pass any historian's microscope. The great original horse, Justin Morgan, was brought to Vermont in 1795. That date like other facts in his life history is established by written records based on the testimony of many contemporary witnesses.

The first thing to say is that the name Justin Morgan was not, to begin with, a horse's name. It was the name of a man, who would have been completely forgotten except for a colt which came oddly into his possession. Justin Morgan, the man, was born in Springfield, Massachusetts in 1747, of a poor family. Like other New England youngsters of that century, public-school classrooms gave him a sound elementary education. Physically he was what we call "rather pindling," thin, hollow-chested. But he had, along with a good mind, a gift for music, and was willing to work as hard at educating himself musically as other men of his period worked at chopping trees and holding plow handles. For many years, he earned his living as singing-teacher in the Massachusetts district schools near Springfield.

When he was forty-one (in 1788), he sold his home place in Massachusetts. He and his wife moved up to Randolph, Vermont. In 1795 he went back to Massachusetts to try to collect some money due him there.

The debtor said he hadn't any money, but he would pay "in kind," with a three-year-old gelding, and a rather small, three-year-old colt. The colt, a dark bay, unnamed, hardly noticed, followed the other horse without being led, along the trails and rough roads all the way to Randolph, Vermont. Here Justin Morgan (the man) rented the colt for fifteen dollars a year to a man called Robert Evans, who was clearing a heavily wooded lot for somebody else. Two years later Justin Morgan (the man) died.

That is really all that is *known* of the origin of Justin Morgan (from that time on, the horse carried the name). Of course many pedigrees have been invented. They vary greatly. In one story there was a Dutch sire, in another Arab ancestors; a third claimed a French-Canadian breed, a fourth gave our Vermont horse as father a thoroughbred stallion called True Briton. No evidence supports these speculations. It has always pleased the Vermont fancy that not the most insistent pedigree fan has ever been able to prove aristocratic origin for our Morgans. They stand on their own performance.

The first thing to mention about the original horse is his remarkable ability to transmit his valuable qualities to his descendants. This ability is a rare one, its rarity as familiar to horse-breeders as to students of royal families. Flesh and blood creatures — horses, men, women — all of them have two parents, and are as likely to inherit the qualities of one as of the other. They also have more grandparents and great-great grandparents than even pedigree fans can keep track of; and, as like as not, any member of any family exasperatingly inherits the qualities of a not-at-all-esteemed great-aunt, instead of those of an illustrious father.

Here is the place to quote from an article entitled "The Morgan Horse, His Relation to Breeding" by William H. H. Murray. The literary style of this ardent horse specialist may hold your attention even if you don't care much about horses.

Of Justin Morgan alone can it be said that he founded a family. Other horses there have been of note and whose eminence was well deserved, but they passed away and left no sons so like themselves as to be distinctively theirs. "Messenger" was a remarkable horse. America owes him more than words can express. But "Messenger" lacked one thing, the power to take of other bloods and dominate them, stamping them with his imperial likeness. "Diomed" was a wonderful animal ranking on a level with "Messenger." But "Diomed" lacked that royal something which when existing in a horse makes all other families tributary to himself, that power to allow turbid currents to be mingled with the stream of his life, and yet flow on in the same pure majesty. This, neither "Diomed" nor "Messenger," nor "Bashaw," nor any other imported horses from which we trace our trotting action ever had.

Not one builded a throne and founded a nation whose population was abundant and all his children. But Justin Morgan did this thing. He stands the progenitor of a mighty

race, spread over all the land from Maine to California; and
wherever you find a Morgan horse — whether in city or
country, East or West, North or South, you know he is a
Morgan. One glance is enough; color, shape, style, limbs,
feet, head, all suggest the little horse from which he lineally
descended — Justin Morgan. How other bloods bowed in
submission to him! Ask Mr. Wallace, one of the most honest
and painstaking students of the horse, what is the superlative
test of blood. He will tell you the power to MARK descendants with its own characteristics. This is the crucial test,
beside which mere verbal pedigrees are simply bits of paper.
Apply this test to Justin Morgan (there are many horses
today who walk with plumed heads who cannot —) etc. etc.
etc.

Well, that is enough to show you that what I may be moved to
say about Morgan horses I did not invent out of whole cloth.
Justin Morgan himself lived to the great old age (for a horse)
of twenty-nine years, and died then of an accident, not of any
infirmity. He had worked and played hard all his long life, and
to the end kept his light elastic step, the brightness of his quiet
eyes, his eager willing spirit, his fabulous powers to transmit his
qualities to his sons and daughters and their offspring. As long as
horses were useful parts of human life, their numbers increased.
In the first half of the nineteenth century, Vermont stallions were
taken to California, some overland, some by ships around the
Cape. Later on, by railroad. Their sons and daughters were everywhere along the Pacific Coast. When crossed with mares descended from Spanish horses, a mount of great value for cowboys
was produced. The resolution passed by the Vermont Legislature
mentioned a number of other places and other breeds to which
the Morgan contributed. They throve especially well in Iowa
(Vermonters always have) and there was a powerful Iowa "Morgan Horse Association."
But they were not "fine horses" in the horse-show meaning,
not at all too fine an article for everyday usefulness around a working home. Some few Vermonters earned their livings by breeding, training and selling them. But that was a business. On the
farm, the Morgan, or part-Morgan horse was like Old Shep the

dog, a valued and beloved member of the family. Hardly a Vermont farm but had some part-Morgan colts and horses. They did whatever needed to be done. The saying was that "you can teach a Morgan anything, s'long as you don't take a whip to him." This lack of submissiveness made them respected by their Vermont families as well as loved.

These were farm horses. They were not taken out to daily light exercise by hired attendants. Their splendid muscles were kept in condition by raking hay, hauling logs, pulling the farm wagon or sled, or carrying the daughter of the family, riding sidesaddle, up over a mountain-pass on a social visit. Show a Morgan something that needed to be done, his head went up, his eye brightened as he tackled it. As long as horses were used on farms, the Morgan character had a notable influence on Vermont life.

I do not apologize for speaking of "the influence" a kind of horse had on the people of a region. I am trying to write something like the biography of the Vermont personality. The biography of a man often speaks of an aunt or an older brother or a teacher who, by example, helped develop certain traits in his character. Vermonters have been influenced by the example of the Morgan character.

Here are some traits of the Morgan personality. Hardiness to begin with. Unlike most valuable horses, they had no need to be coddled, or spoon-fed. They grew a winter coat of fur like a bear's, and reveled in snow and cold as an active collie dog does. They had excellent teeth and good digestions, ate what there was to eat and got the good of their food.

They walked fast. For a horse, a fast walk corresponds to the heartening cheerfulness of a person who can without boredom endure that routine which is a vital part of any human achievement. Learning to sing in opera, or to cook well, doing the minute, detailed, laboratory research necessary in biological or chemical experimentation, raising vegetables, caring for the sick — the acquiring and practicing of these and every other skill depends on the ability to endure without impatience long stretches of monotonous hard work. People without that ability never learn to be more than inept amateurs.

In the day of every working horse, there is a good deal of

walking to be done. The Morgans were working horses. Like human beings with routine, some horses turn walking into listless plodding, or make it unstable, jittery fidgeting. Anybody who has ever seen a little Morgan, stepping cheerfully along in his fast walk through mud or snow, has something in his memory to help him through inevitable dull stretches of life.

But a cheerful acceptance of routine carries neither man nor horse over the strain when work suddenly demands great strength under accurate control. There too the Morgans, to a horse, have been inspirations to those who lived with them. Justin Morgan, the father of the family, first emerges from obscurity with an astonishing record of pulling logs in clearing a piece of woodland. People who did not know him always lost money betting against his ability for such heavy work. He made a handsome, distinguished appearance (the Morgans have fine, intelligent, spirited heads), he carried himself proudly, and he was small in size. He did not look like a work horse. But his muscular equipment was wonderful. Even more important than muscles, he had to a high degree, like a gifted athlete, the focused power of suddenly concentrating his energies with split-second accuracy of timing.

No Morgan, of course, can pull like a modern Percheron. Those imported mammoths perform heavy work as millionaires buy a newspaper, without thinking. Like an ox, one of these big horses leans forward against his collar, and lets his poundage (tonnage!) make the effort. But like an ox, that poundage makes him slow and unwieldy for activities in which quick reactions are needed. Also his magnificent size costs his owner what, in Mr. Murray's language, might be called "an imperial amount" of oats and hay.

The Morgans never had the weight to work without thinking about it. But they enjoyed thinking about it. In drawing logs, for instance, they set their trigger-quick brain centers on the job. When the time came, they exploded into power, pulled the log a third of the way on impetus, stopped, drew breath, set themselves again (their bright, clear, kind Morgan eyes sparkling with pleasure in the exercise of their wits), pulled, drew breath again, pulled a third time — the log was safely on the logway at the mill, the bet was won. The little horse was drawing in deep, quiet breaths, all his mighty muscles relaxed, arching his neck to receive the rough, calloused hand of his owner, stroking him in the open gesture of fond pride all Vermonters felt for a good Morgan.

These Vermont horses had another psychological ability needed by people who do not shirk hard work — the ability not only to bend the back to heavy tasks, but to straighten that back afterwards. The Vermont boy of the first half of the nineteenth century worked all the week with his part-Morgan horse at farm drudgery, much of it heavy and dirty. But he was no clod. Nor his horse either. On Sunday afternoon, bathed, clean-shaven, in his good suit, his shoes shined, he drove the same horse, curried, sleek, stepping like a deer in light harness, to take his best girl for an outing. Or perhaps, if the boy had not come to the best-girl age, he would put the saddle on, and go off alone with his working partner for a long solitary ride over back roads and up steep lumber trails to a sun-flooded, lookout place on a mountain. For people of my age such rides are unforgettable memories of youth in Vermont. Or perhaps his little sister went for a canter along the valley road, in friendly unity with the gentle, well-mannered horse. Thus did Morgan traits help nineteenth-century Vermonters live up to their tradition that human society does not inevitably need a heavy-footed class, deformed and dulled by work, and another class to suggest by physique and bearing a doctrine revolting to us, that uselessness is in itself something to aspire to, to be proud of.

My Vermont Great-uncle Zed, whom I quote once in a while in these pages, once took me, in my childhood, to a horse show which was part of a circus, "over the line in York State." The skilled circus personnel, used to handling horses, had trained a collection of equine performers new to me then, but since seen in many a horse show. The light-harness horses filed first before the spectators. They lifted their forelegs absurdly high, their knees crooked in a grotesque caricature of a well-organized horse's elastic step. I had just been brought back to Vermont from a trip to the Berlin art galleries with my artist-mother. Berlin at that time (it must have been early in the nineties) was echoing to the Prussian ideal. On every street you saw files of soldiers, painfully lifting their legs high in the extraordinarily hideous, parade-ground walk called the goose step. These anxious horses, tensely remembering to fling up their knees in that ugly gait — I looked into the face of the old man beside me, to see what in the world he thought of it. He was gazing impassively at the spectacle in the silence which is "Vermont manners" in the presence of something unfamiliar which you don't appreciate. I got the idea. Children generally manage to get the idea which lies back of their elders' manners. So I, too, gazed silently at the rest of the show.

There were satin-coated riding horses forcing their necks into a cramped curve which could only have come from hours and days and months of training to this unlovely attitude. Used to the muscular good breeding of Morgans who were at ease when standing still, I was astonished by the fidgeting of these fine animals when they were brought to a halt. And I was distressed by the incessant tossing of their heads which flung back flecks of foam from their mouths. Why in the world, I wondered, didn't somebody see that their bridles and bits fitted them, so they could act natural? Above all, we Vermonters were shocked by their eyes, flickering nervously in their sockets, with an expression which looked to us like that of a maniac.

According to the standards you accept, our attitude was either that of Boeotians gaping doltishly at works of art, or that of the little child in the Hans Christian Andersen story of the "Emperor's New Clothes." Psychiatrists call remoteness from reality one kind of insanity. To us rural Vermonters that horse show looked genuinely crazy. "Distinction" defined as and limited to obvious uselessness which had cost a great deal to produce; "beauty" which distorted with enforced nervous tension the flow of natural lines — we were glad to leave that place long before the end of the performance.

We walked away hand in hand, the old man and the little girl who, watching him, was absorbing his tradition through her pores. For a long time after we were back in the low old phaeton, on our way home, nothing was said. Then Uncle Zed remarked, thoughtfully, "No man ever lived who could make a crazy fool like that out of a Morgan."

You know as well as I do what happened to the Morgan horse, because it happened to all horses. Elsewhere the automobile made its first appearance as a more or less fancy vehicle for extravagant sporting youth, or for moneyed maturity. That first phase of the motor-car era was hardly seen in Vermont except as it passed our homes on the way to somewhere else. The gasoline-driven wagon which drove into our farms and villages to stay was the early Ford, the old tin-pan Lizzy. Outside of Vermont, people who lived by traditions unlike ours used to say, "No car at all, rather than one of those cheap-as-dirt Fords." I have written all these pages in vain if you do not know that the Vermont tradition has always denied that cash cost is the same thing as value. Nobody ever scared us off from something we saw the use of by calling it cheap. We are brought up to try to judge things-for-sale, as we try to judge people, by their worth, not by their price. We don't always. But that is what we mean to do.

The miraculous inexpensiveness of the Ford, which like the small stature of the Morgan horse made it valueless for conspicuous display, endeared it to Vermont. From 1912 on, with increasing speed, gasoline replaced horses here as everywhere. Practically no general-utility horses are left. I motored the other day to Rutland and back (about a hundred miles) and saw only three horses. And they were idly grazing, not at work. Probably waiting, I thought to myself, for next spring's maple syrup making. So far, no motor-driven vehicle can replace the plod, plod of horses in deep snow, pulling in the tank of sap to the sugar-house.

A few oxen still lived out their time. They had been used for very heavy work, being strong as the mighty Percherons, but vastly less expensive to buy and feed. If we had had any sense of showmanship (which, as you must have noticed, rates lower than zero in the Vermont tradition), we would have subsidized a few span of oxen just for summer visitors to take snapshots of. How those first auto-tourists did carry on about the few ox-teams they sometimes met, as they drove cautiously around a curve in one of the narrow, dirt roads of those days. But of course as soon as motor trucks were available, the oxen vanished, the saving of time being almost unimaginable.

The saving of time in general was an immense psychological jolt to country folks used to gauging distances by the speed of horses. It could scarcely have been greater if we had been snatched off to another planet where the force of gravity was suddenly less. We all knew the distances to this and that settlement by the horse-time required to get there. Our house is about three miles from the village. The road was often dusty or very muddy, always stony; we used to calculate twenty-five minutes to go out to the field, catch the horse (yes, a part-Morgan), harness him, back him into the shafts, and get to town; and the same time to drive back, unharness him, hang up the harness, and get him into his stall, let alone feeding him and watering him. The road is now just as long as it ever was; but it is made of concrete. We glance at the clock, see that we have six or seven minutes before the post office closes, snatch the letters to be mailed, step into the car, and arrive at the post office in time.

Vermont doctors were the first among us to use the automobile for their work. Formerly (I mean when I was young), when someone in a farmhouse fell ill at night, it meant saddling a horse and racing him through the blackness to the doctor's, helping him hitch up his buggy, and coming back on the run. There are no words to describe the torture of the wait in the farmhouse. Now with the telephone and the car, the doctor is within half an hour, or less, as close as he is to city-dwellers.

The nearest hospital was then fifty miles away, to be reached only by infrequent trains. How many people died before train-time? And in transit? The nearest dentists were seventeen miles away in Bennington. According to the weather there were mud-holes along those seventeen miles, steep stony hills, huge snow-drifts.

It was an all-day trip to get there and back. Now an aching tooth can be transferred from its home to the dentist's chair in twenty-five minutes. In the old days the snow on the winter roads between towns was seldom plowed out. From December to late March, each town, all of them small, was shut up to its own resources, social, intellectual, medical, as if behind bars. Now the human resources of the State, such as they are, can be pooled. We have a State Symphony Orchestra, where musicians get together from homes scattered from one end of the Green Mountains to the other. Our high-school students, some of them, sing and play in an annual Music Festival where they meet thousands of other young Vermonters. Our high-school basketball teams exchange games all winter, each making the trip in its school bus. Our State Library Commission has book-mobiles constantly moving from one rural school to another, from one small public library to the next. Our State capital was an eight-hour (or longer) drive in a horse-drawn vehicle from many Vermont towns. The elected Town Representative was the only person in most towns familiar with it. Now any of us can get an early breakfast and be in Montpelier for a ten o'clock meeting. Vermont can function as a State as never before.

Of course much the same transformation took place everywhere in the United States. My justification for describing it here is that Vermont, although because of our love for Morgan horses we had more emotional reason to resist the change, showed itself not at all the stubbornly set, narrow, conservative community outsiders sometimes think it.

Everywhere, at all times, some people have tried to prevent inevitable change. When long trousers came into style, gentlemen of a certain temperament staged a sit-down strike. They went on wearing knee-breeches (which are, it must be admitted, much more becoming to a man with a good leg) long after other men had succumbed to the revolutionary tube. Again when traveling by private chaise and stagecoach went out, certain ladies of the age and personality which is shocked by change refused to submit their persons to the degrading promiscuity of railroads. This kind of human brake seems generally connected either with extremely primitive backwoods personalities, or with people who have some superfluous, unearned money, and who claim to be socially superior to others. Vermont has not often seen it. When horses vanished before cars, there was here but one human brake, Mr. Joseph Battell.

He was a Middlebury man, who loved Morgans as we all did. But he had money enough to think he could plant his armchair on the economic beach and command the past to stop ebbing away. When the smell of gasoline was first wafted over the Vermont landscape Mr. Battell knew (as did the earlier wearers of knee-breeches) that something he valued was in danger. He took steps to try to protect it. He owned thousands of acres of woodland. He forbade the use of automobiles on any of the roads he established in his forests. He established a fine breeding farm for Morgan horses. And he gave a large and valuable tract of land to the United States, which, as unaware as any of us in 1906 that automobiles and jeeps would eliminate horses from light work, had at that date established through its Bureau of Animal Industry, a station for Light Horse Investigation, in co-operation with the Vermont Agricultural College. At that time the "project of perpetuating and maintaining the qualities of the Morgan horse was deemed of national importance." So writes the Supervisor of the Morgan Horse Farm. One of the aims of the Federal Government was the production of cavalry horses for our Army.

For twenty years, from 1915 through 1935, the Morgan Horse Farm worked to place the breed on a permanent basis. During those years the farm was carefully run by the Federal Government. Those equine members of our Vermont families were there, by professional breeding and training, skillfully transformed into high-priced, fancy riding stock.

But presently there was no horse-mounted cavalry in our Army. We hear that riding is not now one of the subjects taught at West Point. The White House now has no stable for the President's horses because modern Presidents have no horses, use automobiles. Even the Federal Government can't go on forever spending tax money for obsolete purposes. Furthermore individual private breeding and interest in riding horses (Morgans included), as luxury items, has greatly increased. The Bureau of the Budget closed out funds for light horse investigation in 1951. All that fine plant which had been built up to a value (shown by the inventory of 1950) of five hundred thousand dollars — livestock, land, buildings and equipment — became "surplus property."

By law it was necessary that the U. S. Department of Agriculture offer this surplus property to the State Agricultural Experiment Station. But only if the State gave definite intention to use such facilities permanently, rather than just receiving the property and discarding it within a few years.

This meant the appropriation for its maintenance of Vermont tax money. The lid blew off with a bang. You should have heard our alarmed protest. We, who so desperately need money to give

our children constantly improving education to fit them for constantly more complex modern life; we, who can't take care of
our insane as we should; we, who can't keep up to modern standards in salaries for hard-working State officials; we, whose roads
and bridges are far too narrow for the modern traffic which
pours over them, and who can't imagine how we are ever going
to have money enough to make them wider — *we* to keep up an
expensive establishment for perpetuating animals whose sole use,
in our time, is for leisure-time pleasure and for conspicuous
display?

Washington professed to be shocked by Vermont penurious-
ness. Did we not feel it an honor and a duty to keep up our own
special breed of horses? No, unanimously, we did not. Our tradition bids us look sharply into the relative importance of things.
Vermonters could not afford and did not want an expensive
breeding establishment for fine riding horses, any more than you
want or could afford a personal masseur. It did not go with our
style of life.

The Morgan horse had become a white elephant. What to do
with white elephants is a riddle nobody has solved. An ingenious
compromise has been effected. The farm is now a part of the
Agricultural Department of our University of Vermont, and that
is supported partly by Federal money. Only fifteen Morgan mares
and a few young stock were taken over. The major project at the
Morgan Farm is now concerned with dairy heifers. I doubt if one
Vermonter in a hundred, in a thousand, could tell you now the
present status of the breeding of Morgan horses.

Do you think we are unfeeling thus to turn away from what
was a comely part of our culture (no less), an emotional outlet
for many of our people and an integral part of our past? How
"feeling" would you be, if it were suggested to you that you
deprive your son of college education and let the younger children's teeth go unattended, in order to spend your money to
keep intact just as it was, the house in which you spent your
youth?

I don't claim that this episode was a pretty passage in Vermont
history. There are not many pretty passages in our rather hard-
pressed life. But I'm not ashamed of it. I recognize in it a com-

munal realization that a part of the bygone past, no matter how skillfully embalmed and propped up, should not take precedence over real, living and present needs.

No hard and fast line can be drawn between a reasonable sense of proportion, and a meager, ungenerous, gritty realism. No hard and fast lines can ever be drawn between one kind of attitude towards life and another. One shades into the next, like the colors of the spectrum. But in the end, red is different from yellow. It is inevitable that different traditions will take different attitudes towards the past. Many people who look at us from the outside think that we have old-fashioned ways. They will be surprised to hear that the Vermont tradition would not, if it could, have the State climb back into the cocoon from which it has emerged. Vermont does try to save from the past any part of its essence still valuable to the present. But that is not the same thing as pretending that all of the past would be valuable to us now. There is no harm in that pretense, we feel, for people who enjoy it, and can afford it. We don't, and we can't.

Did you ever hear of the recurrent attempt to raise in Vermont enough money (it would take a lot) to make a well-run, carefully preserved Mount Vernon for tourists out of President Coolidge's place? It always fails. We hear non-Vermonters saying derisively (they take no pains to prevent our hearing them), "Too penny-pinching even to show decent respect for their own past."

To that reproach we make our answer in the medium in which we express ourselves most accurately — in what we do and don't do. Calvin Coolidge was no George Washington, and we know that as well as anybody. He was a creditable part of a bygone past. We don't contribute money needed for other things to pretend the past is still with us.

This expression of a basic principle of ours is a rough kind of gesture, like our refusal to spend a lot of money breeding fine saddle horses. But it is honest, it is in accord with our deepest purposes, and it requires a kind of courage which we highly prize, the courage to ignore blame based on standards which we do not accept. Each of us must sort out as best he can those elements of the past which seem to him still valuable, and hence worth preserving. Mostly the ones we feel we can't afford to lose are spiritual and intellectual ideals, hence immortal, never obsolete. Gilded as all the past is in the seductive light of sunset, it is hard to distinguish what is undying in the spirit of the past from buildings, animals, special garments, table manners. And even when you think you can see which parts of the past are mere exterior fact, you must get your nerve up to pay little attention to contemptuous blame from those who don't agree with you.

We don't believe in blaming them in return — not openly anyhow, not enough to tarnish their enjoyment of harmless pleasure which we can't understand. There is, I have heard, a real sure-enough Hunt Club in Vermont, complete with scarlet coats (I mean pink, of course), foxhounds, horns, M.F.H. and all the works. Wherever it is, I know that its Vermont neighbors will never make fun of it (except among themselves), will never interfere with anything its members seem to enjoy, "S'long's they pay their taxes," and do no harm to crops and fences. But I am also pretty sure that they will watch its tootling passage across their stone-walled upper pastures with that poker-faced silence which, in certain circumstances, as I learned from my great-uncle, is "Vermont manners."

CHAPTER 14

Thrift Meets Apollyon Straddling Quite Over the Whole Breadth of the Way

> Economy is the first virtue; without it, genius
> is a meteor; victory a sound; and all courtly
> splendor a public robbery.
> ARTHUR YOUNG, *Travels in France*, 1783

WHERE did we Americans — many of us — get the notion that it is glamorous to spend more money than we can afford? Did it result, as some social historians suggest, from the age-old worship by commoners of the titled nobility, culminating during the eighteenth and nineteenth centuries, in a desperate attempt by the upper middle class to keep up with the conspicuous spending of fabulously wealthy peers of the realm? Thackeray, expert observer of London life, traced that line of descent for senseless extravagance. Perhaps a compulsive belittling of thrift did travel, along with many another British habit of thought, some of them admirable, deep in the subconscious of many who crossed the Atlantic to become Americans. Its roots and buds never dried out. As soon as the young nation had centers of wealth, the transplanted seedling burst into new life. Revolutions, political and industrial, can change laws. Only long passage of time can change habits of thought.

More likely the growth was spontaneous. It is a form of exhibitionism and that is widespread — among the immature. Most of us have marveled to see a child far too young to talk, yet managing by waving arms and wordless babble, to convey the message "Look at me, at Me!" He is informing us that the desire to attract attention is deep-seated, even in babies.

It certainly is in adolescents. That subject is too painful to pursue.

Fortunately the passage of time civilizes most people. The need to earn the family living, to cook its meals, to rear its children, forces most show-off boys and girls to develop into worthy, even self-forgetting fathers and mothers.

But some people never grow up. And for such, the ostentatious spending of more money than is needed is one way to say "Look at Me!" There is a legend of the new-rich millionaire after lunching at a famous restaurant, showily lighting his cigar with a twenty-dollar bill. The story can hardly be true, factually. That it ever was invented and is still told (with variations) means that a man wanting to be admired as a success quite naturally thinks of free and unlimited spending as a means to that end. Conversely, to count your change, either in fact or figuratively, is held up as mean. Most of the stories about the Scotchman are based on the idea that it is ridiculously beneath human dignity to take care not to spend more money than you can afford.

Astonishing how tyrannically that idea rules and ruins people who know better. Because of it, the young husband winces but accepts without protest a suite at a resort hotel, instead of the modest room for two which is within his budget. He cannot endure the humiliation — *why should it be a humiliation?* — of having the room-clerk suspect that his limited resources must be allotted with care, if they are to cover this vacation. So he signs the register.

The room clerk is not fooled. While the bellboy leads the couple towards the elevator, he murmurs, "There's still a sucker born every minute."

No well-managed corporation apologizes or feels mean and niggardly for not maintaining factories or office force twice what is needed for the volume of business reasonably in sight. No architect makes it a matter of pride to specify floor-girders ten times stronger than called for by an amply figured factor of safety. In every branch of art, the ideal is the accurate fitting of means to ends. Why shouldn't that principle hold good for the spending of money in daily life?

One reason that it doesn't is a preposterous and frequent misconception that thrift means shady dealing to get the best of every transaction. "The canny, thrifty Vermonter" means that he is a sharp bargainer. The dictionary gives no support to that definition, nor is there anything of the sort in Vermont character. The

Green Mountain man is no bargainer at all. He has neither liking nor skill for market-place haggling. As a buyer he supposes the other man's asking price is final, because his would be if the case were reversed. As a seller — of apples, maple syrup, firewood, his working time — when anyone tries to beat him down, he does not argue. He silently goes away and does not come back.

One other fixed misconception is the notion that to be thrifty at all is to be too thrifty, is to be stingy, is to be a piker, a cheapskate, a tightwad. That is assuming that a trait of character cannot exist at all, except in excess. The stingy tightwad will not spare a few dollars to buy shoes for his children. But Vermont children, most of them, have shoes when they need them. And the reason there is money to pay for shoes is because that family's cash and credit has not been dribbled away on one or another gadget, not needed, not especially desired, but bought because some salesman insisted that all self-respecting neighbors owned or were about to own a model equally costly.

It would be absurd to claim that Vermonters have any monopoly of thrift. Yet it is true that it is taken here, more than in most places, as a matter of course, needing no apology. Can that be because here, by a lucky chance, thrift became fixed as a habit during many generations who never came into contact with people who spent without counting the cost. The members of such a class elsewhere were perhaps disliked, or even hated, but at the same time were envied, were thought of as models to be copied, at least in daydreams.

Whatever the reason for the habit of thrift in Vermont, and whatever the allowances for exceptions among us, this much is true: nowadays when newspapers, radio, television, movies, have exposed us to all the big-world frenzies of sales pressure, few Vermonters lose their heads. Cars, washing machines, vacuum cleaners, are bought on installment payment contracts here as elsewhere. But almost always only when careful figuring has shown that after the deduction, the reasonably-to-be-expected pay checks will be enough to live on.

The habit of thrift here, and respect for the principle, frees us, to a great degree, from a fear that threatens many other Americans. On occasional trips to Boston and New York, Vermonters do not cringe — not as cravenly as many people anyhow — before those modern robber barons of the road, the headwaiter, the taxi driver, the saleslady. Before getting mixed up in any deal, little or big, we ask, without swallowing hard either, "How much will it cost?" When answered, we are conditioned by generations unashamed to admit that they have compared price with value and with pocketbook. We are able to say, "That is more than I can afford," and turn away, without blushing.

All through Vermont's history, thrift has served her well. It has enlarged scanty resources to ampleness. If in the earliest days, wild sprees in river-front dives had taken the potash money, the families back in the hill country might have sunk to the level of untaught, un-cared-for shanty dwellers. Instead, out of it grew those plain but substantial, low-ceilinged, well-kept, much-loved Vermont homes, and all that they meant, books, tools, clothes — savings too. For, poor as Vermonters have always been by big-commerce standards, something has always been put aside. At first the nest egg of extra cash was kept under the hearthstone. Later it was put into savings banks, as soon as there were any.

These small but humanly priceless savings, growing year by year, have, time and again, allowed Vermonters to rise to special emergencies in ways they consider right and decent. To select one illustration from many, John Dewey, the greatest man Vermont ever gave to the world, received at Johns Hopkins the postgraduate study which shaped to scholarliness that extraordinary brain of his. The money to pay for these years of higher education came from the small savings-bank account of an aunt.

The Deweys are Burlington people. I never knew them personally, never met John Dewey till he was an old man. But from our folk tradition I am sure that Burlington neighbors thought the aunt was only "acting sensible." This is high praise in our vocabulary. And, although I did not hear the aunt say so, I have heard other Vermonters use the accepted speech-formula with which she almost certainly cut short her nephew's thanks, "That's what money's for, child."

There are perils in every human trait if good judgment and good feeling do not keep it in proportion to the whole. On occa-

sion, the greatest moral virtue may become grotesque if carried
to excess. Even in a merely practical, sensible habit like thrift,
there is an ugly danger. It is a sound, reasonable companion in
everyday life. But it is not heroic. And there are, individually and
communally, occasions in human life which can be met only with
heroism.

In *Pilgrim's Progress*, Bunyan shows his hero pressing forward
through perils by the help of such mild qualities as patience,
perseverance, prudence and the like. But then he "espied the
great foul fiend of evil, Apollyon, straddling quite over the whole
breadth of the way." And now the Pilgrim must needs stand his
ground, draw his two-edged sword, and fight for his soul's life.

All through the early decades of the nineteenth century,
Vermonters had shaped their lives according to sound, reasonable
principles. Who could tell whether in those years of quiet re-
pressed discipline, thrift had not shrunk into parsimony? Where
would they stand when confronted with danger to spiritual values,
when the tocsin struck the hour for violent and noble recklessness?

Hardly a Vermonter can talk of his State without mentioning
proudly that the clause in the Vermont State Constitution (1777)
forbidding human slavery on our soil was the first of its kind
on the North American continent. We were all brought up on the
story of the Negro woman and her child, slaves of one of the
British officers, taken prisoner as they retreated from Ticonderoga. A vote was taken among her rustic Vermont captors
as to what to do with her. They were unanimous in favor of
freeing her. Their captain (he was one Ebenezer Allen, brought
up as a blacksmith) thereupon gave her a "written certificate of
emancipation." You can see it if you ever pass through Bennington on an auto trip, for it is recorded, along with other legal
documents, in the Town Clerk's office, original spelling and all.
Neither the blacksmith-captain, nor anybody else, had up to that
time made out such a document. He did not know exactly how
to phrase it to make it legal. To cover all contingencies he used
so many words that, to my regret, it is far too long to give it
here in full. But one statement of principle, because it was written
in the eighteenth century in Vermont, by a Vermonter, should

be quoted — "I, being conscientious that it is not Right in the Sight of God to keep Slaves, I therefore, obtaining leave of the detachment under my command, I give her and her child their freedom." If you know your American history, you know that 1777 was early for such words.

Later, but before 1800, a Vermont judge was approached by a slave-owner, wanting to secure the return of a slave of his escaped to Vermont, and showing his bill of sale to prove his legal right to his property. To him Judge Harrington replied that he would order the arrest and return of the slave only if he were shown "a bill of sale from God Almighty." Vermont memories have allowed no dust to fall on these episodes.

In the early years of our State there were several similar incidents. As the nineteenth century came on, they merged gradually into the Fugitive Slave problem. A branch line of the Underground Railroad ran up through Vermont to Canada. Here, as in some other regions, the farm homes which were safe stations on this secret road to freedom were marked by an unobtrusive white line around a chimney. Nobody spoke openly about the meaning of this line, till after the close of the Civil War. My father was the one who told me about it.

There were Negroes living in Vermont, several hundred, here and there, but since they were felt to be like anybody else, there is nothing special to report about them. They were of all sorts, just like their white neighbors. The town of Manchester, to the north of my home town, had for many years a Negro preacher in the pulpit of its big old First Congregational Church (still standing, still active and thriving). But the most indefatigable cross-questioning of older Manchester people, by a little girl full of curiosity, never turned up any interesting item about him. Apparently nobody had thought the color of his skin made him different from other clergymen. A Negro boy named Saunders, brought up in the town of Thetford, turned out to be one of the especially brainy youngsters who occasionally appears in any Vermont (as in any human) group. Helped by his fellow townsmen to get a good education, he became a lawyer and in the end held for nineteen years an important official position as Attorney General in the Republic of Haiti. Another Negro Vermonter, of the town of Highgate, committed murder, was tried and hanged in 1820. One of the best schoolteachers we now have is an attractive Negro Vermonter, good wife, mother to three fine children, who is teaching a district school, up north, back of Essex Junction. Like the people around them, there were among Vermont Negroes all kinds of differing personalities.

During that long first half of the nineteenth century, everybody in Vermont was — do you need to be told this? — antislavery in opinion. But, at first, here as elsewhere, the possible consequences of a split over slavery in the American Federation were so terrifying that reasonable people often opposed fiery abolition speakers. Moderate Vermonters, like other moderate Americans anxiously looked this way and that, to find some decent, nonviolent way both to save the Union and not to go on with human slavery. Up to the 1820's and 1830's, people hoped that a solution might be to send American Negroes back to their own continent to live in freedom in a country of their own.

During this time an extreme abolitionist tried to speak in Montpelier. The report has always been that mob violence broke up the meeting. When investigated, "mob violence" seems to have taken the form of a noisy hissing and stamping to drown out the speaker's voice and one egg thrown through a window. Shortly afterward, in the town of Randolph (one of our finest quality Vermont towns with a first-rate record of civilized living), another speech by the same orator was announced. That meeting too was broken up — no egg this time, just hissing and stamping. But in Randolph lived a farmer (a former officer in the militia) who, because of his personal character, was a man of influence. He was not in town on the evening when a speaker's voice was drowned out. When he returned and heard about the episode, he said, "I'm not for or against abolition, but as long as I am alive, nobody is going to be refused a chance to state his opinions in my home town."

Other Randolph men of similar temper flocked to him. The speaker (he was the Reverend Mr. May of Boston) was invited to return, and mounting the same platform spoke to a silent audience seated, and to a standing-up group of substantial citizens, ready to throw out the first man who stamped.

But as antislavery feeling rose, the opposition to the violence implicit in abolition talk died down. By 1841 an antislavery ticket appeared in the race for governor. All through the 1840's, all through the 1850's, Vermont Legislatures continued to pass resolutions condemning slavery. They sent them to Congress to be read aloud by their representative, and also to the governors of slaveholding states. The war of words was fierce; in 1855 Georgia passed a resolution to send the Vermont communication back "to the deep, dank, and fetid sink of social and political iniquity from which it came." Virginia voted for a resolution that "able-bodied Irishmen be hired to dig a ditch all around Vermont, till the thing could be detached from the rest of the Union and towed out into the middle of the Atlantic Ocean."

So far, you see, nothing but words, which, unlike "sticks and stones" break no bones. The opposition to human slavery in their nation had cost Vermonters no more than the breath to talk about it.

In 1856 the Vermont Legislature passed an act "encouraging" formation of militia, and also appropriated twenty thousand dollars (a big sum then) for the relief of Free State Vermont settlers in Kansas. The two gestures expressed, we take it, the same emotion. That year two "companies" left Rutland for Kansas. 1857 was the year of the Dred Scott Decision, bitterly resented in Vermont. Two more "companies" of Vermonters left to settle in Kansas.

By 1860 the Legislature increased militia companies to seventeen in number and later to twenty-two. (But the expenses of these companies were to be taken on by the men in them and by the towns which organized them.) The twenty thousand dollars voted by the Vermont Legislature had been forwarded to the Vermonters in Kansas whose homes, household gear, and other equipment had been burned in proslavery guerilla raids. They sent back word that they were much obliged, but could manage without help and preferred to. The twenty thousand dollars came back into the State Treasury.

The Vermont Legislature resolved that "the Fugitive Slave Law being a violation of the Constitution, the people of Vermont will indignantly rebuke any Senator or Representative of theirs

who does not use his influence to bring about its entire repeal." They also highly resolved "that the slave who treads the
soil of a free state by the consent of his master becomes thereby
at once forever free and entitled to the whole power of the
State."

Fine sentiments. Fine phrases.

For almost a century, Vermonters had been safe in their pleasant, small, well-kept old mountain communities, looking out over
carefully tilled fields and pastures bright with green from the
melting of last winter's drifts to the first November snowfall.
With the exception of echoes from the War of 1812, these much-
loved farms, these elm-shaded village streets had never, from
their founding, heard an enemy drum-beat, the rattle of rifle fire,
nor a cannon shot, save to celebrate the Fourth of July. From
this comfortable security, Vermonters had hurled verbal attacks on slavery as a moral wrong. Their unanimous conviction
on this point had so far cost them not a penny of money, not a
drop of blood.

In 1860 the sum of all taxes raised by Vermont towns, counties and State totaled a little more than nine hundred thousand
dollars. This was to last the State for two years. There was — of
course — practically no State debt. Industry, patience, ingenuity
and thrift had sufficed. So far.

Then War, the enemy of God and man, straddled quite all
across the breadth of the way on which Vermonters had been
cheerfully trudging forward with industry, patience, ingenuity
and prudence.

President Lincoln called for volunteers on April 16, 1861. On
the next day the Governor of Vermont sent out a summons for a
special session of the Legislature. As early a date was set as
possible. It would take time for the legislators to assemble. Many
of them lived on back roads. Most of them were in small communities far from the few slow railroad lines. In many cases the
best way to get to Montpelier (certainly the way which cost the
least) was to hitch up the lightest farm horse and drive there.
The horses toiled up the steep roads which led over the Green
Mountains from one side of the State to the other. Up there

snow still lay on the northern slopes. The horses slowly dragged the light buckboards through the valley roads deeply rutted with April mud; they held their heads up as they trotted into the streets of Montpelier. The legislators drove to livery stables where they arranged for care (to cost as little as possible) for their horses. Most of them, carpetbag in hand, then walked to the plain, cheap, rooming house which had sheltered them during the last session. A small number, lawyers and men of other professions, went to the old Pavilion Hotel — as they mounted the steps they remembered that Lafayette had slept there, remembered that he had there spoken of Vermont as one of the earliest champions of freedom. In our turn, as we look up at the old Pavilion Hotel, we think of this emergency Special Session of our Legislature and their not-to-be-forgotten action.

Then, their faces sober, their mouths tightly shut, the legislators walked heavily in their great country boots up the fine wide stone steps, into the beautiful State House, the "Home of our free government," as with affectionate pride it was sometimes called in those days.

No one knew beforehand what they would do there, these countrymen whose life for generations had been based on industry and frugality. They themselves did not know beforehand. They lived on isolated farms and in villages separated from others, by roads which in winter were blocked by unplowed snowdrifts, in spring and autumn were often deep in mud, which in all seasons, were threatened by unruly watercourses. Few representatives saw their fellow legislators except once in two years at Montpelier. They knew how the people of their own towns felt about this terrible crisis. In small communities not much time is needed to pass the word around. But who could be sure about the feeling even thirty miles away, let alone in the almost two hundred and fifty electoral districts spread from the Canadian boundary to Massachusetts?

Their first meeting was on April 23, six days after the Governor's summons. They assembled under the gilded dome in the carefully wrought, classically beautiful Statehouse. On this day, more was at stake than any stone-and-mortar "Home for free government." These countrymen, their weather-beaten faces grave, went patiently through the prescribed traditional routine for the organization of the Legislature. Until the session was in legal order, nothing could be done. By the end of the first day, April 23, they were ready to take action.

The second day (April 24) the motion was made (by one of our Arlington Canfields) that in answer to the appeal of the President of the United States, the Vermont Legislature appropriate half a million dollars with an additional half million on call. Sober and self-contained, the assembled countrymen voted "Aye."

That first sum voted was 110 per cent of the largest total taxes ever raised by the State. Pennsylvania at this time voted 34 per cent, Ohio 31 per cent, New York 20 per cent of their total taxes.

Vermonters had made thrift the foundation of their daily life. But this was not "daily life," and they knew it. Thrift was now no more than a pebble in their path. No man even glanced at it, as they surged forward into literal, physical danger of their lives, and into what must have looked to men of their tradition like certain ruin for their State. The day and hour and human history put a grim question to these farmers, storekeepers, small-town lawyers, sons of blacksmiths, carpenters and schoolteachers, "Do you mean what you say?" With one voice they answered yes, drew out their two-edged swords and stood their ground to fight for the life of their souls.

They had based their State on their belief in human freedom. During the long safe years, nearly a century of humdrum, rural, earning-a-living life, the tradition had struck roots deep into their hearts. They saw it threatened, and were instantly on their feet to defend it.

But by that tradition, human freedom is based on individual personal human dignity. They had been brought up, and had brought their children up, hating anything which might try to force legal or social inferiority on any man, any woman, any child. Before leaving the Statehouse that day, those grandfathers of ours safeguarded such intangible rights with an imaginative, almost poetic divination of their value. They pledged the State "to give any support necessary to the dependents of soldiers, so that not one shall become a pauper, but *all shall be considered* 'wards of the commonwealth.' "

At this stage of the war, no other state took this action. Of course, all states arranged that soldiers' dependents should not starve, but, like other poor people, they would be cared for under the "poor laws."

A modern Vermonter knowing the relative value of money in his state and the total absence all through its history of any large financial resources, is staggered to incredulity by the thunder of those "ayes" rolling down through the ninety years since that vote was taken. Where — he asks himself wildly — did they expect to get a million dollars from one day to the next?

It was humdrum thrift which put the dramatic two-edged sword into their scabbard. They themselves had that million dollars, because they had saved it. And most of the eight million more which, in the four terrible years ahead of them, they were to spend.

The towns, those small sedate towns, many of them hardly more than hamlets, raised five million dollars. I'll set down some of the names and sums. The town of Wells with a rural population of less than seven hundred people (men, women, children and babies all counted) in the next four years raised fifteen thousand dollars which they personally and directly voted on themselves at their Town Meetings. Mendon with six hundred and twelve people, raised thirteen thousand dollars. Greensborough, with a little over a thousand people, raised (always by taxes voted by themselves) twenty-two thousand dollars; Hubbardton people, six hundred sixty of them, voted taxes on themselves for eight thousand five hundred dollars, and raised nearly two thousand in addition in spontaneous personal gifts.

Like John Dewey's aunt, these plain country towns had the money in hand not in the least by a miracle, but by the practice of thrift. And in an emergency, like John Dewey's aunt, they did not hold fast to it, as they had held hard to the pennies and dimes and dollars, which, one by one, had been not-spent for comfort and ease. Now they opened their muscular working-hands for a cause worth more to them than thrift. "That's what money's for," they would have said — if they had said anything.

By that time there were in Vermont some others besides small-town village and farm people. There were bankers, there were men of commerce, and manufacturers. They too opened wide their desk-workers' softer hands. To finance that first bonded debt of their state, the Fairbanks Company of St. Johnsbury turned over ten thousand dollars; James Langdon of Montpelier twenty thousand; Thomas McDaniels of Bennington ten thousand. T. W. Parks living in San Francisco sent back a thousand as a gift. Here is a passage from his letter to the Governor, "Enclosed you will find a check for $1,000 which the State of Vermont will please accept as my contribution toward defraying the expenses of fitting out her sons for battle, or supporting the families of those who may fall in defense of the flag of our Union. Although nearly six thousand miles from Vermont, I love Vermont and her people and take pride in being counted among her sons." W. C. Harding (I put in all these names and initials to try to make this seem as literally real as it was) of Winooski sent a thousand, offered "ten thousand more if needed"; the Bank of Burlington offered 10 per cent of its capital "and more if needed." The Bank of St. Albans did the same. Two Montpelier banks pledged twenty-five thousand each.

These facts would not seem in the mid-twentieth century what they accurately were in the mid-nineteenth century, without a reminder that this State-bonded debt was the first in the history of people who borrowed little money and never unless they were sure it could be repaid. What they voted that day was to each man of them like putting a mortgage on his own home. It was a mortgage on the family home — the first. Those legislators had no illusions about easy money somehow appearing in the future any more than in the past. By that time they knew Vermont's economy through and through, and knew that the future was to be about like the past. This — like all borrowed money — must be repaid. The sums for its repayment could be made only out of taxes, and taxes could be paid only out of hard work and thrift.

In some states of rapidly growing population and wealth, this might not have been true. Americans have had an easy hope that their posterity could somehow swing it with less effort than they, out of some unexpected windfall of economic development. Not Vermonters. They themselves were going into debt, to an amount that seemed crushing, that might really be crushing to the old communal home. The sum involved, the larger later sums, looked to them so huge that it might be materially impossible to repay them. But that home, and what it stood for, was in danger of being crushed by more than debt. They made their vote unanimous.

So far, this has been easy to set down. Money clinks or rustles. It does not bleed or weep.

But more than money was needed.

In January of 1861 the Vermont State Arsenal had only nine hundred fifty-seven muskets of various vintages, seven six-pound cannon, one hundred four tents, and five hundred three Colt pistols "of no practical use." Uniforms, almost nonexistent. There were in this rural state no contractors who could be called on to produce large numbers of uniforms. Vermont women, all of them accustomed to making most of the clothes worn by their families, set to work with intense concentrated effort to make with their own hands uniforms "out of Vermont grey cloth." In words un-Vermont in passion, Burlington women passed a resolution, "We further resolve that we will consider *All* our time and *All* our energies sacred to this object." (These italics are not mine.) The cloth for the uniforms of the first three regiments was made in Vermont mills. Thereafter all soldiers were clad in the blue which was the regular army issue.

But more was needed than money, weapons and uniforms.

Enlistments poured in. The historian Benedict says that of every two Vermonters of military age, one served in the army. Many a town set down in its records that their entire quota throughout the four years was met without recourse to the draft. Two assembly centers were designated. To them the tall, untrained country lads (their average height ran over five feet ten) hurriedly walked, rode, drove, took the steam cars. They received their uniforms, procured what arms there were, spent a short, short time learning the rudiments of marching and obeying orders, put into their buttonholes the sprig of evergreen

which became their especial mark, and were off, from the east
side of the State to Boston, from the west side to Troy, Albany,
New York.

The journal of a Boston woman, covering in detail the anxious
first few weeks of the war, speaks of everybody's spirits being
lifted, by the appearance, *already!* of tall Vermont boys marching by, green pine-twigs in their buttonholes.

It was murder, of course, to send raw troops into the furnace.
But all states, Northern and Southern, did it. Such heroism and
such military idiocy were no monopoly of Vermont. Again like
those from all the states, the Vermont soldiers during those
nightmare years were brave, almost all of them. It is not valor
that is lacking in the collective heart of man when the "forward
march!" is sounded; it is wisdom in their collective minds during
the long years before that summons. The Vermont record was
what is known technically as "good." That means that they were
in constant engagement in hot sections of battlefields. The proof
of this is shown by tragic figures: in the number of men per
one thousand population killed in battle or dead from wounds,
Vermont is next to the highest (New Hampshire had a few
more). In numbers of deaths from all war causes, Vermont stood
third among the states. The First Vermont Brigade lost more
men killed and mortally wounded than any other brigade save
one. Of fifty-four regiments which had had each over two hundred men killed in battle, four were from Vermont, the Second,
the Third, the Fifth and the Sixth.

Here, as in all the other states, Northern and Southern, intense
local attention has been given to the military details of the war.
The plan of every battle and skirmish, the total number involved,
has been preserved in print. As far as possible, the names, even
to the middle initials, of the soldiers are on record. Civil War
anecdotes, tragic, ribald, heroic, comic, are as thick in Vermont
reminiscences as in those of Georgia, New Jersey, Ohio — anywhere. Recurrently there appears, all details given, the statement
that Vermont troops at Gettysburg broke Pickett's charge. But
I don't set that down here. Every State cherishes some such story.
Vermonters did their part, others did their part also. A friend of
mine, born and brought up in Duluth, told me that, till he was

a man grown, he believed that the First Minnesota Regiment won the Civil War.

But I would not dare (or wish) to write of Vermont in the Civil War without setting down one saying which is always told to the younger generation as a precious part of their tradition. It is short, it has been easy to remember, "Put the Vermonters in front and keep the ranks closed up." Such was the order issued to a detachment of Union troops suddenly summoned to Gettysburg to head off Lee's surprise invasion. The commanding officer could not have paid our State a finer tribute than by choosing Vermonters to set the pace on that all-night march. He knew they could be trusted not to drag their feet when headed once more into the known hell of a pitched battle. It is a very young Vermont schoolchild who does not proudly know this saying.

This story, this saying, this challenge — it is part of our inheritance, something to live up to.

There was another specially-Vermont detail of those four war years — the method of caring for part of our State's sick and wounded. All soldiers in that time suffered horribly from the ignorance of sanitation, from dirt, from infection and disease, as well as from actual wounds operated on without anesthetics. The devoted doctors knew no better. Nobody knew any better, Vermonters no more than others. But, acting on a powerful folk instinct, they invented a homely device which saved many and many of their sons from the nightmare military field hospitals, and carried them on strong natural currents away from death up to life renewed.

Here is the account of the "Vermont system," about as it is set down in history books, where, of course, it is only one of uncountable details. "As early as 1862, the number of deaths among wounded Vermont soldiers became so alarming that a new system for their care was adopted. Vermont agents went in among the wounded and choosing those who could be moved without danger, sent them back to their own State for care in Burlington, Brattleboro and Montpelier hospitals — some of them improvised out of roughly built barracks. The result was at once so remarkable (75 per cent of their number were able to return to the battle line) that many other states later adopted the same plan."

Thus, factually, in percentages, do you find that Vermont "system" described in print.

In Vermont life, this is what happened: They rose before dawn, the family who were to go to see their wounded boy. After a hurried breakfast the mother put up the lunch, the father and the younger brothers of the soldier harnessed the two work-horses to the farm wagon. Stout kitchen chairs were put into the springless box-body, ankle deep in clean straw. Precious blankets (carded, spun, woven by the grandmother) were taken out to wrap up the thin old woman. She should not have undertaken the cruel fatigue of the long trip, but she would have gone on foot rather than be left behind. The hired girl, of course, the blooming daughter of a respected neighbor. She and the wounded soldier had "a sort of an understanding."

The jogging horses drew them slowly through the dark. Dawn came. Food was passed around among the travelers. The horses were watered at a roadside "iron kittle," filled with clear water from a little spring.

"Grandmother, wouldn't you better lie down in the straw for a rest? I brought a pillow along for you."

"I'm all right."

The sun rose over mountains they did not know. Late in the morning, they drew up before the sheds called the hospital.

The grandmother's face was white with fatigue when her son lifted her down. She said, "Here, let me carry one of those boxes."

The mother's lips were trembling. She straightened them to composure, as she drew out from under the seat the wrapped-up home-goodies — his favorite cookies, doughnuts, maple sugar. One of the little sisters carried the posy of red geraniums cut from the blossoming pot on the kitchen windowsill.

They stood waiting, till the father came back from the horse shed where he had fed and left his team. After consulting a register, the man in uniform at the entrance told them, "Down there — sixth door to the left, eighth cot beyond the door." Trying to walk quietly in their thick-soled shoes, they set out along the corridor.

He was lying straight in his narrow cot, his white face turned towards the door. At the sight of him, their first-born, the parents' hearts, that had been set in stonelike endurance, were torn to bleeding tatters. But their inner wail of misery made no sound. They smiled, they said quietly, "Well, son — " and took his hands in theirs, his thin, strengthless, sick man's hands, which after this day they might never touch again.

"I don't know where you're going to sit, all of you," said the soldier. "We're not long on chairs here. Take off your things. My! You look good to me. How are *you*, Lyddy?"

The father stood up, by the foot of the bed, the rest sat on the floor, all but the grandmother and the mother who had chairs. These hospitals were informally run. The long room full of cot-beds, every one with its tomblike effigy under its blanket, was of rough wood, with a chunk-stove in the corner. It did not stink of pus and fermenting filth. It had a country smell of wood smoke and fresh air. The nurses were men in shabby uniforms, a little nearer to recovery than the men they cared for. No one objected to the long family visit; there were no rules against their eating lunch together out of the home-packed lunch boxes. The soldiers in the nearby beds turned to watch the country family. Sometimes they smiled at the overheard talk. The geraniums were put into water in a jelly glass and set on the windowsill. "There!" said the soldier, looking at them, "I can fairly see Mother's stove and smell the gingerbread in the oven."

"Oh, we brought some gingerbread!" cried one of the little sisters, finding her voice. They all found their voices (but not the grandmother silent on her chair, her sunken eyes fixed on the young man, whose new-born, baby body she had been the first to wash and clothe). They told the home news, the kind that never gets into letters. All but Old Shep. It had been agreed that they were not to tell him that Old Shep was dead. Perhaps — perhaps he would never need to know.

In his turn, he told them the things which never get into letters — how well his home-knit socks had worn, what their army cooks gave them to eat, how the Vermont troops always hid any runaway slaves who found their way into camp. "Some of our high-up officers from the big cities keep a-sayin', 'This is no abolition war,' and, 'Respect other people's property. Those slaves are property. You wouldn't steal other people's spoons.' Let 'em talk, we boys say, we do as we please. Sometimes those colored men have bloody marks all over their backs. We're not a-goin' to send them back to the folks who whipped them."

He told them of a fellow Vermonter who had, against orders, gone out after dark and brought back canteens full of cool spring water for his mates, parched with the heat. "They took his arms away from him for that. And the very next day didn't we get into battle, and there he was without arms. He grabbed him a hatchet and went into action 'long side the rest of us. He got his rifle back all right."

The boy in the next bed said "Tell 'em about that light-fingered New Jersey regiment and Colonel Morrison's big dog." So he told them that absurd tale.

In return they told him about the day the pigs got out of the pen, and the whole family ran their heads off trying to catch them. Grandmother hobbled to the corn-crib, got a pan of yellow ears, went to the pig-yard, opened the gate and called "He-ere pig-pig-pig!" and rattled an ear against the pan. "And didn't the hull kit and b'ill'n of them run back as fast as they could leg it, and fall over each other, gettin' to the trough."

They all laughed. Except the grandmother. From her stillness and closed eyes you might have thought she had dropped asleep. But not from her face. The listening soldiers in the nearby beds laughed, too. By this time other families had come in from long drives to visit a son. Each group, eating its lunch beside the bed of a wounded soldier, laughed over its own home jokes, told its especial news.

An army doctor appeared to make the rounds. He looked pleased to hear the laughter. "This Vermont system really does work," he thought. He joked as he passed from bed to bed. He was no dapper city man. From his easy, homely ways, he had been brought up in the country; from his accent he was from the Middle West. The Vermonters liked him. So many Vermont children and grandchildren were living in the Middle West that all people from Iowa and Ohio and Wisconsin and Illinois seemed, as they still seem, like cousins in the Green Mountain family.

Arrived at "their" bed, the doctor drew back the sheet and, neat-fingered, lifted the bandage a little to see the wound. "Couldn't be better," he announced. "We'll have you back in the line of duty in no time."

The grandmother shrank together. The mother's lips began to tremble. The father put his hands into his pockets and clenched his shaking fingers to stillness.

The doctor pointed to a ragged old scar, just below the bandage. "If you got over that," he said jovially, "you can get over anything." He passed on to the next bed.

The parents sat silent. They were seeing again their little boy, their only child then, fallen across the scythe blade. How terribly his blood had gushed out! More than they would have thought was in his tiny body. They would have been helpless, except for the grandmother. Although father and mother, they had been but ignorant young people. She had steadied them through the long horror of thinking their child lost. They had not gone to bed for four nights. They gave all they had. They would have given their lives. The hurt little boy had done his best, too. He had lain still as Grandmother told him. He was lying still now, in his narrow soldier's bed.

And then, the long-ago dawn of the fifth day of their vigil, the grandmother-nurse-seer had turned away from the child's bed, saying, "He'll pull through."

She could not say that now, the old grandmother fallen together in her chair, her eyes closed.

The sun was low over that mountain they did not know. The mother said "Come children, let's pass around what doughnuts are left. Maybe Lyddy would like a minute of him to herself."

They moved along the row of beds, stopping at each one which had no family around it. The soldiers near their son's bed turned over, looked discreetly away from where Lyddy leaned close to her sweetheart's face, her voice a low murmur.

"Seventy-five per cent of them were returned to the battle line."

* * *

The soldiers helped themselves eagerly to the homemade doughnuts, with the stiffly decorous, nongreedy, folk phrase of their tradition, "I don't care if I do. Thank you ma'am." One of them said, "That fellow with the bandage on his head, he saw President Lincoln once. Close to. Ask him to tell you about it."

"Yes, I did," said the boy with the bandaged head. "He came to inspect our division. I happened to be in the front rank. I could have touched him as he went by."

The father asked, anxiously, urgently, "What does he look like? What kind of a fellow *is* he?"

The soldier closed his eyes, thought a moment, and told them, "He looks like one of the neighbors."

The father drew in a long breath.

They went back to the bed of their soldier. They told him they would come again if he was kept here longer. But they knew that he would not be. They got the grandmother up from her chair. She went to the side of the bed. "You've always been a good boy," she told the wounded man, earnestly. The children's shyness was gone. They babbled around him. The parents reached over their heads to take their son's hand.

They were gone, tiptoeing along the corridor out into the mountain twilight. "We'd ought to have left before," said the father, responsible for their welfare.

The grandmother said, "Where's that pillow?" She was too tired to sit up on the hard wooden chair. To the mother, stooping to settle her in the straw, the words which all day she had kept silent burst from her in a bitter whisper, *"Why can't we old folks be the ones to die?"*

The mother answered with a wordless sob, and turned to help the worn-out children lie down in the straw. In spite of the jolts, they were soon asleep. The old woman lay as quietly as they, but her eyes were open.

The parents, in the years of responsibility, sat on the backless driver's seat and took turns in holding the reins over the slow-moving horses. Freed by the darkness, they said aloud, like the grandmother, words which they had kept silent. Once the husband burst out "I can't stand it!" He felt his wife's hand on his. "But I know I've got to," he added.

A long time afterwards, the wife murmured in bewildered despair, "Seems as though there must be a better way than fighting."

Sometimes one or the other fell into a half-coma of tiredness. Once they both slowly became aware that the jolting of the wagon had stopped. The horses were standing still in the middle of the road, their heads hanging. The night was black. But by the sixth sense of home, they knew they had come to Mattison's crossroads and the horses were waiting to be told which way to go.

The father turned their heads up the home-hill. It was steep. The horses climbed slowly, slipping and stumbling on loose stones. They panted, stopped to rest, and went on again with weary, sighing breaths. "This is what life is like," thought the father (but he did not say it aloud). "Tired as dogs, everybody's heart broken, but a long steep hill ahead you've got to stumble up, somehow — in the dark."

In the dark.

For Vermonters of the parents' age, of the grandparents' age, the Civil War brought darkness. They had paid a tragic price in shock and pain, more than anyone had realized at the time. All older Americans, on both sides, had suffered shock and pain. But for the older Vermonters it was a larger part of their emotional lives. And like their soldier sons, they had undergone the terrible operation without sedatives, without stimulants, without anesthetics. They had been far from the field. Their hearts had never once been numbed by the loud vehemence of brasses, drums and fifes. Never for an instant had their nerves been deadened by the stupor of watching endless lines of marching men. They had just taken it. It had been too much for many of them.

They had never even seen the human slaves they had done their best to free. Now that the Negroes were legally free, it seemed that they needed — everything. An Army officer, whose home was in Burlington, founded what later grew into the great Howard University. But he did not live to see its success. It was no more, at first, than a primary school. Vermont teachers went south to Negro classrooms. These girls wore themselves out

there, many of them, as their brothers had in the Army, and yet
no change was reported in the black swarms of illiterates, who
had no skills, no civilized traditions. Perhaps — who knew? —
they lacked, just as advocates of slavery had always claimed, the
capacity to learn.

Lincoln was shot to death. The Capital was reeking with
political corruption, especially despised by Vermonters because
of the horrid waste of public money. Of the Vermont sons in
the Army, death had taken about twenty able-bodied young men
from every small Vermont town. The older generation felt that
they could not be spared, that the future could not be faced without them. To people of the parents' age, it seemed as though
Vermont could count on but few of even those soldiers who did
not die. Some came home just long enough to take one dismayed
look at the rocky farms and poor little towns, and go away
again, often taking a Vermont wife along. Some came back to
stay because, drunken, foul-mouthed, demoralized by Army life,
they no longer cared where they lived. Some — crippled by a
wound, or by an ill disease, morose, silent, misanthropic, lazy —
were scarcely to be recognized.

To Vermonters of the parents' age, darkness hung over the
years just past. What had they meant? Sorrow and anguished
anxiety more than a man's heart could stand, sacrifices more than
a family could endure. And what had it come to?

Darkness hung over the future, too. All the best of the younger
generation (it seemed to their elders) were going away. The
left-behind old folks had not strength enough to carry on the
home farm, with its small stone-walled meadows that must be
cut mostly by the scythe, with its miles of fences to be kept
up. Brush began to creep in on the edges of pastures, foxes multiplied in the woods as though the settlements had already been
deserted by men. The farm down the road was given up, and the
one beyond that, and the one on the other side.

Some farms were taken by French Canadians, not one of whom
could sign his own name, not a word of English in the whole
family of them, children swarming by the dozen (so it seemed
to older Vermonters). Down in the valley towns, the Irish were
taking over, they who had built the railroads. They too were

wholly unschooled, none too clean, many of them sickly and strengthless; they also had shoals of sons and daughters. "They'll vote us out of the town as soon as those children grow up."

The price of wool dropped to nothing, or almost. Small, much-cherished industries — hat-making, leather-tanning, woolen mills, tailoring, iron forges, potteries — vanished like a dream. Towns which had manufactured twenty different kinds of useful things had now one sawmill and a wood-working factory, this last barely holding on. The State was deep in debt.

"It'll last our time out — maybe," people of the age of the parents told each other. "But when we're gone — "

They dreaded to think what it would be, when they were no longer there to keep up the old ideals of cleanliness, hard work, honesty, education, and those rights of man, won by their forefathers. Only the shiftless would remain, like meager, dim-colored lichens clinging to rocks. Shiftless Vermonters and ignorant foreigners who knew not the tradition into which, passive and purposeless as so much seaweed, they had been washed up by the tides of destiny. The Vermont experiment had failed. They had made an effort great beyond their strength. They could no longer go on with it.

Tired as dogs, they were all stumbling up a steep, stony road — in the dark.

PART IV

PART IV

CHAPTER 15

Introduction

NOT at all. Not in the least. That's the way the future looked
to the soldiers' parents and grandparents. But that is not what the
future turned out to be.

Many of the older generation here, like older people in other
American states, were emotionally and materially broken by the
Civil War. It had been too much for them — the tension and effort,
the death of many of their sons, the shock of seeing with their
own eyes the almost mortal wounds, psychological and physical,
inflicted by war on many of those who survived, the bewildered
alarm about the changes in American society which followed
dizzingly on this war. They had the tendency common to all on
the downward slope of life to think that change is another name
for death. They were right, of course. Change is death for all
things old which are material — for everything except ideals.

But, by definition, every older generation is on the way out.
If this one, sooner than most, was ready to drop into hopeless
inertia, the stage was left all the more open to the forward rush
of youth, who welcome change as another name for life. They
too are right. If the traditions (another name for the dominating
life-ideals) in which they and their parents grew up have the
vitality to outlast the literal, worn-out garments of the past, if
their inherited standard is rooted in real values, the young are
sound in their certainty that it will serve them as they plunge
forward into the always new, uncharted years ahead.

A good deal of what older Vermonters who survived the Civil
War foresaw in dismay did, factually, come to pass. But it did not
mean what they assumed it would mean. The century (almost)
of Vermont since the Civil War has not been in the least like
what was dreaded by Green Mountain elders.

What has that century been?

How can an intelligible report be made on the myriad of

heterogeneous details of any hundred years in any community's life? To reduce the sprawling pile to some kind of orderliness, perhaps as good a way as any is to sort the details out into four categories according to the four great Vermont forebodings of the post-Civil War decade. That decade is recent enough for many people still living (I am one of them) to hear, still fresh in our ears, the echo of our grandparents' troubled laments at what they thought they saw threatening the progress, the continued existence of our State. These four categories can be used as natural chapter headings. Here they are:

1. Financial ruin. Although the four war years had brought sizable profits to some Vermonters from the enlarged sale of woolen goods and cavalry mounts, this market collapsed with a crash at the end of the conflict. And while it lasted, it benefited only a minority.

Furthermore those who returned from service in the Army brought back reports of enormous actual and potential riches in other sections of the country, outstripping beyond comparison the lean resources of their native state. For the first time, Vermonters generally took in the hard fact that their own home country could never hope for any easy-to-come-by prosperity or wealth. And wealth was needed to pay the State war debt. Like all debt, this was a horror to them. Each of them felt that every cent of it was his own personal obligation.

Weeds and brush were taking possession of acre upon acre of farm land. All could see with their own eyes that the encroachment had gone dangerously far while man power was away at the front. How could those acres be won back?

2. What they saw as "the ebbing away of the lifeblood of communities" in emigration to the cities and to the West.

3. The crushing and obliteration of the Vermont way of life by "hordes of immigrants" of "inferior stocks." Let me say loudly that the words between the quotation marks above, and the ideas back of them, are not mine. They were constantly used by many serious books of that period. Even Stilwell's *Migration from Vermont*, published in 1948, repeats the old theme in words chosen for their tragic color. After 1850, he states, "Community after community was growing sadly conscious of the way in

which emigration was leaching its best blood." Of the immigrants he remarks with an evident effort to sound moderate, "Whatever the moral or physical virtues of these newcomers, they were undeniably persons who maintained and expected a lower standard of living than the native stock." Professor Stilwell's observation apparently stopped short with the very first generation of the newcomers. We shall see that there is a thing or two about the later phases and developments in the life of immigrants which he did not take into account.

4. Finally, in the back of the minds of many older Vermonters was an anxiety lest the Southern contention be proved true — that Negroes are inherently incapable of taking on freedom with its responsibilities. After the Proclamation of 1863 all the North had, to some degree, accepted the assumption that Negroes are fully human; but for many, probably a majority, the chief issue fought for was the nobly political ideal of the Union, indissoluble, eternal. That ideal was reinforced, not tarnished, by the practical consideration that it would be a long economic step backward to break up the Federation. But in Vermont, from the very first of the Civil War — from long before that, from its own beginnings — the unquestioned folk tradition had, with much more clarity than elsewhere, set itself against any form of human slavery. The few Negroes seen by Vermonters in their own state had been just like anybody. They had assumed that all Negroes were. Now they were horrified by their own soldiers' reports of the massive ignorance, superstition, instability, and animal-like indifference to all the problems of civilized life shown by the "contraband" hordes. They did not put it down in written words anywhere, but a part of what broke the hearts of many older Vermonters in the years after the Civil War was the anxious question, "What if Negroes are, after all, only fit to be slaves?"

CHAPTER 16

Financial Ruin

COMPARED with more emotional types, Vermonters seem to have few passions. But those they have are great and burning. The greatest is their conviction that without freedom human life is not worth living. Debt is one kind of servitude. A man cannot hold his head up (so our axiom goes) until he has paid what he owes.

By the end of the war, Vermonters had paid in taxes, from their earnings and out of their small, slowly hoarded personal savings-bank accounts, seven and a half million dollars. That was grim for a State with a population which had been static for a decade, at a little more than three hundred thousand — less than that of even a moderate-sized modern city. This sum seemed very great to Vermont eyes, but to their dismay it had not been enough. In 1865 the State still owed a million and a half dollars. An honest man pays his debts, but they simply did not see how more than a million dollars could be wrung out of the stony, thin-soiled countryside, being abandoned by their sons and nephews, being taken over by penniless, sickly, illiterate foreigners.

How else could they interpret their situation, those older people who, like all mature men and women, naturally assumed that the future would be like the past they had known, at least like the present around them?

As a matter of statistical fact, it took the State of Vermont only fourteen years to pay the last dollar of that indebtedness. By 1879 the grandparents of the Civil War soldiers were, most of them, dead. But the parents were not yet even venerable. When the last of the war debt was paid off, there was left, to boot, in the Vermont treasury, nearly eighty thousand dollars surplus. Since then the State of Vermont has been forced to follow, along with everybody else, the frightening spiral rise of yearly state expenditures. It has had its share of disheartening setbacks. In the great flood of 1927, for instance, it suffered a financial loss almost beyond computing, borrowed ten million dollars (by that time this did not mean to Vermont imagination anything like the incomprehensible greatness of the million dollars voted at the beginning of the Civil War), paid it all off, and this present year our Treasury has a larger surplus than ever before in its history.

Another arithmetical fact is that the total of individual Vermont savings-bank accounts has risen moderately but steadily every single year (with one exception), from the early nineteenth-century invention of savings banks to the present time.

In the ninety-odd years since the Civil War began, Vermont roads have been made better than people in the horse-age could imagine any road might be. Good roads cost a great deal of money. Our public school system has been improved beyond the dreams of the most hopeful. Our teachers are still paid less than they should be, but, even so, their salaries are fifteen times what they used to be. Our public institutions (for the insane, for convicted criminals) are so much more efficient, humane and intelligently conducted than those of the nineteenth century that there is no comparison. The money appropriated for public health and for dependent children would alarm our grandparents who spent practically none for these purposes; and the resultant improvement in health conditions would dazzle them. Our State Public Library system now, with its circulating book-mobiles, covers areas never before reached by books-on-loan; the town libraries have more books, are better organized, and much more used by schools and the general reading public. Among our other tax-supported State services, we have had for a quarter of a century an active, efficient Forestry Department. Our forefathers would have asked blankly, "What's a Forestry Department?" and when told would have exclaimed "Nonsense!"

Part of this advance is only to be expected. Economists point out that goods, values, and per capita income always have soared enormously when machine power has taken the heaviest loads off the backs of men and their domestic animals. Vermonters certainly make use of machines — wherever they can. But for the most spectacular returns, machine production should be on a large scale, and any economic survey of our whole country would have to class Vermont fields and factories as markedly undersized.

In a "standard-of-living" rating then, we should not be surprised to find Vermont's standing rather low on the list of states. Actually, taking up one after another the material items on which such tables are usually based, we find that in telephones, magazines, books, automobiles, bathrooms, and so on, Vermont homes are about on a level with the average American rural and village homes *in the North Central States*, which seems a fair measure of comparison. They are notably above the level of a great many rural and small village homes in other states. In the matter of electrification, inside running water with plumbing, radios, mechanical refrigeration, and central heating, statistical reports show that Vermont farm and village homes stand slightly above the average of the North Central States. In the number of young people who attain a high school diploma and, after that, some specialized advanced education, Vermonters rank about in the middle of the American gamut, below the richest states, like New York and Illinois, far above the less advanced. There is practically no illiteracy in the State, except among the congenitally subnormal (who, alas! do not fare well in the closely figured Vermont scheme of life). As to percentage of school-age population in school, in 1910, it stood, here, at 70 per cent of the youngsters. (In Pennsylvania of that year the figure was 57 per cent, and in Ohio 60 per cent.) In 1940, more than 97 per cent of Vermont children from ten to thirteen were in school, 86 per cent of the fifteen-year-old group, and 12 per cent of the twenty-year-olds. In 1940 the national average of adults who had had less than five years' schooling was nearly 9 per cent. In Vermont it was 6.1 per cent.

It sounds mysterious beyond belief that there can be enough income in the Green Mountains to keep up to — sometimes stand above — the national average enjoyment of all these expensive modern services.

One element of the problem is easily solved. None of the money we get our hands on is slathered on nonessentials. To be sure we do allow ourselves the luxury of having the dome of our

Statehouse regilded from time to time. But that is something more than an ostentatious frivolity. To us our beautiful Statehouse is the symbol of achievements and aspirations in which we take justifiable pride. No member of the General Assembly would refuse to vote the money needed to keep it from looking shabby, any more than he would grudge an Easter hat to a loved and respected wife. Passing over a few, a very few, such exceptions, money both public and private goes where a sober outlook on life decides that it will do the most good. This is our old friend "thrift" again, but now with a quaint new angle. As we see it, we manage substantial results on a comparatively slim income, largely because our tendency is to play safe. Our resources are not cut down by gambling losses. Suppose two ladies go shopping and one of them loses a handbag stuffed with ten- and twenty-dollar bills. Her friend who keeps tight hold of a modest pocketbook is the one who can afford to pay for the luncheon. The money Vermont businessmen have not lost explains many chapters in our economic history.

Consider banking for example. It was not brought in full-grown from the outside as in later organized territories. It grew here slowly in answer to definitely felt local needs. In really early days some of the banker's functions were performed by the general storekeeper — the much respected merchant — the only out-and-out businessman in town. The rest of the community were producers. They were engaged in the primary services of growing food, making objects out of metal or wood, perfecting one or another kind of mechanical device, caring for animals, teaching school. Only the storekeeper made his living by buying and selling. He took what was raised or made around him, paid for it in goods which could not be produced in Vermont. After the first generation, individual heads of families no longer were forced to make long trading journeys themselves. The storekeeper lived up to his name by keeping on hand a store of exotic merchandise — tobacco, fine lawn, tea, silver spoons, books (many books), scissors, needles, silk ribbons, thread and so forth. He procured this stock once or twice a year (no traveling salesmen in those early days) by a laborious, carefully planned wagon or sledge expedition to Boston, Albany, Montreal, or perhaps one of the Connecticut towns like Hartford. In those cities he sold the merchandise manufactured or grown by his neighbors.

Accounts were balanced three or four times a year. Between these settling dates, the merchant often advanced credit in goods, much as a bank today supplies pay-roll money to a manufacturer. In order to stay long in business he had to be absolutely honest. His customers had records showing, to the ounce, how much maple sugar and salt pork and butter they had put into his hands, to the inch how much woolen cloth, how many knit stockings, and all the rest. They could read newspaper market reports and add columns of figures as well as he could. At any sign that he was not dealing fairly, they withdrew their trade and went to the next town with it if the storekeeper there had a better reputation. Their fixed resolution never to get into another man's power through owing him too much money left each of them almost without exception, free to choose his middleman.

In addition, the storekeeper needed a sense of values, actual conservatively figured values, not hopeful guesses about the swing of the market. He was successful if he bought in his town only woolen cloth or maple sugar or butter or salt pork (in early days potash) of a quality he could sell in the city. In city shops he must know how to buy only goods acceptable to his home-town customers.

These qualities, this in-the-field training, its lessons sharply enforced by the immediate loss of money when judgment was faulty, made merchants the natural organizers, the trusted directors of the first Vermont banks. The step was natural. They merely added money to the list of commodities they handled. The shaping influence of this origin has never been outgrown.

The need for some sort of banking system was felt early in the nineteenth century. People began to consider their savings more secure in a central vault, than in a strong-box at home. The danger was not burglary, it was that the individual hoard when needed might be found to contain bogus coins and bills which would never have passed the sharp eyes of a trained cashier. The amount of bad money in circulation was a serious matter. Early lists of prisoners in the State Penitentiary show few charged with crimes of violence, an astounding number of counterfeiters. I am sure I don't know how that fact can be reconciled with our citizens' generally high standard of honesty, unless — just possibly — on the theory that if the fraud was good enough to go undetected, no actual man or woman would suffer by it. The loser, as with potash smuggling, would be a disembodied abstraction called government. At all events, no matter how they stifled their consciences, Vermonters were adepts at counterfeiting. One of them was so extremely skilled — so goes the story — that instead of letting his talent languish in a prison cell, he was offered a job in the United States Mint.

Linked with the idea of safety for savings went the cognate advantage offered by a pool of capital ready for loans to those who could put it to use. In 1803 the first bill to charter two banks (one in Windsor, one in Burlington) passed the Legislature. But old ways of thought die hard. The Governor vetoed it. Repassed, he vetoed it again. Some of the reasons for his disapproval are both quaint and illustrative of a type of conservatism by no means extinct. "Broadening the base of credit," he claimed, "would weaken the moral fiber of business"; the presence of bankers and large amounts of money to invest would "facilitate gambling"; there would be a tendency to shift the moral responsibility of the individual debtor; money would tend to get into the hands of the already wealthy and weaken democracy; "banks would help only the strong."

But of course no gubernatorial veto can long hold back the hands of the economic clock. By 1827 ten banks had been chartered in Vermont. Eight of them had local businessmen (which pretty certainly at that date meant retail merchants) for president. The two other presidents were lawyers, always the useful advisers and close associates of businessmen. Later, when transactions grew larger, an experienced cashier had to be brought in from a distance. Preferably he was a Vermont boy who had learned the trade in a larger center. He was never in the least the "financial wizard" type. For two reasons: the limited opportunities for high finance kept that type from wanting a job in Vermont, nor did Vermont want him. Taking a whirl in watered gold-mining stock was not considered sound banking by the solid, serious directors.

who understood their title literally and really directed. When people came in to "hire money" (in Calvin Coolidge's old-time phrase) their character and reputation were considered as thoughtfully as the tangible security they offered.

These banks grew slowly, but they grew. As time went on, more savings accumulated than nearby borrowers could use. This meant investments (mostly in the newer northwestern states) backed by collateral beyond the reach of minute personal inspection. Fortunately it was the cautious rule to spread these distant loans far and wide with no single commitment dangerously large, and to keep their over-all total only a small fraction of the bank's assets. So it happened that those recurrent terrible bank panics where long lines of despairing depositors battered at locked doors in vain, took place elsewhere in the United States — not in Vermont. Not every bank flourished here. Some of the smaller ones were merged in an orderly manner with stronger institutions. A few had to go out of business, but so few that each case stands out, well-remembered. In 1851 the South Royalton bank failed, but "no depositor lost any money." In Brattleboro, just before a system of bank inspection began operating, a dishonest cashier unsuspected in a community whose business was based on trust in the prevailing financial probity, got away with a sum of money, three hundred thousand dollars, which seemed enormous to Vermonters of that time. But again, "no depositor lost a penny." Following the imperious bidding of the tradition in which they were brought up, that all transactions with other men are human relationships, hence subject to the code governing decent human conduct, the Brattleboro merchants and lawyers responsible for that bank little by little made up out of their own pockets or later profits what was due the depositors.

Nowadays our Vermont banks look thoroughly up to date. Their accounts are kept by calculating machines. They sell or cash traveler's checks and United States bonds over the counter. Through connections in New York or Boston they arrange for their customers all sorts of investment transactions. With only a few days' waiting they will get you a draft on Amsterdam or Johannesburg. But beneath all this modernity the viewpoint of their merchant founders has not fundamentally changed. The cashiers and directors still think of the stock in trade they handle as other people's money, as the equivalent of known and real values — never as mere symbols printed on adding-machine tape. No doubt over the years some handsome profits have been missed. But losses — right through the Great Depression and up to today — have been kept low, so negligible that you wouldn't believe the figures if you saw them.

For general business, wholesale and retail, the line of development has been much the same. There are, to be sure, plenty of establishments dealing in electric appliances, automobiles, oil burners and other contraptions never dreamed of by our forefathers, but beside them are to be found many firms which, like our banks, were founded generations ago on a shoestring, grew with careful management until they reached some kind of organic relationship with the need for them, and from that point on stayed put. Contrary to orthodox American business-dogma that unless a company keeps constantly getting larger, it will start running downhill fast, they continue at the same unspectacular level — comfortably solvent. When outsiders scold us for accepting what they call an atmosphere of stagnation, we brush them off by saying that there's something about the climate of Vermont which makes people who get past sixty-five live on, no better but not much worse, up into the high eighties, and maybe the same principle works with business activities.

But when we talk things over seriously among ourselves, there are not a few of us who wonder whether our critics may not be falling into the familiar error of confusing "the way it was" with "the way it had to be."

When they ask us, "Where would our nation have been without the free, wide, reckless gambling spirit which in a scant century pushed the frontier across the Great Plains, across the Rockies, to the Pacific?" it isn't just the sour-grapes complex which rouses our unspoken comment, "Maybe it might have been better off." The spirit of "Pikes Peak or Bust" undoubtedly speeded up that westward march and the utilization of our continent's fabulous riches. But after all, what was the hurry? Slogans of a different type, "Make haste slowly," "Look before you leap," might have prevented the hideous material loss, with the accompanying human sorrow, frustration, bewildered defeat, of trying to farm Michigan's cut-over territory, and the Dust Bowl.

We have the same narrow, provincial dislike of the economic cycle. It is all very well for some theorist to point out that periodic business failures do not diminish but merely redistribute national wealth. We are sure that almost every bankruptcy crushes the spirit of some individual. We have seen that happen close at hand, although — goodness knows — the business mortality rate here is far below the national average.

Authorities differ in their calculation as to just what life expectancy a new-born business can look forward to. Some of them say that out of twenty new ventures started in our America, nineteen will fail at least once; many, more than once. Others put the death rate lower, but it is always very high. Pondering these astonishing figures, we wonder what would be thought of marriage as an institution if nineteen out of twenty — or even 75 per cent — of the couples joined in wedlock were fated to be parted again by the Divorce Court.

But no amount of money not lost will provide cash for living expenses, keep them ever so low. Some money, relatively a lot of money, must have been earned in Vermont to pay for the widely distributed, constantly more comfortable ways of life — doctor's bills, tuition fees, refrigerators, books, automobiles and all the rest. How has that new wealth been created? By the only method there is. By the intelligent use of labor to shape raw material into a form somebody needs or desires enough to pay money for. That is good economic theory — or was when I went to college. But to make it cover all cases, a rather flexible definition of labor and raw material is needed.

For instance, from our grandparents' point of view it was actually the absence of labor which brought back a steady income-return from parts of our real estate. Just as the foreboding mid-nineteenth-century elders predicted, those thin-soiled, rocky, back-road farms became useless for crops, even for pasture. Work on them was given up. But before they had time to revert to scrub forest, many of them were bought as summer homes by people from outside the State. Too small and simple to serve as "estates" for the wealthy, they accurately suit the tastes of business and professional families. The personal qualities of such Americans are valued and admired by their Vermont neighbors, who, not being rubbed the wrong way by fancied condescension, "act natural" and show their best side. The newcomers in turn usually have a cultivation and intellectual background wide enough to appreciate (often with a smile) the distinctive Green Mountain character.

The taxes on these rejuvenated back-roads farms seem anything but exorbitant to the doctor or lawyer or businessman from a Michigan or Illinois city. They are enough to help out greatly in Town-Meeting deliberations over the always-rising cost of roads and schools. Not to speak of the moderate but very welcome employment they give to Vermont carpenters, plumbers, dairy farmers and eighth-grade boys who want a job mowing lawns.

This sounds cheerful, doesn't it? So it was, so it is, in the long run. Although only a smallish fraction of the up-hill country has found homemaking new owners, most of us agree heartily with our Forestry Department that it is only good sense to let trees take over the rest of it — land that never should have been cleared, never would have been if Vermont had been settled later when the existence of the open flat lands of the West was known.

But the transition, like most changes in a way of life has been a great wrench to several kinds of people. Those who have suffered most have been the slightly feeble-minded or feeble-willed. Confronted with any kind of change, people who are not equipped with a normal amount of energy and competence feel only a limpetlike instinct to cling to the familiar. Such were the most numerous of the few who went on living on infertile hill farms. But even they did not stay long. The economic suction of wages to be earned lower down on gentler slopes or in the valleys was too much for them. After a few years they slid down hill where life is easier.

To the old, also, change was often simple heartbreak. The widower grandfather in his seventies, unable to carry on alone the farm on which he was born and on which he worked all his life, was forced to move to his son's fine farm home in Iowa, his daughter's comfortable city apartment in Rochester, New York. It was silent anguish for him to turn his back forever on the old home where he had spent the long years of his life. To step for the last time over the threshold where he had sat as a little boy watching the sunset, to think that the windows would fall in, the floor rot away, that foxes would make their strong-smelling den in what had been his cellar, fragrant with stored apples — for him it was truly the death of the past. He made good fiction stuff for the 1890-and-later, Mary E. Wilkins school of short stories, tense, hopeless, tragic, but not sordid.

A third kind of victim to economic good sense is now in literary fashion. This group is made up of those with an unbending personal pride (or vanity?) which demands that circumstance must yield to them, never they to circumstance. Every once in a while on some steep back road one finds a solitary farm still carried on by the victims of a fierce-eyed, strong-jawed fanatic member of the family (grandparent, parent, or maybe just a dominating older brother) who expends on resisting a necessary and reasonable alteration in life, a last-ditch determination which would be admirable in a crusader for social justice, but here is malignant egomania. Such a situation is, of course, for what might be called with all due respect to a nobly gifted author, "the Faulkner school," what candy is to a child. The past can never go on living in the present, no matter what the framework of society is. The old man who, behind his set face, wept over the death of his past, soon died himself. Old men do. In some cases his old home died, also, as the forest closed silently in on it.

But in many cases it rose again as a home, a much-loved summer home where children once more slept under the eaves, and fished in the brook, and their parents sat, vacation-quiet, on the grass under the big oak-tree, reading not Horace Greeley's *Tribune*, as the Vermont family had, but perhaps erudite books printed in a foreign language, or mystery stories for the idle rest-hours.

And whatever the fate of those high hill-acres, think of the ordinary men and women, never mentioned in print, who had always felt imprisoned on those sterile, steep, remote farms and who welcomed with joy the change to a more animated, stirring life, full of new interests, new enjoyments, new opportunities. You never read a short story about any of them, did you? But there were many of them. Naturally. When you have not been especially happy in the present, you don't mind a bit the death of that present as it turns into the past.

Considered in its total effect then, the passing of those stony fields, those upland pastures is not tragic. All the rest of Vermont's agricultural story is positively exhilarating. There are fewer farms now in Vermont than there were, but those which exist are richer and more productive than any our grandfathers could have imagined. The dairy farmers, in close touch with expert county agents, have larger monthly checks from their milk sent by special milk trains to Boston or New York than old-time farmers used to handle in a year. Human voters are considerably outnumbered by the cow population, and these carefully bred cows give milk in prodigiously greater abundance than the nineteenth-century scrub cows. The hay is baled by machinery in the field itself and hoisted (also by machinery) to the lofts of the barn. Tractors, manure-spreaders, silos are taken for granted. When some power device, designed for large-scale operation, proves too costly or too unwieldy for our fields (for there is a good deal of up and down even in land we consider flat) it's a pretty dumb Vermont farmer who doesn't manage to rig up some sort of workable substitute by expert tinkering based on the rear assembly of a twenty-year-old Ford.

The farmer's daughter and son go to college (agricultural or liberal arts), his wife has a permanent wave in her hair if she wants it. Dairying is confining — no vacations in Bermuda — but during the winter months there is quite a little free time between milkings for trips in the family car to the village for shopping, for church, for a lecture, for the movies. On such occasions there is nothing markedly rustic about their car, their clothes or their actions. No one would take them for anything but a modern American family. Of course, exactly, that's what they are.

How could any prophet in the 1860's have foreseen that money — big money — would be earned by providing food and lodging for visitors coming into Vermont to catch trout, to enjoy the harmonies of color and line as mountains blend into well-kept valley land, to shoot deer, and most fantastic of all to slide down hill in winter?

The main volume of early tourist trade bypassed the Green Mountain country, touching it lightly only here and there, as at Woodstock and Manchester. Clusters of huge barracklike hotels, such as dominated Saratoga, Atlantic City and many parts of the White Mountains, never were built in Vermont. Looking back, we are as relieved that our Vermont tourist business "detoured" the big-hotel era as that our industrial production similarly detoured the long nineteenth-century period of bloody, violent strikes. It was certainly fortunate (given the quality of our tradition) that our young people escaped the hectic, tip-crazed atmosphere pervading those big resorts. I do not mean that there is anything degrading in accepting a couple of dimes or more for carrying luggage or serving a meal — routine, regular services. Both tip-taker and tip-giver understand that wages from the employer are set very low just because the public is expected to make up the major part of a fair day's pay. It is a silly and highly unsatisfactory system. The full cost of service should be included in the official bill. But where it is a minor matter of routine, it is no more than silly, unbusinesslike and unsatisfactory.

The case is entirely different when tips are large, vary greatly in amount, and depend on the passing whim of the traveler. In the "big-hotel era" of the summer resorts, notably well-to-do people sometimes spent a month or more in one place. This sort of vacation is not unknown, I am told, in the winter resorts of today. The effect is the same on the tip-expecting "servants." If the "guests" are free-spending people, they are soon spotted and fought for. Their waitress has to subsidize the chef's assistant to get them the best servings of meat; somehow, by gang-rule, an unpopular bellboy is never given the chance to answer the call bell from their rooms. For them all sorts of rules cease to exist. Cocktails are smuggled upstairs to them long after the bar is supposed to be closed. The distinction between tips and bribes becomes very faint indeed. That sort of experience — and there is plenty more of the same sort — is not at all good for high-school and college boys and girls in their teens and early twenties. Vermonters in general never would have fitted in to a way of catering to vacationers of which a large professional servant class is a part.

There are hotels in Vermont, of course. A few of them cater to people with expensive tastes. But many of our hotels are no more a part of Vermont life, no more dependent on or expressive of Vermont ideas than the useful chain grocery stores. Like the supermarkets, many of our hotels are branches of a heavily capitalized national organization. Their policies are decided outside of Vermont, and a number of their employees are professionals brought in by the management. It is not a bad way to organize a business which is more economically done on a very large scale, and for which Vermonters have no special aptitude; although some of their policies clash resoundingly with Vermont principles.

But in the vacation-guest field, all over our country, hotels are fewer in proportion to the whole. Most vacationers now drive their own cars and change from place to place as the spirit moves them. For the night's lodgings, increasingly large numbers of them pass by the hotels and sleep in farm or village homes, or in tourist cabins, or now, as Vermont grows more twentieth-centuryish, in motels.

There is much to be done after a vacationing car has driven on from a farmhouse, a tourist cabin, or a motel. Sheets have to be washed, bedding aired, mattresses turned, floors and plumbing fixtures cleaned. But this is work. And most Vermonters are not at all afraid of work, are very glad to have it, and greatly need the pay for it. There is in it almost no element of the very chancy effort to make a personally pleasing surface impression on a stranger, who will pay or not, as he takes a notion. It is a business matter, a set price agreed on beforehand, by the two sides of the transaction. The relation between the worker and the vacationist is satisfactory to Vermonters only when either side of it is one which any American would be willing to accept or to have a son or daughter accept. We can't see that we are unreasonable in setting this standard, and we certainly are thankful for the growth, along these lines, of the Vermont "tourist business." It is true that no one family spends any considerable sum at any one stop. But the total spent by those unceasing lines of summer vacationers and winter skiers already amounts to big business (on our scale), nor is there any sign of its growing less.

Once in a while, in a musing moment, the idea crosses a Vermont mind that, since a good many Americans — the kind who really don't like luxury hotels and all that they imply — seem to us just like Vermonters, possibly many of our summer vacation tourists like this way of managing the human contact between country folk and strangers as well as we do.

It would take a book at least as long as this one to sketch in bare outline the story of Vermont's industry. I shall not attempt it. I have space only for a few examples suggesting the general trend.

Back in the eighteenth and early nineteenth centuries the village blacksmith was an all-round worker in metal, essential to the life of the community and highly valued for his skill. He endlessly shod horses and oxen; he also manufactured runners for sleds, pungs and sleighs, hinges, latches, bolts for doors; he mended the primitive machinery in the primitive sawmills, fullingmills, carding mills, gristmills. He was no unlettered peasant handcrafter. Because of the ever-present district schooling, he knew, as every Vermonter did, how to read and write and figure. Like his neighbors he had books in his house. Respecting "book-learning," he took his citizen's share in providing, somewhere nearby, the opportunity for bright youngsters to go a step further towards higher education.

The story of the Taft family is an illustration. The grandfather of William Howard Taft, President of the United States, was the blacksmith in the tiny town of Townshend, Vermont. His son, father of the President, was the first Chairman of the Trustees of the Seminary (equivalent to high school) founded by the citizens of that community, to provide advanced education for their young people.

Later generations of the Taft family went into the professions, law or education. This often happened in Vermont families. But more often, in and out of Vermont, the early-nineteenth-century blacksmith's son concentrated his excellent mind and great energy on the ever-expanding progress of mechanical invention, industrial production, engineering. In the classrooms of an academy or seminary, he mastered enough mathematical theory to recognize general principles underlying and supplementing the inherited handskill learned at his father's forge. Such a man came to maturity at a time in human history when the western world (as contrasted with the oriental world of the same dates) was crackling with the electric possibilities of machinery, just as centuries earlier the air of the Renaissance crackled with the urge towards intellectual and artistic development. At the time of Vermont's early life, men along the Nile and the Ganges, in China, in Russia, were straining their muscles to do the work needed by human society. In the western world, young men were intoxicated by the possibility of using power-wheels to avoid humdrum drudgery. The lever, the screw, the wheel were not new to humanity. What was new was the rush to increase the application and combination of these mechanical forces. By the time the early Vermont blacksmith's son was a grown man, he was an expert, theoretical and practical machinist and inventor in a world which needed such men and paid them well.

"Inventor" is a fighting word. Nations and localities hotly resent any passing over of priority claims made for their favorite sons. Often all parties in such disputes have some measure of justification. The confusion arises because the word itself is so indefinite. Does the title inventor belong to the dreamer with a hazy vision that something desired could perhaps be accomplished by a method of which the details are still to be thought out; or to the first person completing a working model; or to the Henry Ford type of genius who by design and production improvements makes an expensive luxury available to mass consumption?

Whatever the definition, Vermont has furnished every variety: Davenport with his functioning electric motor, unusable only because in his lifetime no source of power to run it was as yet in existence — the Fairbanks brothers, shipping from St. Johnsbury (population about eight thousand) their reliable platform scales which did their part in weighing the produce of almost every country on the globe.

For the general picture it makes no great difference who first thought of what. The important point is that a great many people were having bright ideas and acting on them. All over Vermont, wherever there was water power, blacksmith's sons and nephews were branching out into one or another small manufacturing enterprise, very often based on patented inventions of their own. First-growth, hardwood forests were turned into furniture, smaller trees and the scraps and edgings from large ones went into crating stock, tool or brush handles, spools, toothpicks — every conceivable wooden knickknack.

Iron and steel had to be brought in from a distance. What of that! Handling hard metal was in their blood. The brisk young men enlarged the family metal-working shops to turn out the latest models in modern machinery, "modern" in the 1830's, 1840's, 1850's. Machines, machines, machines — the word was in everyone's mind, on everyone's lips. The most skillful among these Vermonters designed and produced the extremely accurate machinery which manufactured the machinery, which manufactured goods. This finest form of tool-making has never died out. Today the air of Springfield, Vermont, hums with the vibration of precision grinders, gear-shapers, automatic lathes.

Those early industrialists succeeded greatly. Why wouldn't they? They had what the world of their generation needed — a mechanical skill as instinctive to many Vermonters of that period as breathing. Their factories were never run by the treasurer's office. The boss was part draftsman, part production manager. A smart foreman could look forward to being taken into partnership, or to starting an independent factory of his own, next door to the older one — both of them on a tiny scale compared to modern industrial units. The field was new, demand far in excess of supply. Orders for their products came in from all over the growing American Federation.

Many such orders came to a Connecticut Valley Vermonter of a blacksmith family who had invented ways to manufacture rotary pumps of great size and in great numbers. These were used in many city water works. Philadelphia bought quantities of moderately large models, and St. Louis (already Midwest ideas inclined to the grandiose) ordered the biggest rotary pump ever manufactured. Do you wonder how such a huge piece of machinery could be carried so far, before the days of railroads? It was transported (in pieces of course), under the watchful eyes of an accomplished Vermont machine-manufacturer, over the Green Mountains to Albany; thence by canal to Buffalo; thence by the Lakes to Chicago; thence by great wagons across the plains to St. Louis, where it was set up and put to work by the Vermonter from Windsor. There is a lot more to that story, many amusing details of how St. Louis paid for the pump, and what the Vermonter did with the money, but I would be lost if I included all the colorful anecdotes connected with these transactions.

I really must add just one more — this one with a transatlantic flavor. The Duke of Wellington at last (1852) died, and took down to his grave his never-budging opposition to any change in military equipment. What had been good enough to beat Napoleon and save the world at Waterloo, must be (so he naturally believed) superior to any modern tomfoolery. Just at this time the British government, hard-driven by the crisis of the Crimean War, was ready to try anything to increase the fire-power of its regiments. The machine shops of Windsor, Vermont, were able to manufacture small arms equal to any in the world. Their range was long, they hit what was aimed at, their parts were so closely machined as to be absolutely interchangeable. Also the organization of factories was such that rifles and pistols could be turned out with what was then extraordinary speed. The new Windsor machine shops were fairly swamped by the size of the contracts with the British government. Windsor boomed with prosperity. The sequel to this story is not at all comic. The manufacturers were overextended. With the sudden end of the Crimean War, they crashed. You see we do have bankruptcies even in Vermont when we wade out into deep rough water! Windsor's boom days were over. They would not have lasted long in any case. The failure of one firm merely speeded up and focused attention on a movement beyond human power to prevent. When competition stiffens, costs have to be figured to the fraction of a cent. Vermont's promising arms industry and most of its metal-shaping factories as well, went down the river — literally — down the Connecticut to centers where raw material and the coal needed to replace limited water power could be brought together at lower transportation cost. Granted the faster, faster, *faster!* business doctrine of the time, Vermont did seem to be falling behind in the race for prosperity. Prosperity? For actual existence! Well, it's a long race — forever — and many of the sprinters lack the stamina to keep grinding on, lap after lap.

Was that page of history so tragic, after all? Again I repeat the cliché that it is idle to speculate about what might have happened if — . All we can be sure of in this case is that certain ugly phases of worker-employer discord, almost universal in the early days of big industry, did not happen in Vermont. No adult American can have forgotten the class war in those huge nineteenth-century enterprises with armies of workers (called "hands") so big that the impersonal discipline needed in any army seemed required to keep them in order; with employers convinced that those who paid the wages (they, themselves) had the absolute right — the duty — to enforce that discipline. Class war it was! No human contact bridged the gap between domineering management and the huge masses of resentful, suspicious industrial workers. Often it broke out into terrible, hate-filled struggles between the two. Many strikes were bloody and violent. Most of them caused widespread human privation and suffering. All of them were incalculably costly in money lost. The Colorado coal strike of 1913–1914 meant civil war for months. At Ludlow, many men, women and children lost their lives. In the end Federal troops were sent to end the anarchic chaos. The "massacre" at Herrin, Illinois, was not a case where wage earners were killed by their employers' mine guards during riots over workers' grievances, but the killing of unarmed, nonunion, workingmen by armed fellow workingmen, belonging to the unions, sincerely convinced that only through unions could the human dignity of wage earners be upheld. So hot was local sympathy there for the union members who did the shooting, that the courts, after five months' trial of the case, gave up, defeated, admitting that the processes of law were powerless. The strike of textile workers in Lowell, Massachusetts, lasted, as recognized lawless warfare, for two months, involving thousands of people. The railroad strike of 1877 gravely disorganized our country's business, and became so violent that this time also Federal troops were needed to safeguard life and property. In the one year of 1937, more than a million and a half persons were involved in more than three thousand strikes, which cancelled out from productivity forty million work hours.

The worst of it seems over now. Organized labor and entrenched capital realize that it is poor business to be always at each other's throats — that neither side can insist on having everything all its own way. But the truce is still uneasy. Old resentments rankle. Though there is less open violence, distrust and hostility lie just below the surface. Is it entirely fantastic then, to count it not altogether a hardship that the facts of geography prevented Vermont from becoming a center of big industry? If good fortune it was, we have only our luck to thank for it. Certainly our grandfathers did not plan it that way. Yet, here we are, in spite of their efforts, free from the passionate unreason, from the subconscious wounds left by bitterly contested labor wars — free as our ancestors were (also by a stroke of pure luck) from the earlier nightmare of war to the knife between whites and Indians.

Do we never have "industrial unrest" in Vermont? Yes, occasionally. The first case occurred long ago when workmen building a railroad laid down their tools with loud and vigorous protests that their wages were not being paid. No evidence here to show capital conspiring to grind the faces of the poor — or the other way round. The reason for the lapse had no social significance whatever: the subcontractor for that stretch of roadbed had run out of money.

I don't mean to imply that Vermont's infrequent labor troubles have always been as simple as this one — as unlike the collective action called strikes, elsewhere. A few of them roused indignant anger, slow to cool. But even these, greatly as they are to be regretted, no more resembled the lurid Elizabethan horrors of great strikes in great industries than a scuffle over a close decision at an intervillage baseball game does the bloody ferocity of a prize-ring battle to the knockout for the heavyweight championship.

As for the future it is a fair guess that as in the past some of our long-established sources of income will dry up or at least diminish. The lumber cut is greater than the growth rate. All over New England, textile mills are closing down to move South. Twentieth-century taste in building materials seems to have turned to steel, concrete and glass, away from marble and granite. For years those two noble stones have been considered the outstanding natural resources of our old State. If the modern world no longer wants them for post offices, banks and courthouses, only for tombstones and war memorials, it will be a body blow to a sizable part of Vermont manufacturing, and a dislocation hard to stand to many highly skilled, intelligent, stable quarrymen and stonecutters.

And yet — and yet — the crape-hangers were wrong once, they could be wrong again. The fact stands out that there are very few deserted factory buildings in Vermont. Many of the old firms are still operating. New ones constantly take the places — and something over — of those which go out of business or move away.

Sometimes this show of prosperity is questioned because even though factories may be marked with the familiar trade name, ownership has shifted, and what used to be an independent industry, controlled by local capital, is now in fact only a branch plant of a large out-of-state corporation. Absentee ownership has an ugly sound. Very likely in the past it deserved its bad name. Now, however, when the younger generation of business executives is awake to the importance of public relations, the dangers from sudden and arbitrary shifts in policy are much less to be feared. For obviously there are two sorts of public relations, one important in selling a product, the other in making it.

Efficiency engineers tell us that unnecessary labor turnover — the constant losing of experienced hands, the cost of training new ones — adds enormously to production costs. Their researches show that with wages pretty much standardized as they are, the chief reason given by workers for shifting from job to job is that they have been unfairly treated. This chronic state of dissatisfaction results, so these experts believe, less often from friction inside the factory than from discontent with living conditions outside it. The search for a satisfied, hence stable, working force is behind the present wide movement toward branch plants. In Vermont it brings good results. I don't pretend that all our young people prefer the perhaps excessive tranquillity of village life. Far from it! Quite a few of them can hardly wait until they are of age before chasing off to big-city bright lights, But many, free to move, remain. As they grow older they more and more appreciate the opportunity to work in groups small enough for them to be treated not as names and social-security numbers typed on office filing cards but as individual men and women. Rural elbow-room is grateful too — no garage fees for the family car, a freezer bringing to your midwinter table peas and sweet corn grown in your own garden. What does it matter if directors hold their meetings in a distant city? They are not likely to meddle as long as a profit can be reported by the local manager. And he — a paid employee only a few rungs higher than you on the ladder, the only hiring and firing boss you come in contact with — doesn't put on airs. He rolls a good game on the plant bowling team. You sit beside him and his wife in church, vote and discuss community matters with them at the same Town Meeting. His children and yours go to the same school, study under the same teachers, yell their heads off together in the cheering section at basketball games. What's wrong with that? Running a punch press is no harder than other ways of earning a living!

Vermont is filling up with this newer type of smallish factory, turning out all sorts of products light enough to keep transportation costs from being prohibitive. Molded plastic objects are made in every variety of shape, maps, special types of gelatine films sent — insane though it seems — all the way to Hollywood, millions of capacitors. Here I ought to pause and explain, for it is ten to one that you do not know what a capacitor is. Neither do I exactly. But I think I know that it is a sort of booster like the condenser in a car's electrical system, a very small basic part of electronic equipment — television, radio, radar. And I am sure that, being made of extra light material — rolled paper, bakelite, tiny wire — they are shipped thousands at a time by airplane.

Most of us think of Stowe as Vermont's pioneer ski center and nothing else. That small mountain community at the foot of Mount Mansfield is filled with ski-lifts, ski-tows, ski-trails, ski-lodges, hotels, rooms to rent. It is a genuine surprise to read the figures and find that Stowe's income is based on farming, woodworking and winter tourists — in about even amounts. What in the world can woodworking plants make profitably, ten miles from a railroad station, and that station far away from any large urban centers? Do you remember that in many retail stores when your purchase is wrapped and tied up the salesclerk twists into the string a wire running through a small wooden handle, so that your fingers will not be cut by the thin cord? Such handles, in astronomical numbers, are daily produced and sent out from Stowe.

This is the right time to break off my catalogue of the many, many "specialties" made in one town and another. For Stowe's example serves well to illustrate the economic pattern which is taking place over the State as a whole. Like an old-fashioned milking stool, Vermont's earning-a-living program has three supports: small industry, farming and the tourist trade. It is extremely easy to kick over a three-legged stool. And if one of its legs is broken — !

As a matter of fact, even as I write this chapter, a cold shadow thrown from very far can be seen although not yet felt in the dairy farming industry so flourishing in Vermont. It looks ominously like the shadow cast from afar which blacked out the flourishing Merino sheep industry here. Or, like the scientific technological change in the production of potash which obliterated that industry from our State. No, really, it is like both of them together, the head and the handle of a great, threatening hammer.

Here are the scattered digits in the modern scene which we are beginning to add up to a sum which alarms us: science and industrial production, working hand in hand for profits, are exploring the field to see what might be done about exploiting the fact that milk is mostly water, and that water is heavy and expensive to transport. Ways of making milk-concentrates are, in the vividly expressive medical word, "proliferating" at top speed. Condensed milk and milk powder can now be turned into an increasingly close reproduction of milk right from the cow. All that is needed is to put back into it, from any faucet, in any kitchen, the water that was taken out by scientific procedures far away, the water which, therefore, did not have to be rushed at top speed in express milk trains from the barn to the milk distributors, who then by a costly, intricate system of perambulating milk deliverers get it to the home, hotel or restaurant where it is to be used.

This "essential extract of milk" is sealed in cans. It does not spoil till the can is opened. So it fits very well into the new-style way of housekeeping which does not, as the earlier style did, always have a woman (wife or wife's helper) waiting in the kitchen every morning for the milkman and his bottles of quickly perishable milk, to transfer them speedily to a cool storage place. Canned milk, dry or in a syrup, can safely be kept anywhere in any climate, can be transported over great distances by ship (water transport is always a cheaper way to carry merchandise, especially from a great distance).

And what is there, off in that great distance, which threatens the Vermont cow, now numerous beyond the human population just as sheep used to be? There is, in New Zealand, in many places in South America, in many places in our own Southern Piedmont region, a climate where alfalfa, the great dairy-cow food, can be grown and cut all the year round; where cows need no tight shelters from cold and snow, where many of the other costs of producing milk in a zero winter climate like ours are cut to a minimum beyond anything within the power of Vermont to meet.

This new blow of technological unemployment has not yet fallen. Maybe it never will. But we see the upswing of the hammer off there, beyond the horizon.

And we brace ourselves. It startles and dismays us, but it does not spread panic amongst us. The family which is stricken into demoralization by the loss of a large part of its income is the family which has always been well off, living in ease, which never dreamed it could be poor. Vermonters have always known that we could be poor because we have never been well off. This is, oddly, a "psychological protection to the psyche."

If the whole aspect of our dairy business changes, as the Merino sheep business did, if fluid milk is seen to be too cumbersome and expensive to use, as ash-produced potash became, what then?

It will be a terrific blow. But if experience has taught us anything, it is to keep cool and not lose our heads in ticklish situations. We have jackknives and strong hands that do not fear hard work. We will just have to whittle out another leg to hold up our three-legged stool.

CHAPTER 17

The Lifeblood Drains Out

ONE of the blackest forebodings of our great-grandparents, after the Civil War, was that young Vermonters were leaving the State. Even now, most books on this subject, in speaking of the emigration of the younger generation to the Middle West, use such dreary phrases as "the draining out of the lifeblood of the communities." Nobody doubted that it was.

This conviction was inevitable, granted the usual interpretation of facts. The population of Vermont was small and for thirty years before the Civil War had been almost static. Between 1830 and 1840 the increase was less than 4 per cent; from 1850 to 1860 it was three tenths of one per cent; alarmists began to think that soon it would actually dwindle. (But it never did.) By 1860 42 per cent of people born in Vermont were living outside the State; as early as 1846 twelve hundred Vermont girls were working in the textile mills of Lowell, Massachusetts, alone; Stilwell's carefully accurate report on emigration from Vermont says that by 1850 more than a thousand Vermonters were in California, gold-rushing. (Stewart Holbrook's *The Yankee Exodus* gives the number as 3419.)

To old Vermonters, their young folks seemed to be pouring out of their homes by every possible outlet; by water transport from Lake Champlain to Chicago (the Erie Canal was a link in this), by stagecoach (as in the 1830's my own grandfather left Vermont to attend a theological seminary in Virginia — because unlike the New York seminary, it was Low Church, and his mother, my great-grandmother, had been brought up as an eighteenth-century, fiercely Low Church Anglican); by train for Albany to Utica and farther West; driving a wagon with an entire family aboard; single young men on horseback, or simply on their own two hardy feet, their few belongings tied up in a bundle.

Sometimes whole colonies moved west together to transplant a piece of Vermont to Illinois or Michigan. In 1836 from East Poultney and Castleton a sizable part of the towns moved out together to Eaton County, Michigan, taking their clergyman with them. A "colony" left Benson, Vermont, in 1832 and settled in DuPage County, Illinois. The same year a large group, traveling together, went to Michigan. In the town of Brownington (Orleans County) the seminary (equivalent of high school) was closed because of the emigration to the West. Stewart Holbrook says (although he gives no names or places) that "a hundred more similar schools" were closed for the same reason.

Fully to understand the consternation caused by these removals, it must be remembered that back of the English people who became British colonists in North America, had been a medieval idea about shifting population which for centuries had never been doubted. This idea was that it is a calamity to have people move from the place where they were born and grew up. Up to the time of the Black Death in England, it was more than a calamity, it was a punishable crime. The peasant (the serf, the villein) belonged to the soil, to the actual geographic spot where he was born, and since the soil legally belonged to the landed aristocracy, he belonged to them legally, so that for him to move out of their territory was stealing their property. They thought so, and he did too. This idea that staying put had an actual social and moral value had lasted long enough to become encrusted with those associated emotions which are hard-to-change standards. Long after the villeins had won the simple freedom to move from their homes, without incurring legal penalties, it was still considered socially "nicer" for everybody to stay where he was born. To this day, a good many Bostonians feel it is "nicer." In a vague way (but how those vague feelings do color human lives!) it was thought to be part of a conscientious man's duty to stay near where he had spent his childhood. The feeling that it is inherently a mournful event for children to grow up and leave their parents' house is not unheard of, even now.

There was another emotionally depressing factor in the nineteenth-century emigration from Vermont of its young people. This second factor was not an old idea, but brand-new, a by-product of the fantastically rapid rise in population elsewhere in the United States. Although new, it was as little subject to rationally sceptical examination as if it too had come down from the Middle Ages. This new, nineteenth-century American idea was that an increase of population is, anywhere, just of itself, reason for rejoicing. Even now, very few people ask themselves whether the idea doesn't perhaps come from a long-ago society in which a large number of human beings were necessary for their muscle power, to do, as beasts of burden, the work now done by machines. Even when it is plain that an increase of population means crowding in slums, potential recurrent unemployment, bad blood between those who pay and those who earn wages, greater uncertainty as to decent opportunities for workers and their children, less human relations between human beings — even so, a larger figure in the census is taken as an advance.

Certainly not one doubt as to the need and glory of an increasing population helped our Vermont grandfathers through the startling experience of being practically the only early American state which did not grow larger in numbers. The fact that the population of Vermont increased very slowly, at a time the population of Illinois (especially of Chicago) grew with fabulous speed — this was a subject for unqualified Illinois pride and for abashed Vermont self-doubt (although of course Vermonters tried not to let outsiders see this). When I was a little girl, sixty-odd years ago, well-bred Americans did not, in the presence of a Vermonter, openly refer to the State's small and almost static population, any more than they would have referred to a dwarf or hunchback among the children of a family. The misfortune was so manifest that the only decently kind thing to do was to look the other way.

Enough time has now gone by to make it possible for us to see — not what the doleful books tell us happened when so many Vermont young people moved away — but from our own memory of events, from our own family records, what really did happen.

The first item we see is what no book of statistics ever mentions — that the two modern factors of universal literacy and a rapid postal service gave an entirely different emotional color to emigration in modern times. To read the statistical book reports on the "draining away of the community's lifeblood," you'd think that the departing sons and daughters, when they crossed the state line and stepped upon non-Vermont soil, had fallen into the black pit of oblivion, never to be a part of the family life again. Or that an ocean barrier stood between them, as between our seventeenth-century colonial forebears and the families they had left behind in England, an ocean crossed only by slow, infrequent sailing vessels, carrying few letters because of the high cost of postal service (such as it was). In literal fact, life flowed on along channels of continuous affectionate relations.

Hardly a Vermonter but has been confronted, after the death of the last of his older generation, with the unsolvable question "What *can* we do with all those old family letters?" Boxes and trunks full of them, great packages tied with string or faded ribbon, hundreds in each family, covering many, many years. And so dull! As we leaf them over, we think of the old letters which get put into history books, and feel that other people's old family letters are much more interesting than ours. Sitting on the floor under the eaves, in an attic which, after a century and more of accumulation, must be "cleaned out" at last, we feel that the old letters in our family have nothing in them but "Little Sue's sore throat is better this week" or "Our Mary is getting on well with her school-teaching. She is going with the son of the family where she boards — a fine, sober, hard-working young man, studying to be lawyer. His folks moved out here from a town near Rutland." Or "Henry, Jr., has just won the election for Congressman from this district. He will take his wife and children to Washington when he goes."

We, great-nephews or great-nieces of little Sue with the sore throat of 1849, or of Henry, Jr., the Congressman, leaf over dozens and hundreds of such letters, asking ourselves rebelliously, "Who cares whether or not Petey got over the measles and went outdoors last Thursday" (in 1852). What if "our Martin" did become Justice of the Ohio Supreme Court ninety-two years ago!

How long it takes our torpid human imaginations to see the meaning of facts! A couple of generations had gone by, before we saw that the patently obvious answer to our impatient "Who cares?" was that Vermont families left behind cared. They would have cared about the health of their grandchildren if the grown-up son or daughter were living at the other end of the village street. They cared when the children lived in Ohio, or Wisconsin. Why not?

It is only now that we understand how these streams of letters, incessantly coming and going by a rapid (relatively rapid) modern postal service, made a great web of intimate personal relationships, living in letters instead of in face-to-face meetings. The reason why their letters are not now interesting to us is because they were conversations-on-paper, concerned as family talk always is, with the events of everyday life. It was no momentous event for these ancestors of ours to write a letter. Their pens were practiced, they wrote the news of this day or this week to their families, as they would have called from one house to the next if they had lived next door. They did not write of historical events which would now be interesting for us, because the Vermont and Michigan-Vermont family read newspapers and magazines, and found that sort of news in print. They did occasionally comment on the news, as we all do even in familiar talk. If we their descendants can summon the fortitude to keep on reading how many jars of currant jelly were put up by Great-aunt Helen in Iowa in the summer of '67, we do find an occasional informed comment, sometimes pungent and discerning, on the national elections that year, and what folks in Iowa thought of them.

This sharing life with the older generation, left in the old Vermont home was by no means only in letters. When a young Vermont family, living in Minnesota, expected a new baby, as likely as not the Vermont grandmother (then a vigorous young middle-aged woman) was asked to go out and take care of the household, the mother, the new baby, the husband, the other children, exactly as if the new baby were to be born "over the mountain" in Vermont. The trip to Ohio or Wisconsin made in well-heated trains or comfortable canalboats was considerably less of a hardship than an expedition in a jolting farm wagon by back roads to a remote Vermont farm. A neighbor or cousin "helped out," during her absence, the expenses of the journey were usually paid by the

Illinois or Michigan young folks; it was altogether a stirring inter-lude in the Vermont grandmother's life. And once out in Iowa or Kansas, she worked no harder to take care of the Midwestern household than to take care of her own at home.

She came back full of new ideas, her horizon wider, her mind stirred with new facts about living conditions "out there." As like as not, she brought back with her one of the grandchildren for a visit at the old home, to go to school for a season, where his parents and grandparents had learned their letters, to have a little red sled of his own and the fun (unknown in the prairie country) of breathless slides down steep hills.

Sometimes the Vermont grandmother was captivated by the "go" of the new Western countries and came back only to per-suade her family to move from slow old Vermont and settle near the married children. Sometimes she had "nearly died of homesick-ness in that flat, flat country," and shed tears of joy when, out of her own Vermont kitchen window, she saw again the beautiful long line of the mountains she had loved from her childhood.

Now that we are far enough away in time from all this to un-derstand what it really was, we see that the essence, humanly speaking, was that our nineteenth-century Vermonters acted from free choice — as life-giving an element for human beings as air to breathe. Just as some of our first Vermont forebears had left the old settlements of Western Connecticut and Massachusetts to come along Indian trails to new homes of their very own, while others, brothers, sisters, cousins, had stayed behind, more and more deeply rooted in the old soil — so the nineteenth and twen-tieth century Vermonters have moved on or stayed rooted, as the old local phrase runs, "just as they felt to."

There are those (I am one of them) who find something com-forting in the unchangingness of an old, old background, who love to follow a road every turn of which is part of childhood memories, and for whom a certain ancient elm, growing out of a mossy rock split in two a century ago by the tree roots, is dear because it is one of the first things seen and remembered. There are others (my Vermont mother was one) for whom an unchang-ing and stable background has the monotony of a painfully well-known prison courtyard, and for whom emigration is freedom beckoning through open jail doors.

Those who have crowded out along the westward trails did not go because they were failures at home, or on the contrary because they were the hardy, bold, superior intelligences leaving behind the passive, timid, uninventive dull-wits. For a long time American writers of history glorified the people who moved on "to conquer the continent" as the best, strongest, bravest, and belittled those who stayed put as second- and third-raters, cautiously clutching at what they had, and fearful of the new. Then, perhaps twenty years ago, the historical-literary fashion changed; those who left their old homes and went West became the ne'er-do-wells, running away from their debts and other obligations with the half-baked adolescent idea that just by moving on to another place they could escape from the heavy responsibilities of being adult human beings.

This matter of moving or of staying put, as far as it took place in our State, seemed to be mostly based on personal taste and preference. In a Vermont family which had two sons and three daughters, those who moved West were not necessarily the more energetic ones, the brainier ones. Sometimes they were. Sometimes they weren't. It seems to have been a question of whether "they felt to." Some did. Some didn't. The toweringly vital fact is that circumstance and social tradition left the door open for everybody to choose freely whether to go or stay.

This freedom of choice, exercised for more than a hundred years, has had a wonderful result not at all planned for — the absence, by and large, in Vermont communities of men and women who do not like the Vermont way of life. There are many, of course, born in Vermont, who do not find the social atmosphere congenial. My mother was such a Vermonter. Just as a man is liked by some people because he is gay, cheerful and animated, and disliked by others with different tastes as being noisy and restless and tiring to have around, so the same "way of life" can greatly please some and bore and annoy others. This "Vermont tradition" about which so much is being said on these pages, is dearly (although silently) loved by many of us. But in the nature of things it is extremely distasteful to others of different temperaments. It has been a blessing for everybody that those who dislike it have not been forced by circumstance, social pressure, or public opinion to stay here. (Occasionally family pressure has been the millstone.)

The resultant easing of tensions, because the gangway here in Vermont has been freely let down for those who wish to try another way of life, suggests cheerful possibilities inherent in the "one-world" way of life which, perhaps, is before men and women everywhere on our globe.

Here are some instances of people who did not wait for a gangway. Many years ago I knew a highly cultivated German, of an old Prussian family, who fell in love with the Chinese way of life. He moved to China (this was long before China became modern), made himself as Chinese as possible and enjoyed every moment of his new life. The Danish father of the distinguished Danish writer whose nom de plume is Isak Dinesen had in his young manhood a period when he was suffocated by the Danish way of life, predictable, reasonable, self-controlled, about which so many American authors have written admiringly. To escape that well-planned future, he fled out of Denmark and for years lived rejoicingly, well-oiled with bear grease instead of washed with soap, among the American Sioux Indians. Once in so often, a French man or woman on growing up and becoming, as all of us do when we grow up, a new adult human being, finds the set French way of life (which many of us enjoy) quite unbearable because of its lack of adventure. Such were the early French explorers. Nowadays, when Canada is hardly more adventurous than the Isle-de-France, they escape to African spaciousness, turn up under the palms of the South Sea Islands or (like the son of the great Dr. Charcot) take with passion to Arctic and Antarctic voyages.

Of course, in actual life, it often happens that inexperienced youth makes a mistaken choice. In our Vermont memories and records, with their many personal lives laid out clear to the eye, we see occasional — many, indeed — instances of such mistakes. A neighbor's great-uncle, in his young manhood, went down to New York City, entered the stirring life there with enthusiasm, made good money in interesting work, and in his thirties, when the age of reflection began to dawn for him, found that city life simply had no savor for him. Well, he did not need to stay there. By letters and visits home he had remained in close touch with his Vermont family, he knew the exact business situation in his Vermont town or village or small city, he was able to find a job there, not probably so well paid in cash (but cash goes farther) which allowed him to go trout-fishing when the season opened, to have the uncommunicable satisfaction of direct self-government through Town Meeting, to join the hunters of Vermont escaping from domesticity to the woods during the annual "deer-week," and to take his turn at representing his Town in Montpelier, in the Legislature.

Nobody thought the worse of him for going or for coming back. Whose business was it, his or his neighbors'?

Since nobody lives to himself alone, the matter of going or staying, or returning, was, and is, never so simple as it has sounded in the preceding paragraphs. Misery — sometimes tragedy — follows on a difference of personal opinion. When husband and wife differ, when one is of the temperament which wants to go and the other to stay — there are heartaches.

The son of one of our farmer-neighbors married a pretty, lively girl, who had lived all her life, as he had, on a farm. When they stood up before the minister, making their vows, they knew as little about themselves and each other as most young folks of the marrying age know. As they grew older, through their twenties, into the thirties, and had children, each became, as usually happens, somebody else. The wife was more comely even than in her girlhood, had developed a flair for knowing in every detail what was the "right" thing to wear, the "right" way to do her hair. The movies had been invented. She adored going to the movies. From their Vermont farm it was a long slow trip to the nearest movie theater. She hated to go to bed dully, in the early evening. As a plant drinks up sunshine, she drank the sparkling flare of street-lights. We all knew how she felt, for she talked a great deal about it. Her husband said nothing of what he felt.

A "city person" looking for a Vermont summer home liked their farm, offered a price for it that seemed enormous to all of us. The wife clamored to accept it. The husband said nothing, thought about it silently for a fortnight, accepted the price.

But the wife was no vampire. She had a heart for her husband's feelings, which she probably knew better than we did. She would not, she said, dream of asking him to go to *live* in the city. Her idea was what seemed to her a reasonable compromise, they would use the money to buy a *good* farm, with rich level fields, near a small city in York State, near enough so that she and the children could get in to shops and movies by the trolley, and her husband could go on farming.

He said nothing. They moved. Some months later, happening to meet his sister, I asked her how her brother and his family were getting along. She said sadly, "He don't like it there," and gave me his last letter to read. I have never forgotten what he wrote: "I hate this place. There's only one thing about it I like — there's an old apple tree in the back field that looks like home. I can't bear anything else here. I hate the ground. I hate the way the sky here looks." For once he had found words to say what he felt.

Two days later she came running to our door sobbing uncontrollably. "He's hung himself," she cried wildly. "He took the log chain and walked half a mile to that old apple tree and hung himself."

A grim tale. A stark modern novel ready-made. Yes, clear away as much as you will from the path of men and women, barriers of social prejudice, social barriers, material needs, they can continue to make each other unhappy because there will always be unfathomable mysteries in our own hearts and in the natures of those we live with.

To set against this tale, it must be recorded that these Vermont young people who went West, all through the nineteenth century, almost without exception succeeded, in the good meaning of the word. In most cases their folks back home were proud of them. Hardened to work as they were, every one of them literate, most of them with several special skills, manual and intellectual, young, vigorous, not penniless, they went through the Middle and Far West (very few, almost none, went to stay in the South) like experienced berry-pickers in a rich berry-patch. Their baskets were seldom empty.

It was to be expected that the (relatively) few who had had medical training should become doctors in the Michigan, Wisconsin, Iowa, Minnesota regions where for the most part they settled. Being early arrivals, they got in on the ground floor, medically speaking, and "did well." Young Vermonters who had studied law also had special openings — and they took advantage of these opportunities. To cite a few titles, a man from the small (good-quality) town of Poultney became a justice of the Supreme Court in Michigan. The tiny mountain hamlet of Weston sent out to Iowa an Adams who became a judge on the State Supreme Court. A Martin went out from Middlebury, an especially good town background, and became Chief Justice of the Supreme Court in Michigan. These are only a few out of the many legal successes.

The surprise is the long, long list of emigrating Vermonters who, without having been especially trained for teaching or administration and without having had experience in that profession here, became educators in Ohio, Michigan, Wisconsin, Minnesota and all the rest. However did they manage it, their homefolks wondered, seeing their emigrating sons and daughters with only a high-school (academy or seminary) education become organizers of state public-school systems, founders of teachers' colleges and universities. A man from Minnesota once told me laughingly, "Every Vermonter, when he started for the West, knew how to read and write. Of course he had to teach school." I choose at random a few samples from the long list. From Pawlet, one of the Stewart family went out to Ohio and with another Vermonter founded Oberlin College (first to admit women with men as students and Negroes with whites). From Athens (this is a Windham County town, the population of which is now one hundred and thirty-six, and which never was much more populous) came a Balch who founded Kalamazoo College for training teachers. James Strong of Brownington emigrated to Minnesota and built Carleton College. Charles Kendall Adams, a Vermont boy, was President of Cornell and of the University of Wisconsin. Miss Harriet Bishop from Panton (population three hundred and twelve) opened the first school in St. Paul, Minnesota.

Such successful, widened-out, transplanted Vermonters did not break off their connection with their old homes. Why should they? They came back for summer vacations with their children and later with their grandchildren. And when they were once more in Vermont, most of them again became Vermonters with a normal enjoyment of working with their hands and backs as well as with their heads. Their children rode the farm horse to the brook, learned to go off with the farm collie up to the back pasture to bring back the cows at sunset time, they themselves sprayed the potatoes, ran the hayrake, their soft college-president or school-superintendent hands first blistering and then growing callous on the hoe-handle. A familiar folk anecdote has become one of the themes-with-variations for a "Vermont story." It relates the conversation of a sweating gray-haired farmer in work-shirt and overalls hoeing corn who stops work to answer, poker-faced, the questions of motorists who are unaware that the farm-laborer is Attorney General of Minnesota, or the president of a famous college in Iowa — or perhaps editor of a Montana news-paper, or mayor of a large Minnesota city. I once asked a gray-haired overalled Vermonter who came out of a plain little farmhouse to sell us gasoline for our car if he thought a thick haze in the air came from forest fires in the Adirondacks. With one eye on the indicator in the filling-station pump, he answered casually, "No, I think it is an atmospheric condition prior to rain."

Of course these emigrants from Vermont were by no means all members of the professions. In their home towns Vermonters were often handcraft people. During the first generation, many of them continued hand-workers after their transplantation: millwrights, blacksmiths, stonecutters, coopers, cabinet-makers, machinists, inventors, woodchoppers. There were farmers, of course, but mostly these Vermont farmers, not natural-born lovers of the soil, who were also craftsmen, soon left the farm to practice some other skill. They took to politics. Their experience at serious, responsible, annual Town Meetings made all kinds of political meetings familiar to them. There were Vermonters who, to the extreme (and to tell the truth astonished) pride of their Vermont older generation, became governors and lieutenant governors of states. They were elected to the House of Representatives in Washington. The Tafts are among those who went into politics. Like the family of Professor Bailey of Cornell, they were Townshend people. The father of the Taft who became President of the United States helped organize the academy in Townshend (the town population was less than seven hundred and the village numbered less than three hundred) and was the first chairman of its board of trustees. Moving then to Ohio, he took an active part in the always lively Ohio political doings, and later became a member of President Grant's cabinet. Please bear in mind the almost frantic political corruption of poor General Grant's administration, and remember how members of his official family, near and remote, transferred public moneys to their own pockets, and you will understand how proud Vermont tradition is of the fact that our Vermont Taft, after being Secretary of War and Attorney General under Grant, minister to Austria Hungary and to Russia under President Arthur, died leaving a fortune of $482.80.

When I say that not so many of them went into business and finance, that does not mean that none of them did. There have been successful Iowa and Indiana bankers of Vermont origin. The stirring and creative effort to build up transportation and communication systems especially appealed to many a Vermonter. These men who became influential in railroads in the nineteenth century became — as does not often happen to people from our State — really wealthy, with fortunes astounding to their Vermont relations. Henry Wells of Thetford (a sweet, dreaming old town of about a thousand inhabitants) went to California and established the great Wells Fargo business. One of the Bennington Henrys, a contemporary and friend of my father, built railroads, was a lumberman on a grand scale on the Pacific Coast, ended by being a tycoon and booster of Seattle, one of the richest men on the Pacific Coast. His almost annual summer returns to Vermont were part of my childhood experiences. His attitude towards his old home was one of the several varying ways in which transplanted Vermonters "take" their old State. Each time he returned, he seemed to find it smaller, more static, shrunken — as a college senior finds the desks in his fourth-grade class-room. "Could *I* ever have sat in such tiny chairs?" He always spoke of Vermont, as "the poor little State."

"The Vermont trees look like matchsticks, compared to the Douglas firs in the Northwest," he used to exclaim, and, as he saw a village street which still looked very much as it had when he was a little boy, "Good Heavens, don't you ever have any *new* buildings in Vermont?" Every time he looked at one of our little, silver brooks, with its cowslip-gilded, forget-me-not-embroidered borders, he cried out, "You just ought to see the waterfalls out our way! Fifty, a hundred feet deep, lots of them." Of the Vermonters here, young and old, who listened to this disparagement of the small scale of our landscape, some were seized with a longing to go out where things are big. Very well, they went, if "they felt to." Vermont public opinion neither favored nor disapproved of emigration. It was a matter for each individual to decide for himself, and nobody else's business. But others who heard Horace Henry thought silently, "Because I like a rose, would I like it better if it were twenty feet across?" A few of the old folks who had known the millionaire when he was a North Bennington boy, surmised with sympathy, "He's homesick. Why else does he keep coming back?"

Hardly a Vermont family here but had — still has — one or many family connections with the region west of our state. The young Vermonter who wants to try his fortune elsewhere knows doors that are open to him by personal relatives almost anywhere he wishes to go in the towns and cities and professions and trades scattered all across the northern tier of American states, from the Green Mountains to the Pacific Ocean. And further afield yet, I know one of our own Arlington boys, grandson of our former blacksmith, who is now in Iran, working for our State Department, helping administer a Point Four project.

Leaving to one side the occasional inevitable clash between individuals in personal relations — on the whole, and in the long run and in general, the effect on stay-at-home Vermonters of having large numbers of relatives and neighbors scattered all over the United States and beyond has been cheerful. It has provided a life-giving broadening of the horizon, a lengthening of personal perspective, a freedom for individual lives, an opening of doors to that "chance to start over" which often is the simple, geographical solution for a situation which, if not changed, would end in sour stagnant frustration.

We have an old folk-jingle which runs:

> Some like red, some like blue,
> I am I, you are you.

A clause in the tradition I am trying to translate from life into words is that there is no reason why people whose taste is for red should be disapproved, or blamed by those who like to dress in blue.

CHAPTER 18

"They'll Vote Us Out of Town"

CAREFUL statistics have been compiled, books have been written, about the movement of population away from Vermont. I can't find in print more than a few brief mentions of the movement into Vermont of the Irish, the Italians, the Scots, the French Canadians, the Welsh, Poles, English, Finns.

But the absence of book-information need cramp nobody's style in thinking about it. For, in a state like ours, where people are well acquainted with their grandparents, the single century since the appearance in Vermont of people from across the Atlantic is well covered by family, town and neighborhood memories. We older Vermonters heard from our grandparents what they feared from immigration (none of them welcomed it). Our parents' talk told us what, in their youth before our day, they saw happening. As to what really happened, in the long run, that we know from our own observation.

In the late 1840's, a few railroad lines were being built here. The contractors brought in (as was done everywhere in the nation for this kind of work) gangs of foreign laborers. In Vermont these were, at that date, mostly newly arrived from the rural areas of Ireland. They lived in rough barrack-camps, their food and lodging provided by the contractor. This system is now familiar to Americans. Vermonters of the 1840's had never seen it. The conduct of the men living thus crowded together, far from their families, was about what was to be (is still to be) expected from such conditions. They fought a good deal, they drank a good deal, and the tough fellows who occasionally made nuisances of themselves were (as is true now of similar large groups of migratory lumberjacks) the ones most conspicuous. General public opinion here as elsewhere lumped the whole group together as all of one kind, and that kind not desirable. When with pick and shovel and wheelbarrow they had made the roadbed and laid the rails under the orders of supervisors as alien to Vermont as they were, most of them moved on to other contract jobs, far away.

But an occasional man, or an occasional small group connected by near or distant family ties, came to know something of the life in the quiet country villages through which the railroad tracks passed. They had learned that land could be bought and owned by anybody, and that work was to be had, on farms, in the small factories, in homes, in the blacksmith shops, in the forests. They were born and bred country men and many were family men who had brought wife and children with them across the Atlantic and settled them poorly and precariously in crowded city tenements. Looking around for a Vermont roof under which the beginnings of family life in the New World could be made, such Irish fathers of families found here and there in Western Vermont towns and villages a shelter which might be available — a hired man's house on the corner of a farm, left empty because the Vermont hired man had taken his family out to Ohio or Wisconsin; a little ancient empty dwelling left to tumbledown decay because the old owner was dead and his well-to-do heirs lived in Iowa or Michigan and had no interest keeping up the old place; or perhaps a tiny shack run up for some temporary purpose and then abandoned and forgotten by the Vermont builders, always careless of anything made of wood, because that material was plentiful and cheap. Out of their wages the workers saved enough to bring to Vermont the family crowded uncomfortably together in the city. These Irish were the first — by thirty years — people of another race to come to live in Vermont, in largish numbers.

When the wife and children arrived and took over the plain small shelter the husband and father had found, they did not look promising to their Vermont neighbors, would not have looked promising to any Americans. Many of them were illiterate, a condition shocking to the Green Mountain tradition. Just back of them were long, tragic famine years. They had escaped from famine to a dreadful, nightmarelike transatlantic crossing. The memoirs of educated Europeans who came to America by steerage at the same time the Irish began to flee from starvation and political tyranny speak with incredulous horror of the treatment given by captains and crew to the despairing Irish, crammed together below decks. The drinking water given to the political refugees of '48 from Germany, and to the skilled, clean, literate Danish and Scandinavian migrating hand-workers was boiled. To the Irish it was served as it came from the foul-smelling cask, long strings of green slime hanging down from the cup to the floor. On several of the ships which brought the first Irish, plague broke out and swept over the ill-treated men, women and children, already weakened by malnutrition. Many of those who lived to land in America were gaunt, ragged, white-cheeked, dirty, demoralized.

The Vermonters assumed at first, naturally, that their forlorn aspect was an indication of their innate quality. It was generally thought in those first early years that they were "naturally" tubercular. Their household gear and clothing were meager beyond anything known even to quite poor Vermonters who were passably used to meager material possessions. In these families, the children "swarmed," so many of them that no mother on earth, let alone an undernourished mother with next to no money, could possibly keep them clean according to Vermont standards.

Vermont, like many rural American regions before the railways, had never seen foreigners. The one exception was the occasional unmarried French Canadian hired man or chopper, who nearly always returned to the Province of Quebec after some years of saving his wages. These "Jombatistes" were so rare and so impermanent that their presence scarcely broke at all the dense provincial ignorance as to other races of our inland, rural grandparents. To Vermonters the appearance of whole Irish families was an event they had never dreamed of. For their treatment of these astonishing newcomers, their tradition had no precedents for them to follow.

Of the terrible causes in Ireland for the poverty and ignorance of these first immigrants, the Vermonters had little idea. I gather that the same ignorance was common among most other ordinary mid-nineteenth century Americans. The Irish potato famine of the late 1840's and early 1850's of course made occasional headlines in American newspapers. Americans, a fair proportion of Vermonters too, made some relief gestures, contributed to the stream of ships which crossed the Atlantic taking gifts of food to the "starving Irish." But these contributions were made very much as we Americans later made contributions to Chinese flood victims, with human good will but in an almost total ignorance of the actual men and women involved.

The first Irish appeared in Vermont about the middle of the nineteenth century. At that date the British reform-effort to improve the living conditions of working people, now successful, had barely dawned in England. In rural Ireland, it had not dawned at all. Those Irish "hands" who built the Vermont railroads had lived for generations on a plane described by the *Encyclopaedia Britannica* (usually colorlessly factual) as "miserable and deplorable, the relations between landlords and farm-tenants being of a most unhappy kind." Of the thousands of rented farms in Ireland at that date, half were under three acres in size, and almost all the other half from three to fifteen acres. From the men and women living in those "miserable and deplorable" conditions, with so little land to cultivate that they were always close to the verge of starvation, the rent collectors of the leisure class, absentee landlords, annually took away forty million dollars in rent. This lasted up to 1881, a whole generation after the first Irish came to Vermont.

In 1846 and 1847 these melodramatically poor working people were pushed down into an even blacker pit of misery by the failure of the potato crop, their main food.

From 1841 to 1851 more than twenty thousand men, women, and children died in Ireland of literal physical starvation; and from 1846 to 1851 "the total Irish mortality was close to a million." (*Encyclopaedia Britannica*.) In the ten years after 1847 more than a million and a half emigrated from the small Irish island.

From this million and a half, one smallish wave washed up into west-side Vermont towns along the new railroad track.

The startled Vermonters who watched them come in had already heard about Irish immigrants in New York, Boston and other big cities. These tales were grim. It was reported that the

Irish took no part in the American way of life, that they clung together in clans, partly due to their belonging to a church different from that of most rural American people, partly to their very temperament. This clan spirit, so the early folk tales about them ran, bound them together into a ready-made political bloc, voting at the command of a leader of their own race. To him, as to their priests, they gave an implicit obedience in all things, shockingly alien to the American tradition. In their ignorant docility they presented a political danger such as Americans had never faced. It must be understood that all this was not real news, it was no more than highly colored gossip.

Constantly reported in this gossip was the anecdote of the Irish immigrant who on landing in Boston (or New York or Baltimore) inquired, "What kind of government do yez have here? I'm agin it." Wouldn't you think that Vermonters who had been agin the government of the Province of New York for exactly the same reasons, and who had warmly sympathized with the New York State tenant farmers agin their government, would have seen more in this familiar anecdote than other Americans who took it as an evidence of congenital political contrariness among the Irish? No, they seem to have been too ignorant of the situation in Ireland to see the analogy with their own history.

You might also think that the generalized anti-British feeling left over from the Revolution would incline them to sympathize with the newcomers. It is true the "British aristocracy" was often berated in Fourth of July orations or Commencement addresses. But this was formula-talk, patriotic ritual. It meant nothing definite. Hardly a Vermonter who sat broiling in the July sun to listen with satisfaction to such stylized denunciations of over-privileged lords and ladies had ever seen a single human being who did not work for his living — except the infirm, the sick and very old, who were pitied for their incapacity to be useful. They knew as little of idle aristocrats as of dinosaurs. As to rich landlords taking the bread out of the mouths of oppressed tenant farmers, their idea was that such parasites were a peculiarity of the banks of the Hudson River and had just (1846) been put out of business by new laws in York State. If they had understood (what everyone knows now) that the dismally low plane of living of the first Irish they saw in Vermont was caused by a system of land tenure very much like that which all Vermonters abominated, they would have felt differently about the new settlers.

But they did not. The beginning could scarcely have been more unfavorable. The Vermont tradition could scarcely have had a more rigorous test of its universality than — in the beginning — this strange, unexpected human relation, such as our founding Green Mountain fathers never foresaw. At the first, the mid-nineteenth-century Vermonters fumbled ineptly with the knot. The human beings on each side were too average in quality to untie that knot by conscious informed intelligence. But many human problems not to be solved by intellectual analysis vanish before the mightiness of great general principles embodied in a tradition.

One of the basic principles to which Vermonters are brought up is that every human being is to be considered separately; that there are no classes made up of those foreordained to be superior; that only individuals are superior, and that such individuals are likely to make their appearance anywhere. In the application of this idea to the problem of immigrants from abroad, the numerical smallness of Vermont communities was, as has so often happened here, a material help. There never have been racial or class or nationalistic ghettos in Vermont. The newly arrived Irish family lived anywhere they could find a roof, and that was as apt as not to be just down the road from the old farm home of a Vermont family.

I am not saying that they or any other Vermont farm family gave the newcomers a friendly welcome. All was not sweetness and light, not by a long shot. Never since the dawn of human history, as far as I can find out, did people long settled in any region give a friendly welcome to newcomers. One of the disagreeable traits of our human nature seems to be to dislike on sight people who come later than the first settlers. The English workers in wool of the fourteenth century not only disliked the Fleming weavers, brought in to improve the quality of English woolen goods; at times, when they could (as in the Wat Tyler rebellion), they got rid of them by murder.

What can be said for the Green Mountain State is that this first hateful, alarmed reaction to strange neighbors passed more quickly, and above all was less violent than in many old American regions. The well-to-do Boston bourgeois of the mid-nineteenth century lumped "the Irish" all together as hardly better than Iroquois, and laid the foundation of a lasting hostility. The Irish adults and children in the tumble-down Vermont shack were soon known as individuals, at least by sight, to the people of the story-and-a-half, white, green-shuttered farmhouse. This was mostly because there were so few human beings living along that mountain road that the ups and downs of everyday life there made them more or less personally known to each other.

The young Vermont farmer fell from the hayloft in his barn and broke his leg. His distracted wife sent one of her children flying up the road to ask for help of the Irish neighbors. The accident, temporarily, for a healing day or so, put the two families on a common plane of pain, anxiety and sympathy. One of the Irish babies fell ill (those innumerable babies who so alarmed the older Vermonters with the idea that when grown they would as voters take over the Town Meeting). When he went into a convulsion, the young mother screamed in panic. The Vermont mother, her own baby in her arms, climbed breathlessly up the road to help, obeying the unspoken command of her tradition always to respond to a cry of distress from a neighbor.

Beyond the elemental humanity of this sort of relation, an economic condition brought the old and the new Vermonters together. The big sons of the Vermont farmer were vanishing into the West. Come haying time, help was needed on the farm. There were big Irish boys in the new family. Like Vermont boys, like all boys, they were of varying quality. Some proved to be reliable, quick-witted, hard-working, genial and friendly; others dark and sour, given to drink, slow on the uptake. It did not take long to learn which was which. The reliable, capable ones became much-liked neighbors and helpers. The grown-up Vermont girls were emigrating along with the boys. The Vermont farmer's wife had no one to help her in the rush of summer work. In one or another of the Irish families in town were girls old enough to be useful as household helpers. They too, like all girls, varied in personality. Some were pretty, truth-telling, soft-spoken, lovable and eager to learn; others were notional, lazy, disagreeable, "trouble-makers." The pretty and sweet ones among the Irish girls got from Vermonters their fair share of admiration and affection. During the difficult twenty years after the Civil War this first Vermont-born Irish generation helped tide the State across the gaps left by the emigration of their own young people.

Yet in the social relations of this first phase of adjustment the old Vermont traditions bent and gave way — for a time. Their English conquerors had for generations branded the Irish en masse as inferiors. In Vermont they found themselves among neighbors who till then had admitted no class inferiority. The daughter of a neighbor who in early days became a household helper in a Vermont farm home was no social inferior. She was, in literal fact, one of them, and was so accepted. So was the son of a Vermont neighbor.

But the Irish girl, the Irish boy, who did not go to church with their Vermont employers, who, after work hours returned to a house entirely different from the Vermont home — were they treated as social equals, did they go along to picnics, sugaring-off parties? The only honest answer can be, as so often to questions about complex human relations, yes — and no. Compared to the full rigor of the Vermont ideal, the answer would need to be "no." Compared to what lay just back of the new-comers, the answer could honestly be "yes." We ancient Vermonters, old enough to remember the "Irish help" in our grand-parents' homes of sixty years ago, realize that although they were never called "servants" (any well-brought-up, old-time Vermonter would be ashamed to call any other human being his "servant") still in some respects they were not treated as "Vermont help" had been. We of today can make this admission with less shamefacedness because this was a strictly temporary deviation from the hard-and-fast principles on which our State was founded. We who in our childhood saw these traces of social class discriminations have lived to see them vanish. There is no slightest racial difference made, now, between one or another kind of part-time household helper who, here as elsewhere in the twentieth century, comes in from her own decent home to help other people take care of theirs.

Although we did not realize it at the time, the first, mid-nineteenth-century Irish did not see the situation exactly from the Vermont point of view. They were freshly come from a social structure in which they and their parents had been, with brutal baldness, labeled as inferiors. They were spirited people. They fought (in vain) against this label. But the air around them was thick with the miasma of social discrimination. The English workers, themselves labeled by their "betters" as class inferiors, could and did, consider themselves superior to the Irish. I can remember reading in the London newspapers of the 1890's (Alas! They also appeared in America too, in Boston and New York) advertisements for help, household, clerical, agricultural. At the end of almost every one stood four ugly words: "No Irish need apply." I was a little girl then, no more given to sociological reflections than any other ten-year-old, but I can still feel the sick qualm of shame given me by this repudiation of the Irish, even for the humblest employment. To me it was a shock of surprise as well as of dismay. It was no surprise to the Irish. They had grown up in the midst of that pervasive insult, resenting it, loathing the people who used it, but dismally familiar with it.

Because of this familiarity, it is certain that there was much less bitterness for them in that first passing phase when Irish-American boys and girls working in Vermont homes were not treated exactly as Yankee boys and girls had been. In many ways this intermingling in daily life of the younger generation of the newcomers with old, established local homes was an efficient social agency to speed up their adoption of the standards of Vermont. The slight social discrimination against them (which we are now ashamed to remember because it ran counter to principles we were taught to respect) was little marked compared to the background of "No Irish need apply" in which their people had been living for generations. They had taken a first step. The next step took them all the way.

Because they were seen by old-time Vermonters as individuals, the differences between them were as plain to the eye as the wide differences between individual Vermonters. Nobody could deny that the native stock varied from ignorant, shiftless and unreliable to intelligent, thrifty and upright. Many Irish immigrants were illiterate, yes, but Vermonters soon learned that there were, even among the very first, some with as good an education as anybody. Most Irish newcomers were practically penniless, destitute and unskilled, yes, but in every group there were some who brought along savings from the Old World, enough to buy decent farms which they proceeded to manage competently. Some were careless and improvident (there has never been a Vermont community without a sample or two of such qualities) but many of them seized with a passionate eagerness (much approved by Vermonters) on the opportunity to earn wages and save money to buy land of their own.

Another clause of the Vermont tradition proved to be a solvent more universal than our forefathers dreamed of. This was the institution of the free public school. We sometimes lack-wittedly forget that illiteracy is not an inheritable quality. Each little boy and each little girl entering a first-grade class is illiterate, be he Irish, Vermont, French-Canadian, Italian, or Welsh. By the end of the first year in school, practically all of them can read and write a little. By the end of the second and third year all except the congenitally incapable can read and write well. Illiteracy, which had seemed to Vermonters so appalling a characteristic of the newcomers, proved to be no more a permanent personality-quality than dirty hands. Soap, water and a nail-brush make any pair of human hands indistinguishable from another. By the time the Vermont local district school had had the "immigrant" children for even a few years, illiteracy had vanished from the Irish boys and girls as well as the Vermont ones.

More than just readin' and writin' was accomplished by the Vermont schoolhouse. To sit together in a classroom is a social contact and not only with those present in the schoolhouse. With their families too. And that meant most people in the town. To talk about the school, about the quality of the individual children in it, is in Vermont as ordinary a gambit for conversation as the weather. In that first decade (during the 1850's) when the Irish families were arriving, our grandparents here used to say, "I hear that little Patrick Malone — you know his folks live down in the old Hurd house — can read like a streak. He's only in the fifth grade, but he reads aloud to his folks. They take the *Rutland Herald* now — know what's goin' on as well as anybody." The Vermont tradition (once more largely because the groups involved are not numerous) has always kept its people alive to the value to the community of superior individuals, no matter where they appeared. Trevelyan, in *English Social History*, says, "The Charity Schools had the merit of trying to do something for all, but they had the demerit of too great an anxiety to keep the young scholars in their appointed sphere of life, and to train up a submissive generation."

Submissiveness (in anybody) is the last quality Vermonters have ever wished to inculcate. To use schools for the purpose of training working people's children into docile acceptance of a subordinate social position — they did not repudiate such an idea, they had never heard of it. Each community has always felt pleasure, pride and forward-looking hope at the appearance of any specially bright boy or girl among the town's children. The second-generation Irish families had a fair share of such children. To them, as to any other superior individuals, Vermont tradition took satisfaction in trying to open the door of opportunity. You may be sure that this was noted by their parents.

The Irish in Vermont who took the "Freeman's Oath" became voting citizens, not members of a hostile political bloc. Their tradition of being "agin the government" had been priceless to their self-respect when the only government they knew held them down to despairing poverty. In the Green Mountains an Irish voter could scarcely be against the government since he was the government himself, as much as any of his neighbors. Vermont imposes no literacy test on voters. Provision is still made at elections for responsible, accredited helpers for those who cannot read and write. Nowadays such helpers are mostly anachronistic relics, sitting by at the polls and yawning idly. In the earlier days of immigration they provided the folk-solvent for the frustration and resentment felt by foreign-born elsewhere, which never developed in Vermont.

As to their church, which in the mid-nineteenth century was feared and resented by many Americans, it is to be remembered that the Vermont tradition has no fiercely held theological clauses.

In many Vermont settlements, schools and libraries and even academies were founded before a church was organized. Yet if there was no religious eagerness in the early settlements, no slightest obstacle was put in the way of any group which, after a while, decided to establish "the social worship of God." The first Catholic priests seen by Vermont pioneers traveled occasionally from town to town, to keep in touch with the few scattered French Canadian workers. In a Catholic history of the Catholic Church in Vermont, a specific mention is made of their friendly treatment. They were taken in overnight by Vermont country people, like any other voyager who needs a shelter. As more Catholic newcomers appeared, Catholic parishes were founded. Catholic churches were built, like other churches, to the accompaniment of not-very-attentive good will. The very first one, in the city of Burlington, was burned the day after it was finished. There was, naturally, talk of the possibility that it had been set on fire. If so, it was done with such an absence of open hostility that not a single proof has ever been found that it did not burn down, like so many hundreds of wooden buildings, because of some fault of construction. Except for this shadow of a shadow, there has been no interference with the Catholic Church in Vermont.

As I set down these phases of the adjustment to the old American Vermont life of nineteenth-century Europeans, they sound much too clear and too obvious to suggest what actually happened. Of course the startled Vermonters of the 1850's had, in the thick of the process, as little idea of what was really going on as most of us have when we are living through the thick of any social change. They did not realize the elastic vitality of their own traditions which were to help them, so mightily, to move on into a new phase of life.

After the Civil War they saw more clearly what was going on. A saturated solution can remain a formless liquid for a long time, until some shock crystallizes its elements into new and definite shapes. Such a shock to Vermont (as to many other American communities) was the Civil War. As the armed forces of many a community outside of Vermont, in Minnesota for instance, contained a sizable percentage of Vermonters newly come to the West, so the armed forces from Vermont contained a sizable percentage of new-come Irish. Many of the broad-shouldered, older Irish adolescents in the West Vermont towns went off into the Federal Army along with their Yankee neighbors. Some of them went for adventure, some of them for the small pay or just because they had, already from the ages of nine to nineteen, become Americans who knew what the fighting was all about. The O'Haras and the McCarthys put on the blue uniform and marched beside the Hawleys and the Deweys into battle; they were sent back wounded, to lie in the same rough Vermont barrack hospitals. Some of them were killed in battle and their names were put on the bronze tablets of the town Roll of Honor. Some of them lived through and came back to stay in the old town where they were brought up. Some of them, like other Vermonters, came back only to say good-by to childhood and youth and to go West or to a city to seize opportunities they'd heard tell of in their Army service. The shock which had been too much for the older generation of Vermonters crystallized the solution. The Irish soldiers, now G.A.R. men, were no longer immigrants; they were Vermont boys.

Vermont stopped being old-American and became American. From the end of the Civil War on, the transformation into Americans and Vermonters of the younger generation of European-born immigrants was rapid, almost unconscious and thoroughgoing. You might think from my account, so far, that the Irish were the only non-English-stock immigrants. That is because the Irish were the first, by a whole generation, to come in sizable numbers. Hence, in the parts of Vermont where they settled, they made the most dramatic impact, being the first foreign fellow townsmen the Green Mountain people had ever lived with. But they were the first, not the only new settlers here.

Forty years after the first railroad-building Irish arrived, the Italians in considerable numbers began to appear (in the 1890's) in a few Vermont regions. Like most of the granite workers of Barre, particularly like the Scottish, they were superior people, finely skilled as stoneworkers. They found well-paid jobs in the marble and granite industry of Vermont. Most of them were from Northern Italy. In my youth a folk-saying was that "Carrara gossip is as well known in Proctor, Vermont, as in Carrara, and anybody in Carrara knows the latest Proctor gossip." In 1850 (when the Irish were arriving) the census report showed seven Italians in the state. By 1910 there were three thousand Italian-born, by 1940 a little more than two thousand. It was about 1920 that the principal of the high school in Proctor happened to tell me that the Italian boys and girls there were among the most intelligent of the students and that a slightly more than the customary percentage of them went on to further educational training, many of them entering the professions. Hard for education-respecting Vermonters to look down on them as dagos, you see. The English and Scotch arrived, steadily, in small numbers, year by year, melting at once into the life around them.

Open to them all were the same plain, rustic, nineteenth-century, sometimes primitive classrooms. They sat beside Vermont children, studied out of the same textbooks and played the same games. Vermont boys and girls were not taken out of school to prevent their "associating with foreigners." Foreign names, if they were hard for Anglo-Saxons to spell or pronounce, occasionally slid into some Vermont-sounding syllables — Gauthier became Gokay, in some places Marchant became Walker. But not always. Sometimes the Vermont ear became so accustomed to a non-English name, that it no longer seemed foreign. Rutland people never speak of the Koltonski family (who have given fine public service there) as though the name was different from Perkins and Fowler.

As these children all grew up together, it became apparent

that about the same proportion in each group (a very small percentage) proved mentally incapable of profiting by schooling. About the same relative number in each group (the majority) turned out reasonably able and useful citizens. About the same relative number (a small group) of each racial group proved exceptionally brainy and energetic.

As often happens with human beings who for generations have been notably oppressed and underprivileged, the sudden removal of old barriers seemed to cause (at least in the first and second generation) a startling leap forward. This was especially true of the Irish in Vermont, perhaps because they arrived here in the 1840's and 1850's at a time when the governing authorities in the rural regions in Ireland made no provision, quite the contrary, for the education of poor farmers' children. When, in Vermont, the door to normal learning was opened by the district school, the Irish young people burst out of the cocoon in which most of their parents had been forced to live and became, in personality and way of life, unrecognizably different from their older generations.

There proved to be — of course, by the law of human probability — a normal percentage of Irish parents who, although illiterate, had good native intelligence. With dramatic speed their children raced through the open doors of opportunity to success. In a very few years, many of the first generation of Vermont-born Irish young people had become clerical workers, railroad station agents, salesmen, independent businessmen. When they married and had children, such parents saw to it that those of their children with good head-pieces got more advanced education. The members of that second generation have become college graduates, technicians, professional people, doctors, lawyers, trained nurses. By the same process, from the first generation to the second, all the variegated racial stocks became Vermonters — English, Irish, French Canadians, Italians, Poles, Slavs, Finns. One might have expected the children coming from non-English-speaking families to be at a disadvantage in school. No, in the end, it seemed to make no difference. Those individuals, Finnish, Polish, Italian, no matter what race or nation, who had good brains and stable personalities, became pillars of their communities, whether they stayed in Vermont, or went to Illinois (and as many of them as of their old-Vermont neighbors left Vermont for the cities or the West). Of course there were families and individuals among each racial group as among every group of old-Vermonters, who did not have brains, or stable personalities. They developed, if at all, very slowly, remained on about the same level as similar Vermonters.

A special paragraph should be given to the French Canadians in Vermont, because their situation is different from that of all the other non-English-stock newcomers to our State. The Irish, the Italians, the Finns, the Poles were separated from their old home by the definitive, irrevocable barrier of the Atlantic. The French Canadians had moved only a short distance away. They were in constant touch with the non-English-speaking families and villages they had left. It was easy for them to go back there for visits, for weddings, for funerals; it was easy for their older generation to come to visit the Vermont-French homes. This continued closeness of contact influenced both sides of course. It probably is the reason for the rather slower "assimilation" to Vermont folkways of newcomers from the Province of Quebec. This has never caused friction. The French Canadians have proved, in Vermont, to be singularly noncombative citizens, sticking to many of their old ways, but in a peaceable, non-aggressive manner. And their assimilation has been only slightly more slow than that of some other stocks. They gradually became quite as Vermont and American as anybody — basketball fans, eager bowlers, readers of the morning newspapers and an assortment of ordinary American magazines, owners of cars and as much given to driving them far and fast as any of their fellow citizens. Look through the telephone directory of larger Vermont towns, you will find a number of names obviously French in origin, and a good many others that might be; and in the list of graduating seniors from our high schools there are always some French names. Perhaps the most significant item to report is that most of the Vermont-born French younger generation now speak English only. When they speak French, it is as any of us speak French, from having studied it out of books.

By 1900 there were twice as many born-in-Canada French in

Vermont as Irish, but their numbers have steadily decreased, are distributing themselves more evenly over the state.

Between 1890 and 1920 nearly four thousand Poles and Slavs somehow heard of Vermont, and came here. Their children too have become Vermonters. Too few Finns to put down in statistical thousands, but quite present to the Vermont mind because nearly every family of them lived (during the first generation) in the rural regions, turning farms abandoned by Vermonters into fertile, high-production land. Boys and girls of the second generation of all the foreign-born leave farming for other pursuits about as Vermonters do. There have never been more than a thousand-plus Scandinavians here. And — I've never heard even a guessing hypothesis as to the reason for this — hardly any Germans.

At no time was the total number of foreign-born residents here more than 15 per cent of the population.

This page of statistics gives the explanation for the fading away to nothing of the gloomy fears of a whole generation of old-time Vermonters, who were young adults in 1850, and died between 1890 and 1900. These old Vermonters looked at the swarming children in the poor little homes, gabbling a strange language many of them, and thought with fear of the future, when they would grow up and out-vote "us," at Town Meeting, and overturn or neglect Vermont institutions, dear to native-born Vermonters. If, as I ardently hope, some small rays of understanding may be cast on the general problems of conduct of human life by the report made in this book about what has actually happened in the Vermont human laboratory test tube, it is worth setting down here how completely the heterogeneous foreign-born additions to Vermont population have not remained heterogeneous, nor foreign, but have become united in Vermontism, for good and for not so good, some more than others, but not one threat to their adopted state among them. To be accurate, no *more* threats among them than among the occasionally erring grandchildren of those who saw with uneasiness the arrival of their foreign grandparents.

By the time those first startlingly numerous children grew up, they had gone through Vermont schools, had lived and worked among Vermont neighbors. All kinds of earning-a-living possibilities were open to them. No more than the Vermont boys and girls round them did they all wish to stay passively on the old farm, or close to their parents' home. Like their young Vermont contemporaries, they too looked out over the state line, into the United States, and in about the same proportions joined the ranks of energetic, literate, young Vermonters, moving on to try their fortunes elsewhere. It is to be assumed that the foreign-born parents tried their best to have them settle close to the older generation. They had no more success in this than American-born parents. Vermont towns and neighborhoods were not (except very exceptionally and only for a short time) transformed into little Italys, or Irish settlements, or French-speaking villages.

There turned out to be not more voters among them than among those of the Vermont-born who stayed on in the old place, and it wouldn't have mattered if there had been, for they would not have "voted down" in a bloc the old Vermont neighbors. They had become not hostile to our institutions, but devotedly attached to them. In about the same relative numbers as the descendants of the Connecticut and Massachusetts men, they have joined with all their hearts in the desperate struggle to keep up in our State, on too little money, the necessary modern roads, modern public-health service, modern education, modern traffic control (an unheard of new and expensive complication in our life), decent care for the insane and subnormal, and all the rest of the insoluble problems of maintenance of modern life which — so far — somehow get more or less solved by the end of each Vermont year. They hold public office about in proportion to their relative numbers, and give as good service as anybody. Nobody nowadays even notices whether a selectman has an Irish or Italian name. The need is pressing for selectmen of honesty, with a working amount of gray matter and with public spirit enough to serve the community for practically no pay. When one of the younger people, on growing up, looks like material for a town clerk, or member of the school board or tree warden, it is assumed that he will, if put into office, wish to forward the best interests of the town as much if his name is Koltonski as Lawrence. The assumption has proved accurate. There are all kinds of difficulties in Vermont life, which never runs smoothly along straight rails laid on good ballast. But the problem of a foreign population is not one of them. On the contrary, the children and grandchildren of those newcomers who alarmed our grandparents have turned out remarkably like the children and grandchildren of our own grandparents — mixed pickles, good, bad, mediocre, strong and weak, about like everybody else in modern Vermont — no matter where their ancestors were born.

And altogether there can be no doubt that their coming into the State was one of the factors which made it possible for Vermont to keep up its slow but equable and unfaltering advance from the past to the future.

CHAPTER 19

Fit Only to Be Slaves

THE last one of the five post-Civil War forebodings was nothing connected with Vermont's survival or welfare. It was an unspoken question terribly daunting to them: "Are human freedom and equality before the law not, as we have believed, universal needs for all men for which it is worth giving one's life? Is it perhaps as foolish to give it to some kinds of men as to horses and dogs? Are Negroes, after all, as we have so often been told by those who claim to know them best, fit only to be slaves?"

Till an authentic answer could be given, this doubt tarnished not only what they had done at such cost in the Civil War, but an axiom on which their whole tradition was founded, over which no shadow — not even in their most difficult, struggling, endangered early days — had ever before fallen.

Seldom has a foreboding been disproved so completely, and so rapidly. It was gone before the last of those who suffered from it were dead. No American of today needs statistical information about home ownership or numbers of high-school graduates, or bank accounts, or prosperous businessmen, or gifted writers among modern Negroes; nor tabulated facts about Negro universities and the success in the professions, in the arts, and in daily life of their graduates. The rise of our Negro fellow citizens has been spectacular, beyond anybody's imagination to foresee — from destitution and ignorance almost total, first into literacy, then to higher learning and the professions — first to humble hand-labor, financial independence, then to small savings, thence to a constantly increasing share in the economic life of our country. There are still many unjust, often absurd, sometimes tragic barriers to be cleared away from the roads to completely normal American life for Negroes. But the idea that they are innately fit only to be slaves is not one of these barriers. Not a shred is left of the idea that, as a race, they are incapable of directing their own lives and depend like children on the superior judgment and wisdom of white people — I should think not!

In fact, most American young people (except in a relatively few states) have never even heard of that theory about Negroes; and if they did, would be as astonished as if they had heard someone seriously claiming to have seen an old neighbor rise from the top of her chimney and float away on a broomstick. Negroes have turned out to be just what Vermonters took for granted, like anybody, like everybody, of all kinds, according to personal inheritance of intelligence and energy, but much more according to the opportunities given them. Like other Americans of today, Vermonters have forgotten the heavy-hearted doubt of their grandfathers and great-grandfathers which was the reaction from the emotional excitement of the Civil War. Or to be precisely accurate, neither the question or the answer to it is consciously in the Vermont collective mind. Judging from what is to be heard and seen in our everyday life here, both excited exaltation and reaction from it are of the past.

And yet — ! The conscious mind can, so we have now learned, shove back into dusty oblivion emotions, convictions, meaningful past experiences, which nevertheless the subconscious knows on occasion how to find.

A few years ago Dr. Ralph Bunche came for a day or so into Vermont. It was shortly after his extraordinary success in averting war in the Near East. His errand was an academic one, to take part in a three-day discussion conference on modern international relations, carried on in one of our Vermont colleges. Several very distinguished public servants of the white race also accepted the invitation from the college to share in the serious question-and-answer periods, lectures and seminars at the college. But the Vermont public, most of it, is too steadily engaged in earning its living to have free time in daylight hours. Not many Vermonters found their way to the campus.

The last event of the conference was arranged, not at the college, but in a large hall in the center of the town. It was thought that perhaps an open meeting within walking distance of many homes, in the evening, might make public attendance more possible. But no one expected a large audience to assemble for an austerely serious program consisting of just one feature — Dr. Bunche's report on the situation in Palestine. This was hardly a subject of burning personal import to everyday Vermonters. No singing, no music, no film shown, no other speaker, no other subject.

I shall not soon forget the aspect of that Vermont town when we drove in and slowed our car down to look for a parking space. Up and down the streets around the Armory the automobiles were solidly parked, bumper-to-bumper, along the curb. The sidewalks were full of sober crowds making their way on foot to the hall. By the time we had found a place in a distant street to leave our car and had walked back to the Armory, the big hall was full as I have never seen it, before or since. Not a vacant spot on the floor. Only the chairs in the gallery available. Hundreds of quiet, mature people were still steadily streaming in.

One does not often, in Vermont, see crowds of hundreds of people attending any gathering. More than a thousand were there that evening. When the well-built, brown-skinned Harvard Ph.D. in the businessman's tweed suit stood up on the platform, the big audience settled down in an intense Vermont silence, not only to listen to what he said but to take in through their pores, as is our folk-custom, every visible indication he gave of personality and character. I don't know what Dr. Bunche saw in his almost formidably attentive Vermont audience, but he must have seen that it was no college crowd. They were just everybody — as their grandparents who had marched off to the Civil War had been just everybody, not the select or elite in any way.

I do know what his audience saw in him; no spellbinding orator (they would have detested oratory for such an occasion), but a cultivated, intellectual man, obviously full of his subject, not of himself. He was an able speaker, not notably eloquent, whose every intonation, turn of phrase, and restrained gesture bespoke the quality Vermonters most prize — sincerity. His subject was not exciting, not materially adventurous. To tell his story, many complicated details of historical, political, social lore were needed. He did not try to popularize it. Like a scholar addressing his equals, he did not try to make these necessary details dramatic or entertaining. He told us soberly what we as responsible Americans needed to know to understand what the situation had been, its terrible danger to the world, what had been done to avert catastrophe.

Most of his listeners were not learnèd in international politics and law. Some of what he said was over our heads. When, for a passage, his audience could not follow what he said, they took in what he was. Nobody stirred, nobody coughed, nobody shuffled his feet.

I don't know how long Dr. Bunche usually talks to an ordinary audience such as he had that night. To us he spoke, in his audible, unemphatic voice, for the full sixty minutes which few speakers of today feel like risking. And for full sixty minutes the plain men and women before him kept their eyes fixed on him, listening in unmoved silence. At the end, there was a long peal of applause, minute after minute of it, from people who continued sitting down firmly in their chairs. No man reached for his hat, no woman settled a wrap around her shoulders. No one moved to go.

A man in the middle of the hall stood up and asked a question about something he had not fully understood. Dr. Bunche answered it. Another question was put from the floor. He answered that. And now, we thought, we hoped, a kind of radiance was in his face. Had he divined something of the quality of his reception? After the long hour of his talk, he stood for more than thirty minutes more on the platform, answering question after question. Some of them showed ingenuous ignorance of the many legal and political details involved. All of them showed seriousness of interest. To every one he gave an informed, fully satisfactory answer.

It was a veritable conversation. It was a true contact in talk between a Negro who was a visible proof of what Vermonters of Civil War days had hoped, and the descendants of people who had believed in the humanity of his slave-ancestors. His audience was made up of the grandchildren of men many of whom had risked, some of whom had given, their lives to strike the chains from his grandfather. A cloud, a twilight shadow which had hung over one aspect of the Vermont Tradition, blew away to nothingness — forever.

Dr. Bunche, experienced speaker with, I suppose, hundreds of audiences in his memory, may not have noticed anything special about that evening in Vermont.

We did.

CHAPTER 20

One-way Social Street

HAVE other people, I wonder, idly watching a little boy or girl enjoying one of the modern playthings, been struck by its symbolic representation of human society? You must know the contraption to which I refer — a short length of plank with large and small square and round holes in it, and enough large and small square and round pegs to fill the holes. The task for the child is to set the pegs into the holes which fit them. ("And for statesmen and sociologists, too," you murmur fancifully to yourself.) By the time a child is old enough to go to kindergarten, he has, if he is normal, learned how to perform this exercise accurately and rapidly. ("Human society is still baffled by it," his grandmother reflects.)

Once having thought of this analogy, I can't get it out of my mind. Of course analogies are dangerous if they are taken as more than stimulants to thought. But that they certainly are! This one has set my wits to turning around and around the question of how the child learns that skill. He does not have it to begin with. A two-year-old goes at the problem slam-bang, hit-or-miss, violently trying to pound misfits into wrong holes with the hammer, even if the peg gets splintered and damaged. But as their bodies grow, so do their brains. By the time he is four or five years old, he knows enough to pick up each peg, look at it attentively to see what its shape and size are, and then look back at the plank to find a hole to fit it.

It is simple. Why don't human communities do that?

Any eye can see that they don't. We have all seen large human squares brutally mistreated when society tries to cram them into small round holes. And the other way around, small round human pegs are often left loosely rattling around in large square social holes, their presence there keeping out the personality which would really fit that position.

Why have we not, collectively, advanced to the five-year-old reasonableness in this matter? I don't know why. Does anybody? Would it be presumptuous to give some pages of this book to nonerudite, grandmotherly wondering about this question?

Is it perhaps that men and women were for centuries misled by another analogy — the hereditary idea? It is a plausible one. Elm tree seeds always produce elm trees. And the seeds of those elm trees never produce anything but more of the same kind. It might have seemed reasonable to expect from observing such an obvious fact that the children of upper-class parents would always fit upper-class life, with its monopoly of ease, responsibility and authority; and lower-class parents who had never known ease, responsibility or authority would have none but children suited to docility, obscurity and drudgery. To accept this principle required shutting the eyes to the fact that those elm trees which, sure enough, always grew out of elm seeds, varied according to what they got in the way of food, water, sunlight, free space to develop. Some were starved by the soil or climate they lived in and became feeble, scrawny, graceless early-decaying specimens. Some of the same seeds, surrounded by what they needed, became majestic king-trees of magnificent presence.

Of course one glance back into earlier centuries shows even so unsystematic a thinker as a musing grandmother that shrewd observers of human life have always been able to see for themselves that the hereditary principle doesn't hold water as a guide for getting human pegs into the holes they fit. Our British forebears were well served by their gift for doing one thing while saying another. They steadily burned incense before the idea that nobody can be a gentleman save a gentleman's son. But in real life the British aristocracy has always been renewed flexibly and frequently by admitting to the nobility people born to ordinary families, who had acquired cash or influence.

Up to Napoleon's time, it was honestly believed that no man was capable of being an officer save a member of the gentry. Napoleon had no nobles' sons on his side of the fight. So he officered his army with tavern-keepers' and blacksmiths' able sons. With them he swept away armies officered by lords' sons, and also swept out of human history the idea that a man's ability to command troops depends not on his personality training and experience, but on what kind of people his parents were.

We Americans never did have that notion about army officers, and hence the pre-Napoleonic idea seems inexplicable to us. The hereditary principle really did not survive the transatlantic crossing. And yet we still do not question some current separations of men and women into groups according to old prejudices, not according to any really observed differences between the individuals making up the group.

With the impassive objectivity of science, biological research hands on to us a laboratory-discovered fact so new now that we don't know what to do with it, can't see how, in practice, to fit it into our way of life. This fact is that because of the fortuitous combination of genes in each new human baby, individual *native* ability (or the lack of it) may turn up anywhere, in any human group, not at all according to family, race or color. This fact throws a monkey wrench of doubt and question into the arrangement by which even in our theoretically democratic America, we group human beings not according to their individual qualities but "by association."

Responsible people all around the globe have long realized that humanity is in grave danger, and that we can survive only if we succeed in creating that cyclone-proof shelter called a "stable, civilized society of free people." In view of what modern biology tells us about heredity such people begin to wonder if perhaps our failure, so far, to build up this shelter, may be caused by our leaving undeveloped and unused too large a proportion of the abilities latent in men and women — all men, all women, everywhere.

What biology tells us is that it's as wasteful as growing potatoes on a plot of ground rich in uranium, if we allow our prejudices to decree that all brown-skinned little boys should become Pullman-car porters. One of them may be Ralph Bunche. And our darkly threatened human community can't afford to lose his special abilities which, if given free scope, could help open the way to world peace. We know now that it was dangerous to humanity to accept the idea that pretty little girls needed only to learn to play the piano a little and keep house nicely because, "Oh, they'll marry anyhow." Any pretty little girl may be Madame Curie, whose chance for intellectual development gave us the epoch-making discovery of radium.

We peer out from the dark opening of the ancestral human cave, startled by this enormous diversity of human beings. A few men and women, those with prophetic vision, begin to guess that this diversity might turn out to be not just a puzzling liability. If we could learn how to utilize all the intelligence and patent good will children are born with, instead of ignoring much of it — why — *there might be enough to go around!* There might be enough to solve our alarming human problems, to put an end to poverty, to stop waging wars.

Do you wonder what this vast, global, life-and-death question has to do with Vermont? Is it possible that the small group of rural people in the Green Mountains has developed anything by living together from which a helpful suggestion might be drawn? I think there is.

Only in the climate of freedom — I mean not only political and economic freedom but specifically freedom from caste lines — can our political and educational opportunities bear their full fruits. No, I don't claim — I couldn't — that Vermont has any monopoly of freedom from the caste idea. All over America, class lines have been triumphantly thrown down, and the social thoroughfare opened to ability, as never before, anywhere.

But only in one direction.

We boast that no American is a slave, a serf, or even a vassal to the class into which he was born. We tell the world that our nation leaves him free to move out of it, if he wishes. That is true only if he moves one way. The son of a blacksmith can become President of the United States. Yes, that has been known to happen, and we do well to be proud of it. But would we have thought it fine for the President's son to earn a comfortable living as a mechanic, no matter how much he likes that work? No, our free country will harry him in various ways if he wishes to go in that direction. Yet all the grandmothers who have watched human life would bear witness that there are young men whose lives would have been more satisfactory if the road had been open both ways.

We glow over the emergence from his father's tailorshop of a greatly gifted orchestra conductor. But suppose he has a son not greatly gifted in music, but sound and capable along other lines. What "sympathy for the family" would be felt if the musician's son took up tailoring because he really liked his grandfather's occupation! He would not be happy in it, nor would his wife and children. They are all members of society, dependent on society's approval for much of what makes life tolerable. And society has not yet outgrown in practice ideals which we claim no longer to value.

Except for freaks and oddities, treated as such, the sons and daughters of twentieth-century, well-to-do, conventionally educated families are as helplessly serfs of the class they were born into as any mediaeval villein or vassal.

But not in Vermont.

No, I take that back. That's claiming too much. Vermont cannot be exempt from any idea which is almost universally held by the rest of the human race, like the strange, crippling idea that to earn one's living by working with one's hands is a mark of inferiority. I'll change my phrase to "Anyhow much less in Vermont."

Note that I say that narrowing, crippling idea is "almost" universal. An observer of American life as old as I can see some rebellion against this idea. Once in a while a member of the younger generation is restive under this caste line restriction, as normal youth is under other limitations of freedom of choice. Many a son or daughter of well-to-do city or suburban family tries in youth to get out of what in their own expressive lingo they call "the rat race" of savagely competitive business life, where the physical effort of the fight with rivals is restricted to pushing buttons and tipping back in swivel chairs.

These young rattlers of social shackles even have a slang name. When they try to earn their livings out of a city, partly by some manual skill, they are called "escapees." Every country region in the U.S.A. now recognizes them when they appear in the neighborhood. Question and answer about them runs about like this:

"Who're the new people just bought the Wilkie farm?" "Oh, they're young folks who want to get away from it all."

They are labeled.

The label means neither approval or disapproval. It means only "temporary." For their effort to move across a caste line has, as yet, a pathetic quality of futility. It lasts only as long as they are childless. Experienced elders let them alone in what looks to conventional eyes like a notional but relatively harmless new way to sow the wild oats of youth. But let babies appear — social pressures are brought to bear, as heavy as though morality were being flouted. The time has come for them to quit their nonsense. They are, like all sensitive young fathers and mothers, overwhelmed by the sudden responsibility for their children's future, not only for their present. Daunted by the social threat that their children "will be penalized," they surrender, and take the first office job they can get.

What is the plain meaning of that phrase, used to frighten young parents trying to escape from caste lines, "You must not penalize your children?" Doesn't it mean, in understandable ugly words, here in our free America, that their children must not be threatened with the danger of growing up in a "lower class" than the one to which they are entitled by their "birth"? It does.

What can truthfully be said for most Vermont communities, I think, is that the grim and un-American implications of that word "penalized" are less in the Green Mountains, fewer and less somber.

Americans laugh when they come across the fact that, until modern times, in England, the surgeon (who works with his hands) was not allowed to call himself "Doctor." That title had come to admit its bearer to social equality with the upper classes, hence long after the surgeon's training and skill was as fine as the M.D.'s the medical man who never used his hands except to write a prescription had a higher standing. We Americans see that this distinction is absurd; but does a well-to-do American banker or broker, with a marriageable daughter, admit that the veterinary doctor who now is as professionally well trained as a doctor has the same social standing? He does not. We don't talk about this. But it is so.

Take it from me, Vermonters are uneasy about lines drawn on this principle. We do not take them for granted. Our tradition makes us ashamed to find one still lasting on. We are brought up to avoid any act, word, intonation, facial expression which suggests that work with the hands or inaction of the hands means less — or more — human dignity in individual human beings.

These cherished folkways of ours are the origin of many a misunderstanding between Vermonters and those who come into the State from elsewhere. Our ideal of good manners repudiates, rather roughly, the definition of "courtesy" which limits that quality to contacts with social equals. We resent, and we don't care who knows it, the person who feels that pleasantness to his social inferiors is "kindness" not courtesy. The Vermont ideal (we don't always succeed in living up to it, but we wish we did) is to treat people who work with their hands with as much, and as little, and the same kind of pleasantness as anybody else.

Perhaps I might begin by saying — what always shocks non-Vermonters, we find — that the motto of *noblesse oblige* infuriates us; unless it means (which it does not) that *anybody* with some form of temporary or permanent good fortune not shared by others, is under an obligation to give a less fortunate brother man a boost over a hard place. If a neighbor's roof catches fire, your obligation to help him extinguish the flames is not as his superior protectively kind to a subordinate, it is because your roof is not on fire. And there is no occasion in that fact for you to put on condescending, complacent *"noblesse"* ideas about it, either. He would be bound to give you help, if the situation were reversed.

This conception seems simple, seems self-evident to us. But we often see non-Vermonters who are puzzled by it. A banker from Ohio, who came to call on us last summer, was fresh from such a bewilderment. On his way to our house he had taken the wrong turn, and found himself on a narrow muddy back road. His Cadillac had slithered into a mud-hole. No garage, telephone, house at hand. The jack was no use. Instead of lifting the heavy car, it sank into the soft earth. A farm wagon came rattling up behind, edged into the brush and started to pass. The desperate motorist appealed to him. The driver in faded blue jeans got out, tied his horse to a tree, looked the situation over, got an ax out from under the seat of his wagon and set to work cutting logs for a cribwork. The Ohio man said, apprehensively, "But ought we to cut trees on somebody's land?"

The Vermonter answered, "Sure. To get somebody out of a fix."

Finally, the portly banker sitting on the end of the lever-pole, one wheel was raised, the hole filled in with stones, lugged by the farmer from the old wall at the side of the road. An hour's hard work was put in. The car crept forward to solid ground. The banker offered payment. The farmer, wiping his muddy hands on his overalls said, casually, "No, I don't cal'late to charge you anything. Might have happened to me," and went on his rattling way.

He left the man from Ohio petrified. "Why, they are so grim, so close-mouthed," he told us, "I always thought they hated strangers. I can't make them out at all."

No, he could not make them out. And I didn't try to explain. His mind was too confused with a new fact which wouldn't fit into a rigid theory of his. It would take, I reflected, a whole book to help him grasp what seemed self-evident to us.

That Vermont farmer was from another town, far from ours. We had never laid eyes on him. But I understood him as if he were my brother. Particularly after I heard he had used the formula, so full of meaning for us but just words for the motorist, "Might have happened to me."

Many a Vermont woman, if able-bodied and capable of sitting down in a chair without help, is not at her ease when the "courtesy" is shown her of holding a chair for her at table, because she knows very well that the courteous gentleman who does it would not dream of showing this politeness to a woman who really needs it, like the weary elderly cleaning woman in the kitchen, beginning the task of polishing his wife's silver knives and forks. What we don't much like is a custom that puts on the air of a wish to be helpful but really is only a gesture, and a class-restricted gesture at that!

Vermonters often shock other people by their lack of formal "good manners." In their turn they are shocked by formal good

manners which are based on the house-dog's feeling that it's all
right to bite a stranger's leg if his trousers are ragged. The polls
and our law courts offer one kind of protection to the principle
of fair play for all. We think that principle should be also protected in every human contact. By the unspoken, mostly unconscious but cherished Vermont code, one of the bases of decent
manners is not to imply that a greater share of prosperity means
superiority of person, or the other way around.

Did I say "manners"? Yes, and I meant it. An abstract dictionary definition of that word is "living up to a polite social
code." In some circles, "manners" means making affable conversation about nothing in particular with people you pretend to like
better than you do. To the pre-Civil War plantation-owner it
meant elaborate punctilio while he got ready to shoot last night's
boon companion with a dueling pistol. Measured by either of these
rules, the Vermonter has no manners at all. Just the same he has
his code. A Vermont farmer does not "order" his hired man to do
some specific piece of work. If he did, he would not have a hired
man. Of course Vermonters understand, as every sensible person
does, that when work is to be done, somebody must plan it and
see that his helpers carry out the plan. How do they manage this
without ordering people around? As any manners are carried out,
through turns of phrase to which they have been trained since
their childhood, just as everybody is trained to write "Dear Mr.
Smith," or to say "Glad to see you."

The Vermont farmer has a lot of folkways to avoid a drill-
sergeant's way of issuing commands. He can say, "What say we
get the upper field plowed this morning?" Or, "How'd it be to
cultivate the corn while the good weather holds?" Or, "When I
got up this morning, I said to myself, 'It's about time to — etc.
etc.'" Once in a great while a command in Vermontese happens
to be given outside of our state. Other people find it an oddity.
One famous instance is the momentous order given in Manila
Bay by Admiral Dewey (born and brought up in Montpelier).
We are always taken aback to have American schoolchildren set
to memorize, among other historical sayings, the Admiral's perfectly natural words, "You may fire when ready, Gridley." What
is there so remarkable in that, we wonder.

To this day a Vermonter, asked what he's doing nowadays, does not say "I'm working for so-and-so," but "I'm helping out over at so-and-so's." There are so many "Vermont stories" on this point, one could fill a book with them.

But before I tell some of them, I ought to explain that we consider such stories as fables. Everybody knows that a short fable throws more light on the culture of any group than a chapter full of abstract scholarly exposition.

Our Vermont fables sometimes sound rather like the funny stories dragged in, hit-or-miss, by after-dinner speakers. But they are different in purpose. The after-dinner anecdote is told solely to make the listeners laugh. Vermont anecdotes also purpose to make the listener laugh, but their main intention is to focus attention on a clause of our tradition we wish to perpetuate. Since we do not pretend to monopolize this tradition, we occasionally get an excellent "Vermont" story from quite another country, sometimes even told in another language. Here is one told in French. It emphasizes a clause in the Swiss tradition, but also in ours. A famous Swiss heart specialist is called out of his inner office to quiet a disturbance among the patients in his waiting room. He is confronted by an elaborately dressed lady who says imperiously that she must see him at once. With a wave of his hand the doctor indicates a number of sick people waiting their turns, and at the end of the line several vacant seats. "Just take a chair please," he says pleasantly. The lady draws herself up. "Don't you realize that I am the Countess of Something-or-other?" The eminent doctor smiles, bows, says gently, "Oh, I see. In that case take two chairs," and turns back to his office.

Just the other day, I laughed to read this fable ascribed to a pompous politician calling on a poor family in the Southern Appalachians. In either locality the story is at home. Probably it never literally happened anywhere; but it *could* have happened in Switzerland, in upland Kentucky, or in Vermont. Perhaps, after the passage of a few years, it will have happened here.

Some people tell "Vermont stories" because they sound funny. Some others, who dislike the spirit of our way of life, tell them as instances of Vermont bad manners. For us many of them are means to an end, to undermine the idea that a person who does manual labor or looks as if he did is inferior, and that a person who looks as if he never worked is superior.

Here is one out of my own experience. One summer, years ago, before automobiles, I was back in Vermont from a year's research work for my doctorate in France. One morning, I rode my small, part-Morgan horse several miles up the valley to visit a cousin of my father's, a farmer. In those days horses were means of transportation, not labels of leisure-class rank.

I found him with his hired man working at tense top speed. The hay was down and dry, the weather looked rather like rain, and — calamity! — the man who was to come with his horse to drive the rake hadn't appeared. Well, I had a horse. I got him into light harness, backed him into the shafts, borrowed a gingham skirt from a cousin in the house, climbed up into the metal seat of the rake, and, not for the first time in my life, started to rake hay. My little Morgan was a riding horse, but equine Vermonters, like their owners, have never drawn lines between "menial" and other useful activity.

With an anxious eye on the darkening sky, we raked and loaded, pushing ourselves hard. A three-seater carriage came slowly up the hill with a load of summer people out for a drive. They motioned the driver to stop, and beckoned to me. Assuming that they needed directions as to the road, and that they were elderly or infirm, I drove the clumsy hay-rake to a tree where I could fasten the horse, and walked back, rather impatiently, across the field to the road.

They turned out to be perfectly able-bodied. They did not need directions. They wanted to tell the gingham-clad girl, graciously, how they approved of an American farm woman working on the land. "The peasant women do in Europe," they told me, and explained what "Europe" meant. "In Germany and France, you know. It looks *so* picturesque over there to see the peasant girls helping harvest the grain."

I was not seasoned enough yet to have at my tongue's end a correct Vermont formula for the occasion, but I was thoroughly trained in the Vermont tradition that it is not manners to tell even a very foolish person to go to hell. I stood silent, wondering if they knew the difference between harvesting grain in late August and making hay in June. Presently they said they *would* like to have a photograph of a Vermont farm girl. "Just step over here, will you? Henry, where is my camera?"

I saw my chance, said neutrally, "I'm afraid I haven't time for that," and escaped.

During this incident my farmer cousin and his hired man continued to load hay at top speed. Nor did they turn their heads as I hastened back to the hay-rake, unfastened the horse and climbed to the seat. But out of the corner of his mouth the hired man said, in a flat tone, "I hope those nice kind folks gave you a good-sized tip." We all laughed noiselessly — it wouldn't have been manners to laugh loudly — and went on haying.

If you say, "Why, what are you talking about? All Americans feel this. We draw no caste lines," I can only answer sadly, "Yes we do, too, although we look the other way when we do."

Not long ago the head of a Middle Western manufacturing company was telling me, with the most generous pleasure, about the favored life of the skilled employees in his factory. He gave me the amounts of some of their large yearly incomes — my Vermont ear pricked up to notice that he used the word "wages." He went on, "They have as much money as many a family on our street."

"*Our* street?" silently exclaimed the Vermont tradition.

He was beginning to list their expensive possessions, their high-powered automobiles, their costly kitchen gadgets, when I asked him a question my great-grandmother might have asked. "Do any of these wage-earning workers live on your street?"

He was surprised. "No. No, I don't think so."

"Do their wives belong to your wife's Woman's Club?"

"No, oh, no."

"Would your wife's Woman's Club accept as member the wife of a man who was paid wages, even large wages, not a salary? Would your Golf-Club accept a wage-earner as a —"

The dismay in his fine, open, sincere American face touched me. I stopped my disagreeable questions. Nor did I say what was in my mind: "They do in my Vermont town."

The point I am trying to bring out, without much hope that I can make myself understood, is that in Vermont, from the beginning on, there has been a purpose, both conscious and unconscious, so to run our communities that one end of the social street is as good as the other. If you label one end as inferior, anybody whose natural tastes incline him to live there knows that a move in that direction would cost him and his children a painfully high price.

Last week, in a chat with one of the three selectmen of a Vermont town up beyond Rutland, he told me that a likeable summer resident from another state had asked the selectmen to take a moderate action in regard to housing, which, in effect, would stratify their town, so that wage-earners would live in one part and white-collar folks in another.

"What did you do?" I asked.

"Oh, I told him we couldn't do that. 'In Vermont', I said, 'the hired man still eats with the family.'"

"Did he see what you meant?"

"I dunno." He added mildly, "It's no matter, whether he did or not."

That selectman was, in 1951, carrying on a tradition begun here when Vermont began about 1763.

Our first Governor was Thomas Chittenden, born and brought up in Salisbury in Western Connecticut, close to the New York line. He was elected our governor at a time when other American governors wore brocaded waistcoats, coats of broadcloth or silk, lace ruffles, silk stockings. They rode in coaches with a liveried driver on the seat. Their wives wore silk dresses, never cooked a meal or washed a dish.

Governor Chittendon was a working farmer. He wore homespun clothes and a loose farmer's smock-frock. Once a finely dressed gentleman on horseback came along the road. A load of hay blocked the way. To the elderly farmer on the load the traveler called out, "Can you tell me where Governor Chittenden's house is?"

The farmer called back, "I'm goin' right there now."

The man on horseback followed the hay wagon till it turned into a barnyard. The gray-haired farmer slid down, handed the reins to a waiting boy, dusted off his hands, and said pleasantly, "Now what can I do for you? I am Governor Chittenden."

That this was no personal oddity of his, but a purposeful living up to a recognized principle is shown by another well-remembered, often quoted Chittenden story. Some fine people had come to see the Governor on business, their elegant wives with them. These ladies, so goes the story, were surprised to see the Governor's middle-aged wife, aproned from chin to hem, cooking dinner with the help of a neighbor's wife. They were more surprised when, as the food was nearly ready to serve, Mrs. Chittenden rang the dinner bell to call in the men hoeing in the cornfield.

Their surprise was so visible that Mrs. Chittenden said to them with the unobtrusive, low-relief irony practiced by Vermonters, then as now, "I know, it must seem strange to you ladies that the field-workers are to eat at the table with us. Of course, since they have been working so hard in the hot sun all the morning, while we have been comfortable in the house, they should, by rights, eat first, and we should wait and eat at a second table. But since you are company, I thought probably they wouldn't mind having us eat at the same time."

I don't know whether that story has ever been put into print. But hardly a Vermonter in the hundred and seventy-odd years since Mrs. Chittenden made that remark but has heard it repeated, and nourished his spirit on it.

A few years ago, an anthology of humorous New England anecdotes was published. There were hundreds in the thick volume. I could find only one told of a Vermonter. In the mid-nineteenth century, a well-to-do Boston family, despairing, even then, of getting household helpers, had taken on a tall Vermont country lad. He seemed full of good will, with no prejudices against any kind of work he was asked to do. To try him out, he was given, one evening after a dinner party, a small tray with sugar and cream, and told to follow the maid who was passing cups of coffee, poured from an urn by the mistress of the house. She told him exactly how to present the tray, how to stand waiting till the right moment came. Everything went according to directions. The expression on the Vermont boy's young face had not quite that zero-with-the-rim-off blankness which denotes the correct servant's temporary abdication from the human status. But on the whole, he was presentable enough, until, taking his responsibility seriously and not sure that all the guests had been served, he called genially, across the room, "How you comin' for sweetenin', over there?"

One more Vermont story. A neighbor of mine, who lives on a nearby farm, told us about a project suggested to her by a well-to-do summer resident. We thought it an excellent idea. A class was to be formed with a competent teacher, where our farmers' daughters and village girls might learn the housekeeping skills needed by the city people who come to spend the summer in Vermont. We liked the way she put it, "Here we summer folks desperately need household help. All around us on farms and in villages are nice Vermont girls who need money. Why can't we get together?"

Why not indeed? My neighbor and I were enthusiastic; especially when we heard what big wages would be paid. A Vermont girl, after one summer paid as well as that, could finance her way through a whole year of normal school. My neighbor's daughter was halfway through a Vermont teachers' college. There was more than money in it, too. Our local girls would learn, we assumed, skills valuable in themselves — cooking, probably dishes we didn't know at all, housekeeping in a more complicated pattern than ours, and, in general, the ways of well-educated, widely traveled people. It looked fine. My farm neighbor and her daughter went to talk over the details with the helpful city lady.

But when I next saw them, they shook their heads. No go.

"What was the matter?" I asked.

The mother said, "Well, I'd *thought* what she wanted was help in the work. But it turned out it was something else. We said we were interested to know what kinds of things our Vermont girls would learn in such a class. She said first of all, to stand up whenever the lady of the house came into the kitchen, find a chair for her, and keep on standing while she gave her orders. Suppose you were hurrying to shell a pan of peas for dinner. You'd stop to stand up and stay standing while she told you which windows she wanted washed. Every time she came around, you were to stop your work to do that."

As so often in my Vermont life, I could hardly wait to hear what happened next. "What did you tell her?" I asked.

"Oh, I didn't *tell* her anything. I didn't want to hurt her feelings. Maybe she never heard any different. I just said we'd think it over. The next time I saw her, I said I guessed Vermont girls couldn't ever learn to do things her way, not enough to be much good to her." She added dryly, "I didn't say *which* things."

The teacher's college daughter, in her advanced history course, had been studying the development of social customs. She now said with the accent of intellectual curiosity, "Mrs. Fisher, where does that idea come from anyhow, that it is manners to stand up and let richer people sit down? I can understand — anybody can — their not wanting their kitchen help to eat at the table with them. We certainly wouldn't want strangers eating with us, three times a day. But this standing up. Where do you suppose the idea started?"

I had never asked myself the question, and hazarded, "Could it go back to the early days when the most important person had the only chair? Like the 'chairman' of a committee you know."

"Would it have lasted on till now? Must be hundreds of years there have been plenty of chairs."

"In the Army, a private soldier stands up when an officer speaks to him," I reminded her.

"Yes, but there's some point to that. What the officer has to say *may* be life or death. It may be awfully important for the soldier to hear exactly what he has to do. When you are standing, your muscles are taut, and you are apt to pay more attention. But for housework — anybody with sense enough to do it doesn't have to stop shelling peas to hear about getting the bed in the spare room made up. No," she went on in casual speculation, "I'm sure they mean it to show that the person who pays wages is better than the person who takes wages. But I still can't see why standing up is the best way to get that idea across. In a classroom, the teacher stands up and the children sit at their desks because she can keep her authority over them better. There's some sense in that."

I made another guess, "At church, you know, we stand up to sing the hymns."

"Yes, but when we want to show real respect — when we pray, or the minister prays — we kneel down. There's an idea! Why wouldn't they have their help kneel down when they come into the room to tell them how the potatoes are to be cooked. They'd *have* something, then."

For a silent moment, we three gazed at the imaginary picture, and burst into light-hearted Vermont laughter.

"Well anyhow," said the mother, responsibly, "Marion's got to make what she can to help pay for her normal-school expenses next winter. We calculate to go berrying a good deal. Would you maybe want to buy some blueberries for deep-freezing?"

The little incident was over, was forgotten, as any slight happening is forgotten. They had not resented the upper-class purpose to mark a worker as inferior, because they were not in the power of any kind of upper class, and could, with ease, avoid it, as any of us make a detour to avoid a person likely to have disagreeable manners.

So far, I have given negative examples of the way in which the Vermont tradition watchfully patrols the social frontier as formerly it did the political frontier, to repel smaller or larger attempts to introduce caste lines here. Do Vermont communities also find positive ways to reward by their approval ways of life in which the conventional caste line is disregarded? I'll say they do. Not in words, not perhaps in conscious theorizing awareness. In action.

One such is going on in my home town. I am just back at my desk after having driven down the valley a few miles to see the Vermonter concerned, to ask his permission to cite his life. I found him in his carpenter's work clothes, about to start off in his light truck, with one of his helpers, to a barn he is putting up. He stopped to hear what I had to say, standing at ease in the hot summer morning, the collar of his work-shirt open, his muscular body relaxed, his quiet eyes calmly attentive. "I'm writing a book about the way we manage life in Vermont," I told him, "and I've come to a place where I'd like to put in the way you manage your life."

He looked blank and asked, "Why would anybody be interested?"

"I mean your giving up being a professional man and deciding to be a carpenter and housebuilder."

He got my idea. "Oh — that." He gave the matter a moment of

silent thought. Then he nodded, swung himself up to the driver's seat in his truck, and in an easy, good-natured tone answered me through the opened window, "Sure. If you want to. Why not?"

So here is the story of that Vermonter. After his graduation from our State University in Burlington, he came to teach in our local high school. He was successful in his class work, also successfully coached the basketball team. The students greatly liked him, he was admired and valued by the people of the town. About how to spend his summer vacations he had his own idea, we noticed. He went to work for a local carpenter, coming and going in wage-earner's blue jeans, earning day's wages. Everybody took this as a matter of course. If he wanted to.

After a while, he accepted a position in a city high school (a small Vermont-style city, Barre it was, I think) where the salary was considerably larger. We were not surprised. He was going up the professional ladder, as competent men do. Some years later our principal was old enough to retire. John Moore (that is his real name) was invited to come back and be Principal. Everybody was pleased when he accepted. His success was as great as before, his teaching as excellent. His orderly mind made him an admirable administrator.

But after some years he resigned. He put his reasons for this change into plain folk-words, although psychiatrists often resort to rather complicated technical language to explain the same things. He told us that he had noticed that at the end of every school year he was rather pale, had lost weight, had warnings of trouble with his digestion, felt and looked tired. Yes, we had noticed that too.

Every summer, as he worked at carpentry, he had noticed (we had too) that, although as he grew more experienced he assumed more responsibility, this did not take out of him the nervous vitality which his professional work seemed to cost. By September he was again calm, brown-faced, hearty and life-enjoying. Why not change from one way of earning a living to another which seemed to fill his individual needs more accurately?

In a prosperous suburb, inhabited by white-collar workers, in a state where any form, even skilled, of manual work is connected with social inferiority, to stop being a professional man, in order to work with saw and hammer, would, we gather, have caused him and his family as much nervous tension, as many sleepless nights, as to continue in it. Psychiatrists are all too familiar with patients caught between two mighty forces, pulled one way by a painful maladjustment in their work, pulled the other way by well-grounded dread of social penalties if they change. What I am trying to say in this chapter is that everybody will be benefited and nobody will be hurt, if such penalties are lessened, and that the Vermont tradition tries and, to an extent surprising to many people, succeeds in making that momentous decision a free choice.

Consider how that social tyranny complicates another "natural" (I'll say it is natural) need of humanity — to marry. To be reasonably fulfilled, mature men and women should live with a mate. Finding the right mate in the unknown unexplored world which lies before each individual coming into marriageable age is so difficult that many people take unsuitable mates — and suffer. Their chance to find someone with whom they are personally fitted to live happily is infinitely lessened if their choice is shackled by a rigid, unacknowledged prejudice against usefulness of the hands.

Our poor magnificent hands! Anthropologists tell us that the usefulness of our hands is one of the few human endowments which absolutely differentiate us from animals. The physical and nervous connection between the use of the hands and the normal development of some brain-centers is so beyond-imagination ancient that psychologists often teach re-use of the hands for the mentally disturbed exactly as doctors prescribe vitamins for the physically undernourished. A wrong turning in our human road, taken hundreds of centuries ago, has starved many of us of this vitamin of personality. The "therapeutic busy-work" prescribed by psychiatrists is no substitute. What is needed for many a troubled human life is creative usefulness of the hands and body, given dignity by social recognition.

Well, in Vermont, there was no need to consult a psychiatrist. Our former Principal had but to say to himself as he said to me, "Why not?"

So he did. The town raised a clamor of protest, but only because he was needed as Principal. Naturally we thought of our own needs first. As far as I could see, his fellow townsmen took his decision about as they would if he had changed from a red necktie to a blue one. Many of us thought that red was more becoming to him than blue. But for goodness' sake, whose business was it — his, or ours?

He set up as a building contractor and so has continued with steady success to this day. You must remember that in small Vermont towns a "building contractor" does not wear tweeds and a white collar, does not merely tell working carpenters what to do. He is a working carpenter, using his hands as well as his head.

I think I know what, at this point, may be — naturally enough — in your mind. You may be thinking that there is in Vermont, or is in me personally, a subconscious, Jacobin, resentful wish to tear down people of the upper classes because their superiority is envied. You must remember that upper classes have never succeeded in getting the power here to enforce the idea that they are superior. So they are not envied. Do you envy a Moslem who has been to Mecca and so has the right to wear the green turban or whatever it is such pilgrims wear? Yet in his own society he is considered very superior. Green turbans are nothing to you. Soft, white and incapable hands are nothing to us.

To disprove this possible idea you may have, let me set down here, still from real life, the corollary of John Moore's story. It is that of the present Principal of our high school.

He is also a graduate of our State University. He is, as it happens, just as strong and sizable of body as John Moore. In fact they don't look unlike. But in him, the mysterious and unpredictable action and reaction upon each other of muscles, nerve-centers, glands, gray matter which we call individual personality are not the same. He is just as successful a teacher and administrator, but the multifarious details of school administration do not get him down, any more than the equally multifarious details of building construction get the other man down. He can put up a shelf, if it is needed, but he wouldn't do it for fun, any more than I would specially enjoy shaping modeling clay into statues. He has another way of creating something. He spends his summers in writing and editing school textbooks for an excellent publishing house, to meet classroom needs he has encountered as a teacher. He is a square peg solidly set in a square hole.

Each man is in the way of life which suits the incalculable sumtotal of qualities which makes him a man. Neither of them is in any danger from stomach-ulcers, from nervous alcoholism, from compulsive obsessions, from guilt feelings, from self-punishing tendencies, from psychosomatic something or other. One man is not valued by the community more or less than the other, any more than a fine tall maple is valued less or more than a fine tall oak. From the spectacle of the two of them, deeply rooted and thriving in the special soil which best allows the seed within each to develop and grow, the whole town — men, women and children (perhaps especially the children, their antennae reaching out for indications about what is waiting for them in their unknown future) draw food for their faith in life and a renewed loyalty to American ideals.

In the medium of words it is impossible to comment accurately on something which takes place in the medium of action. In trying to describe the peaceful solution here of a knot of maladjustment which often causes people suffering elsewhere, I realize that, without meaning to, I seem to claim too much for the Vermont tradition. I am only trying to say that less than in many other places, Vermont puts no *needless* barriers in the way of normal growth into natural strength, along natural abilities. But there are countless human problems not in the least helped by this. The texture of human existence is complex in our State, as it is everywhere, a mixture of good, bad and mediocre. Personal perplexities and uncertainties are a trackless jungle here as elsewhere. Of course. Some parents boss their children too much, others neglect them, some children are ungrateful. Business enterprises dwindle and fail as well as prosper. Some people set too much store by material possessions and get punished for this mistake by dry rot of the personality. Some are lazy, others drive themselves and hence others around them, too hard. Some are spiteful and mean, some are generous-hearted. Narrowly respectable people often draw back their skirts self-righteously from the less respectable but perhaps more lovable. Life is life, with all its teasing and tragic perplexities. Why wouldn't it be?

But our folk tradition has perhaps one contribution to make to one human problem in showing that the ugly and unjust mass generalizations involved in caste lines are not inevitable, unescapable elements in the life of ordinary men and women.

Almost everywhere in our America, our nation has done wonderfully in laying out and hard-surfacing one lane of its inter-job highway. But one lane only. The sign on the other, which leads from White-collar to Overalls, still reads, "Road Closed. Proceed at Your Own Peril."

In Vermont we are proud to post the notice — and to try to live up to it, "Open for Traffic in Both Directions."

PART V

PART IV

CHAPTER 21

By Their Fruits—

WHEN people speak of the "fruits" of a certain way of human life, when they ask what have been the "results" of putting into practice one or another standard of values, they are usually thinking about material, tangible objects — temples, fine bridges, pictures in museums — or about single personalities so unusual, so notable (for good or bad) as to be known far beyond the geographical limits of their birthplace. Rarely do they include among results an impalpable, unsensational, widely held standard of conduct. Such a standard — basic respect for men and women according to their individual qualities, regardless of what work he does or what clothes she wears, is cherished in Vermont as a "fruit" of great value. That this ideal has been lived up to (within limits, in a long struggle with human nature), and has been honored through almost two centuries of varied struggle for existence, is for us a subject of proud, if silent, thanksgiving.

Just to mention this much-honored communal fruit would be enough to say about the fruits of our way of life, except for one reason. That reason is a notion about human societies, accepted by many people in spite of the lip-service paid by Americans to the equal-rights, equal-opportunity theory. There is a sizable unreconstructed minority who, claiming that they are the protectors of a high level of culture, object very much to an inclusive, open society. Their idea is that a sterile level of mediocrity is the inevitable result of excluding nobody innately worthy from individual dignity, self-respect and reasonable consideration from his fellows. They point to the great days of Greece, when a small number of the first rank thought deeply or created works of art, and when the hard and dirty work was done by men and women enslaved in semihuman status. Instead of joining those two statements together with an "and," they use a "because."

Now speculations about human affairs cannot be put into one

and another laboratory test tube, cannot be disproved or proved. All I can say about this particular ungenerous speculation is that it rests on an uncertain assumption, drawn from a single example. Plenty of other societies have been based on the separation of privileged leisure classes from servile menials, yet most of the favored groups, far from producing a Sophocles or a Phidias, have been notable only for self-indulgence ruinous to themselves and wasteful spending ruinous to their country. Or to put my denial the other way around, since Vermont has never harbored the idea that enforced inferiority for any group is an essential factor in raising others to superior excellence, since it has refused to admit the necessity for slaves or a permanent lower class to do its hard work, it should by these theories have paid for this refusal by sinking to a low and dead level of human mediocrity. I write this chapter as a comment on that idea.

To begin with, please note that the alternative is not between savorless mediocrity and genius. Genius is like lightning. It strikes without apparent cause. In all human history there have been few truly "great" personalities. No human group has produced numerous men of genius. Such first-raters are set apart from the rest of us by the magic of their special gifts, their mysterious creative (or destructive) powers, their unique combination of qualities. Such miracles as Einstein and Hitler (to cite the two ends of the gamut) can hardly be said to be "produced" in any way understandable to us by the kind of society around them.

What society — environment — tradition — can produce is a number of men and women whose aspirations rise above three meals a day, who have strength, special gifts and good will enough to contribute something of value to humanity; and also a few whose service rises far enough above the ordinary line of duty recognized by all good citizen-soldiers in the ranks for them to be recognized as valuable, all over their country.

Even one such name is above the expected probability for small communities. There are urban centers in the United States with about the population of Vermont which cannot count a single son or daughter as famous enough — or infamous enough, for that matter — for his or her name to be recognized outside his state.

There are similar fine urban centers of the same size in Europe which in a thousand years have been lived in by plenty of people who were able, upright, intelligent, industrious men and women of good will, but anonymous as far as the rest of us know. Have all Vermonters been similarly anonymous? It would seem natural.

Let us first rule out some people whose names are well known, who were born here, geographically, but were certainly not produced by Vermont tradition. Of the many thousands who left Vermont, some took with them the Vermont tradition and rooted it in other soil. Others shook off that tradition like dust from their feet.

The two powerful founders of the great Mormon Church, Joseph Smith and Brigham Young, could never have achieved here what they did elsewhere. The Vermont tradition has never been antichurch, as it has always been antimonarchical and anticaste. But it is considerably more secular than theological or mystical. Our tradition can claim no credit for the extraordinary Mormon achievement of building a large, stable, prosperous community, based on a single religious belief, fervently held by every man, woman and child of the church-state of the desert. Nothing could differ more from the Vermont tradition than the intensity of Mormon belief in the doctrine of a single church, unquestioned, even undiscussed, upheld unanimously, submitted to in enthusiastic docility by all the community. The numbers of the successful Mormon Church are now somewhere near twice the population of Vermont.

Among Vermont-born men with gifts for which a secular background was not suited was Orestes Brownson, one of the most notable nineteenth-century converts to Catholicism, certainly the most turbulent, least humble, most independent, yet most devoutly Catholic in that number. At fourteen years of age, he was taken away by his mother to live in New York State. The influence of Vermont on him can have been nothing more than the large number of good-quality books which he found as a child in the tiny mountain settlements where he lived (yes, Locke's books were among these; they were everywhere a part of early Vermont life).

Another indomitable religious leader was the potent creator and director of the Oneida Community, John Noyes. If there ever was a man absorbed in religion as a way of life, he was, although unorthodox to the limit, and beyond. He was connected with Vermont but not in any way produced by the State (unless perhaps in violent reaction from its ideals). He and his followers were never persecuted by fire and sword in Vermont, as the Mormons were in the Middle West. But their Green Mountain neighbors were entirely out of sympathy with their ideas about sex relations, made them feel very unwelcome here and have never regretted their going somewhere else.

At the other end of the personality-gamut stands Jim Fisk, with his diamond rings and stickpins, and his fancy women. He was a born-and-brought-up Vermonter, but found here, as opportunity for his special personal endowment, no more than the life of an itinerant peddler. He took those personal powers to New York City, leaving behind every shred of the Vermont tradition which, judging from his actions, he energetically disliked and repudiated. In the metropolis he became one of the gaudiest, most reckless plungers and speculators, one of the most unscrupulous, most notorious, most successful spenders of big money, patrons of expensive courtesans, and wreckers of railroads, in the rampant years of get-rich-quick and spend-it-quicker.

Artists too, a few, have been born in Vermont: as many probably as could be expected in a population so small. The Brownings, Hawthorne and the rest of the Victorian English-speaking colony in Italy, admired the statues of a Vermonter, Hiram Powers. Nobody does now. To people used to the angular planes of modern art, his Greek Slave, so famous in the nineteenth century, looks slick and boneless. But art appreciators of its period made it famous with their praise of its beauty, and mid-Victorian prudes made it infamous for its total nudity. Powers came from Brattleboro — literally "came from" there, did not try to go on living there. A marble-worker in Dorset, Vermont, had a gifted son, whose heroic statue of Lafayette stands in a court-yard of the Louvre. But Daniel Chester French's father took him to live in France.

In those days Vermont had, as now, the most tolerant, leave-'em-alone attitude towards artists, as towards other harmless variants from the conventional. ("S'long as they pay their taxes and keep their fences up" is the folk formula.) But the fact was that artists could not in the nineteenth century earn their living here or anywhere in the United States. Only across the Atlantic were to be found a large number of men of wealth who took art seriously enough to spend real money on it. In our day artists can (and how many of them do!) live in the Green Mountains and sell their work in New York or Chicago or Paris. They are not "produced by the Vermont tradition," only left free by it to paint if they want to.

These examples, out of many, of Vermonters whose special personal gifts were not suited to the way of life here, are set down as a reminder of a very important fact, too often over-looked — that no one local tradition can possibly suit all the epic diversity of human possibilities. The very qualities which bring to full flower certain kinds of ability (good or bad) will in the nature of things hamper and frustrate other kinds of abilities. If we forget that any one attitude towards life has this inherent limitation, we fail to see that it points to the need for an open door leading out of all communities. Not only politically open, but psychologically and socially.

Vermonters have kept this door open. Almost from the first (for it was early in the nineteenth century that many in each generation of Vermonters began to move away) our state has had free-flowing emigration and immigration. It is inevitable that some boys and girls as they grow up in Vermont do not find the atmosphere around them in harmony with the best and strongest of their natures. There is not a town in the State from which such boys and girls have not gone out to success elsewhere. The social tradition around them (not of course always the family tradition) leaves them free to choose for themselves whether they wish to go or to stay. Elsewhere, we gather, the remark is peppery and resentful. Here it is easygoing and neutral: "Why don't you try it somewhere else? Maybe you'd like it better. Nobody'd blame you. All folks aren't alike."

* * *

As we people of the harsh, unexpected modern era look forward to the "one world" which is obviously before us, it is often with daunted uncertainty as to what its unknown way of life may mean to individual human happiness and satisfaction. Possibly the Vermont experience of doors wide open for to-and-fro migration may give some evidence that the men and women of the future will profit by freedom to go and come, as the mass of their ancestors never did, seeking out the especial tradition in which each can live most creatively.

Justin Morrill

So much for those exceptional personalities which the Vermont tradition did not at all fit. Have there been any which it did fit? Have any human beings ripened in our climate to that full natural development of their best which makes people noteworthy? We think that Justin Morrill is one.

Wherever you live in the U.S.A. your own life has probably been enriched by what he did for you, or for the people around you who determine your community's level of civilization. It is scarcely possible that not one person in your region ever profited by one of the great state universities. They were created by the Morrill Act.

His notable national achievement, and the international role played by Warren Austin, the Vermont lawyer, in the first years of the United Nations, are based on an unexpected, unplanned-for result of the organization of our nation under the Constitution which seems to me worth the consideration of any American.

We all learn in our high school classes about the compromise finally made at our Constitutional Convention in 1787 between the apparently irreconcilable interests of the large wealthy states and the ones with much smaller population. Our history teacher explains to us that this compromise was intended to persuade the smaller states to join in the Union by assuring them that they would not be bossed around by communities with large numbers of voters. I never heard any teacher point out that in practice this compromise provided something nobody planned for — the possibility that the nation's ideals, standards of values, tradition, would be varied by the ideas produced by communities neither wealthy nor large. A small and not populous state has just as many Senators as a great and powerful one. When a Senator truly represents the standards (good or not good) created by the state of his origin, he can often, through the special position given him by our Constitution, influence the life of our tremendous nation.

The influence of some Senators, reflecting their constituents' standards of values, has been, to speak plainly, bad. We Vermonters feel that the influence of Justin Morrill was notably good. And I'd like here to tell you our reasons.

An explanation of the greatness of his contribution to our American life will not be needed by any American brought up west of the Alleghenies, or having lived in that region. In all that vast territory there is not one citizen whose life has not been enriched by the American institution of the great state universities. Even if he was never a student there, even if his children are not students, the whole level of civilization of his community is higher because of what was started by our Vermont Senator Morrill in 1862. What his community would have become without such state institutions of higher learning is unthinkable to anybody who knows them.

But people east of the Alleghenies have no such flesh-and-bone link with free public higher education. They are, many of them, almost as incapable of feeling that such a link can exist as Europeans to whom Americans vainly try to explain in words certain basic institutions of our nation with which our connection is deep, wordless, organic, more like that of trees to the soil out of which they grow than of men to political theories. One can encounter a roomful of Eastern seaboard people, well versed in booklore about their nation, who have never heard how the state universities were founded, who have no idea what the vast total of their students has been, nor what a miracle it is, was, and will ever be for our whole nation that they came into existence.

It is especially for such readers that I take space here to tell the story of Justin Morrill, and of the Morrill Act.

During the turbulent, yeasty 1850's, the situation of our nation, in one matter of extreme importance, was almost the same as that of England under Henry VIII. For each country there was a similar radiant possibility to seize — or to lose. Sixteenth-century England lost it. Would the crude, ungrammatical, tobacco-chewing Americans, derided by Mrs. Trollope and Dickens, do any better?

What England lost was the chance to use for the nation's education a great treasure which in the 1500's had come into the government's hands. Our nation too, as the 1800's drew towards the mid-century, found itself owner of a vast treasure — the area of enormously valuable public lands. In both cases the government had taken this wealth by force from its original owners; in England from the monastic orders, in the United States from the Indians. The natural comment on such action is not in place in this book, or in the sketch of a Vermonter who represented his State in Congress for forty years. He had nothing to do with the acquisition of the prodigious acreage of the public lands. It was with the use made of some of it that his name is linked.

In England, in the sixteenth century, it was said that a third of the total wealth of England was in the hands of the religious orders. When it came into the hands of the government, there were plenty of Englishmen intelligent enough to see the potential value to the nation of such treasure. Some of the best of them saw what could be done, and spoke up for it. The great Hugh Latimer (1485–1555) cried out, "Here I will make a supplication that ye would bestow so much to the finding of scholars of good wits, of poor men's sons, as ye were wont to bestow in pilgrimage matters, in masses, in pardons, in purgatory matters."

Such men had vision, but the form of their government gave them no power to realize it. In our days Trevelyan says that if even a part of that wealth had been spent on education, "England would soon have had the best secondary education of the world;

and the whole history of England and of the world might have been changed for the better."

But conscientious and farsighted Englishmen protested in vain against the waste of opportunity. The English King had other ideas. Henry VIII sold the greater part of the confiscated monastic lands and spent the purchase price as he pleased. Who could say nay to the nation's sovereign?

Three hundred years of human life — that's about ten generations, isn't it? — were to pass in England before (in 1870) reading and writing were taught to all children. After that, another generation lived its life out before (1902) the meager provision for the primary education of all children was supplemented by opening public high schools.

In the first half of the nineteenth century the North American democracy was raw and new. The people were sovereign, the common people, Hamilton's "great beast." The educational door to the future could be opened by an enlightened use of the enormous areas of public lands. That door could be slammed shut by greed, as Henry VIII had slammed it shut on the youth of his fatherland. There was plenty of greed in the U.S.A. The prodigiously rich national lands were vanishing into the pockets of rapacious private interests. With them was vanishing a chance that would not come again to develop through education the human resources of the nation's future. Would the Sovereign People be more statesmanlike in the use of enormous wealth than the sixteenth-century British sovereign?

In the early nineteenth century, there were plenty of Americans who saw as well as early sixteenth-century English idealists that unexpected national wealth could be used for no better purpose than to raise the plane of education available to the people. But at first they had no leader in a high political office. Speed was essential, or action would be too late. They never could have focused in time their straggling scattered numbers without a leader, persistent, deeply concerned with opening wide the doors of education, not interested at all in getting something for himself not under pressure from his constituents to advance their special, local interests.

That leader was Justin Morrill, for forty years Congressman

from Vermont in Washington. He took on as his own dearest aspiration a campaign for extending to university levels the American principle of providing elementary schooling for all children, by use of public lands. Free primary schooling was now taken for granted. Not free higher education, yet farm and labor organizations stood for this. Horace Greeley used the powerful New York *Tribune* in its favor. Greeley was born in New Hampshire almost the same year as Morrill, lived happily for five formative years of his youth in Poultney, Vermont, just "over the mountain" from Morrill's home. There were in the nation, as there had been in sixteenth-century England, elements of power favorable to extending higher education. But until the Vermonter Morrill arrived in Washington, the cause had no official representative at the National Capitol. It was Justin Morrill who introduced the "Morrill Act" to Congress and after reverses and failures, succeeded in putting it over. By its provisions the land-grant or state universities came into being. States were offered thirty thousand acres of land for each Representative or Senator they had in the National Legislature. The total amount of land given through the Morrill Act by our Federal Government for this educational purpose is nearly a hundred and twenty million acres, about four times the size of the Empire State of New York.

The early story of Justin Morrill's life could have been invented by a story-writer as "typical of Vermont." But it all happened. His grandfather (who came to the town of Strafford in 1795) was a blacksmith. So was his father. One of his brothers, too, during the very years when Justin himself was serving the nation as Senator in Washington.

But early Vermont blacksmiths were not at all like the pious, brawny, edifying peasant, who swung a mighty hammer under a spreading chestnut tree. Longfellow's artisan was partly drawn from life in eastern Massachusetts where a blacksmith had a humbler social status than the bookish and well-to-do Brahmins of his town. Partly he was, like nightingales and primroses, a poetic convention copied from British literature, a docile, honest, horny-handed workingman, esteemed by his betters at the Hall, for his useful work and for his acceptance of social inferiority. He was no Vermonter.

The Morrills were ingenious, skilled, resourceful mechanics who saw no reason why they should have more than their share of manual drudgery. Not when a stream ran past their shop. Before the beginning of the nineteenth century, Justin Morrill's grandfather with a neighbor had dammed the stream and harnessed to this power an interesting equipment of power-driven tools — trip hammer, grindstone, bellows and so on. Using these and head-power rather than muscle-power, he manufactured axes, hoes, scythes, sled-runners, as well as shoeing horses and oxen. In the intervals of metallurgy he and his family produced a large part of their food and clothing on their farm. One of the traditional Vermont life-patterns — not yet archaic among us.

Justin Morrill was born in 1810. He went to school till he was fifteen. Two of those classroom years were in the equivalent of a high school. The right of a blacksmith's son to be there was taken for granted. The community around the growing boy was, like most Vermont communities then, and now, much interested in politics, agriculture, hunting and fishing, education, books, mechanical devices and inventions, and fair play for all citizens; not especially in theological dogma. Religious institutions have not markedly shaped the Vermont way of life. One of the stories often told by the Senator was a variation on the theme familiar, in one form or another all over our State — the disconcerting Vermont response to the emotional revivalists who in the early nineteenth century swept over our nation during the evangelical movement. The story ran this way: a local "character," curious about what a revival meeting might be, attended one held in Strafford. Towards the end, the brass-lunged, hellfire-predicting professional revivalist shouted hoarsely to him, "Brother, have you got religion?" To which the Strafford man called back, with brisk pride, "Not any to boast of, I can tell ye." Morrill himself was a lifelong Unitarian, in a period of our nation's history when many Americans felt that Unitarians were about on a plane with those who believed in "free love."

The boy Justin was slender and bookish, physically fine-fibered. As he grew older he looked rather like Emerson. Anybody could see he was no blacksmith. He ardently wanted to go to college. Dartmouth was close at hand. His father refused to help him financially. This refusal was not based on his authority as family dictator, nor because he did not want a child of his to be superior to him in learning. Taking for granted that his young son, although only fifteen, understood the sanctity of such a basic principle as fair play, he explained to Justin that he had not money enough to send all his sons to college, and did not think that one boy should have more educational opportunity than the others.

It seems possible that Morrill's great service to our country was based on this never-forgotten disappointment and the equitable reason for it, quietly presented by the father, quietly accepted by the son.

But of this he had as little idea as any of us have about the effect upon our late life of events in our youth. He was fifteen. He was expected by others, and expected it of himself, to earn his own living from then on. And he did.

In the hamlet of Strafford (less than a thousand people) his best chance was as clerk in the general store. The owner and manager of the Vermont store was, to his slim, thoughtful, fifteen-year-old clerk, what Dr. Young had been to Ethan Allen at about the same age — an inspiring Socratic teacher. There was nobody — factually not one man or woman — in that Green Mountain community to look down on a man because he sold goods at retail. Old "Judge" Harris, as he was called, stood up straight behind the counter, calmly sure of his human dignity and social standing. He had a small library of good quality. With these books the boy shut out by poverty from classrooms began that effort to educate himself which lasted all through his long, long lifetime. Later on, he published an anthology of favorite selections from his readings. It began with a quotation from Montaigne, always a favorite author of his. His admiring comment on Milton was: "Milton was a giant. Not only among poets. He was a powerful influence in the times in which he lived. He was a scholar, traveling and mixing in the world — a

red-hot Republican, in the days when such principles were rare."
Here was an echo from the old tradition of Ethan Allen and
the other founders of Vermont.

Young Morrill dearly loved books, but when he went to work
in the village store, he did not leave his brains behind him on
his bookshelves. The detail-work of making a living by buying
and selling in small quantities is tedious. He accepted it as part
of the common lot. He learned what he needed to know to be
useful behind a counter. As far as he could see or foresee, he
was and would never be more than a storekeeper in a small
mountain town. In reality he was, during those years, learning
how to rise to a great national crisis by learning how to be dogged
in circumventing material obstacles, shrewd in handling the psychological mechanism of human enterprises, unendingly constant
in purpose.

By the time he was thirty-eight he retired on his savings.
Sounds incredible, doesn't it? It was possible partly because he
knew how to arrange his life with unabashed Vermont thrift.
He bought a farm, and produced from it a large part of his
living. He built a pleasant, substantial house and, the year he
retired, he married an intelligent attractive girl of twenty-seven,
daughter of a doctor. The marriage was happy (Justin Morrill
had a rare gift for the enjoyment of life) and endured to the
great old age of both husband and wife.

For six years he lived thus, enjoying the companionship of a
much-loved wife, reading much-loved books to which he constantly added new ones, running his farm efficiently, and skillfully tending much-loved flowers (the cultivation of flowers
was always a vein of wordless poetry in his life). Occasionally
he wrote what he called verse. These lines expressed his cheerful
zest in life in flat phrases of almost unimaginable ineptness.
Eloquence in words was never one of his gifts. It should be
noted that he and his wife were noted, in a State which for all
its plain ways never has had any esteem for asceticism, for the
excellence of their table, most of the food produced on his
well-run farm.

During these six years, he shared more and more generously
in the life, communal and personal, of the region around him.

His practical shrewdness in business was as notable as his impassioned honesty. The advice of such a man was sought by a wider and wider circle. He became known in Vermont. In 1854 he was elected Representative; and after that re-elected by Vermont voters to represent them, in the House and in the Senate, to the very end of his days, when he was nearly ninety years old.

He arrived in Washington at a time of crisis, the threat of the Civil War black as doom on the horizon. And at once he devoted himself to the advancement of higher education, free to all the children of the nation. At the end of his first two years in Washington Justin Morrill introduced a Resolution about land-grant colleges in which lay the seeds of his great idea of higher education free to all citizens' sons and daughters. Every other Representative and Senator in Washington whom he consulted about his dream discouraged him — or tried to. Without a single recorded exception, they told him, at first, "Why yes, of course, theoretically it would be a fine thing. But you haven't the faintest chance of getting it considered, let alone adopted." There were too many politically powerful people who wanted those public lands for themselves and their sons-in-law.

Just as experienced politicians foresaw, every political device was massively, rapidly and with practiced skill used to defeat the Morrill Act, and to silence its sponsor. He had had little experience in Washington or in politics; and, naturally, no more influence back of him, secret or open, than any other Representative from a small state with little money and few voters.

Yet, in six years, the act providing for land-grant universities had been passed by both the House and the Senate, had been signed (1862) by President Abraham Lincoln and was the law of the land. Hamilton's "great beast" had stood up rather taller in stature than the English King.

For of course the Morrill Act is not the creation of one or a few men. It is an Act of the Nation, something for every American citizen to be proud of. Justin Morrill never dreamed of claiming that he himself had brought it about. Most qualified contemporary observers of the drama said — but he never did — that it would not have been accomplished without him. What he did was to channel into this effort to extend free public education all, every molecule, of what life in Vermont had made of him.

He represented a State which valued education as the open door to human growth. What could he do save to give his heart to the land-grant college idea? His integrity — basis of all lasting creative action — was second nature to him, and hence convincing. The disarming fact that he himself claimed no special credit in this effort drew to its support and kept as workers the many, many superior Americans of good will already inclined to favor the idea. These qualities he brought from the wordless, taken-for-granted ideals of the only background he knew — the little towns of the Green Mountains.

He was recognized as their true representative by the people he had left behind in Vermont. From afar, as voters, they steadily backed him up as he struggled with greedy special interests, with apathy, with the enormous tedium of working through political mechanisms — through committees split by hidden personal alliances for profit — through assemblies swayed by oratory (then much in fashion) not by reasonableness.

As he worked, the national sky grew black with the oncoming horror of the Civil War. Great forces clashed in Washington, thundered around the heads of the men there who were trying to direct the nation's course. At such a time, to try to do something idealistically creative for the future intellectual development of the whole nation must have been like trying to write a poem or teach a child how to read in a house shuddering in a hurricane. Andrew D. White, long President of Cornell, wrote of the calm shining of our Senator's little Vermont candle, "It was the darkest period of the Civil War, and yet, full of confidence in the future of the Republic, Justin Morrill introduced and carried that great measure. There has been no more noble exhibition of faith in the destiny of the republic." A report of the United States Bureau of Education says, "Next to the Ordinance of 1781, the Congressional grant of 1862 is the most important educational enactment in America."

For Vermont as well as for the nation, the hour was one of those sudden, searching tests of character, when what the past has made of a man or a community wrestles for his future. The determination to take a full share in the Civil War had sprung up everywhere in Vermont from the old tradition of devotion to human freedom. Could Vermonters give themselves to the service of that faith, and at the same time stand by their Congressman, undramatically, unoratorically, serving another one of their traditional aspirations — to keep the educational door to human growth open to all? If Vermont voters did not back Morrill up, he would be nobody, a retired country storekeeper. Would his people understand what he was doing? Would they not wish him to use the influence they gave him by their votes to secure special favors for their poor State from the rich Federal Government? Why not? The idea was not at all unknown to American politics.

The answer to these questions is written in the record. His Green Mountain constituents stood by Justin Morrill, as few elected officials in Washington have ever been supported. They returned him, election after election. They were proud of his giving to a great cause the best he had inherited from the tradition common to them all.

He gave the best he had, such as it was. He was not eloquent or persuasive. Like his people he expressed himself best in action. His arguments for free education were no more than clear, sincere, sound, heart-felt explanations. It is to the credit of our nation that such reasonable plain-speaking was convincing. Here is a sample. He pointed out that "most of the existing collegiate institutions and their feeders were based on the classic plan of teaching only those destined to pursue the so-called learned professions, leaving farmers and mechanics and all who earn their bread by labor, to the haphazard of being self-taught, or not scientifically taught at all. The thoroughly educated, being most sure to educate their sons, appeared to be perpetuating a monopoly of education inconsistent with the welfare of American institutions." Through him, in these words defending the idea that "farmers, mechanics and all who earn their bread by labor" have *intellectual* as well as material rights, spoke the voice of

Vermont tradition, magically enabled by the Constitution to be
heard far beyond its own narrow borders.

Psychiatrists tell us that frustration in youth leaves a never-
healed wound on human personalities, which rankles till some
compensation for it has been wrung out from society. What they
do not, perhaps, sufficiently remind us, is that there are different
kinds of compensation.

Justin Morrill's boyhood frustration had been the denial of
education to him in the august name of fair play. "It would not
be fair," he had been told, "for one boy to have a better chance
at higher education than his brothers." No Vermonter could rebel
against this principle. But just as the psychiatrists say, the disappointment had been a traumatic shock. The fifteen-year-old
boy never forgot it, and sure enough, in his maturity when his
chance came, he forced from society a compensation for it. The
principle of fair play had slammed in his face the door to opportunity. In its name he opened that door to millions of Americans.
Generation after generation of our youth have gone through
those doors in the ninety years since Justin Morrill from Strafford, Vermont, stood by Abraham Lincoln's desk and watched
him sign the Morrill Act. For generations to come, the great
universities all over our nation, created by that Act, will go on
providing educational fair play for all the sons and daughters
of the American family.

Warren Austin

BORN nearly seventy years after Justin Morrill, Warren Austin
is in the same bracket. They are both notable for having shown
that the provision of our American Constitution for two Senators
from each state, small or great, is not only a useful cog in a complicated political machinery of federation, but also serves well a
noble spiritual aspiration of democracy — to secure from all citizens, famous or obscure, whatever they have of value to contribute to the whole. How else save through this channel could a

state so inconsiderable in size and numbers have carried into the realm of international politics its old, cherished tradition of resistance to any government not based on the consent of the governed? How else, save through the United States Senate, could this never-wavering Vermont belief in freedom as the only air in which men and women can grow into strength, sanity, and good will, have been heard in America at exactly the time when its affirmation was needed? Mr. Vandenberg's great service to international life was in one field of politics. Mr. Austin's, because he too was a Senator, was in another.

Did you ever wonder why the first representative to the United Nations from the United States of America should have been a Vermonter? Perhaps you didn't know that. Or maybe you never happened to think about it. Perhaps you don't know enough about Vermont to be surprised that he stood where he did, speaking not for the Green Mountain people, but for our vast Federation of States?

If a foreign observer had asked you for the reason for his appointment, you might have been at a loss.

His position in the United Nations was, is, always will be, of historic importance. No man can ever again be chosen the first to stand for our nation in what we hope will be a valid movement towards a more reasonable organization of the world's peoples. However did it happen that a man from a state with a small, nonurban population, with little wealth, with little political influence in the nation, was chosen to represent our wealthy, highly industrialized country of vast, fertile plains?

If our hypothetical foreign question-asker had been unusually well informed about political life in the U.S.A. he might have added, as you hesitated, puzzled, "Hasn't Vermont always voted for the party in opposition to the very administration which chose Warren Austin? That in itself makes his position almost inexplicable."

No matter what you found to tell him, the foreigner would certainly have thought, "Must be some story or other back of it."

There is.

* * *

The story began in 1877 in a small town of less than a thousand inhabitants, up near the Canadian border, where —

No, only in the most superficial view can the story be thought to start in Highgate, Vermont. It began centuries ago, in one of the hopes of humanity, out of which grew the Vermont tradition, small but green branch on the American tree.

In literal fact, the choice by a Democratic administration of a Vermont Republican as the first American official participant in the effort to use ordinary sense in international relations, did start in Highgate, Vermont (population sixteen hundred), where Warren Austin was born in 1877. His father was the lawyer of the tiny town. He himself is a lawyer, his two brothers and his son are all lawyers. This family preoccupation with the law is part of the story. For it was not moral humanitarianism but legal spirit at its broadest best which brought him into internationalism.

Another part of the story is an ancient Vermont grandfather, who lived with the Austins from the age of eighty-five to ninety-one. Because of his great age he provided a personal contact between the Austin boys and the eighteenth-century beginnings of Vermont tradition. Like many another grandfather, he was one of the influences which helped shape, sometimes with rough strokes of the chisel, the personality and ideas of his daughter's little sons.

As a matter of course the Austin boys became lawyers. In 1931, one of our Vermont Senators died in office. At a special election held a little later, the voters elected the able, active, hustling Burlington lawyer. By Vermont standards he was still young, fifty-one years old. Everybody took him to be a typical traditional Vermont Republican, heartily opposed as a matter of course to everything done by the Democratic regime in power in Washington.

But in his past life was an event which made him potentially more than an able, honest, energetic party man of the opposition. It was no more than an hour's informal address heard at a lawyers' convention, but it proved to be the turning point of the Vermonter's inner life.

The story sets the most unimaginative person to musing over ideas as wingèd seeds blown here and there over the surface of the globe, sometimes falling and dying in the salt seas or deserts, sometimes (like Thoreau's book always kept on Gandhi's desk) striking roots in fertile soil and growing tall and strong in distant lands.

Burlington, Vermont, is not far from Montreal. The young Austin, then thirty-six years old, was chosen as delegate to attend a convention of the International Bar Association. The date was 1913, the very last year of international peace, which had lasted so long that Americans could scarcely conceive of a world war. Whatever other ideas may have been in the Vermont lawyer's head, we can be sure that a war of his country with Germany was not one of them. Many distinguished men of law attended this Canadian convention. William Howard Taft (one generation out from Vermont), the elder Choate, the distinguished French leader of the Paris bar who had defended Dreyfus.

Also Lord Haldane of England.

Who was he? He was then nearly sixty years old. He was not the son of an old titled family of renown in England. He had been a commoner till given a title only two years before this meeting; he was a Scotsman — hence more accessible to American sympathy and understanding than if he had been a member of the English ruling class; he had been educated at the University of Edinburgh (not at Oxford or Cambridge) and — this fact is important — at the German university at Göttingen, hence he had had a more cosmopolitan, international experience than most British statesmen.

No more than Warren Austin was he a humanitarian pacifist. For nine years before this Montreal convention he had been a member of the English Cabinet. His effort in this office was concentrated on improving the quality of the armed services of Great Britain. With great political courage, he reconstructed the ancient English military organization along modern lines. Naturally this had aroused against him the embittered fury of vested interests. When the Scotsman scrapped long-obsolete military units and old practices, the Englishmen whose branch of the service was scrapped naturally filled the air with angry resentment.

He had had a sound modern education in Germany, where in

the last half of the nineteenth century the importance of science was more recognized than in the ancient halls of English universities. Set to shape England's military planning to fit the modern world, he gave for the first time an acknowledged place to science in army efforts. He had arranged for the co-operation in war of the Dominions with the motherland. He had recognized the as yet scarcely visible potentialities of aircraft. In general he had made himself one of the most useful and best hated men in the public service of his nation. With statesmanlike energy and brains he had prepared England for a great war as the nation had never before been readied.

At that date American lawyers knew as little about official British governmental goings-on as British lawyers about American politics. We can be fairly sure that when the elder statesman rose to speak on International Law at Montreal few of the Americans who looked up at him knew anything definite about his masterful reshaping of England's military machine or had any idea that the cataclysm of World War I was ahead of them.

Certainly nobody at Montreal that day could have guessed the somber premonitions darkening Lord Haldane's mind as he spoke.

But we know now what they were. The year before this legal convention in Canada, he had been sent on a delicate, responsible diplomatic mission to Berlin. The German war party was rattling the saber. The Scotsman representing the British government was to discuss officially the points of friction which were being exploited by the Germans who thought their army and navy were invincible. He was to see if intelligent, thoughtful, reasonable discussion could help keep the peace. He had done his best. But he came back to England knowing that reason and logic are like straws in the wind against the will-to-war. The threat from Germany had not been lessened and Lord Haldane knew it. Oncoming disaster stood up close before him, as he looked down at the New World delegates brightly unaware of it.

On the day when he cast his wingèd seed-idea out to float or fall, to live or die, he spoke as a lawyer to lawyers. His emphasis was on international law as a logical sequence of the existing legal framework of human life to which all his listeners had dedicated their lives. He made no effort to arouse the emotions of the professional men to whom he was speaking. He drew no horrifying word pictures of human sufferings in war's blood and fire. His mind, brooding over the menace of which he had special inside information, was full of the aspect of war which most strikes the legal mind — its idiocy. How could the total violence of war be countenanced in a world which, in all other human affairs, has given up violence as a solution for human problems, because they cannot be solved by violence? Men who if they disagreed with another over a land survey would never dream of murdering him as a way to decide where the lines ran — how could they, as members of a nation, take to mass murder as a way to settle problems?

Warren Austin says that as he listened to the quiet self-contained old lawyer, speaking of common sense as the basis of law-abidingness for nations as well as for individuals, he saw "a great and splendid vision of the change in the world which would come if nations exercised the ordinary self-discipline needed to respect law, as now the most ordinary men, individually, respect it."

Then the convention broke up. As far as anybody could see, nothing much had been accomplished. The French and English and United States delegates returned to their various homes, and resumed their law practices. The Vermont lawyer returned to his. The wingèd seed lay dormant, or seemed to.

That election of his to the Senate in 1931 was by no means unanimous. Do not for a moment imagine that a one-party State lives a stagnant political life. The campaign of Warren Austin was for the nomination at the primary, not for election, but that fact did not prevent its being hotly and bitterly fought, up and down the State, foot by foot, inch by inch. Out of seventy-nine thousand votes cast, Austin had a majority of eight thousand. Enough, but no landslide. His next campaign, in 1934, resulted in no more of a landslide. This time the fight was the actual one for election. That year a Democrat came as near representing Vermont in the Senate as had happened for several generations. Vermont voters gave Austin a five thousand majority out of their total. This small majority is worth noting, in view of the overwhelming endorsement given him by Vermont after his attitude on international relations had become known.

In 1938 Chicago was, like much of the Middle West at that time, violently isolationist, violently opposed to President Roosevelt. In a speech there, that year, our Vermont Republican Senator announced publicly how he stood on that matter. He did not pussyfoot. He did not straddle. He said outright, "Isolation is impossible. We are inextricably involved in the affairs of the world." Those Americans who knew of Vermont only that it seems irrevocably Republican, said, "He's done for himself. He'll never be returned to the Senate."

The next year, 1939, was the year before the election of Senators. The war came. Senator Austin from Vermont supported the Democratic administration to repeal the Neutrality Act, and cried out on the floor of the Senate, "A country whose boys will not go out to fight to save the principle of freedom from destruction by Hitler — well, we do not find such boys in America."

People asked themselves — who was this Republican, storming out heretically to stand beside an administration intensely disliked by his party? The fact that he was an orthodox member of his party from the most orthodox Republican State was a huge sounding board which magnified every word he said in support of the principle of bipartisan unity in international relations. He was heard all over the nation by Americans who, till then, had paid no attention to the representative of a small, unimportant state. But Austin's heterodox views on international relations were not too alarming to isolationists. The next election in Vermont was at hand. Those dyed-in-the-wool rural Republicans could be counted on to do the right thing.

The people who thus counted on Vermont to "do the right thing" did not know that Vermont had always been too small and too poor ever to indulge in the withering arrogance of self-sufficiency. Its people had been forced to feel themselves a small part of a larger whole, from potash through Merinos and Morgans on. Isolationism either in politics or in economics was no part of their tradition. As early as the eighteenth century their aging Ethan Allen, after spending most of his life in the fight for first-class citizenship for Vermonters, had twice been called on for help by people quite outside of Vermont who were also, they felt, fighting for the principle of equality of opportunity. Vermont has never forgotten that the old Green Mountain Boy did not reply to these "outsiders," "Vermont's liberties are safe. What do we care about yours?" No, he buckled on his old Vermont sword, and as far as his failing vitality allowed him, went out to help those who were fighting for freedom in a new corner of the battlefield.

Isolationists in 1939 had confidently expected that in 1940 the countrified voters of Vermont would unite to push back into private life their Senator who, outrageously, was "on the Democratic side." What happened was that they backed him as solidly in opposing isolationism as they had solidly backed Justin Morrill's work for free public education in the nation. Till then Austin had had a normal share of opposition in Vermont. In the election after he had declared himself against isolationism, nobody at all ran against him in the primaries, and there was very little opposition at the election. The Senator who used all his influence to support a Democratic administration was returned to the Senate as a matter of course, by his old Republican State.

˙ Nor did he have any opposition or criticism from his own people when, after the war was won, he showed why he had wanted it won, by throwing himself into the organization of a world-wide effort for lasting peace. Vermonters supported him in his work for the United Nations as they had supported his efforts for military victory. They valued, as he did, the defeat of the fascist powers because it made it possible to start working for global peace. This connection between wholehearted support of war and wholehearted devotion to lasting peace, never clear to isolationists, was brought out in a phrase of Secretary of War Patterson in a speech he made in honor of the Vermont Senator, when he said, "Without victory in the war, there would have been no organized United Nations."

The voters of Vermont powerfully influenced the course of our nation's development when they steadfastly returned Justin Morrill to the Senate. When they cast their ballots for Warren Austin, it was the development of world peace they influenced, as they stepped soberly in and out of voting booths in their villages and small towns.

This is no fanciful way to dress up a fact. It is literal truth. Either of those men would have become powerless ciphers in the life of our nation and of the world if he had not been steadily supported by the voters at home. Vermonters could as easily, if they had wished, voted for someone less "visionary," more "practical." Neither man knew, on leaving Vermont and going to Washington, what his special service would be. In both minds a dormant seed-idea grew great — the ideal of utilizing national power not for any form of aggrandizement but for human freedom. The ideal is a familiar one to Vermonters. They do not always see in a new situation how they can act according to this tradition. But when they see, there is never any doubt as to what they want to do.

Warren Austin's long term of service to the United Nations is over. When he retired, he was seventy-five, fifteen years older than was Lord Haldane when he had let fall the seed-idea that law-abidingness in an accepted legal system is as necessary and as possible for nations as for the men and women who make up nations. To the cause of international order he faithfully gave his singlehearted best, during the years of his service with the United Nations.

One day an American making his first visit to the United Nations was struck and shocked by the wearing tedium of its long wordy sessions. He had not realized that it would take so much time for peoples of very diverse countries to adjust themselves to the techniques (new to many of them) of effort-in-common. He had not dreamed how hard it is to start from scratch a vast effort involving many people, nor what a handicap is the absence of axioms accepted by all, nor how pervasive a stabilizer is a common tradition, nor how slow, slow of growth tradition is. "Why, people who have grown up in the democratic framework of representative government," he thought, "they must be simply worn out by this talk, talk, talk."

Meeting the old Vermonter who represented the U.S.A. the visitor asked, choosing his words with care, "Don't you — ah — get rather — ah — *tired* during these long debates?"

Warren Austin answered in Vermontese. "Yes I do," he said, "but it is better for aged diplomats to be bored than for young men to die."

John Dewey

MOST people would agree that of all the men produced by Vermont, John Dewey's name is the most widely known. I think there are few who would not be willing to say "and most honored." A large majority would add, "and most loved and followed."

This Vermonter was born in 1859, in the little city of Burlington, on Lake Champlain. He left the Green Mountains when he was twenty-three years old — a man grown.

Till then, John Dewey had been immersed in the Vermont tradition. He could not but be colored by it to the marrow of his bones. That tradition has been homely, rustic, practical, articulate mostly in action rather than in words. Through the greatness of John Dewey's personality, our tradition came to a rich, complex development. By his life and work he proved that the spiritual, intellectual and social implications of the way of life in which he was brought up went far beyond the untheoretic, unsystematic practice of the people who, as best they could, had obeyed its guessed-at basic principles. It was his birthright tradition John Dewey took with him all around the globe from the fields and homes which had been its local habitations. In his person, in his books, in his teaching, it bloomed out to universality.

This statement is not based on mere family pride. During his long life, he constantly became more and more known to the great world. After his death, editorials and articles were full of variations on the theme that he was, as one great metropolitan newspaper put it, "Yankeeism at its best." (But there are variations in "Yankeeism" as people outside of New England sometimes do not realize.) One of the most distinguished of the many philosophers and educators who have written about John Dewey is Professor Sidney Hook. The New York City professor thus described him: "Dewey carries with him the traces of Vermont social environment, not as memories but as habits, deep preferences and an ingrained democratic bias. Vermont shows itself in his simplicity of manner, his basic courtesy, freedom from every variety of snobbishness and matter-of-fact respect for the rights of everyone as a human being and citizen. His simplicity, directness and complete lack of self-consciousness put even the shyest person at his ease. His intellectual humility is so profound that it might seem to be a pose affected by a great man, were it not so obviously sincere — his sense of humor is delightful, although a little unpredictable. A dry chuckle, a grin, a twinkle that lights up the whole face are its premonitory signs."

No Vermonter could ask for a more discerning description of the best qualities we hope are in our tradition — even to the "unpredictable" (to other people) quality of Vermont humor.

What impression on the world was made by this "plain, farmerlike old fellow," as he was often called? Here, set down at random, out of the fantastic number and variety of them, are some of the evidences of his influence on humanity: the Chinese government of thirty years ago, emerging from its age-old isolation and reaching out for the best the West had to offer, invited him to give a series of lectures in Nanking and Peking on his educational ideas. For two years he lived in the Orient, writing and speaking. His lectures in China were printed there and went through ten editions. By official request from Japan, India and Ceylon, he also gave many lectures in those countries.

Following the zigzag trail of his mighty influence, we come upon the fact that the Director of the Brazilian Pedagogical Institute in São Paulo wrote and spoke of "Dewey and the Reform of World Education," as though they were one and the same. At the Belgian University of Louvain and in Holland (and in how many other institutions of higher learning all around the world!) doctoral dissertations were written on his philosophy and educational ideas. His books have been translated into Arabic, Swedish, Spanish, Czech, Chinese, French, Danish, Italian, Hebrew, Portuguese, Turkish, Hungarian, Japanese — too many languages to list. The editions of his works in English are not to be counted, although the *New York Times* calculated that at the time of his death "his published works must have totalled a thousand." Justice Holmes said of Dewey's *Experience and Nature:* "Few indeed, I should think, are the books which hold so much of life with an even hand." Three hundred of these works were written after his "retirement" at the age of seventy. A "school-city" based on his ideas was established in Florence, Italy. More honorary degrees have been conferred on him (the rarely given and much-coveted one from the Sorbonne among them) than anybody has ever catalogued. The Flemish *Encyclopaedia of Pedagogy* declares that the Vermonter is "one of the great leaders of mankind." Of late years he has been an object of violent attack from Russian spokesmen, who call him a "cowardly, hypocritical apologist for brutally materialistic American imperialism." Dewey fought hard openly and courageously against Russian totalitarianism, but what especially rouses Soviet Russian hostility to Dewey seems to be his basic doctrine that change can come only through growth, that growth takes time, and that violence cannot produce any lasting change, even the most desirable. He has also been harshly criticized from within his own country for not teaching definitely that belief in theological dogma is the only foundation for decency in human life.

The quiet professor-philosopher-educator who came to be a figure of his times noteworthy enough to receive such significant widespread praise and equally significant blame, lived to venerable old age, in perfect possession of his faculties, physical, mental and spiritual. Mostly the old Vermonter dodged ceremonial gatherings in his honor, as he always avoided personal publicity. But on his ninetieth birthday (October 20, 1949), he was present in person at a testimonial dinner in New York attended by fifteen hundred people from the most variegated social, national and racial backgrounds. The speakers were of all kinds — a Justice of the Supreme Court (Felix Frankfurter), Pandit Nehru of India, David Dubinsky of the American Federation of Labor, Dr. Hu Shih, former Chinese Ambassador to the U.S.A., Walter Reuther of the C.I.O., Professor Perry of the Harvard Department of

Philosophy, and the Acting President of Columbia University. It was announced that ninety thousand dollars were to be presented to him by his admirers, to be used for education as he wished. The President of the United States and the Prime Minister of England sent warm greetings.

Well, that's enough, and more than enough, about a plain Vermonter who liked to be publicly praised as little as any other Green Mountain man. This Whitman-like build-up of multifarious detail might accurately be ended, "and so forth and so on — ."

What was the man on whom these laureled honors were heaped?

When a modern sociological research-specialist begins work on a biography, one of his first inquiries is "What was the social status of the subject's family during the formative years of his childhood and young maturity?"

This is a funny kind of question to ask about any Vermonter, as I hope the many pages of this book bear witness. But it's an easy one to answer about John Dewey. All the facts are known, and, Vermont-fashion, known back to his grandfather, who left New York State early in the 1780's to move over into Bennington. Anybody who had been brought up in the eighteenth century in the Province of New York, and moved to Vermont, cast his vote almost as definitely as in an election booth against one way of life and in favor of its opposite. He married a Bennington girl (name of Jerusha Hopkins — if you'd invented it, it couldn't have been more Vermont), had a lot of children, and moved to Fairfax (about a thousand people) up north, beyond Burlington a ways. His youngest child was born in Fairfax in 1811. This was John Dewey's father, Archibald Sprague Dewey.

His "social status" was that of a storekeeper. He moved to Burlington and in 1855 married a serious, intelligent, warm-hearted Vermont girl, with a strong sense of responsibility for the welfare of those about her — in her case this responsibility was not limited strictly to members of her immediate family, as it was for many a "good" woman of the mid-nineteenth century.

In Burlington the Deweys lived in a comfortable old house (still standing and as good as ever) built in 1815. It was larger than they needed, and like other families in other New England college towns, they added to their income by renting the extra bedrooms to students at the University of Vermont. Mrs. Dewey's motherliness went out to them as to her sons — especially if, as was often the case, they were country boys with little money. By her own three boys she was not only greatly loved, but respected for her intelligence and literary taste, admired for her dauntless righteousness and for her courageous claim that women are human beings (then called "strong-mindedness"). Her menfolks laughed at her a little, good-naturedly, for her mid-nineteenth-century fanatic disapproval of alcohol, and the boys felt pestered by her emotional piety, rather unusual in Vermont daily life. She had not been brought up to this, since her own family were liberals in religion and belonged to the Universalist Church. It was during a visit to another city that, much against her father's wish, she came under the influence of an "evangelical" friend. When she came back to her Burlington family she had formed a habit of pious questioning which made her sons squirm uneasily. At the breakfast table, or when they came in from long autumn tramps in the woods, or as they were putting their overshoes on, their mother would ask them how they stood with God. But they were always gentle with her. John Dewey was almost invariably kind and gentle to everyone. And they heartily admired their mother's unwearied helpfulness to those in real trouble, rather than hovering and clucking over the minor details of her own family's material needs. She was shamed by the existence of wretched poverty and ignorance in the one slum quarter of her city. Much of her time was spent, often against jeering misunderstandings from the toughs she was trying to help, in the typical fumbling, amateur, lion-hearted effort to help the underprivileged by which the best of the nineteenth-century "good women" prepared the way for modern social welfare work. Her own pleasant home was kept open to students, especially to those in difficulties (financial, educational, social). For them Mrs. Dewey was cordially willing to make hot chocolate and provide wedges of pie, and always had time for them to talk over their problems with her. But her neighbors noticed that her eye was not always caught by a rip in the coat of one of her sons. And even when she saw it, she did not instantly drop everything else to mend it. Do you see her? I do.

John Dewey's father died long ago, but we know what he was, because we have known other Vermont storekeepers who savored life and jovially helped others to enjoy it, and at the same time were serious, responsible businessmen and citizens. His advertisements appearing in the Burlington newspapers were blithely full of high spirits. The new baby John was about two weeks old when in 1859 his grocer-father thus jocularly advertised the salt fish he had for sale.

Turned Up

Not the sea serpent with fabulous tale
but the veritable mackerel without any head,
has been both seen and caught and is now on
exhibition at

Dewey's

One of his advertisements of that year was in jingling rhyme of which the first stanza runs:

Lives there a man with soul so dead
Who never to himself hath said
"Give me, to wet my daily bread
A cup of Dewey's coffee!"

When the neighbors of the lively storekeeper began to make a practice of borrowing his wheelbarrow and forgetting to return it, he made no comment, but on the side of the barrow he painted in very large letters "STOLEN FROM A. S. DEWEY." (Unpredictable Vermont humor.)

This laughter-loving, prankish grocer was also one of the first treasurers of the Burlington Savings Bank, and without pay did much tedious, important detail-work for the financial management of the large First Congregational Church. When the Civil War came, he left his baby son and his wife to serve with the First Vermont Cavalry, and was honorably cited for "coolness and decisiveness under fire."

Can you reconstruct, from the bare bones of these facts, what kind of father John Dewey had? It is all there.

And if you will take time to muse a little, you will see, rising up from the past, the home created by those parents — the genial, joking father, who could manage a bank as well as his grocery store, who had been under fire in battle and was noted for keeping his head in danger. The eagerly intellectual, widely read mother, who loved books and dearly loved her family, but whose finely sensitive heart would not let her relax at ease in her own happiness while so many were suffering.

Burlington was a North Country college town, with the usual college town's doings. The three boys who grew up in their lively, cheerful home and in this college town did about what other boys from similar families did — ranged like young dogs all over the beautiful countryside open to them, played athletic games, earned money for part of their own expenses by odd jobs after school hours, and went regularly to the local public schools.

By the time John Dewey was fifteen years old (nearly sixteen) that public school system had prepared him to enter the local university. He was then physically strong, mentally capable (who ever could guess that he was to be so immeasurably more than "capable"?), full of a zestful enjoyment of life and never-failing warm interest in the human scene, traits which were with him as richly when he passed his ninetieth birthday as when, a teen-age boy, he climbed to the top of nearby Mount Mansfield.

Writing of his early environment in Vermont, Dewey said, "I shall never cease to be grateful that I was born at a time and place where the earlier idea of liberty and the self-governing community of citizens still sufficiently prevailed, so that I unconsciously imbibed a sense of its meaning. In Vermont, perhaps even more than elsewhere, there was embodied in the spirit of the people the conviction that governments were like houses we live in, made to contribute to human welfare, and that those who lived in them were as free to change and extend the one as they were the other, when developing needs of the human family called for such alterations and modifications."

*   *   *

For three years after his graduation from the University of Vermont, he was a high-school teacher, while continuing to be a student — in a class of one, under the stimulating instruction, more like a long Socratic dialogue — of the professor at the university with whom he had as an undergraduate studied philosophy.

When Dewey was twenty-three years old it was plain to those of the older generation who knew him that he had remarkable intellectual possibilities.

Elsewhere, perhaps, in 1882, as nowadays, the family of a grocer in a small, provincial city might have been passably astonished at the idea that a son should plan to earn his living as a professional philosopher. The Vermont Deweys saw no reason why their son should not, like anybody's son, do what best suited his capacities. If he felt he could be a philosopher and if he wanted to be, why not? Luckier than Justin Morrill, a long generation before, the financial assets of the Dewey family made possible his continuing his studies at the finest center for advanced learning then in the country — the newly established graduate university of Johns Hopkins at Baltimore. (That blandly genteel, generalized phrase "financial assets" meant in precise terms the savings-bank account of one of John Dewey's aunts.)

So the twenty-three-year-old Vermonter joined the other young people streaming out from the Green Mountains into the vast American Federation of States. His goal was an intellectual center with very high scholastic standards, established with the avowed purpose of training only the intellectual elite, the especially able, not only those with brilliant brains but those who had been well prepared for advanced postgraduate studies. Nobody here seems to have felt any doubt about the ability of the Vermont student, educated only in local classrooms, to hold his own there. Such confidence proved justified. The grocer's son had — to put it with the pungent understatement typical of his tradition — no difficulty whatever in holding his own in the great world of thought and learning. He went out from Vermont to seventy years of hard work and great fame.

* * *

Such was the house, and outside it such the town, in which John Dewey grew up. Outside home and town was a State the atmosphere of which is the subject of all this book. Outside Vermont was the American Federation of States.

And that was a different kettle of fish. Much of what everybody around John Dewey took for granted during his Vermont youth was approved in theory by those he found outside of Vermont. But in practice it was often decried, derided and greatly feared. Much of what he saw taken for granted after he left Vermont was as horrifying to him as it was astonishing.

About the date when the Vermont boy began to go to the local public school, a high-ranking official in the New York State system of public education published the following statement *as a guide to classroom teachers:*

> The teacher's authority as absolute, must be imperative, rather than deliberative or demonstrative. His requirements and decisions, in whatever form presented, whether that of request, demand, or mandate, must be unargued. What he resolves upon and pronounces law, should be simply and steadily insisted upon as right per se, and should be promptly and fully accepted by the pupil as right, on the one ground that the teacher, as such, is governor. Frederick S. Jewell, *School Government* (New York, 1866), 54.

There, darkly flowing along underground, taught to American schoolchildren, was the doctrine of the divine right of kings, long ago repudiated by their forefathers. There, imposed on the growing boys and girls of our nation, was a nineteenth-century version of the Mussolini axiom, "The Duce can do no wrong."

It was his Vermont background which gave John Dewey his deep burning hatred for all forms of totalitarianism. But Vermont can claim no credit for his bold, simple, epoch-making perception that if to accept totalitarianism is ignoble for men and women, it should not be forced down the throats of children, who are human too, and who very soon will be men and women. Vermont had taught him that all affected by a decision should share in making that decision. But that he saw tyranny to be as poisonous for the children of men as for men themselves — that conception came to him, not from Vermont training, but from the unguessable sources which give original creative power to genius.

Rabelais, Montaigne, Pestalozzi and others had, centuries before Dewey, felt intuitively that children, even young children, are human beings and should be brought up in a way to develop their human traits. But the influence of such radicals had been so slight that, when John Dewey came to maturity, it was still largely taken for granted that boys and girls, like horses and dogs, should be forced by fear of physical torture to perform the actions demanded of them by those who held the whip. Only ten years before Dewey's birth, Horace Mann reported (to his honor be it said with great disapproval) that in the enlightened city of Boston, a typical school of four hundred children had on record, as a routine part of education, sixty-five whippings a day, inflicted by the teachers.

A Dewey maxim, now axiomatic, then shockingly revolutionary, ran, "All reforms resting simply upon the enactment of law or the threatening of penalties, or upon changes in mechanical or outward arrangements, are transitory or futile." Naturally this idea flouts the Marxian dogma of violence as the only possible means to secure reforms. But much of the American attack on Dewey was also roused by this idea, when it was applied to schoolroom life.

It has been said, with some accuracy, that John Dewey had little adroitness in the use of words, that his lectures (although as a whole overwhelmingly influential on his hearers) were, taken singly, dull; that his books are hard to read. It was in action, in reality, in the schools for actual flesh-and-blood children which he and his followers founded, that the meaning of his ideas are clear and compelling. Yet, even in words he occasionally found a terse unforgettable phrase. He was the man who said "The aim of education should be to teach the child to think, not what to think." He summed up his hostility to autocratic government when he said that, in a democracy, school children are "apprentice citizens." Since his mighty hammer struck out such phrases, American schools, all schools everywhere, have never been the same. One of the many learned writers about him has said, "It is doubtful if there is to be found in this country (outside of a very few special schools) a single child whose school life has not been made happier because John Dewey has lived." The same commentator points out that those "happier schoolchildren" can also read and write and spell better, and use their wits more ably than children who were taught by the lash.

John Dewey was aroused to hard-hitting by other absolutely anti-American principles blandly applied to the treatment of the young. One of these was the old, old line of social demarcation between the children of handworkers and the children of the well-to-do. In theory the New World had cast this idea of hereditary upper and lower classes out on the rubbish heap. But John Dewey found it constantly still put into active practice, in education.

The son of a retail storekeeper, whose father had been accepted on his own qualities, saw with his own eyes for the first time that strange line, sharp as an unsheathed sword, separating citizens into superior Americans and inferior Americans, without regard to their individual qualities. Dewey was outraged by the social waste and by the absurdity of the division of education into "theoretic," meaning bookish, for the children of the well-to-do, no matter what their individual aptitudes; and "practical" or "vocational," meaning training in hand skills, for the lower-income group, no matter what their intellectual capacities. For him it was as though he saw the children of the well-to-do with one arm and one leg strapped tightly into uselessness and hence into atrophy; while the children of the less-well-to-do lost the use of the other arm and leg through the same idiotic practice.

Here Vermont can claim a little credit for a Dewey educational theory, because the people with whom he grew up laughed at the idea that manual effort is socially degrading. About this notion, John Dewey spoke out in words the energy of which Ethan Allen might have envied. "President Hutchins calls for liberal education for a small, elite group, and vocational education for the masses. I cannot think of any idea more completely reactionary and more fatal to the whole democratic outlook." It is safe to say that to provide education both for the hands and minds of all children, because they all have both hands and minds, seemed more natural for a Vermonter than for one who had grown up in the social assumption that well-to-do people have minds only, and the lower-income group have hands only. But the step from an accepted practice in daily life, to logical acceptance of the theory on which it is based — that step is too long for any but a powerful, original and well-disciplined brain, like Dewey's.

For another of the great clauses in the John Dewey *Declaration of the Rights of Children*, Vermont furnished the proof of successful practice in everyday life. His personal observance of this practice gave him his realistic premises from which to draw a philosophic conclusion of universal, theoretical truth. He had grown up in a community where men and women were admired by their fellows, not for areas of uselessness in their lives, but for their ability to take their full share of the community's work. The life of that Vermont community was simple enough so that children, too, could be useful in getting needed work done. They were expected as a matter of course to do their share. So they did. It was as fully accepted as any other practice which is wholly sanctioned by public opinion. John Dewey had seen this practice produce practically unanimous acceptance of social responsibility, and he had seen this acceptance produce self-disciplined, orderly, communal life.

The classroom in the modern city child's life is the only equivalent for what used to be "his community." John Dewey, the Vermonter, knew what a child can be in his community. John Dewey, the educator, saw that a school's business is not only to teach the child words out of books, but to provide for him opportunities (real ones, no pretense, since all pretense is poison) to join helpfully and creatively in the work of his community. It was again the sword of genius cutting the tough knot of conventional ideas, now useless, lugged along from the past. "We learn to do by doing," he said in another of his simple memorable aphorisms, the idea of which is now so taken for granted that it sounds like a platitude rather than an exploding bomb, which it was when it was new. The greatest asset of our hard-beset human race is the ability to work together — not physically together as a gang of bodies under the whip of a master, but humanly together, choosing, planning, deciding together as well as working. If human childhood is spent in obeying, under the lash of authoritarianism, the dictates of masters, schools cannot produce persons who on becoming adults have the habit of taking their share of responsibility for communal needs. Dewey's deep, fruitful saying is, "There can be no stable and balanced development of the mind, apart from the assumption of responsibility." (Let intellectuals and artists take notice.)

For more than a century, Vermonters had based their lives on the wholehearted belief in the idea that responsibility is a part of life itself, that to try to evade it is not only base, but self-mutilating. Yet no Vermonter had ever known how to put it into words till the Burlington boy grew to a man who made it his business to find out how to say it, and how to use it to open the door of growth for American children in schools.

Do you perhaps wonder why all my comments are about Dewey as an originating educator, opening with strong thrusts of his sharp-edged intellectual spade new sluice-ways along which lofty intelligence could pour out to enrich fields of human life hitherto overlooked by high intelligence, that is, the education of children. After all he was a professor of philosophy. There are several reasons why I say nothing of him as a professional philosopher.

One reason is the fact that in a folk phrase, "It is like trying to get a feather-bed into a bandbox," to try to say in a few pages anything about so mighty a figure. I am leaving out many another important aspect of his life. For one, his so-called lack of religious faith — he who constantly taught that spiritual development is central to all human experience, especially to all human experience shared with others. For another, there is the vast, absurd misrepresentation of his ideas, both by people who think so poorly of humanity as to accept totalitarianism, and also by certain of his too literal-minded friends.

The only thing to say about the grotesqueries occasionally attributed to Dewey's educational ideas is to ask urgently of every person who hears this kind of gossip that he read and study one of John Dewey's own books. The lack-witted non-

By

sense which perhaps you disapprove of in Dewey's educational ideas you will never find in any statement from his own pen. That nonsense comes from people who have no idea what he is talking about, and he is not the first great "leader of humanity" (as the Belgian Encyclopaedia called him) who has been misrepresented by his less intelligent followers.

A personal reason for the lack of comment here on his philosophic doctrines is that I am so little a metaphysician, I would quite lose my way in any technical treatment of that subject. But I can cite Dewey himself. He is quoted by Alvin Johnson as saying in substance, "Philosophy counts for next to nothing in the present world-wide crisis of human affairs, and should count for less. It needs a thorough house-cleaning and the final, definitive abandonment of most of its traditional values. Those values are class values. They were established in a time when the masses of mankind lived in slavery, or near-slavery, and when a little body of the elect could occupy themselves with speculations on the absolute. The present world belongs to a democracy. And democracy cannot waste time on recondite speculations that have nothing to do with life."

Whatever may be thought of such a hot expression about metaphysics, anybody who knows the Green Mountain tradition needs not to be told that there is nothing in it to surprise a Vermonter.

Have you perhaps noticed, also, that till now I have said nothing about John Dewey's personal life? He might have been a disembodied spirit for anything set down on these pages. That he certainly was not. For many reasons some glimpse should be given of the man he was in everyday life. One of these reasons is his humor. "Dewey stories" are double-distilled Vermont.

An often-told one dates from shortly after World War I, when the first, halting, imperfect efforts at "intelligence tests" had thrown half-erudite people into alarm because such tests seemed to show a large part of the population of our nation to be only about twelve years old in mental ability. A symposium of distinguished educators was brought together at a Middle Western university to discuss this tragic "discovery." John Dewey was to speak first to set the keynote.

His hands in his pockets, he stood, apparently deep in thought, before the large audience. Then he said, "This intelligence-testing business reminds me of the way they used to weigh hogs in Texas. They would get a long plank, put it over a cross-bar, and somehow tie the hog on one end of the plank. They'd search all around till they found a stone that would balance the weight of the hog and they'd put that on the other end of the plank. Then they'd guess the weight of the stone."

All through his ninety years he had as life-enjoying a zest in every day's doings as his laughing father; and he was as devoted to helping the underprivileged as his mother. Yet in all the millions of words written about him, in all kinds of languages, very few are about his human life as a man.

Some of this is due to his Vermont distaste for having strangers to him talk about him personally. The Vermont idea is that people who don't know you just have not the data to understand your inner life. To all men he spoke freely of ideas and principles. But his own inner feelings, his personal relations to those who shared daily life with him — how could anyone glancing in from the outside, know their depths, recognize their meanings?

There may be another reason for this silence on his part, on our part. His personal and home life and human relations were not in the least dramatic, were like anybody's. When he was a young professor, he married a fine, well-educated woman, original and vital. They lived together for many years, till her death, in old age. They had six sturdy, intelligent, straight-fibered children. Two of them died young. To the end of his life, they were mourned by their father, whose grief was apparently a surprise to one of his commentators who called his feeling "an almost womanly sorrow."

From the noise and disconcerting young energy of the four who grew up, their father never asked nor received from their mother that "protection" traditionally needed by a philosopher. He was not a father who would have liked "protection" from his own children. Observers of the Dewey home have said that John Dewey's theories of education were evolved and written with one of his children climbing up his trouser-leg and another dipping his finger into the inkwell on his desk. In other words out of constant, first-hand contact with living children in a stable family framework which allowed them to live naturally. Is there any other great thinker on education who collected such authentic research raw material in the laboratory of the home? He was keenly and unfailingly interested by his growing sons and daughters, as in all young human growth. He wrote once, "I have wondered that philosophers in general, although they are themselves teachers, have not taken education with sufficient seriousness for it to occur to them that any rational person could actually think it possible that philosophizing should focus about education as *the* supreme human interest." Do you hear in this not only the philosopher's voice, but the father's? I think I do.

When he was an old man, when the children had grown up, his wife died. Some time after, he married again. Into this new home, normal framework for normal young life, children were adopted, children who needed parents. And they too swarmed over the old philosopher-educator, played hide-and-seek and guessing games all around him. Like any other Vermonter, Dewey had used action rather than words to express emotional depths within him. In action he said what would have sounded artificial and sentimental if spoken in words to a television audience — "I love children."

Then it became plain to every eye that, through his work, in all the epic length of his many years he had been, with magical, wordless eloquence, saying just that — "I love children."

But was he never so mastered by his feelings that for an instant he forgot to be reticent in the presence of casual strangers?

Yes, from his visit when he was ninety years old, to his home town of Burlington, comes the echo of a cry of love and pain wrung out from his heart.

He was ancient of years by that time, as few men ever are. He had survived to the age when many men have lived clear through their capacity for caring, for feeling, as a garden in a frost-free autumn lives clear through its capacity for blooming, and lies bare and dry, waiting for winter.

After years so many that they would have meant a lifetime for most people, he was seeing again the background of his boyhood and young manhood, seventy years gone by. The students of his old college, their professors, the townspeople, were the grandchildren, some of them the great-grandchildren of those who had been part of his youth. As they pressed around him, eager to see the great man he had become, he was Dr. Dewey to them. Yet a few were left of his age-group or a little younger who called him John. After he had returned to the city, he wrote back to Burlington people that of all the celebrations for his ninetieth birthday, none had touched him so deeply as his welcome home in the old town.

The ancient Vermonter gave little sign, during his visit here, of this feeling. As he was escorted here and there on the campus, in the town, he looked around him with his usual manner at the friendly crowds of younger and older people, at the new and old buildings of the university, off over the blue expanse of the lake, up at the distant mountains which he had climbed in his boyhood. He was as he always was — cheerful, affable, remote, kind, impersonal. A man of ninety has seen so much. He has seen everything.

And then they passed before the old house which had been his home. It had been well kept. It was not changed. He halted, an expression on his face which silenced those around him. Someone finally asked respectfully, "Would you like to go in and take a look around, Dr. Dewey?"

He gazed up at it, the roof under which he had lived his childhood in love and trusting confidence, where the path to growth had always been kept open before him, where growth had given him the strength which had upheld him faithfully all those endless years. He looked at the windows from which his loving-hearted mother had watched the coming and going of her sons, of those other adopted sons to whom she had opened her motherliness. He looked at the door through which his father had stepped out to zestful day after day of life, not one of them tarnished by an ignoble deed. He stood in a long silence before his old home, he, the only one still living of those whom he had loved there, who had loved him.

"It would tear my heart out to go in," he said gravely and passed on.

Robert Frost

VERMONTERS are brought up to be stoically resigned to silence in moments of emotion because our experience is that deep feeling can no more be expressed in words than colors in musical notes. Yet emotion longs for an outlet. Imagine if you can — but I know you can't — our astonished joy when a poet appeared, a great artist, who knows how to speak of the depths within human beings, to speak luminously and yet without losing the ineffable loveliness of silence.

Of course Robert Frost does much more than, by implication, speak out what, wordless as the pulse of human hearts, is felt by North Country readers, or ripens to mellowness in their minds as they grow older. He is far too great a poet to be framed in by geographical boundaries. The man who wrote "I Will Sing You One-O," "Nothing Gold Can Stay," "Fire and Ice," "The Tuft of Flowers," "Mending Wall," writes for the world, for anyone anywhere on the round globe who is fortunate enough to know the language of these master-words. Although Robert Frost has lived all his life, except a few years of his little-boyhood, in the North Country, and for the last thirty years has made his home in Vermont, we make no claim that he belongs to us, any more than Dante belongs to Florence. But there is a special quality of kinsman's love in the feeling Florentines have for Dante, and this book would not be complete without some statement about the special closeness felt for Robert Frost by Vermont and all North of Boston readers. The reasons for that closeness stem from our tradition, from its deep heart's core.

In the layer-beneath-layer of his poems' meaningful beauty there is one which speaks for us so intimately that to find it on a printed page is not like reading something, but like living through a flash of the revelation which comes, in a few especially blessed

moments, even to poor human beings, moments in which we can
see what we are, what we know — what we can only guess.

We can't think what city people can make out of the poem
which begins:

> This saying good-bye on the edge of the dark
> And the cold to an orchard so young in the bark
> Reminds me of all that can happen to harm
> An orchard away at the end of the farm . . .

and goes on, some lines farther down the page:

> I don't want it stirred by the heat of the sun.
> (We made it secure against being, I hope,
> By setting it out on the northerly slope.)
> No orchard's the worse for the wintriest storm;
> But one thing about it, it mustn't get warm.
> "How often already you've had to be told,
> Keep cold, young orchard. Good-bye and keep cold.
> Dread fifty above more than fifty below."

For us this gravely recognizes — always by unspoken implications — one of our hard-won rules of living, not to try to hurry
the miracle of growth, not, in human relations, to snatch for
a flower when all that has been done is to plant a seed. But till
Robert Frost wrote a poem in russet homespun about leaving a
young orchard for the winter, who of us had dreamed that we
would find our axiom thus set down in invisible ink between
printed lines? We, who detest submission for its own sake, we
who are submissive to so little, we submit patiently to the law
that growth can take place only in the dimension of time. We
learn and relearn, from our experience of life, that to try to force
growth sooner than nature wills does not bring an earlier harvest,
but destroys the ability ever to mature and bear fruit. We know
this. Or rather, beyond the limiting exactitudes of knowledge,
we feel it.

We try to act on the knowledge. But in everyday human
relations we fail so often, so clumsily, that we grow bewildered
and disheartened. In moving slowly, our purpose is to protect
from the mortal danger of haste the rich fruiting of comradely
effort-in-common, of friendship, of love, of that rarest, most

exquisite experience in life, all-trusting intimacy. But our skill so often falls below the need for skill! We wished only to surround sacred growth with what it must have to live — time. Yet as we try to embody that noble wish in life, we seem to others harsh and wounding. Too often our inner life is shamed confusion. Yet we are never so confused as to doubt our ideal, clear to us only in rare moments of spiritual insight.

My faltering attempt here is to show how a dimly grasped ideal can shine out plain in a poem, although — no, *because* — its words are only of young apple trees, blossom and fruit sleeping mysteriously within their dormant cells. The poet uses our own language of responsible care-taking for what needs care (language which somehow he shows to be comelier than we knew). On the literal printed page there is not a thought save what any life-experienced farmer might have about his young fruit trees; but the plain country words comfort us with an unspoken mystic meaning.

They tell us that, no matter how inept our efforts, we do well to try to time human life to the slow, in-the-end triumphant pace of growth. Those quiet words about zero-cold and young apple trees steady us. Yes, we think, this is the way things are. To act as though growth had taken place — in a shorter time than it needs and must have — that is pretense, and pretense is deadly. To try to hurry growth is only to maim and mutilate the unknowable core which is its life. It is calming thus to find, expressed by that exquisite side-glance called implication, a basic principle so great that we ourselves have never found words fit to clothe it — only actions.

In that poem the theme is steadfast and strong, as if played straightforwardly in unison on deep strings. In another — "Spring Pools" — it soars as if lifted by the angelic voices of violins.

> These pools that, though in forests, still reflect
> The total sky almost without defect,
> And like the flowers beside them, chill and shiver,
> Will like the flowers beside them soon be gone,
> And yet not out by any brook or river,
> But up by roots to bring dark foliage on.

The trees that have it in their pent-up buds
To darken nature and be summer woods —
Let them think twice before they use their powers
To blot out and drink up and sweep away
These flowery waters and these watery flowers
From snow that melted only yesterday.

We don't know what is made out of that poem by people who
have not, every year of their lives from childhood, come across
such fragile yet everlastingly recurrent loveliness in the still
bare woods of April. Perhaps to them it is just a poem, a beautiful musical poem, one of Robert Frost's greatest literary successes. To us, murmuring its lines over, as we do to greet each
spring's melting snow and small, frail, dauntlessly perfect wild-
flowers, it is a benediction pronounced on the incessant changingness of life. We accept that changingness because there is no
way not to accept it. It is a law of nature. We bow to it because
we must. The radiance of this poem brings us the good news
that nature's law is not harsh and unrewarding, but, if accepted
with hearts reconciled to reality, it is the creator of beauty,
undying, ever-renewed.

But in our Vermont and North Country tradition there are
other elements — many of them. Respect for the principle of
growth is only one of them. Another is the unsparing certainty
that it is not beyond our human power to serve honor, even
when, as happens to many of our human brothers, we find ourselves savagely caught and prisoned fast by life.

Somehow in the maze of our bewilderingly complex relations
with each other, close or distant, we stumble into a coil, which
tightens on us the more we try to escape. Is it by our fault, by
our misfortune? We cannot guess. Our panting struggle with it
leaves us no time, no strength, no peace, in which to try to
understand. We can but pull the strangling noose away from our
necks enough to know that whatever the cause, whatever the
nature of our plight, the wildness of our blood-instinct to escape
and be free must not mutilate or disfigure human dignity, which
is based, in the end, the faraway end, on righteousness. And with

all our strength, our will is to believe in righteousness — unknowable though it may be — even though it kill us.

Many of us move forward as best we can, with such a noose around our necks. North Country people differ from others only in that their tradition bids them live through this ordeal, not talk about it. Each morning when we rise, we find it there beside us, within us, and prepare in silence for another shadowed day.

Whose woods these are I think I know.
His house is in the village though;
He will not see me stopping here
To watch his woods fill up with snow.

My little horse must think it queer
To stop without a farmhouse near
Between the woods and frozen lake
The darkest evening of the year.

He gives his harness bells a shake
To ask if there is some mistake.
The only other sound's the sweep
Of easy wind and downy flakes.

The woods are lovely, dark and deep.
But I have promises to keep,
And miles to go before I sleep,
And miles to go before I sleep.

First there is beauty, calming prelude to the long look at what cannot be seen by the physical eye. It is such beauty as has a special intimate meaning for North Country readers because it is part of our lived-in present, not book-beauty from the literary past. "To watch his woods fill up with snow." We people of the winter know it well, that dreamlike, passive stillness of the blur of falling snow. Those first three stanzas weave a kind of trance. Like a man falling deliciously asleep to his death in the treacherous softness of snow, the reader sinks into the oncoming night and into the blessed illusion that he is solitary, that he has no responsibility for the pain of others. The drowsily falling snow muffles any sound that might wake him, save tiny bells tinkling faintly in ears already almost closed to outer warnings.

"The woods are lovely, dark and deep."

What fatally sweet temptation is it which waits within that lovely darkness? No reader of the poem needs to be told what is his own inner darkness. He leans at the edge of an abyss well known to him, fearing — and longing — to fall.

He leans farther out, more dangerously. What is there to hinder him? The tinkling from the outer world is silent. Only the delicate soundlessness of easy wind and downy flake.

But now, within, a great bell swings for a single bronze stroke:

"But I have promises to keep."

Back to the little horse who — like the flesh of man — knows not what the immortal soul must do. Back to the appointed journey, with its appointed end. Farewell to loveliness dark and deep.

That farewell, resolute though it may be, cannot be said without a sob.

"And miles to go before I sleep."

And again with a long sigh of acceptance:

"And miles to go before I sleep."

The heart bursting with its pain and the greatness of its power to master pain, is stilled to the sober pulse of human strength. What could never be said aloud has been put into a few words about a fall of snow, a man, a horse, and winter trees at nightfall.

But in that vast inner realm which for reticent people is beyond direct expression there is much more than pain and the struggle to master pain. There is love. There is the love of man and wife, of all human intimacies the most incommunicable. Can any man writing within the North Country tradition find new words, words without a single tarnishing finger-mark from the countless hands which since the dawn of our human life have tried to write of love?

At the beginning of one of the volumes of his poetry, Robert Frost put the following eight lines dedicated to his wife. Years later, when his poems were collected and printed in one volume

he put it in again, as first poem, standing alone, not catalogued
or listed in the index.

> I'm going out to clean the pasture spring;
> I'll only stop to rake the leaves away
> (And wait to watch the water clear, I may):
> I sha'n't be gone long. — You come too.
>
> I'm going out to fetch the little calf
> That's standing by the mother. It's so young
> It totters when she licks it with her tongue.
> I sha'n't be gone long. — You come too.

The man is leaving the woman who loves him, whom he loves
too, but whom he is only learning how to love. He turns away
from her as if casually, as if for brief, matter-of-fact experiences
which every human being encounters in the course of the day's
routine. Like all men he is a poet, only this man knows it. Those
routine experiences have a veiled mystic meaning for him. This
he has always jealously hidden from others behind a screen of
prosaic words.

He says lightly, in the habit of his life till then, that he is
going to clear the fallen leaves from the spring. He even mentions, as if it were of no importance, that he may wait a moment
for the water to clear. What he does not speak of — who could?
— is that he will have a glimpse of reality behind its material
surface, as the clear water streams up from inexhaustible underground rivers and seas into that little pool which, like a man,
like a woman, is the small, finite outward sign of infinity. He
knows that at the sight of it, he will feel, in his own nature, the
streaming up of the spirit from sources which he forgets in the
heavy-stepping round of everyday work. He knows that at that
moment he will know that spiritual sources, too, are inexhaustible.

Yet, for sentient human beings, the most exalted reassurance
from the spirit is abstract and remote compared to the intimate
sweet sharing of life with all other feeling creatures on our globe.
The miracle — ! that all of life-to-come is in the feeble, scarcely-
as-yet-living new-born — in all the new-born, here on the farm
as everywhere — life, not frail like the new-born but invincible,
forward-going to what unimaginable goal —

His wife stands waiting, as he turns from the surface of the days and nights they share, to plunge into the rich deepness of his real life. Will he leave her behind, as till now, he has always left behind his fellows in humanity?

She does not know what it is to which he is going out with longing and awe. But because he and she are now one in the flesh, because she is his intimate as no other has ever been, she is shaken by the vibration from the plucked string in his breast.

Is their marriage to be a bridge thrown over the unplumb'd, salt, estranging sea? Or only a convention-approved satisfaction for their lesser needs?

She is silent. She does not plead with him. If he must be asked to open the door and let her in, she would rather turn away than mar the aloneness which has been sacred to him.

He pauses at the door, his face already turned from the room, the house, the bed, the table which he has in common with her.

The North Country woman, reading these lines, waits — waits. It is not a caress she longs for, not a service, not praise, not protection from hardship. It is to be let in where he lives.

The man in the poem remembers the woman who is his wife, remembers what they are to each other, turns back, faces her, holds out his hand — "You come too."

Summing Up

IN nearly two centuries of life in the Green Mountains, the spirit of the community has produced several hundred thousand — no, a million or more if you include those who emigrated when grown up — men and women who, by the act of living together in accordance with local tradition, have made for each other an unvaryingly safe and orderly social framework for widely varying individual lives. The doors of that old home-society have been left open so that those who thought they might be freer in another tradition to develop the best possibilities within them, could walk out unhindered. Those who have wished to stay here have, according to their different tastes and needs, lived like the majority or have been nonconforming oddities, just as they liked.

In every one of the succeeding generations of Vermonters there have been a normal number of gifted, upright and superior personalities never heard of by the outer world, but known, valued, trusted, remembered and often loved (still are) by their neighbors in village, town and state. The rank and file here, detesting and repudiating authority for its own sake, have been notably self-disciplined, successful in assuming the responsibility for their own acts. Those who have stayed at home here, and those who have taken their ideals and standards far and wide over the nation, have given proof that freedom can be orderly, can be beneficent to all who share in it. These ordinary men and women have steadily produced, year after year, out of their very own stuff, the leaders needed by every human group. Am I claiming too much to suggest that such a human fruiting does credit to any root tradition?

That root has also produced some personalities who have served as leaders in the national field. In spite of their very small numbers, practically every generation of Vermonters has produced one figure known and useful to the nation.

The first in date, Ethan Allen, was one of those eighteenth-century pioneers who, in politics, in religion, in social organization, strode resolutely out of the colonial past and into the American future.

In the early nineteenth century, a Vermonter gave his heart to the cause of making advanced education freely available to all sons and daughters of the nation. Because we live under the American Constitution he mightily served that cause.

In our twentieth century, as the world curtain slowly rose on the desperate effort to shape our human future to freedom and to creative peace, another Vermont Senator played a leading role, stepping across political party lines to stand for what was then most needed in our nation and in the world — American unity in international relations. Senator Austin, elected and re-elected by the endlessly Republican State of Vermont, appointed by a Democratic administration as the first representative of the United States to the United Nations organization, served well to refute the doubts of Europeans and Asians hesitating to believe that any American policy could be bipartisan.

In the field of education, venerated for its value to mankind by Vermonters from the day of their arrival in the primeval forests, a genius appeared. Since genius is incalculable, transcending all about it, one can hardly say that John Dewey was produced by the Vermont tradition. What can be said is that his great creative spirit flowed through the channels of the ideals to which he had been brought up in our state.

And, ours only because we are his, that once-in-a-century shooting star, a great poet who, as only a great poet can, speaks out what lies wordlessly pulsing in the hearts of people brought up as he was.

No famous painter, or sculptor, or actor, no multimillionaire, no mighty captain of industry, no glamorous beauty, no master of the abstract like Einstein, no adept manipulator of national politics, no famous organizer of the armies of wage-earners.

Peaches and pomegranates do not, you see, grow on apple trees. But apples do.

PART VI

PART VI

CHAPTER 22

Let's Look at the Record

Is anything left of the Vermont tradition?

Most authors who write about the development of a community prudently stop short at least a generation before the date of the book's publication. For of course nobody can accurately describe the tone and quality of the life around him while he is in it, up to his neck. But facts are clear beyond question; they have been printed right up to this morning's newspaper. If I set down here some of those facts about present-day life in Vermont, your guess as to what they mean will be as good as mine. Al Smith's was an excellent axiom. By all means, "Let's look at the record."

The Vermont tradition is unwritten, mostly inarticulate, to some degree unconscious and instinctive. Nobody ever places one clause in it above the others. Any one of them will do to begin with. For instance the unquestioned right of anyone to practice variations — if harmless to others — from the way of life generally accepted by the majority of his neighbors.

Vermonters agree with all other good American citizens that one variation in standards cannot be tolerated because it cannot possibly be considered harmless to others. This exception is obedience to the Communist party line. Where we Vermonters differ from some American citizens is that in our sincere opposition to Communism and our horror at its threats to every liberty dear to us, we try very hard to keep clear in our minds the difference between suspicion and proof. In some localities we note that people usually sensible and well-balanced have become so worn by long-continued nervous tension that — so it seems to us — any sort of nonconformity to the average level of popular conduct and belief seems to them sure indication of the wish to destroy our government by force. Not so in Vermont. Just because a young man wears a beard and talks rather foolishly about subjects he obviously does not understand, we do not jump to the conclusion that he must be a secret agent of Moscow.

Teachers naturally have great influence in modeling the opinions of the rising generation. Society is right in demanding from them soundness of mind and character. Unfortunately, in the present wave of fear and suspicion, school boards and citizens committees have often gone to such irrational lengths in demanding proof of loyalty, have insisted on the banning of so many impartial textbooks, that in their history classes only the boldest American teachers dare call attention to the Bill of Rights — which is part of our Constitution.

How about Vermont teachers? Let's turn to the record. Here is a resolution voted by the Champlain Valley Teachers Association at a meeting some years ago, just about at the time when the repressive super-loyalty wave was beginning to sweep over our country:

> WHEREAS, we believe that Democracy is strong enough to stand on its own feet, and defend itself by its tested methods of free research and discussion, weighing freely the merits of all questions by open reasoning rather than by taboos, be it
>
> RESOLVED, that the setting up of a code of orthodox doctrine, and the suppression of all differing modes of thought by some censorship — however well-intended — can only strengthen that spirit of intolerance which in the past has always proved a first step towards dictatorships.

The Teachers Association which passed this resolution was (in Vermont newspapers) neither commended or disapproved. Its members were not called courageous, neither were they labeled subversive. No special notice of any kind was given the resolution. As an expression of American opinion, everybody took it for granted.

Let's look at another part of the record. In 1951 an official announcement appeared in Vermont newspapers that the Attorney-General of the United States had directed that a special Grand Jury be drawn up in each Federal District of the United

States, to investigate crime, activities of the Communist Party, violators of the Federal Securities Act, and the like.

The summer before, there had been a spate of accusations, mostly from one person, that Communists were active in Vermont. Our small doings usually go unnoticed by the nation. But this was sensational enough so that it was commented on by newspapers outside the State. Our own Vermont press did not take fire. In their editorials, several Vermontisms appeared which had been appreciatively passed on around the State — such as, "The idea that Vermont, because it has a sparse population and rough terrain, is a good place for Communists to hide in, could have occurred only to somebody who had never lived in a Vermont community, and so does not realize that everybody here knows at any hour exactly where everybody else in the town is, and what he is doing." Another comment which we thought was funny, was, "Anybody who tries to bore from within in Vermont is going to strike granite."

But the anxiety prevalent in the nation is nerve-shaking. Some of the newer residents in our state did not smile at the Vermontisms. They said they had elsewhere gone through terrible communal hysterias starting in this very way. It was serious business. So, when a Vermont Grand Jury was called to investigate subversive activity, they predicted, "Now Vermont's turn has come for a smear campaign. Now *we* shall see citizens called up for public accusations of sedition, and given no adequate chance to defend themselves. Now teachers of history who give their students Thomas Jefferson to read will be told by bullying public authorities that they are fellow-travelers, or worse, et cetera, et cetera." You certainly have heard people talk like this — Elmer Davis, stout-hearted defender of liberalism though he is, occasionally, over the radio, seems almost to lose hope for reasoned examination of any witch-hunting charge — and he usually has good grounds for what he says.

To such prophecies, one brief counsel was made by older Vermonters. "Wait and see what happens." They themselves were not at all sure what would happen, but tradition steadied them to wait.

The first thing which "happened" was the official charge to

the assembled Grand Jury, which we thought very fine. I'll give exact names. It was written by the Presiding Judge in the United States District Court. He is Judge Ernest Gibson, formerly Governor of Vermont, son of a former United States Senator from our State. Such an official charge to a Grand Jury is public property. I could reprint it all, and I'd like to. But it is too long for the pages of a book already overlong. I'll set down some of the paragraphs to which special attention was given by Vermonters, every one of whom reads the newspapers. Those phrases italicized are those which we particularly noted. Please remember that these statements were not made by a "liberal" professor or editor, but by the official representative of the American law. He said:

We read allegations in our state newspapers of Communist infiltration into various areas of our State. The McCarran Act defines the World Communist movement as a world-wide revolutionary movement, whose purpose it is by treachery, deceit, infiltrations into other groups, espionage, sabotage, treason and any other means deemed necessary, to establish a Communist totalitarian dictatorship throughout the world. The same Act further asserts that the establishment of such a dictatorship results in the suppression of all opposition to the party in power, the denial of fundamental rights and liberties, such as freedom of speech, of the press, of assembly and of religious worship, and further asserts that in this country those individuals who knowingly and willfully participate in this world Communist movement, by doing so in effect repudiate their allegiance to this country. None of us here want any real Communists, *as thus defined*, in our midst, and any Communist who *violates our law* should be proceeded against.

However, I want to bring to our attention a second and perhaps more elementary function of a Grand Jury, even more fundamental than that of being an informing body. You may have wondered how the term "Grand Jury" came about. History indicates that originally a body known as a Grand Jury was established *to protect individuals* from oppression by a ruler. It was established thus as a protective body as well as an informing body.

This country can only be kept free and strong if freedom of speech is protected to the hilt. People in this country *must not be afraid to express minority views* because somebody in a position of eminence may holler "You are a Communist." Thus if we have those in this State who brand areas or individuals as being Communists, you, both as an informing body and *as a protective body*, should summons those people in and solicit from them whatever knowledge they may have as to Communist infiltration into this State. If you find some are branded as Communists but that such brand is unjustified by the facts, you should not hesitate in making your report to announce that such has been investigated and proved to be completely erroneous. Maybe some in your localities have told you that different people are Communists. Summons them in and let's arrive at the truth.

The next factual happening was the publication in all Vermont newspapers of a letter signed by the Foreman of the Grand Jury urging anybody who knew anything about subversive activities or any other crime in Vermont, to come forward and give evidence to the Grand Jury.

The next fact to report is a long, long silence. It lasted from February 12 to April 23. Like cats before an interesting mouse-hole, we kept our eyes fixed on the closed door to the room where the Grand Jury was meeting. But it was a Vermont room. There were no sounds from within.

Finally the long-expected public report appeared. Vermonters read this report — there's no denying it — with anxiety. Accounts of similar investigations elsewhere had shown in some of them little wish to protect the American principle of respect for differing opinions. How could we feel sure that our own tradition would stand?

Here is what the official report of the Vermont Grand Jury told us: during the weeks of their session, all kinds of witnesses had been questioned as to crime and subversive activity in our State. From these witnesses, the Vermonters serving on the Grand Jury had learned that the Canadian frontier is not closely enough guarded against smuggling. "There are seventeen inspection stations in Vermont, but there are forty roads leading from

Canada into Vermont on which there are no immigration or customs stations."

But what — how about that Communist infiltration? Vermont eyes hurried down the newspaper column looking for that word. Here it was: "Special consideration was given to the existence of Communists and Communist activity in Vermont. No evidence was presented which seemed to require further investigation by us. It was felt that the situation in Vermont is well understood by the F.B.I. and is properly handled by that Bureau."

The attention-getting position at the very end of the report was given to the following sentence, "It is felt that not only is the Grand Jury a body charged with such investigative power to protect the public from criminal activities, but that it has the further power and duty to protect individuals who may be unjustly accused."

Laying the newspaper down after reading its Vermont record of fact, our impression was — and mine is now — that this needs no comment.

Here is another recent fact from the record: during the 1951 session of the Vermont Legislature, a Representative introduced a bill which — no one could be sure of its provisions, for the first word-of-mouth storm signals flying about the State varied like all scare-talk. We gathered that the idea was to penalize by loss of citizenship anybody who belonged or ever had belonged, "directly or indirectly," to any organization thought to be subversive. That was as inaccurate, as most rumor is. But not too far from the general color of the bill.

When the exact wording was learned, it proved to be:

"No political organization or group shall be qualified as a political party or given a place on a ballot which organization or group is associated, directly or *indirectly*, with Communist, Fascist, or other un-American principles and engages in activities or propaganda designed to teach subservience to the political principles and ideals of foreign nations, or the overthrow of the established constitutional form of the Government of the United States and the State of Vermont."

Well — ! Here it was! Excitable people proposed that pro-

testing letters to the newspapers be written, that mass meetings
be held, that — Other Vermonters took a long breath, braced
themselves — and waited. I heard the following exchange of
views: A newer resident in the State said anxiously, "But you
people who live off here in this small corner, you haven't *seen*
how American principles are being undermined by just such
measures. Those provisions can be stretched to include almost
anything. Who's to decide whether a political party is associated
with un-American principles? On that basis, the administration
can head off all opposition. You don't understand the danger.
You should spring to defend . . . et cetera, et cetera." The older
Vermonter asked patiently, "Why do you take for granted that
our officially elected representatives will undermine basic American principles, unless you scare them, or force them not to?"

We don't know of course what, if any, not-for-publication
talk went on in Montpelier between members of the Senate and
of the House. I can set down here only the published facts.
They are three in number: first of all, the proposed bill was
greatly changed by the committee on Judiciary. Eliminated were
all references forbidding "activities designed to teach subservience to the political principles and ideals of foreign nations."
The House passed the amended bill without comment, along
with a number of others about all kinds of things, one after
another. Then the Senate voted it down, unanimously. Not one
dissenting vote.

But not without comment. A voice vote was called for, with
the public explanation that this was asked expressly in order to
give each Senator a chance not only to stand up and be counted
on this subject, but to make a statement of his reasons for
voting "no."

The general tone of these expressions of opinion followed a
familiar quotation from Calvin Coolidge inscribed on the walls
of the Statehouse, which was recited in full by the first Senator
who spoke:

"If the spirit of liberty should vanish in the United States,
and our institutions should languish, it could all be restored by
the generous store held by the people in this brave little state of
Vermont."

In one form or another, that is about what each of our Senators said, as he registered his "no."

This happened in the 1951 session of our Legislature. The Vermont newspapers have just reported from this year's (1953) session the following incident. A bill was presented to the House, to set up a State board of censorship, with authority to decide which textbooks should be used in our schools. Our locally voted (not appointed) school boards now have that responsibility.

Most of the newspapers of the State represented the feeling of their readers in strongly worded editorials, protesting against this measure. The general idea of these editorials was along the lines of this question: "Since when have Vermonters become incapable of making their own selections for their own schools?" Or, "Why should we have a Board of Censors appointed, not elected, whose ideas we would be forced to accept? We'd rather trust the judgment of our neighbors whom we vote in as School Directors and can vote out, if we don't like what they do."

But as one experienced ancient remarked, "Legislators don't *always* act like people." Nervous Vermonters felt anxious. You never know.

The decision has just been announced as I end this book. Out of the 246 members of the Legislature, eleven votes were in favor of the censorship board. All other votes were opposed. It had gone not only to the Education Committee but to the Appropriations Committee. Their report read that they were "not willing to put the stamp of approval on this Witch-Hunt."

I think I am safe in feeling again that no comment is needed on that part of the Vermont record.

Orestes Brownson characterized the Vermonter of the nineteenth century as "one who has no conservative tendency by nature, who is no slave to public opinion, and for the most part has the courage of his convictions." In trying to answer the question as to whether the twentieth-century Vermonter is recognizably the descendant of his nonconservative ancestors, perhaps one piece of evidence is the fact that the Vermont Legislature of 1953 has a large number of elected women legislators in it, larger (so we read in the newspapers) than any other state in the Union; and also elected a woman as Speaker of the House, the second in the history of the nation and the first in New England.

Modern economists, chiefly interested in large-scale collective phenomena, sometimes in their writings dismiss individual personal financial honesty as a "minor virtue." It is not so considered here. Out of the two hundred and forty-six towns in Vermont, there have been in the last decade a few — three or four — cases where a town treasurer has succumbed to the new, and to Vermonters startlingly large, sums of money handled nowadays by officials even in our small towns. These failures to resist temptation have not been taken with a man-of-the-world lift of the eyebrows, meaning "Oh, what can you expect of human nature?" In the towns where they have happened, they have been dreadful tragedies, the kind of horror which results in suicide and in a feeling of moral disgrace even for those who had no part in the action.

As for the over-all picture of the State in this regard, here are the figures from the latest report by the Bureau of Internal Revenue on tax fraud prosecutions: in all the United States, thirteen thousand cases were reported. The total sum of money involved throughout the nation in that year was ninety-one million dollars. Vermont was the last on the list of states, with a single case involving the smuggling of cigarettes from Canada. Total of tax and fines involved $63.61.

Part of the foundation of Green Mountain life was the idea of a decently human attitude towards Indians. There have been no Indians here for many years. Yet, when we "look at the record," we find a relevant fact, recently reported by our Historical Society. It runs something like this: an elderly Vermont farmer, reminiscing about his boyhood when he used to work with his grandfather, remembered that in one of the hayfields there were some mounds. They were a bother. The mowing machine could not be used on them. His grandfather always mowed them by hand with a scythe. Once the little boy asked the old man, "What are these mounds?" His grandfather said, "Indians were buried here, long before the white settlers ever came into Vermont." The child suggested with practical good sense, "Why don't you just smooth them out? 'Twould make haying so much easier," and learned from some quiet words of his grandfather (as so many of us have learned) something about one clause of our tradition. The old Vermonter said equably, "Oh, I guess not. They've lain there a long time. We'd better leave 'em quiet a while longer."

He who had been a little boy was now very old. To him came one day an archaeologist who told him that because of the great age of the burial mounds, there might be artifacts in them for which museums and collectors would pay high prices. He made the old farmer a proposition: if he could have permission from the owner of the land to dig up the graves, he would share, half and half, any money which came in.

The old farmer delivered no self-righteous rebuke about treating dead Indians less honorably than dead white people. He picked up his grandfather's phrase from seventy years ago and said quietly, "No, they've lain there a long time. I guess we'd better leave 'em quiet a while longer."

Of course here as everywhere, earning-a-living problems are those most constantly present in individual lives. Toward the end of Chapter 16 I have set down the facts which give us reason for cautiously hoping that the spirit of our tradition will not be warped by factory life, cash-crop milk farming, or the tourist business.

How about local self-government in these complex modern times? There we have a problem as yet unsolved. Vermont has about the same number of towns as a century and a quarter ago. But now, although the total population of Vermont has not dwindled, its geographical distribution has changed. Half the State's population lives in only twenty-five towns. Of the other two hundred and twenty-one communities, some are managing pretty well, but many have not nearly enough people or taxable property to keep up local town government, town schools and roads. To support them at a bare minimum civic level they need — and are given — aid from the State Treasury.

The Legislature, where every town has one Representative, is the only body which can bring about the merger of small units into larger ones. Evidently our old political organization no longer fits a changed economic situation. The tax burden is unfairly distributed. More important, the welfare of our schools depends on consolidation, and we do appreciate the importance of schools — why wouldn't we, when Vermont children are about the only "natural resources" we have? Yet at any proposal of enforced regrouping, the air is filled with wails of the sincerest pain, with which we all sympathize: "What! *our* town, which has held its head up and taken care of itself, and done its share since 1781, to lose its identity, its very name!"

Even here, through the emotional uproar of protest, the still small voice of reasonableness can be heard, quietly remarking, as many times before in Vermont history, that there's no use trying to keep a part of the past alive when it is not really alive any more. And several sessions ago, a State Legislature did act on the dictates of this reasonableness, and voted out of legal existence two towns which had so few people in them that their corporate existence was a farce and their representation in the Legislature an inequity to others. A great many foreboding people had thought that no Legislature would "dare" take such action. But they did. Nor were they ever penalized, by public disapproval, or in any other way.

From the "ayes" of 1777 that confirmed the Vermont Constitution with its unique clause forbidding slavery, human freedom has been a concern in our tradition. The only enslaved people Vermonters knew were Negroes. Has that recognition of Negroes' right to freedom and personal dignity lapsed here in the ninety years since the Civil War? No, Vermonters do not overlook the fact — at least some Vermonters do not — that there are still many bristling social and human barriers erected against their darker-skinned fellow-Americans.

Every summer, a trainload of Negro children, from the Harlem district of New York City, travels up to Vermont. One by one, or two by two, they are taken as summer vacation guests into Vermont farm and village homes. There they do what other

Vermont children do — go berrying, swim in the old swimming-hole, help wipe the dishes, feed the hens, play backgammon, go to occasional neighborhood picnics, take books out from the local library. During their month here, our newspapers reporting the news from each town in the region, give their names (no mention of their color) along with those of other local children who may have done something newsworthy — appeared in a play, pitched on the junior baseball team, fallen out of a tree and broken an arm, exhibited something in a Home Demonstration Meeting. When they take the train back to the city, our newspapers chronicle this, report weight gained by any child, pet kittens being carried home to the city, the names of the young visitors who have learned to swim. The next morning we all read such news items, and look at photographs of smiling young black faces upturned in trust to Vermont farmers.

You will notice that I do not attempt to tell you how much, or how little, or exactly what is the meaning of this Vermont gesture of hospitality to members of another race. I don't know. How could I know? The Vermont farm and village families who year by year make the gesture don't know either. They do not theorize about it. They do not try to measure its moral significance. They just do it. And I just set it down here as one of the facts to be seen when we "look at the Vermont record."

Last summer I was asked to speak before a group of foreign-exchange students, many of them from Asia, here in Vermont for a get-used-to-America month before going on to the universities where they had scholarships. From time to time, older Vermonters were asked in to talk about various aspects of our life to these Hindu, Iranian, Indo-Chinese, Philippine, Japanese, Egyptian young people.

As I stood before them, describing our dairy farming and our small industries, it occurred to me to tell my listeners about those young summer guests from Harlem. From their expressions, the young Asian hearers were interested, but not very much. They seemed to take it as just another piece of information, along with how we make a sweet syrup from the sap of certain trees, an item which always astonishes foreign visitors. Then I chanced to mention the fact that some of the Harlem families of the children have begun to invite down to their New York homes for a winter visit the Vermont farm or village families where the Negro children had been guests.

I noticed a change in the young Asians of my audience. They looked suddenly intent. In a neutral voice one of them asked, "Do the Vermont people accept those invitations?"

"They certainly do," I replied. "With interest and much pleasure. You see, it is a wonderful opportunity for them to visit a great metropolitan area such as perhaps they might never have any other chance to see. Yes, they go, last year nearly fifty. They have good times, do a great deal of sight-seeing, and come home full of their new experience."

The young people in their bright Oriental draperies nodded, smiled, exchanged significant looks. Without knowing it, I had passed along something about the Vermont way of life which had a meaning to them far beyond what we had dreamed.

As I looked at them, I had a perfectly definite mental picture of a pebble falling into a pool, the concentric circles about it widening and widening. And then a hope that perhaps one ripple from that circle might have the honor to quench one of the sparks of faraway bitterness and resentment — our small, unpolished, old Vermont pebble.

Postscript

IS there anything to set down in a last report save these tangible items? Has anything else, not planned for but latent, grown out of the old stem?

As I come to the end of this odd book, I find my heart full of something else. I don't know how to speak of it. I am sure I can never find words fit to express it. Might I, perhaps, give some idea of it by implication? Perhaps I could not even do that — not by ever so remote an approach.

Would it do any harm to try?

In a publisher's announcement of a new book soon to appear under the title *Our Common Neurosis*, I found this passage: "There are later developments in Dr. Burrow's investigations, which indicate that despite society's drive towards conflict and impasse, there is a deeper tendency, cohesive and co-operative, in man which can be reactivated as an integrative force in human relationships."

I did not smile over the language. What is at issue is the life or death of our humanity. I thought of our annual Town Meetings.

Take them at their surface appearance, they are often tiresome and vexing. Talk about where to put the new bridge degenerates into quibbling, sometimes angry, unfair quibbling. The wrong people speak, always too long. Clownish jokes are loudly laughed at by people who should know better. The man with a grudge against life once more airs it in the form of objecting to any action proposed, droning on to people sunk into apathetic despair about ever getting home to do the chores. A discussion which seems to be concerned with drawing the material for a new road from one gravel pit rather than another slides down into that same old feud between an elderly citizen and his son-in-law whom he has never liked.

Your chair is hard. Like everybody else you shift restlessly. Like the Moderator you look pointedly at the big clock — are they never going to finish debating those tedious clauses in the Warning about care for the old cemeteries, about how much money to spend on celebrating Memorial Day, and get on, get on to the live nerve of what our taxes are going to be next year?

This is what lies on the top level of your mind. But, even as the meeting fumbles its way slowly forward, you are aware, off and on, in flashes, of something very different from this surface impression, a feeling for which you have no ready-made label. And as you drive home over muddy roads, watching perhaps wisps of mist slowly thinning till the mountain back of them lifts its bulk to view, your surface impression also thins out and blows away, and Town Meeting stands there for what it is — human beings acting together for the needs of all.

The schools are safe for another year, the schools which could not exist at all without the total effort-in-common of all those men and women, any one of whom would be helpless, if alone, to prepare his children for modern life. The roads are planned for, miles of them, any one of the miles costly beyond the means of those living beside them.

The tiresome account-keeping provisions for raising the money to pay for this and that, the attentive, responsible care to have every cent used as the town intends, for everybody's benefit — all those busy-with-their-own-affairs men and women, sitting on hard chairs hour after hour, boring themselves about tedious details — they have been helping each other do what needs to be done. Yet they are members of that human race of whom it is often said that its basic instinct is the dog-eat-dog fight for personal advantage. Not a specially picked group, with the unassimilables left out. Just anybody.

As you turn into your own side road, you find yourself saying wonderingly (every year it is a new wonder), "Why, on the whole we didn't do so badly, somehow." The word "we" has a glint, like something commonplace by day, shining in the dark with reflected light.

Later, after you go to bed, in the musing pause before going to sleep, your heart relaxes enough to let in again that glinting "we" — odd, you dreamily reflect, that a bunch of quite ordinary men and women, if they are not permanently separated into rival, competing classes or groups, are really able, in spite of human rancor, to get together on how to run things — for everybody's benefit, not for any one or any few.

Something else glints in the dark — the paradox that out of a tradition which strictly enjoins letting the neighbors alone should emerge the actual practice of collective action. It only seems odd. It is not odd, it is logical. The point is that the tradition makes human contacts safe. It does not countenance in theory nor permit in fact, except briefly in a limited way for elected officials, the assumption of power by anyone over the others. You do not need to be warily on your guard in closely communal contacts lest that closeness be used by some group or some individual to master or outdo you.

When everybody feels around him this taken-for-granted safety — why, it turns out to be natural — as natural as breathing or eating, to work together, not to try to beat somebody else.

And if, after the prosaic pull-together of Town Meeting, our eyes can catch that glint in the darkness from a light unseen, how much more brilliantly it shines in moments when the achievement of Town Meeting makes itself emotionally felt. Say, at a Commencement of our High School.

It is held in the evening so that wage-earning elders can be there. The ritual is always the same. The tall boys and girls, their senior year finished, march in very slowly while the school band plays — rather loudly for indoors. They mount solemnly to the platform, remembering not to knock their toes on the steps and not to trip over their floating academic robes. These are rented for the night, and worn because they hide any differences in clothing which might mark differences in income.

They take their places in the semicircle of chairs on the stage. In the full glare of the footlights their young faces look blank with inexperience of life. We have all known them since they were born, while they grew up in our communal past. Now we have come together to celebrate the moment when (whether they go on living geographically here or not) they become part of our future.

The man to the right of you, the man to your left, the men

and women beyond them — every man and woman in the twilight assembly room gazes with hypnotic steadiness up at the
lighted stage. All those human eyes which in everyday work
and pleasure flicker aside in a thousand directions, now focused,
now fixed, all in one beam — as if they themselves were one.

The program begins, the glee club, the valedictorian, the
"speaker of the day," the awarding of scholarships. These go
only to a few. No creative co-operation for all, but harsh competition showing its teeth and not in a smile, as one family's son
or daughter wins out over another. Yes, competition. This is a
human scene. There is in it the wish to win out over others.
But that is like one hard-twisted, bright metallic thread running
through the texture of life. The whole fabric is not woven of
those threads.

Singing again. The national anthem. It is the end. Everybody
stands up. The decisive moment has passed. Before our eyes they
have turned the corner. The big boys and girls are no longer
children in our school, but young citizens of life. They begin
to file carefully down the steps, holding those hired academic
robes out of their way. They look intensely serious.

The woman next to you begins, very quietly, gently and joyfully, to cry. The man on the other side, father of a senior,
presses his lips together and stares straight ahead — at what?
Perhaps he does not see it clear. But it is there —

The assembly room is a fine one, the school is a good one.
Astonishing how this smallish group of not-rich men and women
have achieved it.

Perhaps those fixed eyes of the man next to you are staring
back to another gathering of citizens years ago, when the seed
for tonight's celebration was planted. Perhaps he is remembering
— as you are — every detail of that crucial Town Meeting. The
group was divided then, as all human groups are and always will
be. But not logically, coolly, reasonably. It was convulsed, like
a human heart, torn by the passionate wrestling of opposed
desires.

On one side was the feeling that the status quo, the old
venerated community life-pattern, must not be touched.

Against this massive spiritual immobility, the future struggled, as it always struggles, to come to birth.

This was no academic discussion group debating the abstract proposition: "Resolved that every child has the right to four years' schooling beyond the eighth grade." This was a fight over action to be taken now — going into debt for an ideal, an ideal which is almost the only primal urge for which humanity need never blush — sacrifice by the old, to give children a better chance.

Those voters who believed the town could never raise the extra money required for building and upkeep, they were sincere in their mournful admission that, what with wretched train-service, hardly any automobiles, the nearest existing public high school might almost as well be fifty miles off as the actual twelve miles of unplowed winter snow-drifts, and spring mud-holes. But with even more bitter sincerity, they listed our community's urgent material needs one after another. The hill roads should be resurfaced, or they would wash out to stony trails. Care for the sick poor was more costly every year. But above all the bridges!

In a mountain town with flash-floods roaring over the banks of its water-courses after hard rains, bridges have an imperious priority. Our bridges needed reinforcement, not only from recurring high water, but against the great tonnage of modern traffic. It would be dangerous not to rebuild them. It would take all the resources of a poor mountain town to keep our bridges in repair. To add to that expense the enormous cost of a new school — insane!

The tangible needs of the body and the impalpable needs of the mind and spirit stood up to see which was the stronger. The material needs outshouted the ideal. They sounded real and actual. The little flickering flame of responsibility for the future of the town's children died down to a faint glimmer in the hearts of the men and women whose votes would in a few moments make the decision. Those who had longed and worked for the school sat silent, disconcerted by the predicted crashing of the bridges, loud in their ears. What could be said against that?

Then up sprang Patrick Thompson — yes, you are right in guessing from his name that he was Irish, was Catholic, was only one generation away from those who drank stinking water from the ship's barrel, long strings of green slime hanging down to the floor, as they struggled on towards the New World and Vermont. He had worked his way up to partnership in one of our two grocery stores. What education he had — it was sound — he had received in our public schools. We usually saw him in a white apron, standing behind the counter, selling sugar and tea. We have never forgotten and we never will let our children forget how he looked that day, his powerful shoulders squared, his hands clenched. We still remember his exact words, intense as the flame of a blowtorch: "We are being told that our town cannot afford to keep its bridges safe and also to provide for its children a preparation for life that will give them a fair chance alongside other American children.

"That's what we are being *told*. Not one of us here really believes it. We just can't think what to say back. But suppose it were true — Then I say, if we have to choose, 'Let the bridges fall down!' What kind of a town would we rather have, fifty years from now — a place where nitwit folks go back and forth over good bridges? Or a town with brainy, well-educated people capable of holding their own in the modern way of life? You know which of those two is really wanted by every one of us here. I say, '*Let the bridges fall down!*' "

He took his seat in silence, the American citizen, the Celt, whose grandparents had lived in enforced ignorance.

It was a turning point in the life of our town. We knew it was. So we spoke not a word. We sat silent, thinking. And feeling. What we felt, with awe, as though we saw it with our physical eyes was in all our human hearts, the brave burning up to new brightness of the ideal.

Presently the Moderator said in the traditional phrase, "Any further discussion?" The silence was unbroken. Then "Forward your ballots." In a silent line the grave-faced voters moved slowly towards the ballot box, each hand holding a white paper.

The school was built. Years later it burned, and was replaced, almost without opposition, by an even better one. The first battle had been conclusive. As we old-timers look at the building, our hearts bursting with thanksgiving, we can see clearly as if actually carved on the lintel, the words "LET THE BRIDGES FALL DOWN!"

Patrick Thompson has long been in his grave. But he walks at the head of every graduating class in our high school . . . a school for poor as well as rich, open to every race, to every creed, to everybody.

What chance have we — have we any chance at all, we men and women on the globe? — to carry forward the standard which we here call the Vermont tradition, but which is so infinitely more than Vermont's? Our nation calls it the American ideal, but it is infinitely more than American. World-wide, it is the democratic spirit, and that is another name for the guess, the mighty hope, that human beings are capable of uniting to help each other live.

Without that hope what comfort is there in the bewitching, magical human capacity for inventing useful machines and exploring the earth and water and sky, and all that in them is? The settled disbelief that men and women can ever find it more natural to help each other survive and be happy than to exploit one another — that is the death of hope and of the wish to live.

No one can deny that some degree of human solidarity exists. In passing moments of excited emotion, any group of any men and women will act together for an hour or two to help others trapped in a burning building. But human life is not made up of crises which sweep people out of themselves. Can solidarity last day after day, year after year, as the framework for that part of human life which is done in common with others? Not among a few members of the great human family, who, having ideas in common, can act in common. Can the whole of the family ever learn to act for the good of the whole, for that whole made up of ordinary men and women who have in common only that they are human?

❅   ❅   ❅

Anyone who has been part of such solidarity, not as an ideal, a theory, something in a book, a spiritual aspiration, but as a living fiber in everybody's heart — he knows that we have a chance. A fighting chance. Enough. What more is needed for any heart with courage in it?

THE GENTRY'S LAST STAND

Herein the complete statement
from which I deduced
"Chat Between Neighbors."

How It All Began

LET me set down here a brief recapitulation of the reasons for including in this book the story of events which took place long before Vermont was settled. Only the passage of time turns generally held standards into a tradition. Hence the basis of every tradition lies far back in past years. Events and attitudes of those long-ago years decide the shape and color of the institutions and of the attitudes which we call a way of life.

For Vermonters such an event was the struggle to own the land they tilled, with all the social and political implications of landowning in their century. Vermont character and ideals cannot be understood without knowing about the eighteenth-century dispute with the New York landlords. But that dispute cannot be understood without knowing about what led up to it. Our fight was small on the stage of history but decisive for our community then and in the hundred and ninety years since then, because it settled, once for all, which of two contrasting social ideals should prevail here. Those two contrasting ideals have been ever since and are now fighting it out on the huge stage of world history. Hence the land grant dispute has a meaning far wider than its actual events and its literal outcome. In a single act on a small stage, it holds obviously the clue to the underlying motives of many another human drama, shows how inevitable were the parts played by the opposing actor-combatants.

During all of my childhood and youth I had endlessly listened to my old folks talking about early days here and the quarrel with the York State landlords. In my mature years I read the books which all Vermonters read about that dispute. But not till my old age did it occur to me that every one of those folk tales and histories began when the first white settlers walked across the boundary line of our State. You'd have thought that those pioneers had crystallized out of the air, or had sprung full-grown from the top of the Green Mountain pine trees, instead of having had, like all of us, a long line of forebears back of them who had passed on to them the standards by which they lived.

I felt personally well acquainted with the individual quirks and twists of character of my Vermont great-greats. But what kind of great-greats had *they* had? The old Vermont stories gave me their names but nothing about their personalities. Nor did any of the books cover this point. At least I couldn't find one which did.

So I began to look for evidence. First I got together the usual nucleus of history books collected by everybody who wants to find out something about a special aspect of the past. Widening my search from this shelf of conventionally bound volumes, I began to look up, one by one, the volumes or annals or other documents quoted in the text or mentioned in the footnotes of these scholarly books. Not one of these sources was based on interest in what I was looking for, the general outlook on life of the first Vermont settlers compared to the general outlook on life of the big landowners of the Province of New York. I found what I wanted in casual scraps. In these tomes of impersonal, legal, political and social statements, I caught a glimpse, once in a while (as in the Last Will and Testament of the father of Gouverneur Morris), of a human being speaking out his mind; or heard a human voice crying out from two centuries ago, like that of the New York tenant farmer fighting off the New York sheriff — "I will die before I give up."

It was a little like hunting for the pieces of a long-ago-lost jigsaw puzzle. One piece was drawn out from under a pile of legal papers, another came from the autobiography of an impecunious "gentlewoman" writing down her memories to ease her mind of an old grudge as well as to earn in a genteel way an addition to her small income. Or perhaps one sentence was taken out from the twenty volumes of the papers of a Massachusetts governor of the seventeenth century, and another sentence from the book on botany of an eighteenth-century Swedish botanist.

One by one the pieces were located, those scattered bits of the picture I needed to see. In itself not one of them meant very much, but as, through the years of work on this book, they grew in number — well, see for yourself in this section of the book how they look when laid out so that they fit together.

Prenatal Influences

TIME out of mind, men have battled for and against each of those contrasting life patterns. For us, with our background of English history and romance, the Norman Conquest is apt to stand out, at first thought, as a unique example of a nation's subjugation by warrior overlords. But of course it was only a single episode in the long chronicle of western civilization, where, sooner or later, repression has been answered by revolt, where revolt has seldom won the first battle, has always won some measure of long-run success. The names and immediate issues change, yet always it is essentially the same struggle.

Often the clash has been expressed in two or three simple words, as when Zapata's Mexican peon insurrectos rallied under the cry of "Land and Liberty!" Or centuries before that, in 1351, when the plain folk of Kent and East Anglia rose with passion against what they called "servile land tenures," burned manor houses, assassinated "landlords and lawyers" (note the grouping) and in masses marched on London armed and warlike.

At other times the argument is on the level of constitutional theory, as in this proclamation:

> Be it declared and enacted by this Parliament and by the Authority of the same, that the People of this Nation and of all the Dominions and Territories thereunto belonging, are and shall be and are hereby Constituted, Made, Established, and Confirmed to be a Commonwealth and Free State by the *Supreme Authority of their Nation, the Representatives of the People* in Parliament, and by such as they shall appoint and constitute as Officers and Ministers, for the good of the People and that without any King or House of Lords.

To our ears those downright phrases sound like hammerstrokes from our American Revolution. Not at all. They were given out by the then Government of Great Britain in London in 1649. But the mistake is natural. The line of descent is close. Jefferson and Patrick Henry had steeped their minds in Locke's

Treaties on Civil Government, and John Locke, son of a Round-head soldier, was spiritual heir to the best political thought of the Long Parliament.

Cromwell's energy and military genius broke royalist resistance on the battlefield, and for a time he stood acknowledged head of the Parliamentary party. But his "Commonwealth and Free State" ended before he did. He was a practical administrator, with little patience for tedious debate and factional disorder. So he drifted — or felt himself forced by the urgency of public business — into ruling by military despotism. After his death came the swing-back to the reaction of the Stuart Restoration.

That swing-back never took place in New England. There the settlers, almost without exception, had brought across the Atlantic those ideas of republican government, those separatist religious convictions which in the homeland were to stiffen back-bones, first in protest, finally in open revolt against Royal Preroga-tive claimed by Charles I, and the Established Church of Arch-bishop Laud. In the new land these republican ideas took root, flourished abundantly, developed mightily and were never cut down by reaction.

The Pilgrim Fathers were plain farm and village people. Many of them came from yeoman stock. Through bad navigation or in-tention (accounts differ on this point) the *Mayflower* landed them beyond the limits of the territory in which they had legal right to settle. Miles of trackless forest lay between them and any colony organized under British law. Many more miles of angry waves separated them from King and Parliament. Politically they were thrown on their own resources. Fortunately they were re-sponsible, sober men, fully aware that every-one-for-himself anarchy meant death for all. Their one slim chance for survival lay in working together. Hence the Mayflower Compact.

They did survive, and gradually during those early years of trial and error, hardship, near-starvation, they learned to ex-press the spirit of the Compact in a framework of orderly daily life.

All this is true but it does not follow that the Pilgrims were the inventors of democratic government, universal education or ownership of home and fields by the small farmer or villager instead of by an upper-class landlord. Historians have found traces of each of these lines of thought long before the seventeenth century. Neither do the Pilgrims deserve all the credit for developing and passing those ideas on to you and me. The little Plymouth Colony never grew populous or powerful. After the Great Migration got under way in the 1630's, New England leadership was taken over by the much larger, more energetic, better organized settlements crowded thickly around Boston. Those Massachusetts Bay people were opinionated. Doubtless they were ready to try any Plymouth method of doing things — provided that it harmonized with their own fixed conception of the way things *ought* to be done. Not otherwise.

But for this book the much-debated question as to which of them began what has little importance. What does have extreme importance is that — a century later — when the future leaders of Vermont were growing out of boyhood they found certain civic institutions accepted by their parents and neighbors, no more questioned than that water runs downhill.

First of these unquestioned principles of group life was the direct, grass-root democracy of Town Meeting. In New England, a "town" (more or less like a township in other parts of the United States) was, and is, the standard basic political unit. Its limits were always made small enough to allow any citizen to go, a-foot or a-horseback, once a year to the Town Hall. They did go. They still get up from sickbeds to be present. Today, just as three-hundred-odd years ago, they work off steam at Town Meeting, debating every subject conceivably related to community welfare — roads, bridges, taxes, schools. All questions are decided by a majority — one vote to each citizen, no matter how many acres he owns or who his grandfather was.

In early days the town was rather like a little sovereign republic. Now in the twentieth century some of its original powers have been absorbed by the state. Those which remain are jealously guarded. Although Town Meeting debate is sometimes narrow, prejudiced, often wanders away from the subject, it very seldom falls below an honest effort to express conviction. I have never known a demagogue to get anywhere at all, either by bribery or browbeating. In fact every year on the first Tuesday in March, when I take my place among the other citizen-governors of Arlington, Vermont, what comes to my mind is this quotation from Thomas Jefferson, no mean judge of political institutions: "I felt the ground shake under my feet at my first contact with New England Town Meeting."

There is no reason to suppose that the men of Plymouth, or Boston, or Dorchester realized at first how much political dynamite was hidden in this innocent-seeming device. Possibly — probably — they adopted it as a simple obvious way of getting the neighbors together in united action. In the old country they had had two direct personal experiences with the responsibility for the affairs of their own communities. Those of them who were Separatists (most of the early New Englanders were) had themselves governed their own congregations. Those of them who, in England, had belonged to the class of yeomen (most of them did) had, at the village level, been responsible for enforcing the rules and customs of the manor where they lived. It would be giving them too much credit to claim that these plain men had clear, long-range, reforming foresight. It would be giving them too little credit to overlook the lasting quality of the expedients they devised when they found themselves free from the dead weight of precedent, of customs which had become laws, not because they were or ever had been just, but merely because, in the phrase commonly used there in describing them, "the memory of man runneth not to the contrary." That is, solely because they were ancient.

Second on their "must" list was the program of schools for everyone. Here again the New Englanders did not so much originate a social theory as organize the machinery to fill a need which everybody recognized. Wherever the Reformation had destroyed the authority of bishops and canon law, throwing the responsibility for soul-salvation on the individual, it was realized that every individual must be able to read the Bible for himself. Universal elementary schooling was the logical answer. In Holland, the Pilgrims had seen such a system. In New England the religious motive was reinforced by the certainty that even a wood-chopper's boy would, when he grew up, be saying his say and casting his vote at Town Meeting about how to spend tax-money . . . best hammer a little learning into his head while young.

In the seventeenth century, "schools for everyone" naturally meant schools for every boy — though surprisingly early, to judge from family letters, women even on back-country farms learned to read and write, and to spell at least no worse than their menfolks. Naturally also, what with lean returns from thin, rocky soil, with cash hard to come by, the instruction given in these first public schools was (by today's standards) often of pitiably poor quality. Again, every parent who could possibly afford it was called upon to help out either with money or labor, or firewood, or boarding the teacher.

Such weak points have been made much of by certain historians who feel that because New England was outrageously overpraised in nineteenth-century textbooks (written by New Englanders) it is their happy duty to whittle it down to size. Every reasonable person approves that whittling process, whenever it is needed. But down to size — not far below size! With all their efforts, the debunkers have failed to dig up a case where the school door was slammed in the face of any boy because his father was too poor to take his turn at boarding the teacher or to draw in a load of winter firewood. Neither have they explained away the fact that, as resources increased, New England schools steadily grew better, more widely distributed; that their shortcomings even in their worst days were caused only by the delay in carrying out an ideal accepted without any reservations. This ideal of schooling for all was very expressly repudiated by seventeenth- and eighteenth-century England, and hence by the Province of New York. Dr. Andrew Draper, for many years head of the State system of public education in the State of New York, states officially that when the British conquered the Dutch and took over from them, in the 1660's, the Dutch system of elementary education for common people in New York *was stopped*, "in consequence of the apprehension on the part of the nobility that common schools would nourish and strengthen the spirit of independence."

Another item which is not to be explained away, and which became part of the Vermont tradition, as opposed to the New

York colonial tradition, is the fact that as the American frontier moved westward, the surest way of tracing the spread of New Englanders was to follow the chain of tax-supported little red schoolhouses, binding together by a common cultural foundation our sprawling settlements all across the continent from the Atlantic to the Pacific.

The third liberalizing element in group life worked out by these early settlers was a revolutionary innovation then, but today so taken for granted that nobody thinks of it. The innovation was this: that a working farmer, a blacksmith, a stonemason, or anybody, should have the right to buy a meadow or a wood-lot, or a cottage, or a farm, and own it, own it as absolutely and securely as he might own an ax or a scythe or a suit of clothes. He might sell it, all or a part of it, if he saw fit, and (except for his widow's dower right) might pass it on after his death to any-body he chose.

Scholars will object to my putting the label of "innovation" on this notion that you yourself can be sole owner of the fields you plow or the house you live in. They will point out that by 1620 *some* land here and there in England was held by tenures "substantialy equivalent to full ownership." Maybe one of them to make the situation perfectly clear might use the term "semi-alodial." Indeed, unless you keep a firm grip on the reins, any historical expert or legal specialist on this subject will take the bit in his teeth and race away, century after century, through the development of real-property law, coming to a stop only on the right of eminent domain with its "limitations implied" on the conception of freehold.

Now the purpose of this book is not to trace the minute shad-ings in the sequence of legal and political changes, but instead, as best I can, to find out how the character and tradition of New Englanders, especially Vermont New Englanders, were molded by what ordinary men and women thought and felt about the conditions of life as they lived it. But to protect the sensibilities of historical scholars, I withdraw that word "innovation" — or rather I reserve it for use a few lines farther on.

Certainly no historian will deny that the usual pattern of landed estate in seventeenth-century England was very much like a very old patchwork quilt, pieced together at random, in the course of many centuries, without design. The terms of leases held for adjoining farms — often for adjoining fields on the same farm — varied greatly, one from another. In all that incoherent jumble, a single general rule stood out. Everywhere (or, if the specialists insist, "substantially everywhere") the earning-their-living folk had to pay rent to landlords — often exorbitant rent.

Possibly some of the Plymouth or Massachusetts men knew about one or another of the very few, out-of-the-ordinary cases in England where this general rule did not apply. If so, that knowledge must have been a comfort to them, for they were Englishmen and Englishmen are always heartened to find a precedent for doing what they intend to do anyway. However that may be, they did it. And this *was* their innovation: they made it the rule, not the rare, rare exception, that anybody, not only a member of the gentry, but anybody, had the right to buy, hold and sell real estate just as we always (should I say "substantially always"?) do today. A price is agreed on for clear title. You pay the price. You own the land — no matter what your social status.

Why did they do it? Have we any evidence to show that those early settlers had purposeful theoretic objections to the exclusive right of upper-class people to own land?

Captain John Smith, he of the Pocahontas legend, after he left Jamestown, explored and mapped the New England coast. In a book he wrote and published in 1614, he says, "Here are no hard landlords to racke us with high rents, or extorted fines to consume us; no tedious pleas in law to consume us with their many years' disputations for Justice. Here every man may be master and owner of his owne labour and land." And he added that it seemed strange to him that in England men should grow poor paying twenty, thirty, forty, fifty shillings rent *yearly* for an acre of land, when "better, or at least as good, ground may be had here and cost nothing but labour."

Smith was no visionary utopian, no theoretic revolutionary, no city-bred artisan's son. He was a plain, practical rolling-stone soldier of fortune who had knocked about, earning his living in many countries. His father was a tenant farmer paying rent to the Lord of the Manor of Willoughbie, and the son John was brought up on that Manor knowing at first hand the relations between Manor Lords and their tenants, and what the tenants felt about their situation. This book about New England was the work of a real-estate promoter, a come-on statement of the advantages of leaving England to settle in the New World. It is of great significance that as early as 1614 he used a reminder of hated grievances in England to stimulate colonization.

John Winthrop, of Massachusetts, had a very different background from that of John Smith. He had been a university student, was a highly successful lawyer with a sizable income. But he too said very much the same thing when he wanted to induce settlement in that colony. "The whole earth is the Lordes garden; and he gave it to the sons of man to be tilld and improved by them; why then should we stand starving for places of habitation. . . ."

Such statements give evidence of widespread hostility to the exploitation of working farmers by landlords in England. What wonder that the plain men of Plymouth and Massachusetts Bay felt no impulse to set up under this blessedly new sky a copy of what they had known under the old sky of England.

Theirs was not a class favored by English law. Members of that class, fathers, grandfathers, or their friends had all suffered, even the most fortunate, through constant day-by-day uncertainty as to their legal rights to the land they cultivated. The English land laws were in a state of flux almost inconceivable to us now. It is dizzying to read in the contemporary documents what a variety of tenures might exist in one farmer's holdings. Landlords, clever lawyers, rival tenant farmers, or just personal enemies, were always on the prowl looking for flaws or faults in records or leases, technical, legal points which might bring profit to them, heavy loss to the holder.

A yeoman farmer, your ancestor perhaps or mine, as he lay dying, could not close his eyes in peace for fear that his wife and children would be forced from the home and the land where he had maintained them. Under a hostile lawyer's subtle search it might turn out (to cite just one of innumerable possibilities) that the best fields of the farm were held by a tenure which gave the Lord of the Manor the right to exact so large a fee upon the tenant's death that his widow would not be able to pay it.

Uncertainty was the least of the tenant's troubles. Often enough, certainty was worse. For many years radical changes had been going on in English agriculture. "Enclosures" — carving out profitable farm units from the old quasi-communal "open fields" — almost always brought hardship to those country people whose status was below that of yeomen, whose claim to a roof over their heads, a garden plot, pasture for a cow, rested on custom rather than on deeds recognized by law. Disaster for all but a few of the yeomen was caused in many regions by the other type of enclosure — turning large tracts of former plow land into sheep pasture. As far back as the reign of Henry VIII, Sir Thomas More, then Chancellor, had deplored this practice:

"Noble men and gentlemen," he wrote, "Yea, and certain Abbots, holy men God wot, not contenting themselves with the yearly revenues and profits that were wont to go to their forefathers and predecessors of their lands . . . leave no ground for tillage; they enclose all pastures; they throw down houses; they pluck down towns [villages] and leave nothing standing but only the church, to make of it a sheepcote."

Economists, looking back objectively, tell us that the enclosure movement led to improved agricultural practice in England and turned marginal land to use that would pay dividends to the landlords. Hence, in the long run, it created much more wealth than it destroyed. That well may be. The fact remains that the way it was carried out caused in its time a horrifying sum of heartbreaking unhappiness.

To be thrown out from houses which for centuries their ancestors had felt to be "theirs," was all the more bitter and horrifying because tradition, so powerful an element in British life, had always led the tenants to believe that they had with the Lord of their Manor a valid *human* relationship as well as a legal one. The relationship was rooted in long-ago feudalism, when the villein swore fealty, and in return the Lord promised protection. Ever since, handed down from father to son, the connection had been close and binding, almost as valid and lasting as a family tie, which is not broken even if it interferes with cash profits.

With the enclosure movement, the Lord, to make more money, ignored all but the legal aspects of his status. The farmers did not submit to eviction without a struggle. In the law-abiding English way, they turned for protection first to the courts. When their cases fell under the jurisdiction of a local manor court, they were lost before they were begun. There the Lord of the Manor had prime influence — yes, even in disputes where he was one of the parties involved. Farmers who had money or influential family connections — few of those who became our New England ancestors had — might band together and get their cases tried in the King's Courts. Here they had a better chance of a fair hearing, but even here no great prospect of success. Only rarely was their plea sound — from the point of view of an upper-class jurist, surveying the scholarly arguments of well-paid professional lawyers.

What then? Did you ever see a cornered mouse, maddened by despair, stop running away, turn, stand and try pitiably to fight for his life against a powerful active cat, twenty times his size? Over and over from 1536 on to 1607, English country people, crazed by helplessness, were driven, contrary to their deepest English instinct, to open revolt against the law, to snatch up whatever weapons they had to fight the enclosures which forced them from their beloved fields into the filthy slums of the cities. Over and over, the powerful soldier-cats, protecting law, order, and property, needed only one pounce, one crunching snap of jaws, and another of these scattered riots "against the King's Peace" was ended.

But not forgotten!

Out of the *Mayflower*, out of the ships which soon followed, came men and women for whom the words "rent" and "lease" were a festering memory. Biologically, spiritually, intellectually, they were close kin to the Parliament party which only a few years later was to deny the divine right of one man to be superior to all other men because of his parents. The people of Massachusetts anticipated that principle by only one further logical step when they denied anybody's right to be, because of his parents, superior to anybody else.

The pioneer civic efforts of colonial Massachusetts were carried out by normally faulty human beings, hence imperfectly. Town Meetings were full of unmannerly, petty disputes, with attempts to bar newcomers' livestock from pasture on the village common, with grumblings about paying the cost of schools for other people's children. There, as everywhere, individuals drove sharp bargains, made grabs for special privileges. When new towns were organized, the well-to-do sometimes banded together to make an unfair profit out of fellow citizens' land hunger. Those who had gained social, political, economic advantages did their acrimonious best to keep others out of them. In standing up for their new rights, the plain people were anything but tactful. They shouted, they stamped, they wangled for votes to force a more even distribution of advantages.

Yet it is fair to note that no one tried to settle questions by other means than elections, that in spite of continual backsliding, always with continued advance, the unwritten code of the New England way of life was being worked out. While it has never quite brought about Emerson's ideal democracy — "where no one blacks another man's boots" — it has in the main, wherever adopted, made it certain that no one shall be locked into a legal or social inferiority. It allows no bolts on the doors of opportunity. They may be closed and heavy, but a strong shoulder can always burst them open. We in Vermont, who value such things, are grateful for this legacy from the Commonwealth of Massachusetts.

We are also thankful that we did not fall heir to a less admirable element in the life of Massachusetts. The seventeenth century was a period when almost everywhere in the western world, religion was equivalent to bigotry. Toleration (again, *almost* everywhere) was considered sinful. Your particular creed alone was the true faith. So far as you had the power, it was your duty to extend your creed, by force and violence, if necessary.

Since only orthodox church members could vote, and since ministers, elders and deacons had immense influence with their congregations, church and state were identical. Thus with the best of intentions, and with no more, indeed much less, than the usual vindictiveness characteristic of the seventeenth century, Massachusetts justices persecuted Baptists, had Quakers whipped at the cart-tail or hanged.

Even then, however, more modern ideas were stirring in a few enlightened minds. Roger Williams believed in toleration, doubted that the King of England had a better title than the Indians to American land and held other crack-brained heresies. He was exiled to Rhode Island. Thomas Hooker was too distinguished and too orthodox to be exiled, not orthodox enough to feel at home in the Boston climate. From the scanty first-hand evidence which has come down to us, he appears to have disliked and mistrusted the close interrelation of civil magistrates and church elders, the narrow limits placed on church membership (hence on the franchise), and in general to have been more concerned with saving souls than with doctrinal hair-splitting, and temporal political power for religious leaders. There was never an open breach. In the 1630's he and his whole devoted, like-minded congregation left their well-established homes in what is now Cambridge, and set off — families, household goods, livestock — in a slow-moving caravan through the forest wilderness to the tiny outpost settlements along the Connecticut River, there to found Hartford.

Did you ever, on a winter walk, watch your pet dog sniffing along a rabbit track, freshly printed in the snow? All goes well until he smells that some other animal — a deer perhaps, or a fox — has cut across the path and gone off at an angle. Then woe and confusion! The poor dog dashes, yapping from one fascinating scent to the other. But at last, if he has outgrown his puppyhood, he lets out a final mournful howl to show that he knows that he cannot follow two trails at once, and that his best chance of success lies in getting on with his rabbit hunt.

Like that schizophrenic dog, I am tempted almost beyond resistance to branch off here, and undertake a step-by-step research into political developments in the Connecticut "River Settlements," because a great deal about them and Thomas Hooker, their guide, counsellor, and pastor, suggests a close spiritual connection with the Vermont tradition. For example, the Fundamental Orders (the framework agreement on which the River Towns based their union government) set up no religious qualifications for voting. Many bottles of ink and reams of paper have been used up to show that this means little, because each component town had its own tests limiting citizenship; or on the other hand that the mere fact of omission means a great deal — might be the planting of a seed-idea, later to grow into the sweeping religious-liberty clause of Vermont's first Constitution. Again, that first Constitution of ours insisted on the "indubitable, unalienable, and indefeasible right of the community to reform, alter or *abolish*" any government so as to promote (in the community's judgment) "the public weal." Speaking before the River Town General Court (Assembly) in 1638 or 1639, Mr. Hooker (so he was always called — perhaps because to give him the title of "Reverend" sounded too much like Established Church of England formality) spelled out and underlined his consent-of-the-governed theory: "The choice of public magistrates belongs unto the people by God's own allowance," he said. "They who have the power to appoint officers and magistrates, it is in their power also to set the bounds and limitations of the power and place unto which they call them." Translated from the quaint three-centuries-old diction that sounds very like Lincoln's "by and for the people."

These and other similarities are striking. Yet there is always danger of adding modern overtones to words used in an earlier period. When Lincoln spoke of "government by the people," he certainly did not dream of including half of "the people" — women. Almost nobody in his time would have done so. When Hooker spoke of "the people," did he mean to include every single one of his neighbors, or did he, instinctively following town ordinances, intend to restrict popular sovereignty to "householders of honest conversation, taking the trinitarian oath"? And just what are we to make of this quotation, "He [Hooker] was not perswaded that the chief magistrate should stand Neuter and tolerate all Religions"? Is the emphasis there intended to be on toleration (unlike the practice of Massachusetts Bay) of a great many shades of belief, or on the necessity of drawing the line somewhere? Possibly an answer can be found in a law of 1642: "If any man, after legal conviction, shall have or worship any God except the Lord God, he shall be put to death." Did Hooker approve or protest against that law? Perhaps no protest was needed. I have found no evidence that this law was ever taken seriously. Certainly we would know about it if any one in Connecticut had been put to death for heresy. To search the old records for information about these and many other questions would be fascinating, but really beyond the limit of my particular rabbit hunt.

This much at least there is space for: as the years went by, what had been a real danger of autocratic rule by magistrates and clergy dropped out of the New England pattern. Even more to the purpose of this book, when the time came to frame a government for the new settlements in Vermont, the members of the Windsor Convention — all men of substance and standing — agreed to admit to voting rights men with no wealth at all. They also voted to forbid for all time the establishment of any tithe-supported church. Some influence in their background must have prepared them to enact legislation radical far beyond the working average of 1777. In large majority they had been brought up in the West Connecticut hill-country. Is it not distinctly possible that at least the first foundation stones on which they built their open-minded, future-welcoming, social faith were laid by the long-dead Thomas Hooker?

All through the rest of the seventeenth century, on into the eighteenth, the River Towns increased and multiplied. Connecticut men, women and children spread out into the valley of the Naugatuck, the Housatonic, and the hills beyond.

So now we have finished our long detour and have come back to the homeland from which, before many years, those eager young settlers of Chapter 2 were to head north to the Hampshire Grants. In this remote hill and valley country of Western Connecticut and Western Massachusetts in the eighteenth century, the outside world had intruded so little that something like a community habit of mind had grown up, from within. It was so fixed that it inclined even those violent individualists who, taken together, made up the citizen-group, to agree more often than not on the elements needed to make public and private life orderly and satisfying.

They were the ones who made the decisions. They were astonishingly self-governing. The government in faraway London had been much too busy to bother its head about rules and regulations for a handful of backwoodsmen. First it had had the Civil War to settle, then came the Protectorate's involvement in Europe's balance of power politics. At the Restoration, the Connecticut colonists were fortunate enough to petition Charles II when he was newly back on the throne. His long poverty-stricken exile was fresh in his memory. He was still walking very carefully, anxious to appear everybody's friend. The royal charter he gave the Connecticut people confirmed in effect all their laws and customs, and granted them almost complete political independence.

Those laws and customs, confirmed by royal charter, had of course grown out of basic assumptions common to all New England as to the nature of the good life. But years of local self-government had molded their development until they differed, always a little, sometimes notably, from the practice of Eastern Massachusetts, which was much more obviously under British power.

Thus a young man of Connecticut, just of age in the year the Fundamental Orders were signed, would by 1685 have grown into a graybeard of sixty-seven, and all his mature life he would have been familiar with, conformed to, approved the standards, not at all of Boston or Salem, but of Western Connecticut.

What were those standards? To begin with the material side: thrift, few comforts, no luxury, small farms worked by the owner and his family.

After the basic material necessities — schools. Basic education for all of as good quality as could be provided was considered a public responsibility.

Consideration of religion came third in their minds, for by this time the flame of rabid sectarianism was burning low everywhere. At no time had it burned hotly in Connecticut. Only down along the coast around New Haven (different in origin, and politically long separate from the Hartford government) had the inhabitants ever even faintly resembled the thin-lipped joy-killers imagined by modern cartoonists. By the middle eighteenth century, there as elsewhere, the old blue laws were becoming dead letters on the statute books. Already church membership had been extended to cover all baptized persons — a step radical beyond a modern imagination to understand. Soon permission would be granted — this too an enormous step toward toleration — for individual church congregations "soberly to differ and dissent" from the Established Church. More and more people had begun to doubt whether slightly unorthodox views about the proportion of Faith and Works needed for a State of Grace must be punished by hell-fire and brimstone in the life to come.

With the passing of years, the hardening of arteries and brain channels, political views had been somewhat trimmed down from Hooker's popular-sovereignty radicalism, but the west-country men were still set against any government imposed from above, either by bishops or royal governors. They also stuck so doggedly to the belief that Parliament "had the right of it" in its quarrel with King Charles, that for years they successfully gave sanctuary to the regicide judges Whalley and Goffe. Never having known at close range the by-no-means-always republican or democratic methods with which Cromwell had hacked his way through the black and dismal problems of his later years, they kept him in mind as a symbol of the whole Parliamentarian movement — not as dictatorial Lord Protector, but as the invincible leader of his psalm-singing Ironsides, when squadron after squadron they wheeled, charged and broke the Royalist army at Naseby.

That Cromwell they dimly felt to be a champion, the symbol of their most cherished standard of all. This was a social standard: success — not because one man or another happened to be your father — but because you yourself earned it.

I chose the date 1685 for a survey of the ideas likely to travel along with the settlers who, later, journeyed up to Vermont, because in that exact year we have recorded evidence of still another rooted conviction. This one says an angry and determined "No."

James II, less adroit than his elder brother, more straight-driving in his bid for power, came to the throne. All over his kingdom he revoked ancient privileges to towns and corporations granting liberties which he thought dangerous. His wish was to replace local self-government with an administrative system depending directly on the Crown. In line with this policy, his agent called for the surrender of Connecticut's charter.

It was for that colony one of the greatest dangers in its history. As practical, political realists, the members of the Hartford General Court knew that any force they might assemble could not stand a minute against the King's regiments. Resistance was out of the question. But they would try at least to make the best terms they could. They sent King James a petition to this effect: first of all, they begged him to allow them to continue as they were. But, so ran their appeal, if they must be forced to go under the legal rule of another colony, let it be the government of Massachusetts. *Not of New York.*

King James had plans for a wider consolidation than the colonists foresaw. But arrangement for it took time, and, as any schoolboy knows, by 1688 he had so overbid his hand that he was no longer King of England, but a refugee in France, pensioner of Louis XIV. Connecticut's old Charter continued in force until by the advance of time it was outdated, and was replaced by a Constitution voted by the "*People* of the *State*." But this inconclusive little flurry is of great interest to Vermonters. We know that in many ways Connecticut people did not care much for Eastern Massachusetts and its government. Men were still living in 1685 who had made the long perilous journey through the wilderness and endured the first winter's cold and hunger just because they did not like the way things were run in the Bay Colony. Why then did they go on record as preferring union to Massachusetts rather than to New York? What made them so certain that they would prefer living under a government they knew they disliked rather than under that of the Province of New York? The answer to that question will need several chapters.

What's Bred in the Bone

IN 1660 England swung back to "normalcy." The bulk of its citizens wanted a change. They were sick and tired of both the good and the bad points of the republican experiment so eagerly welcomed only eleven years before by John Milton. Somehow the "commonwealth governed by the people's representatives for the good of the people" had resulted in a repressive, army-supported dictatorship. Cromwell was dead. On the throne sat a good-natured, rather battered, not at all scrupulous rake in his early thirties. Unlike most king's sons, Charles II had lived for years as a human being, not as a potentate with a special charter from God. Throughout his youth he had been cold-shouldered by well-to-do, powerful people, who were not at all sure that he would ever be more than a poverty-stricken exile. Nor had he himself been sure of this. Often he had been uncertain of his next meal, homeless, shabby, helplessly dependent on grudging handouts. Naturally then he was glad to compromise in return for the Crown. His "Act of Indemnity and Oblivion" promised pardon to all, except the few directly responsible for his father's death.

But the rural gentry, who made up the majority of his Parliament, were in no mood for compromise. Partly in a burst of loyalist emotion, more in a spirit of revenge, they made their enemies — their late oppressors — suffer in every way not blocked by the King's proclamation. They restored bishops to their sees, to their revenues, to their authority; they restored landowning squires to their autocratic legal power as justices of the peace; they excluded from civil office and from the universities everyone who was not an active communicant of the Established Church; they forbade dissenting religious meetings in public; they decreed that no clergyman or schoolmaster should come within five miles of a city or corporate town unless he would swear that he would not "at *any* time endeavor *any* alteration in Government of either Church or state," thus leaving the nonconformist town folk with the hard choice — either to violate their convictions, or to let their children grow up illiterate. The country districts, of course, needed no such thought-control laws. In them the justice-of-peace squires could be trusted to enforce orthodoxy.

In those honeymoon days of the early Restoration, Royalist enthusiasm ran high. Many of the war-scarred, elderly cavaliers believed that all they had fought for was now won. They were wrong. This wave of reaction stopped short of vindicating all that is implied in the doctrine of kingship by Divine Right. Instead it established, until well on into nineteenth-century England, the *de facto* rule of the upper classes, of wealth expressed in terms of land-holding.

What have these epic, ancient goings-on to do with the small-scale scuffle, a century later, between two American colonies as to land titles in Vermont? Everything! In 1664 the English took over from the Dutch the territory drained by the Hudson and the Delaware Rivers. Since this was a "province, conquered from a Christian nation," it became (by an old English law still valid at that date) the personal property of the King, to do with as he wished, without interference from Parliament. Charles passed it as a gift to his brother James, Duke of York, who proceeded to organize it according to his conception of the ideal form of government.

Dr. Julius Goebel, Jr., Professor of Law, Columbia University, a recognized authority, describes the situation as follows:

The substitution of English in the place of Dutch institutions in New York, during the last decades of the seventeenth century, can be understood only if we take into account two circumstances; first that the province had been conquered by force of arms, and secondly that the whole scheme of government and administration introduced by the conquerors, was planned and carried out by the Stuart kings, whose philosophy of the state and the functions of the crown was exceedingly reactionary. Imagine, if you will, a return of the Hohenzollern dynasty to power in Germany, and I think you will be able to visualize the situation in England after 1660. The Stuarts were bent upon the preservation of all the medieval traditions which tended to exalt the crown above the other departments of the government. At home in England, conditions did not favor the realization of their dreams, but it was otherwise in New York.

Except around Manhattan Island and Albany, the Dutch had done little to establish settlements. They had tried to people the long gap between these points by making extensive grants on both sides of the Hudson to individual proprietors who in turn were supposed to fill them with settlers, but few of the patroonships had prospered. However, the English governors were not discouraged. The principle of large holdings by a few rich men, with working farmers subordinated to landlords, seemed so right to them that they made it the basis of their land policy. So far as new-world conditions would permit, the English Manor, with its archaic rules and customs, and its "exceedingly reactionary" social atmosphere, was to be transplanted to the Province of New York.

Progress toward this end was slow at the start, but steady. In 1683, the New York Colonial Assembly went on record with this resolution: "That from hence forward Noe Lands Within this province shall be Esteemed or accounted a Chattle, or personal Estate but an Estate of Inheritance according to the Custome and practice of his Majesties Realme of England."

Lawyers tell us that this is nothing to get excited about; that the phrase "estate of inheritance" limits nothing except freedom to divide "real property" into small holdings by will; that after all, this endorsement of entail and primogeniture continued in force for a mere ninety-nine years only; that the rest of the resolution is still sound in principle, since the conception of personally possessing land as a chattel is and always has been "quite unknown to English law."

This well may be true in abstract theory, for every cult has its own nucleus of esoteric doctrine, baffling to the uninitiated. But plain Connecticut farmers hearing the news from across the boundary line had no training in the fine points of legal terminology. To them "personal estate" in lands such as they had, seemed reasonable, desirable, to be taken for granted — and the proposal to change this according to the "Custome of his Majesties Realme" sounded an ominous note. They were quite familiar then with what now is known only by historians after long study — the meaning to working farmers of the "Custome of His Majesties Realme" in terms of daily legal and social subordination to landowning gentry. From what their older generation had told them, from reports of people newly come from England to settle in New England, from what they read (for they were all literate) about English land tenure, they were sure they wanted no part of it. It was in 1685, just two years after they had heard about this New York resolution, that they begged King James, if he was set on revoking Connecticut's independence, at least not to put them under the government of New York.

Eighty-five years later, the descendants of those Connecticut farmers had a great deal more to justify their alarm at such a merger. By that date the New York idea had developed to a degree beyond anything which their ancestors could have imagined. Nor was there any guesswork in the information the Western Connecticut men had about living conditions in the province next door to them. Every step in the Frankenstein-like growth of the tenant system had been noted at first hand and reported to those back home living on their own land, by three generations of far-roaming observers.

Something in the air, the food — or could it have been the stimulating vitamin of self-governing independence? — made these West Connecticut men energetic, restless, ingenious, resourceful. Whenever farm work was slack, they turned their hands to producing things to sell, sold them cheaper than anybody else, hustled out to find more buyers than those in their immediate neighborhood. No natural barriers shut them out from the Province of New York. Today, on a vacation motor trip, a longish half hour takes us from Poughkeepsie to Amenia, with Sharon, Connecticut, six miles further on. Or if, coming from the west, we cross the Hudson and drive east through Rhinebeck, only a roadside marker tells us, after some thirty miles, that we have passed the state line. In a few minutes we are in Lakeville, then in Salisbury — a district which sent many of its young people up to settle Vermont in the 1760's.

To be sure, there were no smooth-purring motors, or hard-surfaced roads — for that matter in the eighteenth century there were hardly any roads at all. Those pushing Connecticut traders with their long sinewy legs needed no roads. A forest trail from one isolated farm home to the next was all they asked.

In vain the landlord class tried to bar them out. One early lease specifies that if the tenant let a strange trader into his house overnight he will be "in pain of forfeiting all conditions granted to him, and to be ejected as a perfidious man." Their objection was natural. If the tenants on their land had any money to buy things with, they claimed, by the sacred principle of hereditary right, that the place for it was in the landlord's cash box. However, supervision was too difficult, enforcement was impossible. This early attempt to set up an exclusive "company store" proved unworkable. As law, it lapsed, but the wish and intention which underlay it continued. New York ruling classes hated all New Englanders, and especially Connecticut peddlers.

There was more to that hatred than the loss of retail profit. When one of these "drawling impudent levelers" paid a visit to the tenants on a Hudson Valley farm, who could tell what pernicious, unsettling ideas he might bring, with his talk about plain folk over the line owning their own farms, making laws for themselves at Town Meeting, about free schools for all children, those of poor families too, about sawing out boards for yourself from your own trees, about being able to sell your own farm if you wanted to, and keep for yourself a price that covered the work you had put into it? "Why, the unbridled democrats acted as if they considered themselves as good as anybody!"

Angry sputtering was a waste of breath. Nothing could stop the traffic — not even keeping the tenant farmers so poor that they had practically no cash. These persistent house-to-house salesmen were rightly called "traders." They took goose-feathers to pay for a comb; they traded an ax for wool. Cheese bought calico, or a mirror; or — most vicious attack on propertied landlords who were also shrewd men of commerce — they handled the really profit-making item of fur.

Landowners might fume and curse — little enough the peddlers cared for that. They kept on stepping briskly along the

dim forest paths, well-fed, full of jokes and lively talk, afraid of
nobody. And what they had in those great packs! Knives, pins,
knitting needles, buttons, tin pots and kettles — so much lighter
to handle than the heavy iron ones — ribbons, lengths of cloth.
Even to see the pack opened was a treat for a lonely tenant
family sunk in the backwoods! They brought the news, listened
to neighborhood gossip. Likely enough, as events turned out,
the landlords were correct in fearing that their visits helped to
fan local discontent. Certainly when a trip was finished, they had
a great deal to tell the home folks about how farmers fared under
the system of land tenure in the Province of New York.

Travelers' tales are often spiced. It is only human nature to
pass over the humdrum normal, to turn the spotlight on the
exceptional, the thrilling, especially on the shocking. In this case
not even the mildest distortion was needed to thrill and shock
listeners in Western Connecticut and Western Massachusetts.
Modern historians, who have searched through eighteenth-century land records of the mid-Hudson valley, agree that these
returning peddlers would have been sticking closely to average
provisions of land-leases there if they had summed up the complicated legal rigmarole of "conveyances with reservations, du-
rable leases, letting and hiring forever, leases for two lives in
being, half- or quarter-sale rights, distraint, reversion, mining,
milling, timber-rights" somewhat as follows:

"The big New York owners are willing to sell some of their
land — a little — what they *call* 'sell.' But you have to promise
them and their heirs a fixed rent every year, FOREVER. D'ye
hear that? Rent to be paid '*forever*.' It's down in black and white
in the leases. If the value goes up and you want to sell your rights
to someone else, they take such a big cut out of the new price
that your profit is mighty slim. *They* can't lose. And of course
the new tenant has to sign the same sort of one-sided agreement.
But mostly they won't sell, on any terms. There's more money
for them in renting. Leases can be for as short as a year, or for as
long as you and your wife live. If you don't stick close to the
terms of your lease, any time, the landlord can throw you out and
take over. And the rules are pretty strict. You can't cut a tree
unless he lets you, you have to grind your corn at his mill, he

keeps a tenth part of the meal, and when a lease runs out, he can jack up the rent as high as he wants. Anything you've done to build up the farm is *his* good luck, not yours."

With such a prospect, is it any wonder that settlers in the New Hampshire Grants felt that New York's claim to their land was a threat, dark, ominous, and immediate?

The story of the "Land Grant Dispute" is usually told either with so little detail that its meaning is lost, or with so much that the reader loses his way. The average textbook for a college course in American history, occupied as it is with the conquest of Canada and the taxation trouble with England, can spare only a paragraph or two to this (so it appears to the editor) insignificant local quarrel.

"After the end of the French and Indian Wars (1763)," so may run its bare account, "the land stretching from the upper Connecticut River to Lake Champlain was for the first time safe for settlers. Families (mostly from Western Connecticut, but some from Western Massachusetts, and a few from Rhode Island) bought farms from the Governor of New Hampshire, who said he had a legal right to sell. They moved in, built houses, barns, trails and roads, cut down trees to make clearings for fields. Then they heard that the Province of New York denied that the Governor of New Hampshire had any right to sell this land, that it belonged to New York, and that the settlers now living on it would have to pay for their farms over again, or be legally ejected. There was a long dispute about this.

"The settlers, led by Ethan Allen, a tall, rough-spoken frontiersman with a big voice who constantly drank rum and swore a good deal [hardly anything else is ever told about him] refused to pay twice for their land. The claim of New York Colony was confirmed in the Supreme Court of New York. The Vermonters refused to accept this legal decision, and stood off the authority of the law by threats of shooting. Members of the landowning class in New York who held grants of land in the Green Mountains under New York law kept trying to enforce their legal rights. The settlers kept threatening to fight. The American Revolution came along. In the end, New York landlords accepted a small sum of money to give up their claims. Vermont was admitted to the United States. The End."

On the other hand, special histories, written by native Vermonters, cover that period in detail so minute that, from lack of space, they are often forced to compress everything after 1791 into one short, bare, concluding chapter as if nothing had happened here after the end of the dispute with New York landlords. If your interest is keen enough to want all the facts, you can find them by referring to one of the titles listed at the end of this volume. But I shall not attempt a blow-by-blow account. For one thing, too great concentration on "exactly when and precisely where" this or that individual event took place blurs the over-all perspective. And only that long perspective makes it worth your while to know something about the Vermont-New York land grant quarrel. Only as they are linked with the past and lead forward into the future do the events of those years deserve the attention of busy moderns. They certainly were so linked. No short-lived, neighborhood flare-up across a backyard fence could possibly have passed down through the generations the not-to-be-imitated, not-to-be-forgotten throb of proud emotion in the voices of the Vermont older generation, the flare of indignation and exultation on their usually quite ordinary old faces when they speak of the part played by our ancestors in the land grant quarrel.

Something in the story is more vital than its scenes and incidents, stirring though they are. Our own hearts beat faster, our boys and girls listen wide-eyed, intent, fascinated, to that something — barely half understood, but deeply felt — bringing life and fire to the familiar time-worn words. "See children, that monument is to Remember Baker. Right up this road came the York State sheriff with his posse in the black of night to drag Baker away to prison. Away they raced towards Albany, towards the Province where any court would be on their side. And out from low-ceilinged little homes, like our own homes now — all they had in the world — swarmed our great-great-grandfathers to stand up for the right . . . as they saw the right.

"Don't forget that to resist an officer of the law was then a life-and-death offense. Only five or six years before that night of the twenty-first of March, 1772, dozens of farmers in the Province of New York had been put into prison, fined, pilloried, punished, and one upright, kind, hard-working country man condemned to horrible torture for resisting arrest. But our Vermont fore-fathers were not men to take off their hats to any old rules, just because they were dressed up in legal clothes by men who wanted to keep plain people down. That's what they thought New York laws were.

"They knew that Remember Baker's chances for life were slim if he could be carried off to be tried in the law courts of New York Province where rich landowners called the tune, where poor farmers had no chance.

"Two of Baker's neighbors tried instantly to stop the sleigh. Two against many! One of those two was also taken prisoner and carried along towards Albany. The other escaped, gave the alarm, and a messenger was sent off at top speed to collect fighting men farther down the line. They sprang to their horses and came galloping back to cut off the New York party, and were met — all this still in black darkness — by Arlington and Sunderland men racing south to help in the rescue.

"Keep in mind, children, that all these young ancestors of yours knew that they were risking their necks. Not a man of them could be sure that the others would turn out. The safe thing to do was to stay right at home in bed. They had not a minute to deliberate, to call a meeting, to encourage one another, to listen to a speech by a leader they trusted. Nobody told them what to do. Each man knew what to do.

"Look back at them, snatching up their outdoor clothes, reaching for their long-barreled shooting-irons, shouting to their sons to race out to the barn and saddle the horse. They swung them-selves up, and pelted down the road after the sleigh in which the York State officer of the law was carrying off, perhaps to his death, a man who believed as they did, that it should be pos-sible for an American to own the land he plowed. Look back at them across the nearly two centuries — can't you see them, black against the snow, reining in their horses around the sleigh, shout-ing, scuffling, lifting the wounded and bleeding Baker to the back of one of the horses, galloping home through the night, their hearts bright with pride in their courage. . . ."

No, we do not tell any part of that story with the annoyance of somebody complaining about a twice-presented bill from a dishonest grocer. Our voices, like those we heard as children, are shaking with emotion, our gray heads lift, our old faces burn — the children look up at us, taking in, as we did at their age, an impression beyond words.

When a woman leaps out of a tenth-story window, nobody believes a witness who testifies that she had nothing on her mind except that she couldn't manage to do up her hair to suit her that morning. For such an act of desperation we know — anybody knows — there must have been some grave compelling reason, probably going back into her youth.

Just so, there must be more than a commercial reason involved when for twenty years a number of sober, industrious citizens, ordinary farmers, law-abiding men, load their rifles, grimly determined to back up a spokesman who almost froths at the mouth as he shouts out that they are fighting for human dignity and freedom. When they risk their necks in resisting duly authorized officers of law — and when both before and after this long phase of violence they have always been notably self-contained and close-mouthed, with characteristic English distaste for uncontrolled emotion — why then, the statement, sometimes made, that nothing was at stake during the "Hampshire Grants dispute" beyond the title to some partially cleared farms and a not-too-serious money loss, obviously falls short of covering observed facts.

Money was an item — nobody denies it. Like many colonials (George Washington was a notable example), Baker and the Allens owned wild land which they did not expect to cultivate, hoped to sell to later settlers. But saving or making money was not — could not have been — the compelling motive. To take only one instance can anyone imagine for a moment that his friends turned out for that wild, reckless midnight rescue just to help Remember Baker safeguard his possible profit on a land speculation?

Tub of Butter

Woe to the men who add house to house,
    who join one field to another,
Till there is room for none but them
    in all the land!

ISAIAH, V. 8

YOU must have read — all of us have — literary pictures of life on an English Manor in the eighteenth or early nineteenth century. The jolly, red-faced huntin' and fishin' squire is generally presented (though not by Fielding, who knew the breed) as a masterful but kind, good-natured father to his tenants. From him the farmers (as described by Victorian writers nostalgic for good old days) accepted orders, respectfully pulling a forelock in token of contented submission. Like sturdy, rather subnormal sons, the broad-shouldered, simple-minded country folk were thankful to have knowledgeable upper-class superiors take charge of them in a world far too complex for the slow Saxon brains under their flaxen hair. Novelists of this school show the Lady of the Manor as interested in every new baby born among Manor families, dispensing blankets, soup, fuel, medicine, and peremptory good advice on the most intimate family matters to rosy, aproned matrons who curtsied low to see M'Lady honor the poor but picturesque, rose-embowered, thatched cottage with her noble presence.

No need to comment on the accuracy of these pictures. By semantic devices, which you have certainly recognized as such, I have made it plain that, like most moderns, I think a tall lot of fancy nonsense has been talked about beauties in the relationship between human beings who believe themselves born to have others serve them, and those other human beings born into a social order which requires them to do the serving.

All the same. All the same! Those accounts certainly did not tell the whole truth about what British landlords and their tenant farmers thought of one another, but part of the truth they did tell. They painted the picture as it was supposed to be — that is, according to tradition. And tradition never grows up from no root at all.

No matter how often and how greatly political and legal theory and details of organization might change, there can be no doubt that the deep taproot of the English Manor continued to draw its nourishment from feudalism. For centuries that root had produced stem, branches and leaves. Generations of men and women had been born, lived and died on the same land as their fathers. They, their ancestors and the ancestors of their landlords, were all parts of the same ancient system. They looked forward to a common future. As freedom of movement increased, many of the dissatisfied, the rebellious, who could not or would not fit themselves into the pattern forced on them by their birth, had moved away to the growing cities or to the colonies — a form of selective screening which helped to make the residue remaining on rented land even more passive, unimaginative, more inclined to accept life as they found it.

The life offered them was not so hard, judged by the standards of that age. Eighteenth-century French reformers (even Voltaire who had first-hand knowledge) were entirely sincere in holding up for admiration the liberal institutions of England. Compared to French rural workers, those in England lived in sunny freedom. French peasants were much less savagely kept down than those of Prussia. And as for Poland and Russia!

There was almost always a little human warmth in English landlord-tenant relations. To be sure, in districts where change from plowland to sheep pasture offered substantial increase in income, the landlord's benevolence seldom resisted hard cash. Neither could his temper be kept in control when confronted with the crime of rabbit-snaring. And when he lost his temper, there was nothing in the manor tradition which prevented severe beatings for the lower-class man. But, by and large, he and the country population got along not too badly together because as a rule, landlord and tenant had much in common.

Unlike the French nobility, English Lords of the Manor were country people, desired to be country people. The great landed aristocracy, those with fabulous fortunes, with thousands of acres, with gold plate on their tables, with Van Dyck and Reynolds portraits on their walls, and dozens of house servants, the all-powerful, cosmopolitan elegants of their period — even they spent much of their time in the country. Their careless assumption that it was vulgar to haggle over a few pounds no doubt had a restraining effect on the occasional wealthy merchant, buying an estate with an eye on Parliament (an income of three hundred pounds per year *from the land* was prerequisite to a seat in the House of Commons). With a social climber's eagerness to imitate those already arrived and established, he would no more have ventured to break the unwritten rules as to what was and what wasn't "done" than he would have turned out to ride to hounds without a pink coat and hunting boots well polished by his personal servant. But, for good or bad, the influence of the very wealthy, upper-bracket families never touches directly a large number of the ordinary people of any nation; and to understand rural life in eighteenth-century England, we must look rather to the lesser gentry, the country squires whose whole life was lived close to the soil.

Such squires were cut from the same stuff as their farmer tenants. On their rare trips to London, smart city folk found them rustic, awkward, laughably "clumsie." On their return to the fields, they drew a long breath of relief, comforted to be back with their horses, dogs, cows, sheep and farmers. In country life men are drawn together, whether they will or not, by problems they are forced to share. Side by side, day by day, the squire and his tenants struggled with the inevitable ups and downs of producing food from the earth, with sick cows, with too much rain for spring plowing, new crops to be tried out, new breeds of sheep. They lived together under the open sky, summer and winter. Although the peasants were generally forbidden hunting and fishing for themselves, they were often taken along as helpers on a landlord's sporting expedition, and, as subordinates, shared a joy in outdoor life which often was wordless poetry. Together they fought deep snows and floods. Side by side, they watched the coming up of children to take the place of old folks. Effort and experience in common, long continued, make a living bond between human beings, no matter how absurd the theoretical social barriers between them.

Dismiss such traditions from your mind in considering the Hudson Valley manor life. No such links forged of accepted custom, and deep, shared instinct for the soil, bound the New York landed proprietor and his tenants together in spirit. Nor any other bond, except the business connection customary between the man who has something to sell and the man who buys it. In old England the manors had slowly taken shape under the management of landlords reared, generation after generation, in rural life, landlords who had learned through the centuries that their stability depended on skill in their relations with living flesh and blood — animal and human. The New World manors represented an attempt to create, overnight, institutions which in the Old World had grown up as slowly as ancient trees.

One common element did exist on both sides of the Atlantic. The political motive. Members of the English ruling class, shocked to the marrow of their bones by memories of their loss of privilege during the Commonwealth, found it easy to persuade themselves that the following reaction was a Crusade in which it was their duty to uphold Magna Carta and the British Constitution against any revival of Roundhead republican heresy. As the first articles of their creed, they believed that the powers of Parliament were supreme, and that the Gentry *were* Parliament.

With like reasoning the royal governors of New York felt the need of a solid bulwark against subversive infiltration from the New England colonists who were their next-door neighbors.

Dr. Goebel points out that Colonel Nicolls, Commander of the British Army of Occupation and Deputy Governor of New York, "desired to attach to his Master's [the King's] cause men of substance, *not infected with the democratic virus.*" That policy persisted. Almost a hundred years later, in 1772, we find Governor Tryon justifying enormous grants of land to men of money and influence on the ground that: "They will naturally farm out their lands to Tenants, — *a method which will ever create subordination,* and will counterbalance in some degree the general leveling spirit."

But where in the province could fitting candidates for a wealthy landed aristocracy be found? The only "men of substance" were in the cities of Albany and New York. They knew nothing about life on the land, being capable businessmen (Dutch and British and Irish and Scottish) born and bred to skill in buying material objects for less than the price they could get for them.

Nothing is the matter with that skill in its own field. Human history gives ample evidence that it is socially useful. A great deal of our nation's life — of every nation's life — is founded on skill in buying and selling, in finding profitable investments for money already made. To this ability we owe and always will owe a large part of our American comfort, security and pleasure. But like other skills, it is valid only when working with its own materials. The wizard of conveyor-line production may turn out more automobiles at less money than any competitor, but the chances are that a garage hand with never a cent in his blue jeans more than his current wages, is a far better man behind the steering wheel. A famous opera singer may be a flop on roller skates, a fine cook may be baffled by a card catalogue. Just so, these New York shopkeepers, fur-traders, merchants and lawyers, who bought or bribed themselves into the title of Lords of the Manor or great Patentees in the Hudson Valley, showed little aptitude in their new venture. They had plenty of commercial acumen. What they lacked was the essential know-how in personal and human relations.

In fairness it must be acknowledged that much of their failure was beyond their power to avoid. Unlike their English counterparts, they found no accepted local code to guide them, no experienced neighbors close at hand to use as models in solving their unaccustomed perplexities. They could, of course they did, do their best to follow what they had read or been told about conditions in England where the "triumph of landlordism" was by this date an accomplished fact. They can hardly be blamed for ignoring one vital factor standing in the way of transporting Old World customs across the Atlantic. What they overlooked — what nobody took into account before the era of tabulated sociological analysis — is the fact that only a relatively small percentage of any population likes to obey the orders of other people; that a larger number, but still far short of making up the total, can be forced to take orders, but unwillingly, always close to revolt; and that there are some whose desire for personal independence makes them violently detest and resist subordination. Those who liked to obey orders naturally, for the most part, stayed at home in the English countryside.

Settlers in the new continent tended to be drawn from the percentage of the Old World population who had no natural taste for docility. They were unpromising material out of which to mold a contented peasantry. "Pay a hundred dollars for a dog and you own him," so runs the folk aphorism, "a million dollars will not make him wag his tail." New York tenant farmers did little tail-wagging.

Their tongues, however, wagged freely. There was probably exaggeration in the common talk, though plenty of plain truth as well. Tales were told about the false "metes and bounds" used to stretch Indian deeds out of all conscience, about low or non-existent prices paid by the proprietors for acres on which the farmers were now required to make an inflated book-value profit for the owners. It was not affection nor admiration the "subordinate" tenants felt for the man to whom they were obliged in New York Province to pay rent, to give up their best timber, their mill-rights and all the rest. Nor respect.

Someone has said that a despot is more secure when he is hated than when his subjects laugh at him. Among the personal records of everyday life on Hudson Valley Manors in letters, memoirs, diaries preserved by the Dutchess County Historical Society, there are plenty of gay folk satires ridiculing the social pretensions of the would-be "Quality." The following story strikes an often repeated note. "On a Sunday morning," so ran the instructions issued from the Lord of the Manor, "all tenants were to assemble in front of the church, but were not to enter the building until the Manor family had arrived and taken their places in the Manor pew." The tenants were notified of this rule. As directed they arrived early. But they walked on, silently, into the church and sat down in their own pews. When the Manor family arrived, not a member of the maliciously delighted lower classes gave them a glance. Nothing about not sitting down in your pew, was there, in the restrictive clauses of those detested leases? Let their lawyers put this one in their pipes and smoke it!

But — cruelest disappointment of all — on large sections of every estate there were no tenants, even mocking disrespectful ones, to pay rent. By their efforts to screw the last possible cent of profit out of every transaction, the landowners went far toward pricing themselves out of the market. Agreeing with this interpretation, the brilliant modern historian James Truslow Adams, a New Yorker, condemns:

> . . . the grasping land policy by leading families which kept down the population of New York so that the colony lagged behind almost all the others in proportionate increase in number. With an unrivalled situation both for overseas commerce and for the fur trade, with rich fields and fertile valleys, its natural advantages went for nothing, and it excelled the other colonies only in the short-sighted avarice of its aristocrats who were laying the foundations for family wealth, at the expense of their colony.

Consider these population statistics expressed in thousands:

In 1750 — Massachusetts 180, Pennsylvania 150, Connecticut 100, New York 80.

In 1760 — Massachusetts 235, Pennsylvania 220, Connecticut 142, New York 113.

In 1770 — Massachusetts 265, Pennsylvania 250, Connecticut 175, New York 160.

Even a few of the wiser contemporary observers deplored the trend and had no doubt about its cause. In 1732 Cadwallader Colden, then President of the Provincial Council of the Province of New York, wrote:

> And every year the young people go from this Province and purchase land in the Neighboring Colonies, while much better and every way more Convenient Lands here lie useless to King and Country. The reason for this is that the Grantees themselves are not nor ever were in a Capacity to improve such large Tracts, and other people will not become their Vassals or Tenants: for one great reason for people (the better sort especially) leaving their Native country was to avoid the dependence on landlords, and to enjoy their land in fee to descend to their posterity, that their children may reap the benefits of their labor and industry.

Efforts to bring in new recruits from across the Atlantic had scant success. The ocean voyage was long, six weeks at least on a sailing vessel. Passengers with little to do chatted with members of the crew, and soon found that outside the Province of New York (to which they were bound) lands could be bought and owned by the farmers who cultivated them, could be passed on to their children, intact, with all improvements. Many of them, even though they might have promised before leaving the Old World to go up the Hudson and be tenants on a manor, walked off the wharf at New York and betook themselves straight to one or another of the many places, The Jerseys, Pennsylvania, New England, where they would not need to be "subordinate forever."

No, any way you figure the score, Hudson Valley landlords made a lamentably poor showing, if their efforts were really, according to the theory, directed to building up a thriving farm community. Where they did succeed — and their success taxes our comprehension — was in extending the boundaries of their vast estates.

In acquiring a tract of wild land, first of all, the governor must be persuaded to issue a license authorizing the project. The next step was to buy rights to it from the Indian tribe claiming it as part of their hunting territory. To modern Americans, familiar with the many shameful chapters of our history, in which Indians have been dispossessed so often and so callously, this provision of New York colonial law seems an odd formality. But of course the colony had everything to lose by offending the warlike Iroquois, and even the Wappinger and Stockbridge tribes could be useful as allies against the French. At all events, there the provision stood. No one objected to it. It did no harm. In fact, in some ways it was extremely useful to white estate-builders.

Indian notions of what "owning land" meant were not unlike those one might imagine to be held by woodchucks and bears. They understood the value of cash as little as any squirrel. Against them, wanting to get something away from them, were sharp tradespeople, all of them able to calculate money value down to the last copper coin. For scarcely one of the men who became owners of vast land grants, but came from a family which, in New

York and Albany markets, had bought and sold everything, from fur and molasses to rum and slaves.

It required no special skill on their part so to rig the game as to get land from the Indians for the close equivalent of nothing. By their primitive idea of landmarks, the Indians themselves played into the hands of their exploiters. Here are the boundaries as set down of a great tract of land bought by Cornelius Van Rensselaer:

> The lands beginning at the Beaver Creek, going northward to the great Fallen Plane Tree, Where our Tribe Slept Last Summer; then eastwards to the Three Great Cedars on the Hillock; then westwards, straight to the Wild Duck Swamp; and straight on from the Swamp to the turn in the Beaver Creek where the old dam was.

The Dutch son of a canny Dutch father must have rubbed his hands at the wonderful opportunities offered. The Van Rensselaer claim to the region north of Livingston Manor was either twenty thousand acres or fifteen times that area (three hundred thousand acres) according to the location of "Waranquasick," the Indian word for a place called the "Heap of Stones." Are you surprised that it turned out to be the hugely larger area of which, in consequence, two hundred and eighty thousand acres were never paid for at all. By not mentioning in his deed the words "a marked tree," Adolphe Philipse turned a grant of fifteen thousand acres into one more than thirteen times as big (two hundred and five thousand acres), out of which one hundred and ninety thousand were acquired for nothing.

Robert Livingston bought from the Indians a tract agreed upon to contain two thousand six hundred acres. But according to his manipulation of such boundary terms as "Mahaskakook or Minnissichtanock," where two black oaks are marked with "L" or "Wawanaquassich," "where heaps of stones lie," of "a winding stream running back into the woods," somehow or other the area when later surveyed turned out to be one hundred and sixty thousand acres. Livingston (who began life as a Scottish clerk) paid for the twenty-six hundred acres the Indians thought they were selling less than six hundred dollars (three hundred and seventy-five in wampum, two hundred in axes, kettles, knives, blankets and similar trade goods). He received sixty times the acreage he paid for. The English governor of New York at that time remarked that:

> Robert Livingston has made a considerable fortune, never dispensing six-pence but with the expectation of twelve-pence. His beginning being a little bookkeeper, he has screwed himself into one of the most considerable estates in the province. He had rather be called Knave Livingston than poor Livingston.

Compared with those of his contemporaries, Livingston's holdings were not exceptional. Frederick and Adolphe Philipse (the family were city merchants, making their first New World money out of slaves, selling wampum, and sea-trade) were rated as owning three hundred and sixty-one thousand acres. But the Van Rensselaers (the first one of this tribe in America was a Dutch Reformed Clergyman, but after that they were all traders) sang high C in this chorus by holding title to one million acres.

When we consider that six hundred and forty acres make a square mile, we are forced to admit that this was big business on a grand scale.

These figures answer the question sometimes asked: Might there not have been plenty of room in Vermont for both family-owned homesteads and the larger estates of New York Patentees?

No statement about something which did not happen can be positive. But what does the record indicate? Is there the faintest probability that once they had gained a foothold, the New York land speculators, as mad with greed as nineteenth-century railroad barons, wallowing and guzzling like pigs fallen into a tub of butter, would ever have stopped for breath until they had gulped down every square foot of Vermont farm land?

Where There's Boodle

Where there's boodle, there's graft. Where
there's graft, the police are fixed.
AMERICAN PROVERB

CADWALLADER COLDEN, President of the Provincial
Council from 1721 to 1761, and Lieutenant or acting governor
of the Province of New York, from 1761 to 1776:

> The gentlemen of the Law, both the Judges and the principal practitioners at the Bar, are either Owners, Heirs, or strongly connected in Family Interest with the Proprietors. In few cases a cause of any Consequence, especially where the King's Rights are concerned, can be brought before a Judge entirely disinterested and free from connections with those interested in the Case, or in other Cases similar to it.
>
> It is not then, improbable, that Combinations may be made between the Bench and the Bar, whereby partial Juries may be procured, wholly influenced in favor of the great Interests.

Dr. Irving Mark in his *Agrarian Conflicts in Colonial New York*
(published 1940):

> From 1730 to 1776, of the three chief justices of the supreme court of New York Province, which usually handled land actions of any consequence, two were great landowners. The third held office only sixteen months.
>
> Of eight colonial executives, ruling New York from 1750 to 1776, six were great landlords, holding land in New York exceeding one thousand acres in extent.
>
> Of thirty-three attorneys, licensed from 1730 to 1776, thirty were connected with great landed families.

From the acreages listed in the last chapter, you would never guess, would you, that the English law for the Province of New York expressly forbade large grants of land. But it did. It limited the size of any patent to two thousand acres. In addition, each grant was to be forfeited, unless, in three years' time, three acres out of every fifty should be under cultivation. To comply with this ruling, the Van Rensselaers would have had to provide, in three years' time, settlers and cultivation for sixty thousand acres. It would be simple-minded to imagine that they or any other large owner had the slightest idea of obeying such a law.

In 1701, the Earl of Bellomont, then Governor of the Province, reported as to settling and cultivation:

> Mr. Livingston has on his great grant of sixteen miles long and twenty-four miles broad, only four or five cottagers, as I am told, men that live in vassalage under him and work for him, are too poor to be farmers, having not the wherewithal to buy cattle to stock a farm. Old Frederick Philipse is said to have about twenty families of such poor people that work for him on his grant.

The law of the region had been set up by able lawyers. The British Royal Governor, a titled nobleman sent from London, had full authority to enforce it. How did the New York landowners manage thus to ignore it?

Everyone in those days exchanged gossip about how the trick was turned. Even the tenant farmers grumbling about high rents told one another sullenly that no relief could be hoped for as long as the courts refused to oust their proprietors from land stolen in the first place and still held contrary to law. But that was guessing.

Today, two centuries later, we do not need to guess. We know all about the pulling and hauling, the grabbing, the legal corruption. It was rather like a fiercely played game of poker, this long-ago struggle against His Majesty's Government by His Majesty's especially devoted subjects, the gentry of the Province of New York. They held their cards close to their chests. But bids and bluffs and scheming are no secrets any more. The gamblers are dead. Their cards lie on the table, face up. Anybody can see how they were marked. Throughout its colonial history official reports about what was going on in the province were frequently sent back to the Home Government. At that time they were hush-hush confidential. Today their words are open to us to read, in good black ink on first-quality paper.

These documents show that the majority of the eighteenth-century governors, sent from London to rule over the province, could not resist the incredibly easy money to be made out of their official position.

Now it is well to bear in mind that we only cloud our understanding of any historical period if we try to measure its manners and morals according to the ideas current in our own time, or by some rigid theoretical code. We cannot hope to see the actors of past centuries as they saw themselves without taking into account the whole setting of the stage on which they played their parts. While reserving our right to approve or blame, we are not in the least condoning wrongdoing if we take the realistic position that large areas of human conduct are matters of convention rather than black and white, good or evil.

The truth was brought home to me not long ago by an old friend describing the carefree life of the foreign colony in pre-war Shanghai: "Your Number-one houseboy looked out for everything," she said, "and you paid him very little. He expected to piece out his wages by taking a kickback — squeeze, they called it — so many cents on every dollar of household bills." Here, noting my raised eyebrows, she explained tolerantly, "Why, back here in the States, when you throw a party at a hotel, you don't make a fuss because the extras — tips to bellboys, cloakroom girls and waiters — add quite a little to the printed prices on the menu. That's not quite the same thing, but after all it's not so different from the Chinese idea. Your Number-one boy never let any outsider cheat you. According to his lights, he himself wouldn't cheat you. He thought of his squeeze out of your marked-up bills as part of his legitimate earnings. You knew it. He knew you knew it. Everything was reasonable and aboveboard."

Her face darkened as if at unpleasant memories. "Of course sometimes — sometimes there *were* exceptions. And that was not so good."

In the spacious days when Sir Robert Walpole and Lord North bought rotten-borough votes in the open market to keep their ministries in power, when Clive and Warren Hastings were consolidating the British Raj in India, English public life was run on something very like the Number-one boy principle. An administrator was entitled to the "perquisites of his office." Legally he could collect a substantial fee whenever he signed his name to one of the many papers needed by private citizens doing business under his jurisdiction. Actually in that morally relaxed period of English government, few members of the ruling class saw anything out of the way if he extended the list of his perquisites further — considerably further.

The British Empire was expanding — exploding comes nearer to describing its surge into world-wide colonial domination. Vast sums of new money were pouring in. Is it any wonder that during transit a certain amount stuck to official fingers? We can imagine the shop-talk that went around as the New York governor, his staff and secretaries discussed the latest news from Madras over their after-dinner port wine in Albany or New York. To be sure the Province of New York was not India. The Mohawks' hands were dark-skinned like those of the Maharajahs, but they held no long-accumulated family hoards of diamonds, rubies and gold. Still the pickings were not bad.

The confirming of land grants was in the hands of the royal governors. What then? To borrow the formula of my ex-Shanghai friend, the rule might call for a certain moderation in feathering your own nest out of public money, but sometimes there *were* exceptions and that was not so good. Sometimes? Pretty generally.

To be explicit: Governor George Clinton, serving from 1743 to 1753, reserved shares of land grants for himself under fictitious names, "set the precedent for exacting high fees for land patents," and returned to England with a fortune of eighty-four thousand pounds — pounds, not dollars. This was pretty fair pay for only ten years' chiseling, especially when we remember that money then was worth hugely more than now. Lieutenant Governor Clarke (1736–1743) also made use of dummies in securing grants for himself (one hundred thousand acres in the rich Mohawk Valley) and by this practice got together an estate of a hundred thousand pounds in seven years. William Cosby (1732–1736) reserved for himself a third of all lands patented by him, thus establishing a policy described by Chief Justice Morris of New York as:

First, engrossing great tracts of land into a few hands;
Second, rendering it very difficult if not impossible for any
but a certain class of men to come at them;
Third, rendering them so dear that it will not be worth the
while even of those few that can come at them to
meddle with them, there being better lands and much
cheaper, to be purchased in Jersey and Pennsylvania.

Were there no honest British governors? Yes, a few. It is from their angry reports that we can reconstruct the story of general greed and graft. The Earl of Bellomont, a normally conscientious public official, was one of them. He was staggered by the conditions he found. Writing to the Lords of Trade, he complains about his predecessor's "intolerable corrupt selling away the lands of this Province." And again that he believed three quarters of the whole vast fertile Province to be "in the hands of ten or eleven men."

Authorities in London were quick to answer his appeal for support. The orders they sent back bristled with indignation. Future grants were to be cut in half, no more than *one thousand* acres to a single person. In cases where actual occupation of the land by bona fide settlers was delayed over three years, the provision of forfeiture was to be insisted on. Most drastic of all, conveyances already made beyond the legal limit of acreage, *were to be annulled*. No responsible representative of a home government could have asked firmer backing.

Bellomont was an earl, the fully accredited English governor. Behind him he had all the power of a mighty empire. He started full of zeal. A few grants (to Dellius, Bayard and others) were declared void, and then . . . Well, then it was the story we all have seen enacted in many an American municipality . . . a reform mayor battling singlehanded with an organized, well-established ring of professional politicians. Every holder of a huge estate felt himself potentially threatened in the future by the new ruling. The "interests" closed their ranks for resistance. How could anybody with a grain of ordinary sense imagine that a man who had counted on getting title to two hundred thousand acres would accept limitation to a single thousand? And the insane provision about losing even this pittance if sixty out of that thousand were not under cultivation within three years! Impossible! The authorities in London needn't expect to put over any such tomfool decree under New York conditions! Not while there were sons-in-law, and uncles, and brothers, and first cousins in all the legal key positions of the Province.

The startled Bellomont was shocked to find how completely the Council of New York Province was controlled by the inter-related clan of landowners, members of the assembly, lawyers and judges. This was far more alarming to any responsible representative of the British government than the peculations of an executive appointee, going a little further than others across the line of official probity. To bring the law courts into the dirty business was to compromise the integrity of British justice. If that failed, the very foundation of England's life was shaken. In haste he wrote back to London, admitting that in spite of his authority, so great on paper, he feared that without a peremptory order from the King, "I shall not have strength enough in the Assembly of New York to break them."

By the word "them" the harassed governor was referring to the opposition, whose methods he was just beginning to understand. It was a marvelously well-organized machine. Tammany Hall in its palmiest days never had a better. No numbers racket ever carried on its illegal game more securely protected by the bribed police. The key idea was simple: throughout the province, the legal and political administration was manned by the gentry and its partisans. To the eye, an official might look like what he was paid to be, an impartial enforcer of all laws, including the land laws. But examine the background of one — any one of them, be he sheriff, member of council, judge — and you would find him a well-trained, faithful assembly-hand on the production line of the large landowners. This was called the New York "Junto," and was generally recognized both inside and outside the province as the real government.

As early as 1732, a high official of New York wrote:

Several families in New York are possessed of Land of Great Extent, greater than those of any subject of England; some of them setting up boundless Claims. They are connected by Relation and Kindred with the Gentlemen of the

Law, both on the Bench and the Bar, most of whom are themselves interested in one or another of the great land Patents.

At various later times the same official states:

In my opinion it may be very disadvantageous to Government that any one or two Families should be able to return so large a Proportion of the Members of our Assembly.

And (referring to the manors of Livingston and Rensselaerwick):

It is in their Power to determine every Election in the County [Albany] and may in effect Return all five Members.
. . . The Proprietors of the Great Tracts of land in this Province have united strongly with the Lawyers as the surest support of their enormous and iniquitous claims, and thereby this faction is become the more formidable and dangerous to good government.

Secure though they thought themselves, the bosses of the Junto felt it would do no harm to clear up permanently the matter of regulation at its source in England. Influential men naturally have influential friends. They saw to it that they always had influential friends in London. They now urged such friends to apply pressure on the Lords of Trade. In the Province of New York they were used to getting what they wanted. With confidence, they set out to secure the abolition of the thousand-acre limit.

They instructed their lobbyists in London to point out that the vast open spaces of America called for ideas correspondingly broad, for limits less restraining than might seem reasonable in a snug, small, thickly populated country like England. No monopoly would be created by granting large patents, since, in order to maintain the position in life to which a gentleman is entitled, the holders must from time to time resell sizable blocks — say five thousand acres or more — to men of money, ambitious to enter the landowning class to secure its political and social privileges. Only through personal contact, by personal initiative could such buyers be found. Surely, once they understood what was at stake, the Lords of Trade would do nothing to prevent the building up of a social order — like that so happily established in England — bound together by common interest and common loyalty to the Crown.

Their propaganda was plausible. But it failed. The restrictions were upheld in London. In the Province of New York they could no longer be disregarded.

Not openly, that is.

As an experienced American, you will not be surprised at what followed. To try to lock doors against people who know a great deal about picking locks never amounts to much. Without any interruption, the New York wealthy families went on securing great grants of land far beyond the legal limit. It was only a little more complicated than the old method. A number of obliging friends joined together in petitioning for a grant, each of them decorously putting himself down for less than the thousand-acre maximum. These numerous owners were duly recorded as holding legal title. Then they passed those plots on to the real purchaser — they themselves well paid for their part in the dummy transaction. The letter of the law was complied with. No conspiracy to bypass its clear intent could be proved.

The Junto had been beaten on no essential issue. Just the same its members were annoyed. They were doing what they had been told to do from the day the British authorities had taken over from the Dutch — trying to make New York safe for class supremacy. And what thanks did they get? None. Just the opposite. Those narrow-minded London bureaucrats were always badgering, hampering, strangling their efforts to make the Province of New York a duplication of English society, with fixed upper and lower classes.

Year by year friction grew. Contrary to the all-black-and-all-white, anti-British pictures drawn in the grade-school histories which we read as children, the record shows repeated evidence that the Lords of Trade in London were taking a statesmanlike view, were trying (from a distance which made their efforts futile) with considerable administrative wisdom to get the rich New York farming regions really settled by hard-working citizens of sound quality. The landlords of the Hudson Valley did not see it that way. They felt obliged to be constantly on their guard against the British authority, constantly trying to extend their own. The Director of the New York State Historical Association, in a lately published, carefully documented biography, shows James Duane — well-known lawyer and landholder — cautiously sitting on the fence from the time of the Stamp Act agitation clear up to the final showdown. "In the troubled relations with England following 1763," he writes, "Duane strove for the golden mean which would protect gentlemen of his station *both from British taxation and from domestic upheaval.*" Evidently it was the result of Duane's mental balance sheet which inclined him at last to support Congress. Does the fact that many of his associates also joined the patriot party explain perhaps why such a surprising number of tenant farmers were pro-British?

But I have left unfinished Governor Bellomont's story. What happened to him? He died. Three years after he started his forlorn-hope offensive against the Junto line, a fine funeral was given him.

He was followed by Governor Cornbury. Of him a later and relatively honest governor said that his extravagant grants of land were worse than all the governors before him put together. Lieutenant Governor Colden reported that Governor Cornbury had made large grants of land *without survey*, described by such phrases as "be it more or less," and "profitable land beside woodland." Under this easygoing regime, claims were stretched a hundred times their legal boundaries — remember, these facts are taken from official reports to London. Colden cited one grant of three hundred acres stretched in this way to two hundred times its original size.

What were the reasons for this frenzy to get hold of such quantities of unimproved property which could be counted on to bring in any considerable rent return only in the rather distant future? One reason was that these sons of shopkeepers naturally looked forward to a time when their unpretentious manor houses (few of them north of Westchester had much to offer in the way of "refined elegance") would be replaced by splendid mansions, the scraggy clearings by well-kept grounds, fat crop-and-meadow-lands, advertising to the world their owners' material success. We have not even today entirely outgrown this form of the "conspicuous-display-of-wealth" motive. But surely a tenth — a hundredth — part of those huge grants would have been all a sane man could hope to develop into a show place.

The full extent of the land mania must be explained rather by the consideration that before the rise of factory production, and modern system of finance, only two channels for investment of surplus money were open: commerce and land. Commerce required special knowledge, close burdensome attention, and was always — since much of it was carried on by sea — very risky. But a tract of wild land could be secured at a comparatively small outlay by a judicious greasing of influential palms.

Another factor to be remembered is that it was a period of boom psychology. Just as the bull market of the 1920's filled brokers' offices with clients scrambling to buy on margin shares in any company — no matter if it had passed dividends for the past ten years — confident that quotations on the bulletin board would always go up and up and up, so in eighteenth-century New York, the quick money, the big money came from buying and selling land on which the operator never intended to set foot.

A contemporary American writer (Royall Tyler) knew very well how to get a surefire laugh. In one of his works, he describes a tavern scene where one man in casual talk lets drop the information that he has inherited a vast tract of land in New York Province, without any boundaries at all. Immediately two men drinking at another table, come over and ask him to name his selling price for it. Taken aback, he explains that not only does his deed fail to mention the exact metes and bounds, but he hasn't the faintest idea where the land is supposed to lie. "That makes no difference at all," the others tell him. "We're still ready to go ahead with a deal. We don't want the land to settle on it, but to speculate with."

After the facts presented in this chapter, no one can ask himself, "Why did Vermonters refuse to trust the decision on their titles to the New York courts?" They did, as a matter of fact, make one effort to plead their case in Albany. The result was exactly what was to be expected from an organization where, I quote Dr. Mark again:

Of the one hundred and thirty-seven governors, councillors, assembly-men, judges and lawyers from about 1750 to 1776, one hundred and ten (eighty percent) were large landowners or related to such families: six were small landowners; twenty-one (fifteen percent) held either very small areas of land or no land at all. Against such extensive landlord power, what prospect of improvement did the small farmer have in appeal to executive, legislative or judicial remedies?

Once was enough for the Vermonters. From that time on, they expected what they got from New York courts — nothing. This one "appeal to judicial remedies" gave them all the proof they needed that, as Dr. Mark put it, "landlord power" dominated the legal system of the province. They rode back to the Green Mountains from the Albany court where their case had been decided against them in ten minutes, without any hearing of the documents they had brought, the arguments they were prepared to make. This was the last time. They made up their minds that wherever she might be found, Justice, the blindfolded goddess holding up her even-balanced scales, was not presiding over the Supreme Court of the Province of New York.

Those Connecticut Levelers

DR. JULIUS GOEBEL, "Some Legal and Political Aspects of the Manors of New York":

The grants of land made indicate that a conscious effort was being made to create a land-aristocracy devoted to the crown and its governor, that would offset the republican tendencies among the people, so deplored by all New York colonial governors. Do not overlook the fact that within the Province of New York and about its eastern borders (New England) were settled fellow-countrymen of whose disaffection and republican tendencies, the crown was justly suspicious.

Ethan Allen, 1777:

For nothing which can be done to any people is capable of so effectually inslaving them, as the monopoly of their lands; when this is the case with the people, it is idle for them to dispute any more about liberty; for the sovereign nod from their landlord cannot fail to overawe them, and by degrees erase the natural images of liberty from their minds, and make them grovel out a contemptible and miserable life.

Do not forget — people sometimes do forget it — that the Vermont hostility to York-Staters was solely to New York landlords and their lawyers. New York people — the *people* of New York are excellent neighbors. Always were. More than mere neighbors, they showed themselves true friends to Vermonters in the thick of the troubled years. But from the day of the conquest of the territory from the Dutch by the British, the record of life in the Province of New York shows that the majority of the *people*, the everyday men and women, had little or nothing to do with the running of their government and making its policies. Policies were decided by a small clique, whose every ideal, standard and tradition was the opposite of those which Vermonters had been brought up to revere and serve.

The land issue was not the cause of the hostility between the New York gentry and the Vermont pioneer farmers. It was, rather, a symptom. The angry hate between their two opposing traditions dated from long before Vermont was settled. Each side was enemy to the other because each side was unalterably convinced that its outlook on life was the right one. No board of arbitration could have brought about harmony.

Do you ask, "Were there not *some* subjects on which the ruling class of the Province of New York and Vermont settlers could see eye to eye?" the answer is simple. "No, there were not. They disagreed on just about everything."

Take political theory. Vermont was all for local self-government, with the accent on "local" and "self," particularly on officials elected by unrestricted manhood suffrage. New York on the other hand was organized from the top down. The governor was chosen by a distant king, the council was hand-picked, the assembly (thanks to property qualifications limiting the right to vote) closely tied in with the leading families. Such weak local government as existed was very much soft-pedaled.

Or consider schools. New England, as we have noted, believed in public-supported education. In Massachusetts, by 1642, the law required in addition to apprentice-training, instruction in reading and writing for all. In 1647 it set up machinery toward that end; for every town of fifty families there must be an elementary school, and a grammar school (roughly corresponding to our high school) in every town of a hundred families. The Colonial Assembly of Connecticut in 1700 passed a law authorizing constables in each town to collect a special school tax. Freely admitting that there was considerable delay in putting these paper regulations into practice, the fact remains that by 1750 common schools, under local control, were maintained in every Connecticut district. The fathers who had been taught in those schools had no intention of grudging the same advantages to their children in Vermont. Again they did not at once do everything they wished, but the goal was never abandoned. In practically every town charter — whether granted by the New Hampshire governor or later by the prudently budgeted government of Vermont — at least one share of land (often two or three) was not to be sold, but held in trust for the support of education. "A School or Schools [so runs Section 40 of Vermont's first Constitution] shall be established in each town by the Legislature for the convenient Instruction of Youth."

Meanwhile the Province of New York was purposefully suppressing public-supported education. The purpose of the ruling class was to keep working people ignorant. Andrew Sloan Draper, for many years head of the New York state system of public education, an outstanding authority on the history of education in New York, writes that the Dutch belief in public education flourished in the colony as well as in Holland. So much so that: "Literacy was diffused to a remarkable degree among the hardworking citizens and handcraftsmen. When the Dutch were obliged to surrender to the English in 1664, the educational spirit was so common throughout the Dutch colony, that almost every settlement had a regular school taught by a more or less permanent teacher."

The British conquerors promptly put an end to such a reprehensible spirit. It was easy to do. The majority of the ordinary folk of the Province were not Church of England members. The supply of both teachers and children for schools was cut off at the source by the British specification that all teachers must be members of the Church of England. Local control, even local influence on schools, was also forbidden by instructions from London in the early days (1685). Governor Dongan received, among his other orders, this explicit command from the King: "And we do further direct that no schoolmaster be henceforth permitted to come from England and keep school without your license first to be had."

Down to the Declaration of Independence, "no teacher could be employed until he had proved his affection *for the present government* and his conformity to the doctrine and discipline of the Church of England."

The intention of this careful screening was obvious. The growing generation was to be shielded from any hint that doubt or questionings might be possible. They were to absorb along with ABC's and Two-and-Two-Make-Four, the axiom that the Church, the State and the Status Quo of their time had reached perfection. Plenty of people on both sides of the Iron Curtain accept that policy today, as the end and aim of all education. It failed to produce expected results in provincial New York — but that may be because the children of poor families never had schools where they could learn either ABC, or that the Status Quo was perfect. British governors were uneasy about having ideas — even orthodox ideas — put into working-class heads. As late as 1870 — note that date *eighteen*-seventy not seventeen-seventy — it was estimated that in old England only about half the children of country laborers knew how to read and write.

Another, and realistically perhaps a stronger, reason was that, then as now, schools cost money. Those who had money could think of any number of pleasanter uses for it than spending it on schools for other people's children. The outcome is tersely stated by Dr. Daniel J. Pratt in his official history of education in New York: "It is in point to remark that no effort seems to have been made in behalf of primary education from 1709 during the remaining colonial years of the Colony." In connection with these facts about the lack of free primary education during the British rule in the Province, we must bear in mind the idea expressed by Stuart Noble (*A History of American Education,* 1938) when he says:

> Tradition is no more than habits of thought based on long-continued action. Its color, of course, depends on what the action was. The principle of public-supported education free to all children, denied for a century in the Province of New York, was not fully recognized as valid by the State of New York for almost another century, in 1867.

We have on this subject more than the statements of modern historians, accustomed to today's standards of education. Eighteenth-century eyewitnesses agree with them. In 1713, for example, the chaplain of the King's forces in New York reported: "There is hardly anything which is more wanted in this country (New York) than learning, there being no place that I know of in America where it is less encouraged or regarded."

Fifty years later, in 1762, the President of King's College (now Columbia) in a letter to Archbishop Secker, remarks, in reference to the marked lack of generosity of the Province as to Church and education:

> It is a great pity when patents are granted — as they often are for large tracts of land — that *no provision is made for religion or schools.* I wish that instructions were given our Governors never to grant patents for townships or large manors without obliging the patentees to sequester a competent portion for the support of religion and education.

But this was only a college president writing to a clergyman. The rich people in power seem to have paid little attention to advice from such an unworldly source. I say, "little attention." I mean none.

To be sure, something — if it can be called "something" — was accomplished by the Society for the Propagation of the Gospel in Foreign Parts. Between 1710 and 1776 it managed to organize in or very near New York City enough elementary schools to give instruction to four hundred children at a time. That was the maximum. Often the number was lower. Not exactly educational "coverage," one would think, for a population which increased during the period from eighty thousand to one hundred and sixty thousand. Yet possibly enough to satisfy demand. For (now I quote from Thomas Finegan's *Documentary History of the Free School Movement in New York State*): "In schools directed by the Society, the main purpose was to give religious instruction and to increase the prestige of the Church of England." The large majority of parents in the province, Lutherans or Calvinists in belief, preferred to let their children go untaught rather than have them forced to recite the Anglican catechism, and receive daily indoctrination in a theology their parents very much objected to.

Secure, for the time being, in their political independence and local self-government, Vermonters were free to decide what their children should learn and who should and who should not teach them. They were resolutely unreconciled to schools directed by the Church of England, or any other church. Not that they were opposed to religion. On the contrary, the typical Vermont charter for a new town set aside, in addition to reserved school lands, one share for the first-settled minister (or ministers), and one for the "social worship of God." Your guess is as good as anybody's as to the precise meaning of that last phrase — but certainly it does not suggest atheism.

Favoring religion in general, however, is a very different thing from establishing a particular church. Vermonters wanted nothing of the kind. They were tolerant — they were almost belligerent in stating their tolerance. Article Three of the first Vermont Constitution reads:

> That all men have a natural and unalienable right to worship ALMIGHTY GOD according to the dictates of their own conscience and understanding, regulated by the word of God: and that no man ought or of right can be, compelled to attend any religious worship, or erect or support any place of worship, or maintain any minister, contrary to the dictates of his conscience. . . .

They were **not** completely tolerant, as the twentieth-century understands that word. Membership in the legislature was limited to those "professing the Protestant Religion." This is understandable, considering their historic background. Such a restriction was common enough (with a few notable exceptions) in the other colonies, and was the accepted rule in the home country until much later, indeed in spirit and in literal explicit statement it still lives on in the (rather astonishing) words of the English Royal Oath of Accession.

Just the same, we present-day Vermonters squirm a little with embarrassment when we read that reservation, out of tune as it is with the otherwise broad-minded liberalism of our first "Declaration of Rights." We are greatly relieved to find that only a few years later, during revision, the discordant clause was quietly dropped. There was no agitation, so far as we can discover, no speeches made for or against it. We can only assume that the drafting committee cool-headedly considered the old causes, in English history, for that restriction — the Counter Reformation, with its threat of divided loyalty, the Spanish Armada, Jacobites ready to welcome a French invasion — and decided that they were hardly live issues in Vermont. At all events, the restricting clause was dropped from our Constitution, in a Vermontish silence, with not a protest.

The credit for first denouncing Negro slavery in America belongs to the Mennonites and Quakers of Pennsylvania. Later, Washington, Jefferson and other Virginia statesmen made no secret of their hope that the "institution" would soon wither away. It does not surprise us to find Ethan Allen, temperamentally alert, as always, to any phase of the growing "Rights-of-Man" movement, fulminating thus against the autocratic governments of New York: "Probably a habit of inslaving their subjects has beat it into their heads that it is just: and *thus people commonly conceive it to be just to inslave negroes.*"

But talk alone did not satisfy Vermont. It acted. When our Constitution was adopted in 1777 — very early for such action — it forbade slavery by state-wide law.

I learned that fact as a child in Vermont. You can imagine

how eagerly the old folks called it to my attention. But only as a grown woman, after considerable browsing background-reading in the Dutchess County Historical Society's library, and especially after making the acquaintance of Mrs. Grant's revealing auto-biography, *The Memoirs of an American Lady*, did I realize that here again, Allen and the Green Mountain settlers for whom he spoke were pointedly taking their stand on the opposite side of the fence from the Hudson Valley gentry.

On a New England hill farm, the man of the house, his wife and children — helped out at times by a neighbor's son or daughter scrupulously treated as one of the family — expected to do all the necessary work indoors and out. But by the British, and hence by the Province of New York, social definition, a landowning gentleman could not curry or saddle his horse or milk his cow, nor could his wife wash dishes or take care of her own baby without losing caste. Most of the New York Manor Houses north of Westchester were small, plain and bare. But in each one the Lord and Lady did their best to live up to the social standards established by the Stately Halls of Old England.

But in England, seven centuries of enforced subservience had produced, under the thatched roofs of the Manor farmers, a social tradition which supplied the Manor family with all needed cooks, gardeners, grooms, ladies' maids, children's nurses, chambermaids, washwomen, scullery maids. Rural descendants of the Saxons had become so wonted to social inferiority that it was considered a step up in social status to be accepted as personal servants in the Manor family.

The landlords of the Hudson Valley found themselves sur-rounded by a rural population which was not submissive and subservient in temperament. Quite the contrary. In the Province of New York, the only men and women who could be counted on to give docile personal service to the gentry were blacks, and their docility was ensured by their being legally slaves. They were far from satisfactory substitutes for the sons and daughters of the Manor farmers in England trained for generations to con-sider it an honor to be house servants. But they were better than no house servants at all. Population statistics of the period show a surprisingly large number of Negroes living as slaves in New

York City, Albany and the river settlements between those cities.

For the most part they were neither abused nor overdriven. As much care and thought was taken for their well-being as is usual in the treatment of domestic animals by decently kind owners. An English eighteenth-century writer who lived long in the Hudson Valley cites as an example of the humane consideration shown by the New York gentry towards these black sharers of their family life, the fact that persons of good breeding would never dream of selling a child of one of their black slaves without first consulting the Negro mother about the family into which it was to be sold. Such sales, in the nature of things, were frequent. The two Negro slaves (man and woman) given as a wedding present to a young married couple of the manor class, were expected to furnish enough children to keep up a suitable house and farmstaff for the growing white household. If more Negro babies were born than were needed, they could always be profitably sold, like the surplus of puppies in the dog family.

If one of the dogs owned by a family becomes unruly, surly or incurably disobedient, he is shot. By the eighteenth century, this solution of a problem in personal relations was not acceptable. In the Province of New York the slaves and their white owners lived close together, much of the time under the same roof. There was no provision made, as on large southern plantations, for flogging, off in a distance, out of earshot, carried on by the upper servant called an overseer. And the eighteenth-century New York gentry were pleasant people of normal good feeling. They would not at all have enjoyed flogging with their own hands a woman who had grown up from babyhood as a member of their own household.

Yet when human beings of any color are held in slavery, there are always some individuals among them who do not realize that the duty of a slave is not only to serve, but to appear to enjoy serving. And in any human group there are some who steal and lie and make themselves in other ways uncomfortable life companions. The white masters of slaves in the province had an easy — for them — solution of what to do with slaves who did not suit their tastes or standards. Mrs. Grant tells us in her genial memoirs, "No serious punishment was ever needed." The slaves were kept docile by the threat always hanging over their heads, of being sold for labor on the sugar plantations of Jamaica. This meant being beaten or worked to death in a few years.

It was a simple matter. The Hudson Valley Lords of the land came, mostly, from trading families, and although they had acquired many acres they had not sunk into rusticity. Not at all. They capably carried on the commercial tradition of their city families by doing a brisk business with the West Indies. The ships were loaded before going, at the landlord's own dock, on the bank of Hudson's River. It was noted with much satisfaction that every time a ship bound for Jamaica was being loaded at the wharf of a Manor, the slave population was commendably subdued, submissively eager to please, and did their work with a humble alacrity very agreeable to their white masters.

But no human device is perfect. Mrs. Grant noted that even in this ingenious solution to the problem there was a disadvantage. The master who had sold a slave to be shipped to a Jamaica sugar plantation was often obliged to go to the expense and bother of sending a guard along till the black was actually in the custody of the purchaser, to avoid the inconvenience and financial loss of the slave's committing suicide by jumping overboard.

Well, this is one side of this chapter — a list by no means complete of the ways of life of the New York ruling class which were abhorred by Vermonters. To give a fair account of what New York officialdom thought about New England settlers in the "Grants" is much more difficult. It calls for extreme mental effort on the part of both author and reader, to wipe from our minds much that is now taken for granted, until with fresh eyes we can see the world as it looked to many people of the eighteenth century, when the truths listed in the Declaration of Independence seemed by no means self-evident.

Burke spoke exultingly in praise of the character of Englishmen, for "their awe of kings and priests, their sullen resistance of innovation and their unalterable perseverance in the wisdom of prejudice."

"In my view the surest wealth consists in a multitude of laborious poor. To make society happy and people easy, it is requisite that great numbers be ignorant as well as poor." So in 1714 wrote Bernard de Mandeville, author of *The Fable of the Bees*. He was much applauded in all eighteenth-century London coffee houses, not as a clever cynic, but as a realist — a wise philosopher who said right out what everyone knew. Recent history had convinced the upper classes of England that calamities were certain to follow any weakening of authority. Naturally, Cromwell's Commonwealth regime seemed to them vastly more radical and democratic than it does to us. England had learned its lesson. Those with a "stake in the country" (this phrase means property-owners) must stand firm against "mobocracy." Laws were passed to keep the great heart of the people pure and loyal — at least as far as jail sentences, exile and disfranchisement could do the job. Sermons were preached exhorting good Christians to be content with the conditions of life, in the stations in life where God had placed them.

No — this won't do! In spite of all my good resolutions to be objective, I am slanting my report to fit a post-revolution (American and French), post-nineteenth-century outlook. And that is to miss the essential point that the English conservatives of the eighteenth century were not in the least hypocrites inventing excuses for their own selfishness. Without a shadow of doubt, they believed themselves intelligent patriots saving their country from ruin. They felt that by spending their huge incomes lavishly they were testifying to that country's wealth and power. The best of them did achieve in their lives a measure of that rare quality called *distinction*. They made it a matter of pride to fill their lovely homes with expensive art treasures from the Continent, to have their portraits done by the best painters, endlessly to entertain other gentry in the most delightful manner, to create beautiful gardens, to have fine libraries and plenty of docile, silent servants, in short to further, as Trevelyan puts it, "the great business of making life pleasant for the upper classes, in which the men of the Eighteenth Century were such adepts."

As long as the institution of hereditary aristocracy remained in full flower, its supporters never, so far as I know, thought it worth while to consider weighing its good points against its drawbacks. As they saw it, there were no drawbacks. Only later when — though far from dead and buried — it was being questioned, did serious thinkers suggest that in the decay of the Ancient Regime the world may have lost more than merely the glittering stage setting of powdered wigs, gold snuffboxes, minuets by candlelight. Some such thought is suggested by Goethe's dictum that if both are not possible together, freedom is less desirable than order. More explicitly, with his habitual painstaking thoroughness, Henry James, himself an exile from what he considered America's crude newness, set himself to work out the problem which he saw as still a living issue in Victorian England.

The hero of his novel *The Princess Casamassima* had been in his inexperienced youth a revolutionary radical, opposed to the English institution of an enormously favored upper class. Later he changed sides because (so Henry James has him write) no matter how unjust to the lower classes, the hereditary aristocracy had produced "the general fabric of civilization — the monuments and treasures of art, the great places and proprieties, the conquests of learning and taste." These he clearly recognizes are "based on the despotisms, the cruelties, the exclusions, the monopolies and rapacities of the past." But he feels that the wretchedness of the many is not too high a price to pay for such glories. The little revolutionary sends a bullet through his own heart and dies, rather than strike a blow against a society based on injustice to the majority, because he feels "a deep distrust of the grudging attitude, the intolerance of positions and fortunes that are higher and brighter than one's own."

Some of the best minds — as we now rate them — in the eighteenth-century American colonies and in France thought differently. A few even in England were beginning to question the justice of denying to the "inferior" majority a fair share of opportunity to develop their best abilities, in order to shower upon the "superior" few a great deal more than their fair share of the good things of life. "Because some tough old pirate of an ancestor captured a Spanish galleon, is that any reason," they asked, "why his nitwit great-grandson should be appointed to posts where he draws a huge salary for doing nothing at all, save occasionally sit in the House of Lords?"

But these questioners were few in England, and in the eighteenth century still without much influence. It was not necessary to refute their arguments — merely to shout them down as foul-mouthed, disloyal, atheist dogs.

The members of New York's ruling class kept true to the principles on which the province had been founded. They did their best to copy English institutions — social and political — as faithfully as they followed English fashions in hats, wigs, sleeves, neck-wear. In the motherland the Prime Ministers, Whig or Tory alike, held their majority in Parliament by openly buying votes. This was the "every man has his price" epoch. Only slightly less brazenly they kept the favor of the upper classes by appointing to well-paid government sinecures the younger sons of influential families. Just so the New York Junto controlled the Assembly and saw to it that no laws abridging business enterprise or the rights of property were passed.

But it was hard on them to have for next-door neighbors in Western Connecticut and Western Massachusetts a nest of pernicious democratic levelers. It was almost unbearably hard, because their repulsive republican society was not breaking down into poverty-stricken and anarchic barbarism, as was predicted of republicanism by right-minded European and English conservatives. About this date, a noble German general stated publicly that if the servile condition of the workers on the land were "lightened by a single jot, *Prussia would starve in two months*" because such dumb brutes would work only if forced to by their superiors. To obvious axioms like this, the well-dressed, well-to-do people everywhere solemnly nodded their heads in affirmation. But the small farm-owning Connecticut and Massachusetts communities were visibly not starving, although no "superior class" was forcing them to labor. On the contrary. They were disagreeably on the up-and-up. They were prospering, they were dangerously expanding, they were drawing away new settlers of intelligence and energy from the province to the west of them which was so earnestly trying to duplicate the delightfully civilized, gracious atmosphere of rural life on the Manors of Old England, the admiration of all the world.

Again let us remind ourselves that the newly created upper

classes in New York were sincere. A typical backward-looking lawyer, like James Duane, could see in Vermont democracy nothing but diabolical, anarchistic license, to be put down as rigorously as we now punish arson and burglary. To him and his like, it *was* arson. It was an attempt to set fire to the only framework any decent society could have. It *was* burglary, an attempt to steal from the landed gentry their lawful possessions – money, power, social prestige and, most precious of all, *privilege*, the right to exclude others from these advantages. Conscious of the rectitude of their own purposes (and humanly, of course, of the sizable material advantages to them) the New York would-be gentry hotly resented the "grudging attitude" towards "positions and fortunes brighter than their own" among ordinary New England people. Many open and vigorous expressions of such New York opinion are preserved. Here are a few comments taken from personal letters and memoirs, wills or other documents of eighteenth-century New York. You will note that all of them are savagely disparaging. This is not because I specially picked them out to quote. I didn't find any expressing a more friendly tone.

". . . these ungovernable people [New Englanders] – to say no worse of them" . . . "fierce republicans, if anything sneaking and drawling may be so called" . . . "litigious and loquacious pretenders" . . . "they left the mother country as banished from it by what they considered oppression, came over foaming with religious and political fury, and narrowly missed having the most artful and able of demagogues, Cromwell himself, for their leader and guide. . . ." [I never heard before, did you, that Cromwell ever came close to settling in New England.] "Their illiberal opinions produce manners equally illiberal. All tendencies to elegance and refinement are despised as leading to aristocracy."

"Their indifference to the mother country spreads like a taint of infection." Here we have an aspect of the situation which roused all landlords to understandable fury. At the slightest contact with it, the "grudging attitude of the democratic spirit" rubbed off like wet paint, on their tenants. Illiteracy was of some help in preventing such contacts. But geographically the province was wide open to the contagion.

One of the most striking expressions of this feeling is to be found in Lewis Morris's will, drawn in 1760. In it he provided that his son, Gouverneur Morris, should never be sent to Connecticut for his education " . . . lest he imbibe in his youth that low craft and cunning of the People of that Colony which is so interwoven in their Constitution that all their art cannot disguise it from the world."

What would Lewis Morris have found to say about those younger-generation Connecticut sons and daughters who were soon to carry their still more radical ideas northward to Vermont? The answer to that question is suggested by adding a few more entries from the pages of *The Memoirs of an American Lady*, a book very well received in England, being republished in successive editions, well on into the nineteenth century. The author, Mrs. Grant, was the daughter of an English regular army captain. After a long term of service in the colonies, he had the idea of setting himself up as country gentleman on a four-thousand-acre claim (under New York law) in southwest Vermont, not far from the land which my family has owned (under Vermont law) since 1764. She and her parents spent some years trying to establish their claim to this area, partly by living on it in a camping-out sort of way, in the summertime. Her greatest pleasure — in fact the only one she mentions — was in visits from social equals. "Schuyler visitors," she notes with approbation, "particularly disliked Cromwellian political talk. They always left us in great good humor, for they spoke respectfully of our dear King." This would have been the beloved father of his people, George III.

For other Americans than the Hudson Valley gentry, her mildest emotion was a contemptuous aversion. She scorned the Quakers, "who little pleasure know and feel no pain," because their ideas of human equality reduced their lives to a drab stagnant dullness. She looks down her nose at Benjamin Franklin — a man of low, mean parentage — describing him as "that cold-blooded philosopher, the deistic Franklin, the legitimate father of the American age of calculation."

But at the sight or sound of a New Englander, all restraint is thrown to the winds. Her bristles rise, her ladylike pen drips vitriol. Vermont she describes as a place of refuge to all the "landless and uncontrollable spirits who had banished themselves from general society." Her Vermont neighbors had paid for their acres, but she never calls them anything but "squatters." She always speaks of them as "rude, insolent, and entirely disagreeable people."

If she had left it at that, we would have had only a vague idea of the reasons for her disapproval. Standards of insolence and rudeness vary greatly from one era to another. But she added details, which with accurate precision define her ideas of insolence and rudeness. She complains, for instance, about some "Obadiah or Zephaniah from Hampshire or Connecticut" dropping in unannounced and sitting down without invitation.

A natural objection, we admit. We would today regard a stranger as unpleasantly informal if he came into our house and dropped into a chair without our saying first, "Take a seat, won't you." But for us the illuminating point in the situation is that if the visitor had waited for an invitation from her, he would be standing yet. She believed so absolutely in the social subordination of the lower classes that she never would have pronounced that casual phrase of what we now consider perfunctory politeness. In the code of her etiquette book, it was always insolent for a common man to take a chair in the presence of a lady — the word LADY, we may be sure, capitalized in her mind, and denoting not sex but rank.

Her indictment goes on, "He lights his pipe without ceremony." Again we agree. Modern standards are casual, but even now that is not very good manners.

But then she adds still another instance of insolence to one's betters, "He talks about buying land." Here we must stop, take a long breath and use some imagination to grasp the fact that even to talk about *buying* land was as discourteous to a lady of the gentry as to light a pipe without asking if she objected to smoking.

The most meaningful part of the lady's racy portrait of our great-greats comes in her last phrase. It definitely connects the Western-Connecticut Vermonter of the 1760's and 1770's with the men of the Commonwealth from the 1620's on to 1660. She says, "And finally he begins a discourse on politics which would have done honor to Praise-God Barebones, or any of the members of his Parliament. To hear these people talk, one would think time had run back to the day of the levellers."

By the wish-thought of the ruling class of the province trying to force the people of New York into the then English mold, it was assumed that the ideas of the leaders of the Commonwealth were as dead as their bodies, dishonored by the Royalists who followed them. But if the chatty and genteel Mrs. Grant was very much a snob, she was no fool. A sure intuition warned her that only the outer shell of the Commonwealth movement lay a-moldering in its grave. In the person of her unceremonious Vermont squatter visitor, she saw its soul — its antimonarchical, rights-of-man spirit, very much alive — go marching on.

There the two groups stood, face to face, toe to toe. Yet so far apart in ideals that the contrasting basic principles underlying their two communities were like two chemical elements, compelled by their natures, if ever brought together, to burst into flames. It was on Vermont soil that historical circumstances forced them upon each other, and caused the explosion of fury which the one-volume high-school histories often dispose of in one phrase as "a difference of opinion about the validity of land titles in the Hampshire Grants."

The successful men in the Province of New York who knew how to accumulate wealth and possessions and social rank were living in a way which met with approval from the well-educated, the well-born, the well-mannered nearly everywhere in the western world. They were smoothly in the groove of their historic period, as their class had been for centuries in the groove of the past, that past which for men of their kind was richly encrusted with success-memories of power, and money and elegance, of authority, and of the "distinction of person" created by authority, of social privilege which holds the many in inferiority, so that the few may have the exquisite poison-pleasure of looking down on them. Like all the upper classes everywhere in the world of that period, those landowners in the Province of New York who meant to establish themselves as gentry, were supported by a great past, and by the present, smiling broadly on them.

The homespun young rustics in Vermont had on their side only the unforeseeable future.

Not a Bibliography

ACKNOWLEDGMENTS AND THANKS IMPOSSIBLE

A GOOD deal of meditation has brought me to the conclusion that a conventional list of books consulted and the customary acknowledgments and thanks would be, in the case of this book, out of the question. *Vermont Tradition* has been a book lived as well as written; and lived, off and on, during about all of a long lifetime. To acknowledge with thanks each one of the cloud of witnesses who have in one way or another contributed to it would be to set down a list of names as unsuitable for a reader to look over as a telephone directory.

But of course, in addition to living, such a book as this has required a great deal of reading and study. The contract with the publishers to write it is dated fifteen years ago. At that time I began examining and taking random notes from the Vermontiana available in my home state. For the last three or four years I have been absorbed by serious, more coherent work on all available sources, outside Vermont as well as inside.

To try to set down the list of the documents, reports, books, diaries, letters and the like which have been consulted during all this time would fill many pages most unprofitably. My purpose is stated in the subtitle of this volume — *The Biography of an Outlook on Life;* that is, a chronicle of the growth of a general attitude about how to organize community life in a manageably small human group. Minute statements of small exact details are hence not to the purpose. And the intention of long bibliographies is to prove to erudite scholars that there is adequate evidence for the accuracy of such details. Does anybody except an erudite scholar ever really read a bibliography anyhow? A book of this kind needs to be based on accurate facts, but it is concerned with the human meaning of such facts grouped together.

As I pondered over the way to present the documentary evidence usually printed as a bibliography, I came to feel that it is no more suitable for an author to send such an accompaniment with an interpretation of facts than for an artisan who has constructed a piece of furniture to send along with it the pile of shavings left on the floor of his shop as the completed chair or table is carried out.

Yet in the section on the land-grant dispute I promised to set down at the end of this book the titles of a few conventional histories of that long-drawn-out quarrel. So here are a few of the ones read by most Vermonters and by the small numbers of other Americans who have been interested in that period of our State's history (about the only phase which has seemed important enough to interest historically minded readers).

The first is *The History of Vermont from Its Discovery to Its Admission into the Union in 1791*, by Hiland Hall (Albany, New York, Joel Munsell, 1868). The date of this gives you some idea of its style and manner. It was written by one of the most notable Vermonters of his time, who was governor of Vermont, state's attorney, member of Congress for ten years, judge of the Supreme Court for four years, and so forth. His story, covering like most of these books less than thirty years of Vermont history, is honest, fully detailed, based on documentary evidence, and would have little interest for the modern general reader, but is a fine source book for anyone who wants to be sure that a certain event occurred on a Thursday morning, not a Monday afternoon.

Another covers an even shorter period, from 1778 to 1782, and yet it has more than 550 closely printed pages. This is *Independent Vermont* by Charles Miner Thompson (Houghton Mifflin Company, Boston, 1942). The name of the author would mean nothing to you. To Vermonters it is a familiar one, for Mr. Thompson was the son of the author of that old swashbuckling, cape-and-sword romantic school novel called *The Green Mountain Boys*. Older Vermonters, all of us (I mean *all*) read it in our childhood, greatly enjoying the naïve exaggerated glorification of our ancestors, the marvelous literary digestion of youth untroubled by its extraordinarily turgid, inept style. I am told that now even quite young Vermonters can no longer read it. Certainly any literary-minded American non-Vermont adult would find it an impossible assignment.

As far as I have heard, the author of *Independent Vermont* never told anybody his motive in devoting a great deal of his time and energy to writing a serious history of those years, but many of his fellow Vermonters (like our local historian Dr. Russell) have always assumed from the character of the book that he felt it his duty not to pass away without having debunked his father's rosy picture of early Vermonters as Pure Patriots. It is a recognizably Vermont idea to correct sentimental and exaggerated pictures. We understand his motive; but we think of it as we read his book.

A third book is *Vermont in the Making 1750–1777*, by Matt Bushnell Jones (Harvard University Press, Cambridge, Massachusetts, 1939). It is a fine work and widely read in Vermont for its conscientious research. All the facts are there. But any fact looks very different viewed from different angles. It has seemed to Vermont readers that Matt Jones sees the land-grant quarrel from one single angle – the legalistic one. He applies to everything in it the yardstick of literal, written-down, systematized law. And as the only legal yardstick of this kind then geographically available was the legal system of the

Province of New York, our ancestors did not accept it as an accurate measure of the merits of the case. And we don't, either.

The finest of all the books I have read and studied in connection with this period of Vermont history is not about our State at all, and is not intended to be a "reading book." Irving Mark's *Agrarian Conflicts in Colonial New York, 1711–1775* (Columbia University Press, New York, 1940) is a Ph.D. thesis, and I was as surprised as you probably are that such a thesis can be written not only with meticulous documented accuracy as to every date, place, name, action, but can also give a broadly intelligent and carefully measured interpretation of the meaning of the stream of events set down. About fifty years ago I wrote a Ph.D. thesis myself, and the improved quality of American scholarship as shown in this book heartened me.

As to acknowledgments to those who have so greatly helped me in this long task, my heart overflows with gratitude at the memory of the innumerable people, in and out of Vermont — librarians, historians, professors of economics, and just good Americans interested in making some sense out of our history — who with quick, unfailing, and to me inspiring generosity, stood by with advice and aid — I never could list them all.

To each one of them, still active in beneficent service or dead long ago, I hereby send my deeply touched appreciation and thanks.

Date Due

DE 16 '63			
JAN 18 '72			
APR 13 '72			
MAY 5 '72			
MAY 23 '72			
SEP 22 '87			
SEP 15			
MY 8 '91			
	PRINTED	IN U. S. A.	